Teaching Beginning Readers

Linking Assessment and Instruction

Second Edition

Jerry L. Johns
Emeritus, Northern Illinois University

Susan Davis Lenski
Illinois State University

Laurie Elish-Piper
Northern Illinois University

KENDALL/HUNT PUBLISHING COMPANY
4050 Westmark Drive   Dubuque, Iowa 52002

Book Team

Chairman and Chief Executive Officer:
   Mark C. Falb
Vice President, Director of National Book Program:
   Alfred C. Grisanti
Editorial Development Supervisor: Georgia Botsford
Assistant Vice President, Production Services:
   Chris O'Brien
Production Services Manager: Kathy Hanson
Prepress Editor: Angela Shaffer
Permissions Editor: Colleen Zelinsky
Design Manager: Jodi Splinter
Designer: Deb Howes

Books by Jerry L. Johns and Susan Davis Lenski

Improving Reading: Strategies and Resources (three editions)
Reading & Learning Strategies for Middle & High School Students (with Mary Ann Wham)
Improving Writing: Resources, Strategies, and Assessments
Celebrating Literacy! The Joy of Reading and Writing (with June E. Barnhart, James H. Moss, and Thomas E. Wheat)
Language Arts for Gifted Middle School Students

Ordering Information

Address: Kendall/Hunt Publishing Company
           4050 Westmark Drive
           Dubuque, IA 52004
Telephone: 800-247-3458, ext. 5
Web site: www.kendallhunt.com

Books by Jerry L. Johns

Basic Reading Inventory (eight editions)
Spanish Reading Inventory
Secondary & College Reading Inventory (two editions)
Literacy for Diverse Learners (edited)
Handbook for Remediation of Reading Difficulties
Informal Reading Inventories: An Annotated Reference Guide (compiled)
Literacy: Celebration and Challenge (edited)

Books by Jerry L. Johns and Laurie Elish-Piper

Balanced Reading Instruction: Teacher's Visions and Voices (edited)

Books by Jerry L. Johns and Roberta L. Berglund

Fluency: Questions, Answers, and Evidence-Based Strategies
Strategies for Content Area Learning

Author Addresses for Correspondence and Workshops

Jerry L. Johns
Consultant in Reading
2105 Eastgate Drive
Sycamore, IL 60178
E-mail: *jjohns@niu.edu*
815-895-3022

Susan Davis Lenski
Illinois State University
Campus Box 5330
Normal, IL 61790-5330
E-mail: *sjlensk@ilstu.edu*
309-438-3028

Laurie Elish-Piper
Northern Illinois University
Reading Clinic—119 Graham
DeKalb, IL 60115
E-mail: *laurieep@niu.edu*
815-753-8487

Cover photos © PhotoDisc and Eyewire.

Only the resources pages with the Kendall/Hunt copyright footnote may be reproduced for noncommercial educational purposes without obtaining written permission from the publisher. This license is limited to you, the individual purchaser, for use with your own clients or students. It does not extend to additional professionals in your institution, school district, or other setting, nor does purchase by an institution constitute a site license. This license does not grant the right to reproduce these materials for resale, redistribution, or any other purposes (including but not limited to books, pamphlets, articles, video- or audiotapes, and handouts or slides for lectures or workshops). Permission to reproduce these materials for the above purposes or any other purpose must be obtained in writing from the Permissions Department of Kendall/Hunt Publishing Company.

Photos by JM IMAGES

Copyright © 1999, 2002 by Kendall/Hunt Publishing Company

ISBN 0-7872-8672-9

All rights reserved. No part of this publication may be reproduced, stored in a retrieval system, or transmitted, in any form or by any means, electronic, mechanical, photocopying, recording, or otherwise, without the prior written permission of the copyright owner.

Printed in the United States of America
10 9 8 7 6 5 4 3 2 1

Brief Contents

1 Attitudes, Interests, and Oral Language 1

2 Literacy Knowledge 49

3 Letters and Sounds 125

4 Fluency and Automaticity 207

5 Vocabulary and Comprehension 269

6 Writing and Spelling 341

Contents

Preface ix
Acknowledgments xi
About the Authors xii
Introduction xv

1. Attitudes, Interests, and Oral Language 1

Overview 1

1.1 Desire to Read 3

Teaching Strategy 1: Morning Message 3
Teaching Strategy 2: Shared Reading 4
Teaching Strategy 3: Favorite Book Show and Tell 5
Ideas and Activities 8
Home-School Connections 11
Selected Resources 12

1.2 Background Knowledge 13

Teaching Strategy 1: Object Exploration 13
Teaching Strategy 2: Book Boxes 14
Teaching Strategy 3: Knowledge Chart 15
Teaching Strategy 4: Brainstorming 16
Teaching Strategy 5: Predicting with Pictures 17
Ideas and Activities 18
Home-School Connections 21
Selected Resources 22

1.3 Oral Language 23

Teaching Strategy 1: Show and Tell-Question-Connection 23
Teaching Strategy 2: Expand-a-Sentence 24
Teaching Strategy 3: Progressive Storytelling 25
Ideas and Activities 26
Home-School Connections 27
Selected Resources 28

1.4 Assessments of Interests and Attitudes Toward Reading 29

Assessment Strategy 1: Interviews about Reading 30
Assessment Strategy 2: News about Me 35
Assessment Strategy 3: Elementary Reading Attitude Survey 38

2. Literacy Knowledge 49

Overview 49

2.1 Print Concepts 52

Teaching Strategy 1: Shared Reading 52
Teaching Strategy 2: Language Experience Approach (LEA) 54
Teaching Strategy 3: Learning about Print through Writing 55
Teaching Strategy 4: What Can You Show Us? 56
Ideas and Activities 57
Home-School Connections 59
Selected Resources 60

2.2 Sense of Story 61

Teaching Strategy 1: Simple Story Elements 61
Teaching Strategy 2: Plot Relationships Chart 62
Teaching Strategy 3: Story Star 65

Teaching Strategy 4: Story Faces   67
Ideas and Activities   70
Home-School Connections   71
Selected Resources   72

2.3 Informational Text Structures   73

Teaching Strategy 1: Graphic Organizers   73
Teaching Strategy 2: Expository Frames   77
Teaching Strategy 3: Scrambled Text   78
Teaching Strategy 4: Expository Writing   79
Ideas and Activities   82
Home-School Connections   83
Selected Resources   84

2.4 Assessments of Literacy Knowledge   85

Assessment Strategy 1: Print Concepts   86
Assessment Strategy 2: Retelling a Story   119
Assessment Strategy 3: Informational Text Retelling   121

3. Letters and Sounds   125

Overview   125

3.1 Alphabet Knowledge   128

Teaching Strategy 1: Alphabet Song   128
Teaching Strategy 2: Using Alphabet Books   129
Teaching Strategy 3: Letter Actions   130
Teaching Strategy 4: Identifying Letters   131
Ideas and Activities   132
Home-School Connections   133
Selected Resources   134

3.2 Phonemic Awareness   136

Teaching Strategy 1: I Spy Rhymes   137
Teaching Strategy 2: First Sounds   137
Teaching Strategy 3: Sound Boxes   142
Teaching Strategy 4: Put It Together   143
Teaching Strategy 5: Break and Make   146
Ideas and Activities   147
Home-School Connections   151
Selected Resources   152

3.3 Phonics   154

Teaching Strategy 1: Explicit Phonics   155
Teaching Strategy 2: Making Words   157
Teaching Strategy 3: Whole-Part-Whole Phonics   158
Teaching Strategy 4: Phonics in Context   159
Ideas and Activities   160
Home-School Connections   164
Selected Resources   165

3.4 Assessments of Alphabet Knowledge, Phonemic Awareness, and Phonics   167

Assessment Strategy 1: Alphabet Knowledge   168
Assessment Strategy 2: Rhyme Detection   174
Assessment Strategy 3: Phoneme Segmentation   177
Assessment Strategy 4: Phoneme Deletion and Substitution   180
Assessment Strategy 5: Auditory Discrimination   184
Assessment Strategy 6: Phonics: Consonants   187
Assessment Strategy 7: Decoding   199

4. Fluency and Automaticity   207

Overview   207

4.1 Sight Words   209

Teaching Strategy 1: Explicit Instruction   210

Teaching Strategy 2: Pattern Books　213
　　　Teaching Strategy 3: Associative
　　　　Learning　214
　　　Teaching Strategy 4: Word Wall　215
　　　Ideas and Activities　216
　　　Home-School Connections　218
　　　Selected Resources　221

4.2　Fluency　222

　　　Teaching Strategy 1: Teacher-Assisted
　　　　Reading　222
　　　Teaching Strategy 2: Structured Repeated
　　　　Readings　223
　　　Teaching Strategy 3: Choral
　　　　Reading　227
　　　Teaching Strategy 4: Radio Reading　228
　　　Teaching Strategy 5: Multipaired
　　　　Simultaneous Oral Reading　228
　　　Ideas and Activities　230
　　　Home-School Connections　232
　　　Selected Resources　233

4.3　Cross-Checking　234

　　　Teaching Strategy 1: Making Sense　235
　　　Teaching Strategy 2: Predict-Sample-
　　　　Confirm　236
　　　Teaching Strategy 3: Word
　　　　Detective　237
　　　Teaching Strategy 4: Cue
　　　　Questioning　239
　　　Ideas and Activities　241
　　　Home-School Connections　242
　　　Selected Resources　243

**4.4　Assessments of Sight Words,
　　　Fluency, and Cross-
　　　Checking　245**

　　　Assessment Strategy 1: Basic Sight
　　　　Vocabulary　246
　　　Assessment Strategy 2: Common
　　　　Nouns　252
　　　Assessment Strategy 3: Words Per
　　　　Minute　258
　　　Assessment Strategy 4: Fluency Scale
　　　　Checklist　262
　　　Assessment Strategy 5: Oral Reading
　　　　Miscue Analysis　266

5.　Vocabulary and Comprehension　269

Overview　269

5.1　Meaning Vocabulary　271

　　　Teaching Strategy 1: Preview in
　　　　Context　271
　　　Teaching Strategy 2: Vocabulary
　　　　Connections　272
　　　Teaching Strategy 3: Word Frames　273
　　　Teaching Strategy 4: Four-Square
　　　　Vocabulary Grids　274
　　　Ideas and Activities　277
　　　Home-School Connections　278
　　　Selected Resources　279

5.2　Reading Comprehension　280

　　　Teaching Strategy 1: Think Aloud　281
　　　Teaching Strategy 2: Directed Reading–
　　　　Thinking Activity (DR-TA)　283
　　　Teaching Strategy 3: Story Frame　284
　　　Teaching Strategy 4: Idea-Mapping　286
　　　Teaching Strategy 5: Making Text
　　　　Connections　288
　　　Ideas and Activities　291
　　　Home-School Connections　296
　　　Selected Resources　297

5.3　Monitoring Reading　298

　　　Teaching Strategy 1: Critter　298
　　　Teaching Strategy 2: Monitoring
　　　　Think-Along　300
　　　Teaching Strategy 3: Pause-
　　　　Think-Retell　301
　　　Teaching Strategy 4: Monitoring
　　　　Logs　302
　　　Ideas and Activities　304
　　　Home-School Connections　306
　　　Selected Resources　308

**5.4.　Assessments of Reading
　　　Comprehension and
　　　Monitoring Reading　309**

　　　Assessment Strategy 1: Caption
　　　　Reading　310

Assessment Strategy 2: Passage Reading   317
Assessment Strategy 3: Retelling   336
Assessment Strategy 4: Monitoring Strategies Checklist   339

6. Writing and Spelling   341

Overview   341

6.1 Responding to Literature   344

Teaching Strategy 1: Language Charts   344
Teaching Strategy 2: Getting the Feeling   345
Teaching Strategy 3: Responding to Plot   348
Teaching Strategy 4: Discovering the Message   350
Ideas and Activities   351
Home-School Connections   352
Selected Resources   353

6.2 Writing   354

Teaching Strategy 1: Shared Writing   354
Teaching Strategy 2: Text Tapping   355
Teaching Strategy 3: Writing from Songs   356
Teaching Strategy 4: Parent-Recommended Topics   357
Teaching Strategy 5: Let Me Tell You About . . .   359
Ideas and Activities   361
Home-School Connections   364
Selected Resources   365

6.3 Spelling   366

Teaching Strategy 1: Have-a-Go   366
Teaching Strategy 2: Directed Spelling Thinking Activity (DSTA)   369
Teaching Strategy 3: Spelling Workshop   370
Teaching Strategy 4: That Reminds Me . . .   370
Ideas and Activities   372
Home-School Connections   374
Selected Resources   375

6.4 Assessments of Writing and Spelling   377

Assessment Strategy 1: Writing   379
Assessment Strategy 2: Writing Rubrics   381
Assessment Strategy 3: Writing Observational Checklist   387
Assessment Strategy 4: Developmental Spelling   389

Appendices   393

Appendix A: Professional Organizations and Agencies   394

Appendix B: Word Families   395

References   405

Index   411

Preface

As revision work began on the second edition of *Teaching Beginning Readers: Linking Assessment and Instruction*, we re-defined our goal of helping teachers of beginning readers make their instruction more responsive to the needs of young children. The new title reflects this shift in our focus to link two important components of teaching early learners—instructional and assessment strategies. Teachers continue to provide us with feedback that clearly indicates that they appreciate the practical, evidence-based strategies and assessments that are easy to use and adapt to their classroom needs.

QUESTION AND ANSWER APPROACH

Each of the six chapters begins with a series of questions that an inservice or preservice teacher might ask. These questions are answered with research and expert opinion to help establish the importance of the major areas presented in the chapters.

STRATEGIES, ACTIVITIES, AND ASSESSMENTS

Following the questions and answers, a series of teaching strategies and activities are provided for each of the major areas. If we have identified an appropriate assessment strategy, it is provided at the end of that chapter, thus linking assessment and teaching strategies.

TIPS FOR ENGLISH LANGUAGE LEARNERS

We have noted a growing diversity in many schools, and we planned this revision to aid teachers who need extra assistance in working with early learners whose first language is not English. Each English Language Learners box throughout the chapters contains tips for instruction.

HOME-SCHOOL CONNECTIONS

Many ideas and activities are presented in the form of Home-School Connections. These reproducible pages are placed appropriately in the chapters for you to duplicate and send home. Each Home-School Connection contains several ideas for how parents can help their children improve their early literacy skills.

SELECTED RESOURCES

The selected resource pages are arranged according to topic areas to highlight relevant children's books, web sites, and professional books. These reproducible resource pages are provided for your convenience in locating materials and to give you an opportunity to disseminate information about which resources are appropriate for young learners. We suggest that you refer to these resources for information about authors and publishers.

REPRODUCIBLE RECORD SHEETS

There are blackline masters for the assessment record sheets. You may duplicate these record sheets and use them as you record children's responses to the assessments that you have selected.

APPENDICES

The Appendices list Professional Organizations (Appendix A) and Word Families (Appendix B).

How to Use This Book

It is easy to find and use information in the six chapters—
Chapter 1. Attitudes, Interests, and Oral Language
Chapter 2. Literacy Knowledge
Chapter 3. Letters and Sounds
Chapter 4. Fluency and Automaticity
Chapter 5. Vocabulary and Comprehension
Chapter 6. Writing and Spelling

Take a look at the table of contents to become familiar with the major areas included in each chapter. For example, if you look in Chapter 3, Letters and Sounds, you will find the subject phonemic awareness (Section 3.2). You can see there are five step-by-step teaching strategies followed by an extensive list of ideas and activities. You will also find ideas for Home-School Connections.

A listing of Selected Resources—children's books, web sites, and professional books—related to that particular subject area is included in this section.

The last section (3.4) of the chapter contains assessments related to topics presented in the chapter. Assessment Strategies 2, 3, 4, and 5 all relate to phonemic awareness. There are two forms for each of these assessments as well as a reproducible Record Sheet that provides an easy way to note the child's performance.

Note from the Authors

We continue to be grateful to teachers for their support of our work. Teaching is a challenging profession. We are pleased that so many teachers and prospective teachers have found our books helpful in providing high-quality instruction that can help more children become thoughtful readers.

Jerry, Sue, and Laurie

CD-ROM (Included with each book)

Each book is packaged with a dual platform CD-ROM that contains **all** the pages that can be reproduced for noncommercial educational purposes by teachers for use in their classrooms. Included on the CD-ROM are the following:

- Instructional Reproducibles—forms to use directly with children to enhance your instruction.
- Home-School Connections—twenty resources to send home that help link and reinforce important skills and strategies you taught at school.
- Selected Resources—provides lists of children's books, web sites, and professional materials related to each of the major topics presented in the six chapters.
- Assessment Record Sheets—contains **all** the Record Sheets you need to note children's responses or summarize results from the assessments you select.

Acknowledgments

We wish to thank all those teachers and reading specialists who offered ideas and suggestions for the second edition. Appreciation is expressed to the following professionals who provided systematic and helpful feedback to strengthen the book:

Linda Keddie
EE Oliver Elementary
Fairview, AB Canada

Cheryl Maguire
Centerville School
Chokia, IL

Cindy Dooley
Western Illinois University
Macomb, IL

Bonnie Stiles
Armstrong School
Peoria, IL

Teddy Harpe
Springfield School
Peace River, AB Canada

Susie Emond
Saginaw Valley State University
University Center, MI

Debbie Theodore
Scott Elementary School
Naperville, IL

Jack Barshinger
Northern Illinois University
DeKalb, IL

Kathleen Hagele
Wapello Elementary
Wapello, IA

Audrey Hansen
Area Education Agency #4
Sioux City, IA

Dwight Watson
Hamilin University
Saint Paul, MN

Arlene Saretsky
Chicago State University
Chicago, IL

Trudy Haffer
Regional Office of Education
Jacksonville, IL

Kirsten Williams
Jefferson Elementary
DeKalb, IL

Special thanks to the following teachers and colleagues who assisted in reading page proofs: Dawn Andermann, Roberta L. Berglund, Annette Johns, Linda Oshita, Dottie Priddy, Marilyn Roark, Chris Sears, William Earl Smith, and Joan Will.

About the Authors

Jerry L. Johns has been recognized as distinguished professor, writer, and outstanding teacher educator. He has taught students from kindergarten through grade eight and has held the position of reading teacher. Dr. Johns now serves as a consultant and speaker to schools and professional organizations. An officer of the International Reading Association, he is president during 2002–2003.

Professor Johns is a past president of the Illinois Reading Council, College Reading Association, and Northern Illinois Reading Council.

Dr. Johns has been invited to consult, conduct workshops, and make presentations for teachers and parents throughout the United States and Canada. He has also authored, co-authored or edited 16 books as well as nearly 300 publications that have been useful to a diverse group of educators. His *Basic Reading Inventory,* and *Improving Reading* (with Susan Davis Lenski) are widely used in undergraduate and graduate classes as well as by practicing teachers.

Susan Davis Lenski is an Associate Professor in Elementary Education at Illinois State University. Before joining the faculty at ISU, Dr. Lenski taught in public schools for 20 years. Her teaching experiences include working with children from kindergarten through high school. Dr. Lenski currently teaches undergraduate and graduate reading and language arts courses.

Professor Lenski has been recognized by several organizations for her commitment to education. Among her numerous awards, Dr. Lenski was presented with the Nila Banton Smith Award from the International Reading Association; she was instrumental in her school receiving an Exemplary Reading Program Award from the International Reading Association; and she was inducted into the Illinois Reading Council Hall of Fame.

Professor Lenski's research interests are in improving reading, writing, and assessment in elementary and middle schools. She also conducts research in the field of teacher education. Dr. Lenski has conducted numerous inservice presentations and has presented at many state and national conferences. Dr. Lenski has written over 50 articles for publication and six books.

Laurie Elish-Piper is an Associate Professor of Reading in the Department of Literacy Education at Northern Illinois University. She directs the Reading Clinic and teaches reading courses for undergraduate, graduate, and doctoral students, including practicums in reading assessment and instruction. Prior to her current position, Dr. Elish-Piper worked as an elementary and middle school teacher and an educational therapist in a clinical setting. She has also developed, implemented, and evaluated family literacy programs for inner-city families and their young children.

Dr. Elish-Piper is active in many professional organizations. She serves on the Board of Directors of the College Reading Association and the American Reading Forum. In addition, she chairs the Alpha Upsilon Alpha Committee of the International Reading Association and the Parents and Reading Committee of the Illinois Reading Council. She is the coeditor of *Exploring Adult Literacy* and serves on editorial boards for *The Reading Teacher* and several other journals.

Dr. Elish-Piper also consults with schools and family literacy programs across the Midwest. Her research, publications, and presentations focus on family literacy, reading and writing strategies, and authentic literacy assessment. She has authored over 40 publications including books, chapters, articles, and instructional materials.

Introduction

CONTINUUM OF CHILDREN'S DEVELOPMENT IN EARLY READING AND WRITING

The International Reading Association (IRA) and the National Association for the Education of Young Children (NAEYC) have collaborated to produce a continuum that illustrates children's literacy development in the early years. This continuum is grounded in a view of literacy that is developmentally appropriate. IRA and NAEYC define developmentally appropriate as "challenging but achievable with sufficient adult support" (1999, p. 15). In other words, while children tend to progress along a continuum of literacy skills, they must be supported, instructed, and guided to make maximum progress.

The purpose of the continuum is to help educators understand the goals of literacy instruction and to determine if children are making appropriate progress in literacy growth. It is important to note, however, that the continuum is not a rigid sequence of steps that all children must follow. Reading and writing are complex processes that are influenced by individual differences; therefore, it is expected that children will move through the phases of the continuum at their own rates. In addition, children may overlap phases, meaning that they may exhibit characteristics in more than one phase at the same time.

The continuum and this book are based on the belief that teachers must be knowledgeable about a variety of strategies to assess and foster individual children's literacy development. Effective teachers "make instructional decisions based on their knowledge of reading and writing, current research, appropriate expectations, and their knowledge of individual children's strengths and needs" (International Reading Association & the National Association for the Education of Young Children, 1998, p. 15). This continuum is useful for helping teachers set appropriate goals for literacy instruction and assess individual children's progress toward those goals. The continuum is divided into five phases.

Five Phases

Continuum of Children's Development in Early Reading and Writing

Awareness and Exploration
(Preschool)

Experimental Reading and Writing
(Kindergarten)

Early Reading and Writing
(First Grade)

Transitional Reading and Writing
(Second Grade)

Independent and Productive Reading and Writing
(Third Grade)

Illustrative examples are provided for each phase in terms of what children can do, what teachers do, and what parents and family members do to support children's continued literacy development. We offer this continuum to help you consider the most important aspects of literacy development, instruction, and assessment of the young children you teach.

CONTINUUM OF CHILDREN'S DEVELOPMENT IN EARLY READING AND WRITING

Note: This list is intended to be illustrative, not exhaustive. Children at any grade level will function at a variety of phases along the reading/writing continuum.

Phase 1: Awareness and exploration (goals for preschool)

Children explore their environment and build the foundations for learning to read and write.

Children can:
- enjoy listening to and discussing storybooks
- understand that print carries a message
- engage in reading and writing attempts
- identify labels and signs in their environment
- participate in rhyming games
- identify some letters and make some letter-sound matches
- use known letters or approximations of letters to represent written language (especially meaningful words like their name, and phrases such as "I love you")

What teachers do:
- share books with children, including Big Books, and model reading behaviors
- talk about letters by name and sounds
- establish a literacy-rich environment
- reread favorite stories
- engage children in language games
- promote literacy-related play activities
- encourage children to experiment with writing

What parents and family members can do:
- talk with children, engage them in conversation, give names of things, show interest in what a child says
- read and reread stories with predictable texts to children
- encourage children to recount experiences and describe ideas and events that are important to them
- visit the library regularly
- provide opportunities for children to draw and print using markers, crayons, and pencils

Phase 2: Experimental reading and writing (goals for kindergarten)

Children develop basic concepts of print and begin to engage in and experiment with reading and writing.

Kindergartners can:
- enjoy being read to and themselves retell simple narrative stories or informational texts
- use descriptive language to explain and explore
- recognize letters and letter-sound matches
- show familiarity with rhyming and beginning sounds
- understand left-to-right and top-to-bottom orientation and familiar concepts of print
- match spoken words with written ones
- begin to write letters of the alphabet and some high-frequency words

What teachers do:
- encourage children to talk about reading and writing experiences
- provide many opportunities for children to explore and identify sound-symbol relationships in meaningful contexts

(continued)

From Learning to read and write: Developmentally appropriate practices for young children, *The Reading Teacher*, 52, 193–216. Copyright © 1998 International Reading Association. Reprinted with permission. This is a joint position statement of the International Reading Association and the National Association for the Education of Young Children.

- help children to segment spoken words into individual sounds and blend the sounds into whole words (for example, by slowly writing a word and saying its sound)
- frequently read interesting and conceptually rich stories to children
- provide daily opportunities for children to write
- help children build a sight vocabulary
- create a literacy-rich environment for children to engage independently in reading and writing

What parents and family members can do:
- daily read and reread narrative and informational stories to children
- encourage children's attempts at reading and writing
- allow children to participate in activities that involve writing and reading (for example, cooking, making grocery lists)
- play games that involve specific directions (such as "Simon Says")
- have conversations with children during mealtimes and throughout the day

Phase 3: Early reading and writing (goals for first grade)

Children begin to read simple stories and can write about a topic that is meaningful to them.

First graders can:
- read and retell familiar stories
- use strategies (rereading, predicting, questioning, contextualizing) when comprehension breaks down
- use reading and writing for various purposes on their own initiative
- orally read with reasonable fluency
- use letter-sound associations, word parts, and context to identify new words
- identify an increasing number of words by sight
- sound out and represent all substantial sounds in spelling a word
- write about topics that are personally meaningful
- attempt to use some punctuation and capitalization

What teachers do:
- support the development of vocabulary by reading daily to the children, transcribing their language, and selecting materials that expand children's knowledge and language development
- model strategies and provide practice for identifying unknown words
- give children opportunities for independent reading and writing practice
- read, write, and discuss a range of different text types (poems, informational books)
- introduce new words and teach strategies for learning to spell new words
- demonstrate and model strategies to use when comprehension breaks down
- help children build lists of commonly used words from their writing

What parents and family members can do:
- talk about favorite storybooks
- read to children and encourage them to read to you
- suggest that children write to friends and relatives
- bring to a parent-teacher conference evidence of what your child can do in writing and reading
- encourage children to share what they have learned about their writing and reading

Phase 4: Transitional reading and writing (goals for second grade)

Children begin to read more fluently and write various text forms using simple and more complex sentences.

Second graders can:
- read with greater fluency
- use strategies more efficiently (rereading, questioning, and so on) when comprehension breaks down
- use word identification strategies with greater facility to unlock unknown words
- identify an increasing number of words by sight
- write about a range of topics to suit different audiences
- use common letter patterns and critical features to spell words
- punctuate simple sentences correctly and proofread their own work
- spend time reading daily and use reading to research topics

(continued)

What teachers do:
- create a climate that fosters analytic, evaluative, and reflective thinking
- teach children to write in multiple forms (stories, information, poems)
- ensure that children read a range of texts for a variety of purposes
- teach revising, editing, and proofreading skills
- teach strategies for spelling new and difficult words
- model enjoyment of reading

What parents and family members can do:
- continue to read to children and encourage them to read to you
- engage children in activities that require reading and writing
- become involved in school activities
- show children your interest in their learning by displaying their written work
- visit the library regularly
- support your child's specific hobby or interest with reading materials and references

Phase 5: Independent and productive reading and writing (goals for third grade)

Children continue to extend and refine their reading and writing to suit varying purposes and audiences.

Third graders can:
- read fluently and enjoy reading
- use a range of strategies when drawing meaning from the text
- use word identification strategies appropriately and automatically when encountering unknown words
- recognize and discuss elements of different text structures
- make critical connections between texts
- write expressively in many different forms (stories, poems, reports)
- use a rich variety of vocabulary and sentences appropriate to text forms
- revise and edit their own writing during and after composing
- spell words correctly in final writing drafts

What teachers do:
- provide opportunities daily for children to read, examine, and critically evaluate narrative and expository texts
- continue to create a climate that fosters critical reading and personal response
- teach children to examine ideas in texts
- encourage children to use writing as a tool for thinking and learning
- extend children's knowledge of the correct use of writing conventions
- emphasize the importance of correct spelling in finished written products
- create a climate that engages all children as a community of literacy learners

What parents and family members can do:
- continue to support children's learning and interest by visiting the library and bookstores with them
- find ways to highlight children's progress in reading and writing
- stay in regular contact with your child's teachers about activities and progress in reading and writing
- encourage children to use and enjoy print for many purposes (such as recipes, directions, games, and sports)
- build a love of language in all its forms and engage children in conversation

CHAPTER 1

Attitudes, Interests, and Oral Language

OVERVIEW

Children learn a great deal before they arrive in school settings. They learn how to walk and talk as well as how literacy is used in their homes. They build a rich store of background knowledge about the world from the daily events they experience such as going to the grocery store, riding the bus, and playing at the park. This view of learning aligns with the emergent literacy perspective that suggests that literacy development is a complex process that begins at birth. Furthermore, literacy learning is a social process wherein a child experiences language used for real life processes by other members of the family and community (McGee & Richgels, 2000).

Children bring their attitudes, interests, background knowledge, and oral language foundations to the emergent literacy process. You can enhance children's emergent literacy development by linking your teaching to children's interests and nurturing positive attitudes toward reading and writing. In addition, by helping children build and activate their background knowledge about the world and their experiences, you can assist children with making connections with texts they read and write. By supporting children's oral language development, you increase the likelihood that they will have the necessary foundations to draw from as they learn to read and write (Watson, 2001). Effective teachers of young children know the importance of building on what the child brings to the learning context as well as providing the child with new experiences and opportunities. The following questions address some issues commonly raised by teachers about the roles of attitudes, interests, background knowledge, and oral language in literacy development.

Why are attitude and interest so important for emergent literacy development?

If a child doesn't have a positive attitude about learning and an interest in the topic being studied, it is difficult for that child to get excited and motivated about learning. Certainly all children do not come to school with positive attitudes and interests that parallel the curriculum; however, this does not mean that the situation is impossible. Teachers can do much to help develop positive attitudes by creating nurturing classroom communities, providing scaffolding to help children succeed, and supporting children's self-concepts as learners. In addition, teachers can build children's interest by sharing their own enthusiasm, by making topics personally meaningful, and by providing firsthand or vicarious experiences. For example, if you are planning to teach a unit on farm animals to a group of kindergarten children in an urban setting, you might arrange for a field trip to a farm or zoo so the children can see the animals firsthand. If such trips are not possible, you might bring in videos of farm animals so the children can "see them in action." Such experiences, whether firsthand or vicarious, will increase the likelihood that children will be interested in learning more about the topic, in this case, farm animals.

If a child lacks background knowledge, can I really do anything to make a difference?

Some children come to school with a rich store of background knowledge gained through their experiences: books they have heard, outings they have taken to places like zoos and museums, and activities in which they have participated. Unfortunately, some children come to school with fewer experiences, and, as a result, they may lack some concepts that are taught at school. If a child has limited background knowledge, a teacher can provide firsthand experiences, vicarious experiences through books or videos, and concrete objects for the child to explore. Specific strategies for building and activating background knowledge are provided in Section 1.2.

What is the role of oral language instruction in the typical kindergarten or primary classroom? With all of the emphasis on skills and testing, do I need to address oral language, too?

Oral language is the foundation for reading and writing (Watson, 2001). In *Standards for the English Language Arts* (1996), the National Council of Teachers of English and the International Reading Association address oral language in several of their standards. Teachers can nurture oral language development in a number of ways including Show and Tell, creative dramatics, peer-led discussions, and storytelling. Oral language is typically woven into various activities throughout the day rather than taught as a separate subject. As teachers plan their lessons, they are encouraged to consider how listening and speaking experiences will complement and enhance their lessons.

1.1 Desire to Read

> **Goal** To help children develop positive attitudes, interests, and motivation toward reading.
> **Assessment Strategy 1** Interviews about Reading, page 30
> **Assessment Strategy 2** News about Me, page 35

BACKGROUND

Children are born with a desire to learn. They are interested in the people, things, and events around them. When young children come to school, they still have a strong drive to learn. Two of the things most children want to learn when they come to school are to read and write (Cochrane, Cochrane, Scalena, & Buchanan, 1988).

The desire to read and write is an important foundation for all literacy learning. Children who view reading and writing as interesting, exciting, and meaningful will be more likely to engage in reading and writing. As with any skill, additional practice and engagement with reading and writing leads to improved competence (Guthrie & Wigfield, 2000).

You can capitalize on young children's natural interest and curiosity by providing a classroom environment that invites children into literacy. Classroom environments that contain many types of print, offer easy access to reading and writing materials, provide for choice, and immerse children in literacy activities motivate and support children's literacy development (Sulzby & Teale, 1991).

There are simple strategies and activities you can use in your classroom to arouse and build on children's natural curiosity and interest in literacy. The teaching strategies and activities set forth below provide suggestions to assist you with creating a classroom environment and literacy program that will help children develop positive attitudes, interests, and motivation toward reading.

Teaching Strategy 1

Section 1.1

Morning Message

The Morning Message is a daily classroom routine that provides a meaningful context for reading and writing in the classroom. The teacher writes the Morning Message to the students to share important information about the upcoming day and concludes by asking the children a related personal question. Children may try to read the message on their own, and then the teacher engages in shared reading to guide the children through the reading. Finally, children discuss, draw, or write a response to the question.

DIRECTIONS

1. Write a short message on the chalkboard or on chart paper. The message should include important information about the upcoming day. The message then concludes by asking the children a related personal response question. A sample message is shown on the next page.

> *Dear Boys and Girls,*
>
> *Today is art day. We will be painting pictures. We will use blue, green, red, and yellow paint. I like to use many colors in my paintings. What colors will you use when you paint today?*
>
> *Your friend,*
> *Mrs. Jones*

2. Post the message prior to the children's arrival in the classroom. Provide time for the children to look at the message and informally discuss it among themselves.
3. Gather the children around the message. Read the message aloud to the children.
4. Reread the message. Invite the children to join in with the reading if they would like to do so.
5. Discuss the ideas in the message. Discuss the question in the message. Provide time for students to informally discuss their responses to the question.
6. Ask children to record their responses to the question by either drawing or writing responses in their journals.
7. Provide time for children to share their responses.

Tips for English Language Learners

- Add pictures to the morning message to help English Language Learners understand the context of the message.

- Encourage English Language Learners to partner with another student to explore the morning message before you discuss it as a group.

- If you know any words in the child's home language, consider using both the English language and the child's language for those words in the morning message. This action will support English Language Learners as well as encourage the other children to learn words in another language.

Teaching Strategy 2

Section 1.1

Shared Reading

Shared Reading replicates the bedtime story sharing situation with an individual, a small group, or a classroom of children. This strategy allows children to participate in and enjoy books they cannot read on their own (Mooney, 1990). The emphasis of this strategy is on enjoyment of the story as a whole. Teachers can introduce new, exciting books to children through Shared Reading.

DIRECTIONS

1. Select a children's book with predictable text and engaging illustrations. If you are reading with a large group of children, a Big Book will work well.

4   Chapter One

2. Gather the children into a circle so they all can hear the story and see the illustrations.
3. Show the children the cover of the book and read the title. Ask them to make predictions about the contents of the book. Provide time for volunteers to share their ideas.
4. Read the story aloud to the children, inviting them to read along if they would like to do so.
5. Provide time for the children to share their personal responses and favorite parts of the book.
6. Reread the book, inviting the children to read along if they would like to do so.
7. Place the book in the classroom library so the children can read it during their free time.

Tips for English Language Learners

- Select predictable books with clear illustrations to provide clues for English Language Learners during shared reading.
- Provide time for English Language Learners to engage in a picture walk to see the story before starting the shared reading. The picture walk allows children to look at the pictures and think about what the story line might be before hearing the actual story. To do a picture walk, have the children look at the cover and discuss what they see. Progress through the book, directing the children's attention to pictures that convey important information about the story. After viewing and discussing the pictures, begin reading the story with the children.

Teaching Strategy 3

Section 1.1

Favorite Book Show and Tell

Since literacy is a social process, children benefit from meaningful opportunities to share and discuss books with their peers. The Favorite Book Show and Tell strategy allows children to share their favorite books as well as to learn about what their classmates enjoy reading. This strategy also supports the children's listening and speaking skills.

DIRECTIONS

1. Inform children that you will be starting Favorite Book Show and Tell time each day. Explain to the children that each of them will have a chance to share a favorite book with others. Clarify that the books can come from the children's homes, the public library, the school library, or the classroom library. Explain that the books can be new to the class or ones that have been read and shared together. Allow children to repeat a book if it is a favorite for more than one child in the classroom. Also, explain that children can select books that have been read to them or books they have read on their own.

2. Model the Favorite Book Show and Tell process using a book the children know from the classroom. Show the book to the children and say something such as, "The book *Lily's Purple Plastic Purse* is written by Kevin Henkes (1996). It is one of my favorites because it is funny, and Lily is an interesting character. I also like the pictures because they have some funny surprises hidden in them. The book has a happy ending, and it teaches a lesson too. I would recommend this book to anyone who likes funny books and stories about school."

3. Fill out a Favorite Book Show and Tell sheet (see page 7) to demonstrate the process to the children. Display the sheet in a designated place in the classroom. Sheets can be posted on a bulletin board for the week, and then they can be placed in a binder or folder for other children to consult when looking for book suggestions. If the book is in the classroom library or school library, make it available for other children to check out. If children are unable to fill out the sheet, they can dictate the information to you or to a classroom volunteer.

4. Schedule two or three children for Favorite Book Show and Tell each day. Rotate the schedule through the classroom so all children have a chance to share.

Tips for English Language Learners

- Encourage English Language Learners to bring in books written in their home language, if they wish to do so, for the Favorite Book Show and Tell.

Favorite Book Show and Tell Sheet

Your Name _____

Book Title _____

_____

Author _____

Illustrator _____

I like this book because _____

_____

_____

Draw something you liked from the book.

```
┌─────────────────────────────────────────────┐
│                                             │
│                                             │
│                                             │
│                                             │
│                                             │
│                                             │
└─────────────────────────────────────────────┘
```

From Jerry L. Johns, Susan Davis Lenski, and Laurie Elish-Piper, *Teaching Beginning Readers: Linking Assessment and Instruction*. (2nd ed.). Copyright © 2002 by Kendall/Hunt Publishing Company (1-800-247-3458, ext. 5). May be reproduced for noncommercial educational purposes.

1. Provide daily class time for self-selected reading. Consider using a fun acronym as a name for this activity (e.g., DIRT: Daily Independent Reading Time or DEAR: Drop Everything And Read). Provide access to varied types of reading materials and allow children to find a comfortable place to read in the classroom. During this time, you should also be reading to serve as a good reading model for the children. You can also provide a short sharing time after children have completed their reading.

2. Model your enthusiasm and love for reading. Bring in your favorite books and share them with the children. Discuss how and why reading is important to you. Provide a special display of your favorite books in the classroom. Update the display on a regular basis.

3. Create a print-rich classroom environment that includes access to and displays of various types of print. Possible types of print are listed below.

   - labels for important classroom locations and materials
   - lists of children's names (e.g., who lost a tooth, birthdays)
   - sign-in sheet
   - message board
   - posters with captions
   - displays of the children's work and writing
   - announcements
   - classroom rules and procedures
   - chart and language experience stories
   - children's books and magazines

4. Read aloud to the children at least once a day, more often if possible. Focus on the children's enjoyment of and personal reactions to the story. Consider using different voices and sound effects to make the read-aloud experience highly motivating for the children. Provide time for children to ask questions and discuss their responses to the story.

5. Schedule time for children to share with their classmates the books they are reading and stories they are writing. Learning what their peers are reading and writing often serves as a motivator for students to pursue similar reading and writing tasks. Consider using a special chair such as a rocking chair to make the sharing experience more special. Provide options so children can share with a small group of children or the entire class.

6. Implement a home-school reading program through the use of reading backpacks. Fill several small backpacks or book bags with children's books on specific topics or by particular authors. Include construction paper, markers, crayons, pencils, and a small notebook in the backpack. Attach a short note explaining that parents and children are invited to share the books and write or draw about their favorite parts. When children return the backpack to school, provide time for them to share their responses. Post their responses on a bulletin board or in the classroom library. Change the contents of the backpacks frequently and rotate them around the classroom so all children can take home a reading backpack on a regular basis.

7. Arrange the classroom so children have easy access to literacy materials. For example, consider establishing a writing center that contains different types of paper, markers, pencils, pens, a computer, a children's typewriter, letter stamps, picture dictionaries, scissors, glue, tape, letter tiles,

magnetic letters, and other writing supplies. Label storage areas for materials in the center so children can find and put away materials themselves.

8. Create literacy play centers so children can explore literacy through meaningful play situations. A list of literacy play centers and suggested materials is provided in the box below.

Literacy Play Centers

Post Office Center
mailboxes
envelopes
paper
stationery
stickers or stamp pads
address labels
boxes
packages
cash register
play money

Restaurant Center
menus
order pad and pencil
tablecloth
dishes
glasses
silverware
napkins
list of daily specials
cash register
play money

Office Center
phone
computer or typewriter
message pad
pens and pencils
paper
calculator
note pads
file folders
rubber stamps and stamp pad

Grocery Store Center
grocery cart
food packages
price stickers
advertisements
coupons
cash register
play money
shopping lists
grocery bags

---

9. Implement a message board in the classroom. Consider using a bulletin board with a pocket or envelope for each child. To introduce the message board, write a personalized message to each student in the classroom. Provide daily time for children to write messages to their classmates. To keep the message board going, you may want to write messages to several children each day.

10. Invite children to engage in artistic responses to literature. Provide opportunities for children to explore creative dramatics, art, music, dance, and movement activities after reading a book. These types of responses actively involve children in learning and literature.

11. Introduce children to various genres of literature by doing brief book talks. During book talks, focus on enticing children to want to read the books without giving away the stories. After conducting book talks, make the books available in the classroom library.

12. Develop a cross-age reading buddy program. This type of program pairs a younger child and an older child so they can read together. The focus of this type of activity is on enjoying the stories and making reading fun.

13. Introduce poetry, rhymes, jingles, and jump-rope rhymes to children. Display these materials on chart paper so children can read them on their own during free time. Encourage children to engage in word play by developing their own verses or modifications of the poems, rhymes, jingles, and jump-rope rhymes.

14. Develop a classroom listening center so children can follow along as they listen to a tape-recorded version of a book. Rotate the books and tapes in the listening center on a regular basis.

15. Implement a guest reader program to invite various adults from the school and community to share their favorite books with children. Designate a special place in the classroom to display books shared by guest readers.

16. Establish a well-stocked classroom library and provide daily time for children to browse through the library and select materials. Suggestions for creating a classroom library are detailed in the following list.

Creating a Classroom Library

Specific, named location	The classroom library is in a highly visible area, and it has a specific name.
Partitioned and private	The classroom library is separated from other areas in the classroom by book shelves, book carts, or other partitions.
Comfortable	The library contains comfortable seating such as bean bag chairs, carpet squares, or pillows.
Number of books	Provide a minimum of five to eight books per child in the classroom.
Assortment of books	Provide books from varied genres and reading levels. Be sure to include other reading materials such as magazines, pamphlets, materials written by the children, and class books.
Organization	Organize books and provide labels to show the organization (e.g., genres, themes, topics, authors, or reading levels).
Shelving	Include some open shelving so students can see book covers. Shelve other books with the spines facing out to provide room for more books in the available space.
Literature Displays	Include displays with posters, puppets, felt boards, stuffed animals, and puppets that are related to children's books.

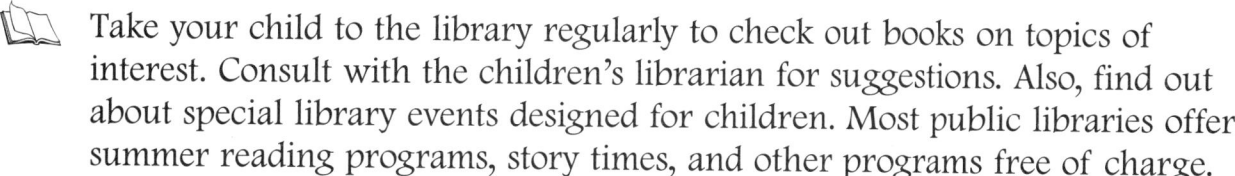

📖 Take your child to the library regularly to check out books on topics of interest. Consult with the children's librarian for suggestions. Also, find out about special library events designed for children. Most public libraries offer summer reading programs, story times, and other programs free of charge.

📖 Give your child books as gifts to show the importance and value of books and reading.

📖 Set aside time to read to your children every night. Right before bedtime works well for many families. Make this a special quiet time that you and your children look forward to at the end of the day.

📖 Write notes to your child and encourage your child to write notes back to you. You can tuck notes in a lunch box or backpack, or you can post them on the refrigerator or bathroom mirror. If your child cannot read independently yet, use a combination of drawings with words such as
I ♥ You!

From Jerry L. Johns, Susan Davis Lenski, and Laurie Elish-Piper, *Teaching Beginning Readers: Linking Assessment and Instruction* (2nd ed.). Copyright © 2002 by Kendall/Hunt Publishing Company (1-800-247-3458, ext. 5). May be reproduced for noncommercial educational purposes.

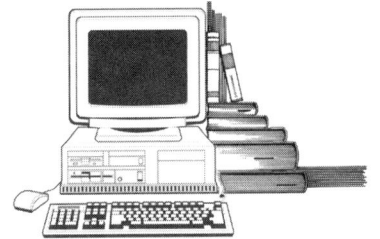

Selected Resources

DESIRE TO READ

Predictable Books

Ahlberg, J., & Ahlberg, A. (1978). *Each peach pear plum*. New York: Scholastic.

Barracca, D., & Barracca, S. (1990). *The adventures of Taxi Dog*. New York: Dial.

Brett, J. (1985). *Annie and the wild animals*. New York: Houghton Mifflin.

Kimmel, E.A. (1988). *Anansi and the moss-covered rock*. New York: Holiday House.

Kimmel, E.A. (1994). *Anansi and the talking melon*. New York: Holiday House.

Slobdkina, E. (1968). *Caps for sale*. New York: Scholastic.

Walsh, E.S. (1993). *Hop jump*. San Diego: Harcourt Brace Jovanovich.

Rhyme and Jump-Rope Rhyme Books

Cole, J. (1987). *Norma Jean, jumping bean*. New York: Random House.

Cole, J. (1989). *Anna Banana: 101 jump rope rhymes*. New York: Morrow.

Cole, J., & Calmenson, S. (1990). *Miss Mary Mack and other children's street rhymes*. New York: Morrow.

Jorgensen, G. (1989). *Crocodile beat*. New York: Bradbury Press.

Wescott, N.B. (1987). *Peanut butter and jelly: A play rhyme*. New York: Dutton.

Professional Resources for Locating Children's Books

Barrera, R.B., & Thompson, V.D. (Eds.). (1994). *Kaleidoscope: A multicultural booklist for grades K–8*. Urbana, IL: National Council of Teachers of English.

Lima, C.W. (2001). *A to Zoo: Subject access to children's picture books* (6th ed.). Westport, CT: Bowker-Greenwood.

McClure, A.A., & Kristo, J.V. (1996). *Books that invite talk, wonder, and play*. Urbana, IL: National Council of Teachers of English.

Pierce, K.M. (Ed.). (2000). *Adventuring with books: A booklist for pre-K–grade 6* (11th ed.). Urbana, IL: National Council of Teachers of English.

Silvey, A. (Ed.). (1995). *Children's books and their creators*. Boston: Houghton Mifflin.

From Jerry L. Johns, Susan Davis Lenski, and Laurie Elish-Piper, *Teaching Beginning Readers: Linking Assessment and Instruction* (2nd ed.). Copyright © 2002 by Kendall/Hunt Publishing Company (1-800-247-3458, ext. 5). May be reproduced for noncommercial educational purposes.

1.2 Background Knowledge

Goal To help children expand their experiences and build background knowledge.

BACKGROUND

Children can learn more effectively when they can relate new learning to something they already know. This type of previous knowledge is often referred to as background knowledge or schema (Anderson, 1994), and it is an important foundation for constructing meaning in reading and writing. Some children come to school with experiences that help them connect school learning to their life experiences. Other children come to school with limited experiences and exposure to events, objects, and books (Salinger, 1999).

The concept of building background knowledge focuses on providing new experiences to children. Building background knowledge is greatly supported by providing children with concrete experiences and opportunities to use their senses to examine materials and objects. Because young children learn by doing, playing, and being actively involved, hands-on experiences are essential for building background knowledge.

Activating background knowledge refers to the process of helping children remember what they already know about a topic. You can help children activate their background knowledge by making connections between what they already know and what they will learn. Simple techniques such as making predictions, discussing, or drawing what is already known about a topic, or brainstorming how two topics are alike are examples of strategies you can use to help activate children's background knowledge.

By planning simple experiences related to a topic of study or book, you can build and activate children's background knowledge, thus increasing the likelihood that they will understand and learn the new concepts. Specific suggestions for building and activating children's background knowledge are provided below.

Teaching Strategy 1

Section 1.2

Object Exploration

The Object Exploration strategy provides children with concrete experiences related to an upcoming area of study. Young children learn through active involvement and hands-on experiences, and this strategy provides them with opportunities to personally explore and examine materials before they begin a new unit of study. In addition, related vocabulary and concepts are introduced in relation to the concrete objects, thereby providing a useful framework for children to understand and learn the new words and ideas related to the topic of study.

DIRECTIONS

1. Identify an upcoming unit of study and gather concrete objects related to the unit. For example, if you are studying eggs, gather raw eggs, cracked eggs, hard-boiled eggs, brown eggs, duck eggs, and magnifying glasses.
2. Tell the children you will be starting a new unit. Inform them of the topic for the new unit. Show them the concrete objects you have gathered and tell them they will be examining these materials to prepare for the unit.
3. Provide exploration time for the children to use their senses to explore and examine the objects. Share magnifying glasses so the children get a closer look at the objects.
4. Ask the children to brainstorm words that describe the objects they have explored. Write the words on the chalkboard, a piece of chart paper, or an overhead transparency. Make a separate list for each object. For example, if children explored eggs as described in step 1, make lists of the describing words on chart paper labeled *raw egg, cracked egg,* and *hard-boiled egg.*
5. Discuss the words on the lists and what the children learned about the objects. Inform the children that they will be learning many things about the topic in the new unit.
6. Display the brainstorming lists in the classroom. Add new words to the lists as children participate in additional activities related to the unit.

Teaching Strategy 2

Section 1.2

Book Boxes

Book Boxes are collections of artifacts related to a story, poem, or informational book. A Book Box is decorated according to the focus of the book, and it contains at least three important objects related to the book. Teachers can use Book Boxes to introduce a book to children by sharing the objects, discussing why the objects are included, and inviting the children to make predictions about the book.

DIRECTIONS

1. Identify a story, poem, or informational book that you will be sharing with children.
2. Read the book to identify at least three important objects that are mentioned in the book.
3. Gather these objects or pictures of the objects and place them in a box.
4. Decorate the box according to the focus of the book. Also, write the title and author of the book on the box.
5. Prior to reading the book with the children, show them the Book Box. Discuss the decorations on the box and the title and author of the book.
6. Remove one object from the box. Discuss what the object is and why it is included in the Book Box. Invite the children to make predictions about what other objects might be in the Book Box and why.
7. Share the objects in the Book Box. Invite the children to make predictions about what the book will be about based on the objects in the Book Box.
8. Introduce the book to the children and read it with them as a teacher read aloud, shared reading activity, or guided reading activity.

 **Tips for English Language Learners**

- Add labels to the objects in the Book Box to support the vocabulary acquisition of English Language Learners. As you discuss each object, point to the label and use the label consistently. By your using the same term consistently, English Language Learners will be more likely to acquire and remember the new words.

Teaching Strategy 3

Section 1.2

Knowledge Chart

A Knowledge Chart focuses on children's prior knowledge about a topic and their new knowledge about a topic after reading (Macon & Macon, 1991). This strategy invites children to share their knowledge about the topic of a book they will be reading by brainstorming words and ideas related to the topic. After the book is read, children then focus on the new knowledge they learned about the topic, thus connecting their background knowledge with new learning.

DIRECTIONS

1. Select an informational book the children will be reading or that you will be reading to them. Identify the topic of the book.

2. Create a Knowledge Chart on the chalkboard, a piece of chart paper, or an overhead transparency. A sample Knowledge Chart is shown below.

Knowledge Chart

Prior knowledge about _____	**New knowledge about** _____

3. Tell the children they will be reading a book about a specific topic. Show them the Knowledge Chart and ask them to brainstorm what they already know about the topic. Write their ideas on the Knowledge Chart.

4. Explain to the children that they should think about the ideas on the Knowledge Chart as they read or listen to the book. Tell them that you will be asking them to share their new knowledge about the book after they have read or listened to the book.

5. Read the book with the children as a teacher read aloud, shared reading activity, or guided reading activity. Discuss the book with the children.

6. Ask the children to share the new knowledge they learned about the topic. Add this information to the Knowledge Chart.

7. Engage the children in a discussion about how their prior knowledge compared to their new knowledge. Remind them that thinking about what they already know about a book or topic is an important strategy that good readers use to prepare for reading.

Teaching Strategy 4

Section 1.2

Brainstorming

Brainstorming allows children to share what they already know about a topic. This strategy is completed in a group setting; therefore, children who have little or no background knowledge about the topic can benefit from hearing what the other children share. During this process, an idea shared by one child will often trigger a related idea for other children. By building and activating their background knowledge, children will be more prepared to understand and remember what is read.

DIRECTIONS

1. Once you have selected a topic for study, present the key word to children by writing it on a piece of chart paper. For example, if you are going to begin a unit on the ocean, write the word *ocean* on chart paper. Draw a circle around the word and be sure to leave space around it to record the children's ideas.

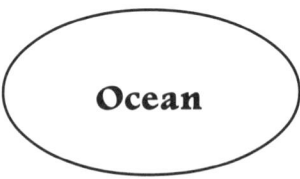

2. Tell the children you want them to share all of the things that come to mind when they hear the word *ocean*. Explain that this process is called brainstorming and that you welcome all responses.

3. Provide time for the children to share their responses as you write them on chart paper.

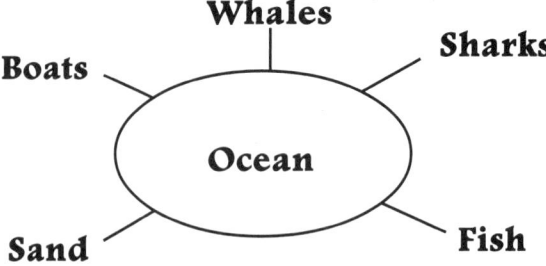

4. After all children have had a chance to share their ideas, explain that brainstorming is a great way to prepare for reading.

5. Tell the children that they will be reading books and doing activities related to the ocean. Explain that some of their brainstormed ideas may be covered in the unit and that they will also learn new information on oceans.

16   Chapter One

 **Tips for English Language Learners**

- Provide concrete materials related to the topic for brainstorming so English Language Learners can use the objects as a springboard for ideas. For example, when brainstorming about oceans, provide a shell, sand, and toy fish.

- Provide thinking time before asking children to share their responses. Give English Language Learners several minutes to think about the topic or to discuss it with a peer, and they will be more likely to have related ideas and the words to share them.

Teaching Strategy 5

Section 1.2

Predicting with Pictures

Predicting before reading serves several purposes. First, it activates background knowledge. In addition, it sets a purpose for reading and piques the child's curiosity and interest in the text.

DIRECTIONS

1. Select a book to share with children that has an interesting title and cover art. For example, you may choose to share *Me on the Map* by Joan Sweeney (1996).

2. Explain to children that you are going to show them the cover and title of a book and then ask them to predict what they think the book will be about and why. Discuss their predictions. Record their predictions on the chalkboard or a piece of chart paper. For example, children may share the following predictions.

    It's about the world because I see water and land.

    I think it's about a girl who is going on a trip because she's in the picture with a map.

3. Have the children read the story (or listen to you read it aloud). They should pay careful attention to see if their predictions are accurate or not.

4. Stop the reading at several logical points and ask the children if their predictions were accurate or not.

5. At the end of the story, discuss how pictures and predictions will help children get ready to read and improve their understanding of the story.

Ideas and Activities

1. Take frequent field trips to locations in the community such as the library, grocery store, dairy, fire station, farm, post office, veterinarian's office, hospital, and restaurant. Exposure to these locations will help to build children's background knowledge about important locations, people, jobs, and things in their communities.

2. Invite guest speakers into the classroom to share information and artifacts related to their jobs, hobbies, or travels. Provide time for children to examine the artifacts and ask questions. Consider speakers with interesting jobs or hobbies and be sure to contact children's parents, community members, and school personnel when looking for guest speakers. Consider the concrete artifacts that a guest speaker will be able to bring to share with children during a presentation. A list of possible guest speakers is provided in the box.

	Guest Speaker Ideas	
Banker	Farmer	Photographer
Musician	Cook	Artist
Receptionist	Nurse	Painter
Dentist	Veterinarian	Gardener
Weather forecaster	Store clerk	Doctor
Traveler	Florist	Secretary
Bus driver	Dog trainer	Astronomer
Mechanic	Computer professional	Construction worker
Hobbyist	Collector	Sports enthusiast

3. Help children develop a picture of a place, event, or person by sharing photos or videos with children prior to reading about the new topic of study. This technique works well when you cannot bring real objects or speakers into the classroom.

4. Create jackdaws to introduce a new topic of study. A jackdaw is a collection of artifacts related to a topic or book. Jackdaws may contain concrete objects, photographs, a list of related words, a time line of events, clothing or personal items related to a character, and various other materials. A jackdaw is displayed like a mini-museum in the classroom, and it serves as an excellent introduction to a new area of study (Rasinski & Padak, 1999). You and the children can also add materials to the jackdaw throughout the unit.

5. Invite children to bring in interesting artifacts and collections to share during Show and Tell time. Encourage other children to ask questions about the Show and Tell objects. Provide time for several children to Show and Tell each day. Create a classroom area to display Show and Tell materials for the students to explore during their free time.

6. Read to children on a daily basis to expose them to new ideas, experiences, and information. Vary the types of books you read to include poetry, fiction, nonfiction, fairytales, folk tales, and other genres. Provide time to discuss the books after reading them. After sharing the books, place them in the classroom library so the children can explore or reread them during their free time.

7. Engage children in filling out a K-W-L chart for a new topic of study (Ogle, 1986). The chart focuses on What I **K**now, What I **W**ant to Learn, and What I **L**earned. Before the children read a nonfiction book, the teacher introduces the K-W-L chart and asks the children to brainstorm what they already **K**now about the topic of the book. Next, the children list the things they **W**ant to learn about

the topic. After reading the book or listening to the book, the children list the things they **L**earned about the topic. This strategy works best as a teacher-guided activity for a group of children. The teacher serves as a scribe who writes the children's ideas on the various sections of the chart. A blank K-W-L chart is provided below.

K-W-L Chart for _____

K	W	L
What I already know:	What I want to learn:	What I learned:

8. Provide access to appropriate reference materials so children can look up information on topics about which they want to learn more. For example, create a classroom research center that contains children's dictionaries, children's encyclopedias, easy-to-read nonfiction books, computer resources, children's magazines, and informational posters.

9. Invite children to complete a Quickdraw or Quickwrite about a new topic of study. In a Quickdraw or Quickwrite, children are told about a new topic they will be studying. Children then draw or write what they already know about that topic. After two or three minutes of drawing or writing time, provide an opportunity for children to share their ideas. Discuss their knowledge about the topic as an introduction to the new topic of study.

10. Ask children to make predictions about a book based on the title and cover illustration to activate their background knowledge before reading or listening to a book. Follow up on children's predictions by asking them to explain how they made their predictions.

11. Supply interesting hands-on materials and place them in the classroom discovery center so children can explore them during their free time. Change the materials in the discovery center on a regular basis. Suggestions for the discovery center are in the following list.

Suggested Materials for Classroom Discovery Centers

Science Materials	Art Materials
Rocks	Paints
Shells	Brushes
Plants	Assorted papers
Magnifying glasses	Markers
Magnets	Glue
Scales	Scissors
Leaves	Crayons
Pinecones	Hole punch
Fossils	Ribbons
Children's microscopes	Cloth scraps
Nonfiction books on science topics	Posters showing various styles of art

Music Materials	Math Materials
Rhythm sticks	Counters
Drums	Graph paper
Materials to make simple instruments	Number lines
Triangles	Calculators
Recorders	Adding machines
Tape recorders	Number blocks
Tapes of various types of music	Math manipulatives
Song books	Abacus
Charts with song lyrics	Pencils
Conductor's baton	Paper

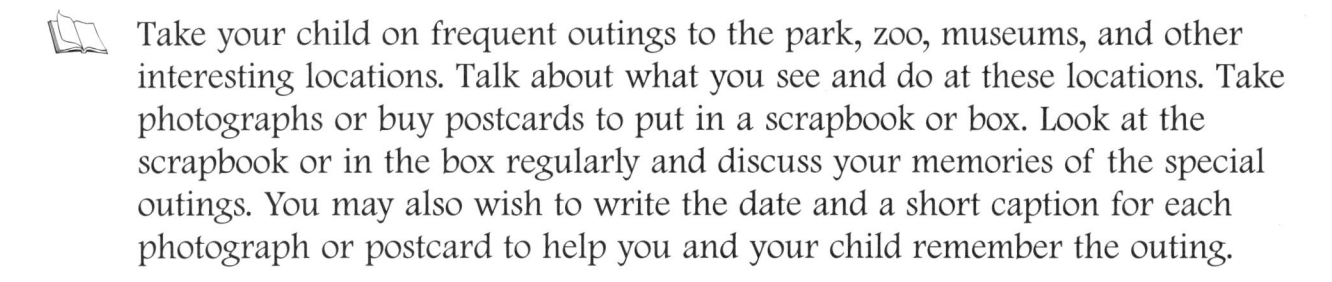

Home School Connections: Extending Background

- Take your child on frequent outings to the park, zoo, museums, and other interesting locations. Talk about what you see and do at these locations. Take photographs or buy postcards to put in a scrapbook or box. Look at the scrapbook or in the box regularly and discuss your memories of the special outings. You may also wish to write the date and a short caption for each photograph or postcard to help you and your child remember the outing.

- Watch educational programs with your child. Discuss the programs to share interesting new things you both learned from the programs. Many excellent informational programs on animals and nature can be found on PBS stations. In addition, many cable channels offer educational programming.

- Check out informational books from the library. Read and discuss these books with your child. Some popular topics for children include animals, weather, food, crafts, how-to books, holidays, travel, history, and famous people.

From Jerry L. Johns, Susan Davis Lenski, and Laurie Elish-Piper, *Teaching Beginning Readers: Linking Assessment and Instruction* (2nd ed.). Copyright © 2002 by Kendall/Hunt Publishing Company (1-800-247-3458, ext. 5). May be reproduced for noncommercial educational purposes.

Selected Resources
BACKGROUND KNOWLEDGE

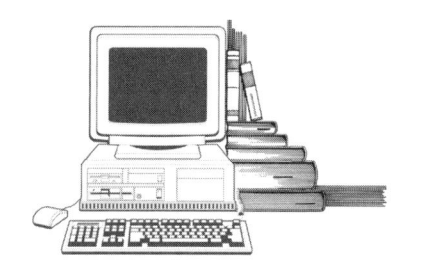

Informational Magazines for Children

Chickadee Magazine
25 Boxwood Lane
Buffalo, NY 14227-2780
Topics: Science, nature, and technology
Ages: 8 and under

Zoobooks
Wildlife Education Limited
9820 Willow Creek Rd.
Suite 300
San Diego, CA 92131
Topics: Wildlife
Ages: 5 and up

Let's Find Out
Scholastic, Inc.
2931 E. McCarty Street
P.O. Box 3710
Jefferson City, MO 65102-9957
(800-651-1586)
Topics: Science, social studies, theme-centered
Ages: Pre-K to K

Sesame Street Magazine
P.O. Box 52000
Boulder, CO 80301
Topics: Games and real-life activities
Ages: 3–7

Your Big Backyard
National Wildlife Federation
8925 Leesburg Pike
Vienna, VA 22184
(800-432-6564)
Topics: Nature, conservation
Ages: 3–6

Crayola Kids Magazine
P.O. Box 37198
Boone, IA 50037-7968
(800-846-7968)
Topics: Art, fact-based activities
Ages: 4–8

Media and Technology

Arthur's Thinking Games (critical and creative thinking activities). Broderbund. Available from Smart Kids Software (*www.smartkidssoftware.com* or 888-881-6001).

Busytown 2000 CD-ROM (readiness skills and activities). Simon and Schuster. Available from Smart Kids Software (*www.smartkidssoftware.com* or 888-881-6001).

Richard Scarry's Busytown Best Activity Center Ever CD-ROM (creative play activities in the neighborhood). Simon and Schuster. Available from Smart Kids Software (*www.smartkidssoftware.com* or 888-881-6001).

Thinkin'Things Collection 1 CD-ROM (thinking skills for young children). Edmark. Available from Smart Kids Software (*www.smartkidssoftware.com* or 888-881-6001).

From Jerry L. Johns, Susan Davis Lenski, and Laurie Elish-Piper, *Teaching Beginning Readers: Linking Assessment and Instruction* (2nd ed.). Copyright © 2002 by Kendall/Hunt Publishing Company (1-800-247-3458, ext. 5). May be reproduced for noncommercial educational purposes.

1.3 Oral Language

> **Goal** To help children expand and enhance their oral language development.

BACKGROUND

Oral language provides the foundation for reading and writing (Clay, 1998). Children draw on their listening and speaking vocabularies as they read and write. In addition, as children develop their oral language, they become more aware of shades of meaning and different ways of expressing thoughts. Some children come to school with well-developed oral language skills in English. Other children may need more support to develop their oral language. All young children can benefit from engaging in activities and strategies that foster oral language development.

Teaching Strategy 1

Section 1.3

Show and Tell~Question~Connection

The classic activity of Show and Tell is an excellent way to promote children's oral language development. Including a question-answer time as part of Show and Tell will further enhance the language development opportunities offered by this strategy. In addition, because children are sharing a favorite object, they are highly motivated to convey their ideas and information to others.

DIRECTIONS

1. Explain to the children that you will be doing an activity called Show and Tell-Question-Connection and each of them will have a chance to bring in a favorite object to share with the class.

2. Demonstrate the process by sharing one of your favorite objects. For example, you might bring in a large pinecone you collected from a recent camping trip.

3. Explain to the children that first you will Show and Tell about the pinecone. For example, you might say, "I got this big pinecone when I went camping in Indiana last fall. I like this pinecone because it is long and sturdy. It smells like the forest, and it makes me think of all of the fun I had on this camping trip."

4. Next, tell the children that you will move into the Question phase of the activity. Invite children to ask you questions about the pinecone or anything you shared. If a child's question is unclear, help him or her rephrase it. Respond to each question.

5. Tell the children that you are now going to move on to the Connection part of the activity. Explain that any of the children who would like to share a personal connection with the object or ideas shared are invited to do so.

6. Develop a schedule so each child has a chance to bring in an object to share.

> **Tips for English Language Learners**
>
> - Meet with English Language Learners before they share in the Show and Tell-Question-Connection activity. Discuss the object they have selected, offering English words as necessary. This preparation should result in increased confidence and clarity when English Language Learners take the lead in the activity.

Teaching Strategy 2

Section 1.3

Expand~a~Sentence

This strategy encourages children to add descriptive words and phrases to a simple sentence to enhance and extend the meaning of the sentence. By doing so, children can begin to understand the importance of using descriptive words and explaining things clearly and completely.

DIRECTIONS

1. Select a simple sentence. Write the sentence on the chalkboard. For example, you may select the following sentence: The boy ran.

2. Ask children to expand the sentence by adding one or more words to make the sentence more interesting and informative. Children may offer words to expand the sentence as in the following examples.

    The little boy ran.

    The little boy ran home in the rain.

    The little boy ran home quickly in the rain.

3. Once the sentence has been expanded several times, write the new expanded sentence on the chalkboard below the original sentence. Discuss the differences between the two sentences. Ask the children which sentence is more interesting or informative.

4. Continue the strategy using several other sentences.

> **Tips for English Language Learners**
>
> - Provide word cards for English Language Learners to use to expand sentences. By providing several possible choices, you can help English Language Learners focus on what makes sense in the sentence rather than on trying to generate new ideas.

Teaching Strategy 3

Section 1.3

Progressive Storytelling

Children love to tell stories, especially those with wild, imaginative events and characters. The Progressive Storytelling strategy invites children to add to an evolving story. They must listen closely to make sure their additions make sense.

DIRECTIONS

1. Gather a group of six to eight children together in a circle on the carpet or around a large table. Explain to the children that they are going to work together as a group to tell a story.
2. Remind children that stories are more fun when interesting words are used and exciting events and characters are involved.
3. Tell the children that you will begin the story and then move around the circle or table in order so each child can add to the story. Explain that children can say "Pass" if they cannot think of something to add at that time.
4. Begin the story by sharing an opening sentence such as, "Once upon a time in a land far, far away, there lived a little boy who had a very special talent."
5. Rotate around the circle so each child can add to the story.
6. When the story reaches you again, provide closure to the story.

Tips for English Language Learners

- Invite English Language Learners to share their additions near the beginning of the story to decrease the likelihood that another child will already have shared similar ideas.
- Provide several props related to the story opening. Invite English Language Learners to select a prop to help them make additions to the story.

Ideas and Activities

1. Display an interesting picture or object. Invite children to orally describe what they see.

2. Invite children to tell a story from a wordless picture book. For a list of wordless picture books, see the Selected Resources at the end of this section.

3. Provide props, puppets, or felt board shapes in a learning center to encourage children to tell stories based on the objects.

4. Institute a "Turn to Your Neighbor" policy in your classroom so all children have a chance to share, even when time is short. Tell children to "turn to your neighbor," share an idea, and then switch roles.

5. Play the game of telephone to promote careful listening and speaking. Have the children sit in a large circle. Begin the game by whispering a message in one child's ear. Have that child whisper the message in the next child's ear, and so on. Continue until the message travels through the entire group. Share the final message. Discuss any differences between the original message and the final message. Emphasize the importance of listening and speaking carefully in order to understand and be understood.

6. Ask open-ended questions to encourage children to share longer, more complex responses. For example, you might ask children, "What would you do and why?" and "What was your favorite part and why?"

7. Provide thinking time before calling on children to share their ideas.

8. Brainstorm lists of interesting words to replace overused words such as *good*, *said*, and *happy*. Display these words in the classroom. Use them in your conversations with children and invite them to use the more descriptive words in their speech.

9. Provide time for role-playing and creative dramatics so children can explore and apply language in interesting contexts.

10. Read aloud to children from a wide variety of books and genres to model interesting, effective, engaging language. Discuss examples of particularly interesting or engaging words, phrases, or sentences from the books.

Home School Connections — Language Activities

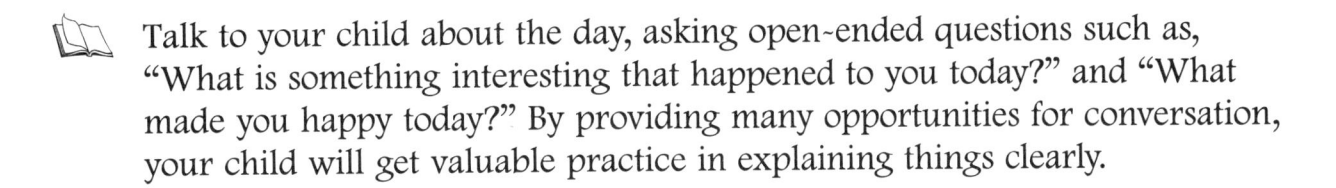

- Talk to your child about the day, asking open-ended questions such as, "What is something interesting that happened to you today?" and "What made you happy today?" By providing many opportunities for conversation, your child will get valuable practice in explaining things clearly.

- Label objects, ask questions, and invite your child's observations as you do daily activities such as grocery shopping, playing in the park, or walking through your neighborhood.

- Read to your child. Describe and discuss the pictures. Share favorite parts. Later, work together to tell the story to another family member.

From Jerry L. Johns, Susan Davis Lenski, and Laurie Elish-Piper, *Teaching Beginning Readers: Linking Assessment and Instruction* (2nd ed.). Copyright © 2002 by Kendall/Hunt Publishing Company (1-800-247-3458, ext. 5). May be reproduced for noncommercial educational purposes.

Selected Resources
ORAL LANGUAGE

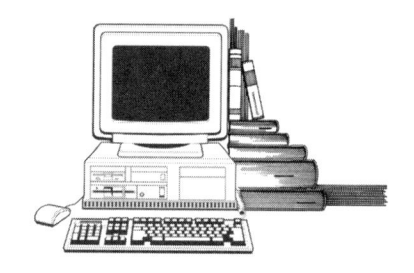

Wordless Picture Books

Day, A. (1995). *Carl's birthday*. New York: Farrar Straus Giroux.

Day, A. (1998). *Follow Carl!* New York: Farrar Straus Giroux.

DePaola, T. (1978). *Pancakes for breakfast*. New York: Harcourt.

Peddle, D. (2000). *Snow day*. New York: Doubleday.

Tafuri, N. (1988). *Junglewalk*. New York: Greenwillow.

Tafuri, N. (1990). *Follow me*. New York: Greenwillow.

Wiesner, D. (1988). *Free fall*. New York: Lothrop.

Wiesner, D. (1991). *Tuesday*. Boston: Houghton.

Children's Songs and Rhymes on Audio CD

Can a jumbo jet sing the alphabet? (1998). Northridge, CA: Hap-Pal Music.

Classic nursery rhymes (1991). Northridge, CA: Hap-Pal Music.

Rhythms on parade (1995). Northridge, CA: Hap-Pal Music.

Puppets and Audio Books

Children's literature and cassette packs available from Houghton Mifflin at *www.eduplace.com*

Children's literature and cassette packs available from Scholastic at *www.scholastic.com*

Puppets with corresponding audio books available from Act II Books at *www.kidsbooksandpuppets.com*

Children's literature with corresponding puppets, puppet theaters, and puppet making kits available from The Puppet Patch at *www.parentpatch.com/puppet_puppets.htm*

From Jerry L. Johns, Susan Davis Lenski, and Laurie Elish-Piper, *Teaching Beginning Readers: Linking Assessment and Instruction* (2nd ed.). Copyright © 2002 by Kendall/Hunt Publishing Company (1-800-247-3458, ext. 5). May be reproduced for noncommercial educational purposes.

1.4 Assessments of Interests and Attitudes Toward Reading

Assessment Strategy 1   Interviews about Reading   30

     Emergent Reader Record Sheet   31
     Early Reader (Grades 1–2) Record Sheet   33

Assessment Strategy 2   News about Me   35

     Child's Copy   36

Assessment Strategy 3   Elementary Reading Attitude Survey   38

     Child's Copy   40
     Scoring Sheet   45
     Percentile Ranks   46

Additional Ways of Assessing Attitudes and Interests   47

Goal   To assess a child's interests and attitudes toward reading.

BACKGROUND

Responsive teachers know the children in their classrooms well and incorporate this information into lesson planning, materials selection, and approaches to teaching. Teachers can get to know children through conversations and daily activities. In addition, interviews, surveys, and questionnaires are helpful tools for learning more about the children you teach. Observations are also very useful as you seek to learn about children's attitudes toward reading.

Attitudes, Interests, and Oral Language

Assessment Strategy 1

Section 1.4

Interviews about Reading

Overview	Interviews about Reading are designed to determine the child's understanding of the nature of reading, the purposes for reading, and the child's attitude toward reading.
Materials Needed	1. Record Sheet (p. 31 or p. 33) 2. Tape recorder (if desired)
Procedures	1. Duplicate the appropriate Record Sheet. If the child does not yet read, choose the Emergent Reader Interview (p. 31). If the child is beginning to read, use the Early Reading Interview (p. 33). 2. You may decide to tape-record the interview rather than write the child's responses on the page in the Record Sheet during the interview. If you tape-record the interview, set up the tape recorder and test it to make sure it is working properly. 3. With the child, say, "Today we're going to talk about reading and your ideas about reading. There are no right or wrong answers. I'm going to ask you some questions. To answer the questions, just tell me what you are thinking." 4. If you are tape-recording the interview, say, "I'm going to turn on the tape recorder so that I can remember what you say. Do you mind?" (Teacher: Be sure to test the tape recorder.) 5. If you are writing the child's responses, say, "I will be writing down what you say so that I can remember your comments. Is that all right with you?" 6. Begin asking the interview questions in the order they are written. If the child does not answer, prompt with easy questions such as "Do you have any brothers or sisters? and What animals do you like?" Once the child feels comfortable answering the questions, proceed with the interview.
Scoring and Interpretation	Record the child's responses as accurately as possible. Then read the responses looking for overall patterns. Informally determine whether the child views himself or herself as learning to read and whether the child has a positive or negative attitude toward reading. Record your qualitative judgment of the child's attitude and understanding about reading with an X on the continuum provided on page 32 or page 34.

RECORD SHEET

Interviews about Reading Emergent Reader (PreK–K)

Name _____ Date _____

1. Do you like to have someone read to you? ____ Yes   ____ No

    Who do you like to read to you? _____

2. What kinds of stories do you like? _____

3. Tell me the name of a favorite story. _____

4. Do you have any books at home? ____ Yes   ____ No

    About how many books do you have at home? _____

    Where do you keep the books? _____

5. Who do you know that likes to read? _____

6. Are you learning to read? ____ Yes   ____ No

    Tell me what you have learned so far. _____

7. Do you want to learn how to read better? ____ Yes   ____ No

    Tell me more about that. _____

8. Do you think you will be a good reader? ____ Yes   ____ No

    What makes you say that? _____

9. What makes a person a good reader? _____
   _____

10. What is reading? _____
    _____

From Jerry L. Johns, Susan Davis Lenski, and Laurie Elish-Piper, *Teaching Beginning Readers: Linking Assessment and Instruction.* Copyright © 2002 by Kendall/Hunt Publishing Company (1-800-247-3458, ext. 5). May be reproduced for noncommercial educational purposes.

RECORD SHEET

Qualitative Judgments of Interviews about Reading Emergent Reader (PreK–K)

Name _____ Date _____

	Not Evident / Low / Seldom / Weak / Poor	Some	Evident / High / Always / Strong / Excellent
Overall interest in reading	⊢―――⊢―――⊢―――⊢―――⊣		
Familiarity with specific stories	⊢―――⊢―――⊢―――⊢―――⊣		
Availability of books	⊢―――⊢―――⊢―――⊢―――⊣		
Knowledge of reading role models	⊢―――⊢―――⊢―――⊢―――⊣		
Confidence in learning to read	⊢―――⊢―――⊢―――⊢―――⊣		
Motivation to learn to read	⊢―――⊢―――⊢―――⊢―――⊣		
Knowledge of purpose for reading	⊢―――⊢―――⊢―――⊢―――⊣		

Observations, Comments, Notes, and Insights

From Jerry L. Johns, Susan Davis Lenski, and Laurie Elish-Piper, *Teaching Beginning Readers: Linking Assessment and Instruction.* Copyright © 2002 by Kendall/Hunt Publishing Company (1-800-247-3458, ext. 5). May be reproduced for noncommercial educational purposes.

RECORD SHEET

Interviews about Reading
Early Reader (Grades 1–2)

Name _____ Date _____

1. Do you like to have someone read to you?   ____ Yes   ____ No

   Who do you like to read to you? _____

2. What kinds of stories do you like? _____
   _____

3. Tell me the name of a favorite story. _____

4. Do you have many books at home?   ____ Yes   ____ No

   How many books do you think you have? _____

5. Who do you know that likes to read? _____
   _____

6. Do you think you are a good reader?   ____ Yes   ____ No

   Why or why not? _____

7. What makes a person a good reader? _____
   _____

8. When you are reading and come to a word you don't know, what do you do?
   _____

9. What do you do when you don't understand what you are reading?
   _____

10. What is reading?
    _____

From Jerry L. Johns, Susan Davis Lenski, and Laurie Elish-Piper, *Teaching Beginning Readers: Linking Assessment and Instruction*. Copyright © 2002 by Kendall/Hunt Publishing Company (1-800-247-3458, ext. 5). May be reproduced for noncommercial educational purposes.

RECORD SHEET

Qualitative Judgments of Interviews about Reading Early Reader (Grades 1–2)

Name_____   Date _____

	Not Evident / Low / Seldom / Weak / Poor	Some	Evident / High / Always / Strong / Excellent
Overall interest in reading	⊢———⊢———⊢———⊢———⊣		
Familiarity with specific stories	⊢———⊢———⊢———⊢———⊣		
Availability of books	⊢———⊢———⊢———⊢———⊣		
Knowledge of reading role models	⊢———⊢———⊢———⊢———⊣		
Confidence in learning to read	⊢———⊢———⊢———⊢———⊣		
Motivation to learn to read	⊢———⊢———⊢———⊢———⊣		
Knowledge of word identification strategies	⊢———⊢———⊢———⊢———⊣		
Knowledge of comprehension strategies	⊢———⊢———⊢———⊢———⊣		
Knowledge of purpose for reading	⊢———⊢———⊢———⊢———⊣		

Observations, Comments, Notes, and Insights

From Jerry L. Johns, Susan Davis Lenski, and Laurie Elish-Piper, *Teaching Beginning Readers: Linking Assessment and Instruction*. Copyright © 2002 by Kendall/Hunt Publishing Company (1-800-247-3458, ext. 5). May be reproduced for noncommercial educational purposes.

Assessment Strategy 2

Section 1.4

News about Me

Overview	News about Me provides information about the child's background, interests, and life. It can be completed as an interview, or older children can respond in writing. Teachers can use the information to recommend books, adjust the curriculum, or make connections between the classroom and the child's life.
Materials Needed	1. News about Me Record Sheet (pp. 36–37) 2. Tape recorder (if desired)
Procedures	1. Duplicate the News about Me Record Sheet (pp. 36–37). 2. Explain to the child that you want to learn more about him or her by using the News about Me Record Sheet to help gather information. 3. If you plan to give the assessment as an interview, you may wish to tape-record the child's responses. 4. If the child will be responding in writing, explain that he or she should seek assistance if any of the questions are unclear. Also explain that in some sections students may not answer all the questions (for example, no pets).
Scoring and Interpretation	Review the child's responses, noting any information that may help you suggest appropriate books for the child. Note any connections you can make to the curriculum.

RECORD SHEET

News about Me

A News Story about _____ Date _____
(write your name here)

News about My Family

I have _____ brothers and sisters.

They are _____ years old.

I like to play with _____.

My mother and I like to _____.

My father and I like to _____.

I (like/do not like) to play alone.

I help at home by _____.

The thing I like to do at home is _____
_____.

News about My Pets

I have a pet _____.

I (do/do not) take care of my pet.

I do not have a pet because _____
_____.

I would like to have a pet _____.

News about My Books and My Reading

I like to read about _____
_____.

The best book I ever read was _____
_____.

I (do get/do not get) books from the library.

I have _____ books of my own at home.

I read aloud to _____.

_____ reads to me.

News about My Friends

My best friend is _____.

I like (him/her) because _____
_____.

We play _____.

I would rather play (at my house/at my friend's house) because _____
_____.

News about Things I Like and Dislike

I do not like _____.

I like _____.

I am afraid of _____.

I am not afraid of _____.

News about My Wishes

When I grow up, I want to be _____
_____
_____.

If I could have three wishes I would wish

(1) _____
_____.

(2) _____
_____.

(3) _____
_____.

page 1

From Jerry L. Johns and Susan Davis Lenski, *Improving Reading: Strategies and Resources* (3rd ed.). Copyright © 2001 Kendall/Hunt Publishing Company (1-800-247-3458, ext. 5). May be reproduced for noncommercial educational purposes.

News about My Travels and Adventures

I have traveled by:

____ bus   ____ car

____ airplane   ____ truck

____ boat   ____ train

____ bicycle   ____ van

I have visited these places:

____ circus   ____ zoo

____ farm   ____ park

____ hotel   ____ museum

____ bakery   ____ library

____ airport   ____ fire station

____ factory, and _____.

The best adventure I ever had was _____
_____
_____
_____.

News about My Hobbies and Collections

One of my best hobbies is _____
_____.

I collect _____.

I want to collect _____.

My other hobbies are _____
_____.

Movie, Radio, and Television Favorites

I see _____ movies each week.

I like to listen to _____ on the radio.

I see _____ television programs a day.

My favorite programs are _____
_____.

News about My School Subjects

My favorite subject is _____.

The subject I dislike most is _____.

I am best at _____.

I wish I was better in _____.

Write any other news about yourself below.

_____
_____
_____
_____
_____
_____

page 2

From Jerry L. Johns and Susan Davis Lenski, *Improving Reading: Strategies and Resources* (3rd ed.). Copyright © 2001 Kendall/Hunt Publishing Company (1-800-247-3458, ext. 5). May be reproduced for noncommercial educational purposes.

Assessment Strategy 3

Section 1.4

Elementary Reading Attitude Survey

Overview	The Elementary Reading Attitude Survey provides insight into children's attitudes toward recreational and school reading. In addition, a total score can be calculated to get an overall idea of a child's attitude toward reading. The assessment can be administered individually or to a group of children.
Materials Needed	1. One copy of the Elementary Reading Attitude Survey (pp. 40–44) for each child and one copy for teacher 2. Scoring Sheet (p. 45) 3. Percentile Ranks (p. 46)
Procedures	1. Explain to the children that you are going to give them a survey to find out how they feel about reading. 2. Tell them there are no right or wrong answers and urge them to be honest in their responses. 3. Display the Garfield responses on the overhead projector and explain what each of the Garfields means: happiest, slightly smiling, mildly upset, and very upset. Discuss examples of when the children feel each of these emotions. 4. Distribute the Elementary Reading Attitude Survey. Instruct the children to circle the Garfield that matches their feelings for each question. 5. Read each question aloud, providing wait time for the children to respond.
Scoring and Interpretation	1. To score the survey, count four points for each leftmost (happiest) Garfield circled, three for each slightly smiling Garfield, two for each mildly upset Garfield, and one point for each very upset (rightmost) Garfield. Three scores for each student can be obtained: the total for the first 10 items, the total for the second 10, and a composite total. The first half of the survey relates to attitude toward recreational reading; the second half relates to attitude toward academic aspects of reading. 2. You can interpret scores in two ways. One is to note informally where the score falls in regard to the four points on the scale. A total score of 50, for example, would fall about midway on the scale, between the slightly happy and slightly upset figures, therefore indicating a relatively indifferent overall attitude toward reading. The other approach is more formal. It involves converting the raw scores into percentile ranks by means of Table 1. Be sure to use the norms for the right grade level and to note the column headings (Rec =

38 Chapter One

	recreational reading, Aca = academic reading, Tot = total score). If you wish to determine the average percentile rank for your class, average the raw scores first; then use the table to locate the percentile rank corresponding to the raw score mean. Percentile ranks cannot be averaged directly.
Norms for the Elementary Reading Attitude Survey	To create norms for the interpretation of the Elementary Reading Attitude Survey scores, a large-scale study was conducted late in January 1989, at which time the survey was administered to 18,138 students in Grades 1–6. Several steps were taken to achieve a sample that was sufficiently stratified (that is, reflective of the American population) to allow confident generalizations. Children were drawn from 95 school districts in 38 states. The number of girls exceeded by only 5 the number of boys. Ethnic distribution of the sample was also close to that of the U.S. population in 1989. The proportion of Blacks (9.5%) was within 3% of the national proportion, whereas the proportion of Hispanics (6.2%) was within 2%. Percentile ranks at each grade for both subscales and the full scale are presented in Table 1. These data can be used to compare individual students' scores with the national sample and they can be interpreted like achievement-test percentile ranks.

McKenna, M.C., & Kear, D.J. (1990). Measuring attitude toward reading: A new tool for teachers. *The Reading Teacher, 43,* 626–639. Reprinted with permission of Michael C. McKenna and the International Reading Association.

RECORD SHEET

Elementary Reading Attitude Survey

Name _____ Date _____

School _____ Grade _____

1. How do you feel when you read a book on a rainy Saturday?

2. How do you feel when you read a book in a school during free time?

3. How do you feel about reading for fun at home?

4. How do you feel about getting a book for a present?

© Paws, Inc. The Garfield character is incorporated in this test with the permission of Paws, Incorporated, and may be reproduced only in connection with the reproduction of the test in its entirety for classroom use until further notice by Paws, Inc., and any other reproduction or use without the express prior written consent of Paws is prohibited.

2

5. How do you feel about spending free time reading?

6. How do you feel about starting a new book?

7. How do you feel about reading during summer?

8. How do you feel about reading instead of playing?

© Paws, Inc. The Garfield character is incorporated in this test with the permission of Paws, Incorporated, and may be reproduced only in connection with the reproduction of the test in its entirety for classroom use until further notice by Paws, Inc., and any other reproduction or use without the express prior written consent of Paws is prohibited.

Attitudes, Interests, and Oral Language 41

3

9. How do you feel about going to a bookstore?

10. How do you feel about reading different kinds of books?

11. How do you feel when the teacher asks you questions about what you read?

12. How do you feel about doing reading workbook pages and worksheets?

© Paws, Inc. The Garfield character is incorporated in this test with the permission of Paws, Incorporated, and may be reproduced only in connection with the reproduction of the test in its entirety for classroom use until further notice by Paws, Inc., and any other reproduction or use without the express prior written consent of Paws is prohibited.

4

13. How do you feel about reading in school?

14. How do you feel about reading your school books?

15. How do you feel about learning from a book?

16. How do you feel when it's time for reading in class?

© Paws, Inc. The Garfield character is incorporated in this test with the permission of Paws, Incorporated, and may be reproduced only in connection with the reproduction of the test in its entirety for classroom use until further notice by Paws, Inc., and any other reproduction or use without the express prior written consent of Paws is prohibited.

Attitudes, Interests, and Oral Language

5

17. How do you feel about the stories you read in reading class?

GARFIELD: © 1978 United Feature Syndicate, Inc.

18. How do you feel when you read out loud in class?

19. How do you feel about using a dictionary?

20. How do you feel about taking a reading test?

© Paws, Inc. The Garfield character is incorporated in this test with the permission of Paws, Incorporated, and may be reproduced only in connection with the reproduction of the test in its entirety for classroom use until further notice by Paws, Inc., and any other reproduction or use without the express prior written consent of Paws is prohibited.

Elementary Reading Attitude Survey Scoring Sheet

Student Name _____

Teacher _____

Grade _____ Administration Date _____

	Scoring Guide
4 points	Happiest Garfield
3 points	Slightly smiling Garfield
2 points	Mildly upset Garfield
1 point	Very upset Garfield

Recreational reading

1. _____
2. _____
3. _____
4. _____
5. _____
6. _____
7. _____
8. _____
9. _____
10. _____

Raw score: _____

Academic reading

11. _____
12. _____
13. _____
14. _____
15. _____
16. _____
17. _____
18. _____
19. _____
20. _____

Raw score: _____

Total raw score (Recreational + Academic): _____

Percentile Ranks

Recreational	
Academic	
Full scale	

From Jerry L. Johns and Susan Davis Lenski, *Improving Reading: Strategies and Resources* (3rd ed.). Copyright © 2001 Kendall/Hunt Publishing Company (1-800-247-3458, ext. 5). May be reproduced for noncommercial educational purposes.

Table 1. Mid-Year Percentile Ranks by Grade and Scale

Raw Score	Grade 1 Rec	Grade 1 Aca	Grade 1 Tot	Grade 2 Rec	Grade 2 Aca	Grade 2 Tot	Grade 3 Rec	Grade 3 Aca	Grade 3 Tot	Grade 4 Rec	Grade 4 Aca	Grade 4 Tot	Grade 5 Rec	Grade 5 Aca	Grade 5 Tot	Grade 6 Rec	Grade 6 Aca	Grade 6 Tot
80			99			99			99			99			99			99
79			95			96			98			99			99			99
78			93			95			97			98			99			99
77			92			94			97			98			99			99
76			90			93			96			97			98			99
75			88			92			95			96			98			99
74			86			90			94			95			97			99
73			84			88			92			94			97			98
72			82			86			91			93			96			98
71			80			84			89			91			95			97
70			78			82			86			89			94			96
69			75			79			84			88			92			95
68			72			77			81			86			91			93
67			69			74			79			83			89			92
66			66			71			76			50			87			90
65			62			69			73			78			84			88
64			59			66			70			75			82			86
63			55			63			67			72			79			84
62			52			60			64			69			76			82
61			49			57			61			66			73			79
60			46			54			58			62			70			76
59			43			51			55			59			67			73
58			40			47			51			56			64			69
57			37			45			48			53			61			68
56			34			41			44			48			57			62
55			31			38			41			45			53			58
54			28			35			38			41			50			55
53			25			32			34			38			46			52
52			22			29			31			35			42			48
51			20			26			28			32			39			44
50			18			23			25			28			36			40
49			15			20			23			26			33			37
48			13			18			20			23			29			33
47			12			15			17			20			26			30
46			10			13			15			18			23			27
45			8			11			13			16			20			25
44			7			9			11			13			17			22
43			6			8			9			12			15			20
42			5			7			9			10			13			17
41			5			6			7			9			12			15
40	99	99	4	99	99	5	99	99	6	99	99	7	99	99	10	99	99	13
39	92	91	3	94	94	4	96	97	5	97	98	6	98	99	9	99	99	12
38	89	88	3	92	92	2	94	95	4	95	97	5	96	98	8	97	99	10
37	86	85	2	88	89	2	90	93	3	92	95	4	94	98	7	95	99	8
36	81	79	2	84	85	2	87	91	2	88	93	3	91	96	6	92	98	7
35	77	75	1	79	81	1	81	88	2	84	90	3	87	95	4	88	97	6
34	72	69	1	74	78	1	75	83	2	78	87	2	82	93	4	83	95	5
33	65	63	1	68	73	1	69	79	1	72	83	2	77	90	3	79	93	4
32	58	58	1	62	67	1	63	74	1	66	79	1	71	86	3	74	91	3
31	52	53	1	56	62	1	57	69	0	60	75	1	65	82	2	69	87	2
30	44	49	1	50	57	0	51	63	0	54	70	1	59	77	1	63	82	2
29	38	44	0	44	51	0	45	58	0	47	64	1	53	71	1	58	78	1
28	32	39	0	37	46	0	38	52	0	41	58	1	48	66	1	51	73	1
27	26	34	0	31	41	0	33	47	0	35	52	1	42	60	1	46	67	1
26	21	30	0	25	37	0	26	41	0	29	46	0	36	54	0	39	60	1
25	17	25	0	20	32	0	21	36	0	23	40	0	30	49	0	34	54	0
24	12	21	0	15	27	0	17	31	0	19	35	0	25	42	0	29	49	0
23	9	18	0	11	23	0	13	26	0	14	29	0	20	37	0	24	42	0
22	7	14	0	8	18	0	9	22	0	11	25	0	16	31	0	19	36	0
21	5	11	0	6	15	0	6	18	0	9	20	0	13	26	0	15	30	0
20	4	9	0	4	11	0	5	14	0	6	16	0	10	21	0	12	24	0
19	2	7		2	8		3	11		5	13		7	17		10	20	
18	2	5		2	6		2	8		3	9		6	13		8	15	
17	1	4		1	5		1	5		2	7		4	9		6	11	
16	1	3		1	3		1	4		2	5		3	6		4	8	
15	0	2		0	2		0	3		1	3		2	4		3	6	
14	0	2		0	1		0	1		1	2		1	2		1	3	
13	0	1		0	1		0	1		0	1		1	2		1	2	
12	0	1		0	0		0	0		0	1		0	1		0	1	
11	0	0		0	0		0	0		0	0		0	0		0	0	
10	0	0		0	0		0	0		0	0		0	0		0	0	

Additional Ways of Assessing Attitudes and Interests

1. Listen carefully to the children and observe them during free-choice activities. Try to incorporate what you learn about children into your instruction and materials selection.
2. Confer with children and ask them to share their interests, hobbies, and daily activities.

CHAPTER 2

Literacy Knowledge

OVERVIEW

Young children learn about print and stories through experience; they don't inherently know how print works. Children need to learn that letters arranged in certain ways form words, that words are separated with spaces, that words form sentences, that print is read from left to right, and that meaning can be constructed from print. These and other print concepts are developed as children have experiences seeing print and watching others read.

In the same sense, young children learn about the structure of stories from experience. Fictional stories have a specific structure, called story grammar (Stein & Glenn, 1979). Young children learn how stories are organized as they listen to older children and adults tell stories and read stories to them. Through multiple exposures to stories, children learn that stories have a plot, setting, characters, and theme. As they become familiar with story structure, children are able to predict events in stories and are able to discern what is missing from the stories that they hear.

Fictional stories are common in the lives of children—they hear stories from grandparents, they watch stories on television, and they hear stories read to them— so learning the structure of fiction is easy for most children. Learning how informational text is organized is much more difficult. Children in the primary grades have had little experience with informational text (Duke, 2000). Informational text, however, is also written in fairly predictable organizational patterns. The most common informational organizational patterns are description, sequence, comparison, cause-effect, and problem-solution. When children understand the structures of informational text, they can more easily make predictions and comprehend text. Answers to questions teachers often ask about literacy knowledge follow.

Language develops naturally in children. Do they learn print concepts the same way?

Yes and no. Children learn language through listening to others speak, but they also have an inherent knowledge of grammatical structures (Chomsky, 1968). Children can learn print in the same way—through experiences. There are, however, some important differences. If children are not exposed to print in their surroundings, they do not automatically develop an understanding of print concepts. Therefore, young children need guided experiences in order to learn print concepts, such as parents reading to their children.

Many of the children in my classroom have not experienced story reading with their parents. What should I do?

When children have had few experiences with stories at home, they need extra story reading in school through a literature-based instructional program (Morrow & Gambrell, 2001). Reading books aloud and showing children that pages turn from right to left, that you read from top to bottom, and that sentences are read from left to right are essential understandings to develop. Provide many experiences during the school day for children to learn these concepts. Frequently read Big Books to children, showing them how to turn pages, sweeping your hand under the print, and illustrating the directionality of the print. Have other adults and older children read to your class as well. In addition, provide children with opportunities to read (look through) picture books, remind them to practice reading every day, and provide a print-rich environment in the classroom.

We spend most of our time in kindergarten teaching the letters of the alphabet, but I know the children in my classroom are weak on print concepts. Will my focus on letters eventually help students learn about print?

Children need to understand how print works before they can benefit from instruction on letters and sounds (Au, 1998), but that doesn't mean you should only concentrate on print concepts. If children have had few experiences with books and have little knowledge of print concepts, you should spend much of your time with these foundational skills. However, you can still teach letters and sounds associated with letters during shared reading. An emphasis on stories, rather than individual letters, will help children develop concepts about print more rapidly.

Do children learn the structure of stories through reading, or do I need to teach story grammar?

Most children develop a sense of story as they listen to stories being read (Stein & Glenn, 1979), but this story sense can be refined through instruction. For example, many children in the primary grades understand that a story needs to have a setting and main characters, but they may not understand that the plot of a story will have a "problem" that needs to be resolved. Teaching children how stories work helps them improve their comprehension of text, and it also facilitates their writing of stories (Pressley, Allington, Wharton-McDonald, Block, & Morrow, 2001).

I don't have many informational books that are easy enough for my beginning readers. Where can I find nonfiction books for them?

Many publishers are currently developing a line of easy-to-read informational books. The Selected Resources (see page 84) include a list of publishers that offer informational books for young children.

2.1 Print Concepts

> **Goal** To help children learn concepts about print in books.
> **Assessment Strategy 1** Print Concepts, page 86

BACKGROUND

As children grow, they learn about the world around them and gradually develop literacy skills. Knowledge about reading and writing begins early in children's lives (Teale & Sulzby, 1989). Very young children begin to notice that reading and writing are part of their world. For example, young children learn that their environment is full of print. They see print material such as newspapers and magazines in their homes, they see print on television, and they recognize signs and logos on products and in stores. As children begin to notice print, they are progressing toward literacy (Clay, 1985). Regardless of their backgrounds, all children are learning about their worlds and how literacy fits into their lives (Taylor, 1983).

Even though all children have important background experiences, they have had various degrees of exposure to books. Some children have participated in thousands of hours of shared reading with caring adults. Other children have had very little experience with books. The amount of experience children have had with books is important in their acquisition of literacy. Most children who have been read to have learned some of the basics of literacy knowledge. They may know that books are for reading, that books open from right to left, where the pictures in books are, what print is used for, and so on. Children need to understand the purpose of books and concepts about print in order for instruction to be effective.

Many young children have learned that print carries meaning, and they know how to open a book and turn the pages. However, many children still do not know the terminology of reading—the concept of a letter, a word, a sentence, or sounds (Johns, 1980). As children begin to learn to read, they need to learn how language operates, that a written word matches a spoken word, that spaces are used between words, and that sentences are set off with punctuation. This literacy knowledge is an important precursor to independent reading.

When children do not know concepts about print, they need instruction in those concepts. Children need a solid base of literacy knowledge in order to firmly grasp other aspects of the reading process. The following teaching strategies, ideas, and activities provide suggestions that promote children's literacy knowledge.

Teaching Strategy 1

Section 2.1

Shared Reading

One of the purposes for shared reading is to introduce children to concepts about print. Many children are unfamiliar with book parts, how books are read, and the relationship between words and speech. Providing children with explicit instruction about the parts of books can help them increase their literacy knowledge.

DIRECTIONS

1. Choose a Big Book to read to children. (A Big Book is an oversized book that all children can see.) Before reading the book, identify concepts about print that you want to introduce. Some of the concepts that children need to learn are listed below.

   - books are for reading
   - the front and back of a book
   - the top and bottom of a book
   - pages turn from right to left
   - the difference between print and pictures
   - print carries meaning
   - pictures on a page are related to what the print says
   - print is read from left to right
   - print is read from top to bottom
   - where one begins reading on a page
   - what a title of a book is
   - what an author is
   - what an illustrator is

2. Introduce the concepts you want to teach as you read to students as in the example below.

   Teacher: Today we're going to read *Little Cloud* by Eric Carle (1996). What do you see on the cover of this book?

   Students: Clouds!

   Teacher: Yes, you see a picture of clouds. The front of the book is called the cover, and on the cover we usually find a picture and the name of the author. What's an author?

   Students: The person who wrote the book.

   Teacher: Right, and the author of *Little Cloud* is Eric Carle.

   I'm going to open the cover. Now what do you see?

   Students: The same picture of clouds.

   Teacher: Yes, this page is the title page and it has a picture and the name of the author again. Now, I'm going to begin reading with my hand sweeping under the words. Notice how my hand moves from left to right as I read to show you how I am saying the words.

3. After children have participated in shared reading, reinforce the concepts you have introduced by asking children to point to the cover of the book, the illustrations, and the name of the author, and by having them sweep their hands under the words to show the direction to read.

4. Give all children their own books to read. Reinforce the concepts you introduced by having students point to the cover of their individual books, the illustrations, and the name of the author. Then have students move their hands under the print of the books, reading if they can.

5. Spend several sessions each week introducing concepts about print. During each session, review the previous lesson that you taught. Some children require many exposures to print before they increase their understanding of print concepts.

Tips for English Language Learners

Children whose home language does not follow the same conventions of print as English may have difficulty learning English print concepts. Identify the home languages of the students in your class and find out the differences between those languages and English. Point out the differences to students as in the following example.

"I know when your parents and grandparents read Chinese at home you read from right to left. That's how you read Chinese, but in English you read a different way. When you read English, you start reading at the top of the page and read from left to right. Different languages have different ways of reading books, and you can learn more than one way to read."

Teaching Strategy 2

Section 2.1

Language Experience Approach (LEA)

The Language Experience Approach (LEA) helps children make connections between spoken and written language (Stauffer, 1970). Children's dictation serves as the foundation for the LEA. The main premises undergirding LEA are that children can talk about what they have experienced, their words can be written down, and they can read what they say. The Language Experience Approach begins with the children's experiences and own language; therefore, it provides a personalized connection between learning about spoken and written language.

DIRECTIONS

1. Provide a hands-on experience for children such as a field trip to an apple orchard or a zoo.
2. Invite children to tell about their experiences with the hands-on activity by dictating a story. This can be done with individual children, small groups, or a class of children.
3. Inform children that you will record their ideas in writing.
4. Write children's dictations on chart paper. Be sure to write exactly what the children say. Do not make corrections for grammar or usage unless you have been teaching a specific writing convention, such as the use of *I* in *Cheryl and I*. An example of a dictated experience follows.

   Yesterday we went to the zoo and we saw lots of animals. We saw a bear and he was eating lunch but we don't know what it was he was eating. We saw a momma giraffe with her baby. She was way tall! We saw lots of other animals too.

5. When the children have completed the story, read it aloud to them, identifying print concepts that you want to emphasize as in the following example.

Teacher: I'm going to read this story back to you. Where should I start reading? Show me where to begin. (Child points to the first word.) Yes, I need to start reading at the top of the page at the first word I see.

(Teacher reads first line.)

Yesterday we went to the zoo, and we saw lots of animals.

Teacher: How many words do I have in the first sentence? Remember, a sentence starts with a capital letter and ends with a period. Which word has a capital letter? (Yesterday) Where is the period? (After animals) How do I tell where the words begin and end? (Spaces between words) Count the number of words with me.

6. Reread the story, inviting children to participate in the reading if they would like to do so. Reread the story several times. Discuss ideas contributed by specific children.

7. Guide children to understand that the story's ideas came from their words and ideas. Discuss how their words can be spoken, written, and then read.

8. Have the children illustrate the story and bind it into a Big Book. Place the Big Book in the classroom library so the children can read and reread it during their free time.

Tips for English Language Learners

English uses the Roman alphabet, but not all languages do. Some of the English Language Learners in your classroom use an alphabet that looks very different from English. Children who are not familiar with the Roman alphabet may have difficulty distinguishing capital letters from lowercase letters, ending marks, and even spaces between words. English Language Learners unfamiliar with the Roman alphabet will need extra assistance learning print concepts.

Teaching Strategy 3

Section 2.1

Learning about Print Through Writing

One of the challenges children encounter when learning print concepts is that children cannot distinguish which direction to read when a book is facing them. When teachers read Big Books with children, they generally face them so they can show the books' illustrations. Children looking on may be confused about which direction to read print, especially since young children rarely have a good understanding about which direction is "left" and which is "right." When children write their own stories, however, they can learn these print concepts quickly.

DIRECTIONS

1. Tell children that you would like to have them write a story. Give children unlined paper or lined paper with space for a picture.

2. Begin by having children write about their family as in the following example.

"Today, I'd like you to write a story for me about your family. When we write stories, we can write words first or we can draw pictures first. You can decide which you want to do. To start your story, tell me a little bit about each of the people in your family."

"I'll show you what I mean. I'd like to write about my family. I have a husband named Larry, so I'll start with a few sentences about my husband."

My husband's name is Larry. He is the band director at the high school. He also plays a trumpet in the community band.

"I also have twin girls who are in third grade. I'll write about them next."

Literacy Knowledge 55

Larry and I have twin girls named Adele and Anne. They are eight years old and look exactly alike except for one thing: Adele has short curly hair and Anne has long wavy hair. Larry and I have lots of fun with our girls.

"Now you write about your family."

3. As children write, help them write from left to right, from top to bottom, and with spaces between words. Encourage children to write several lines of print, spelling words with developmental spelling. (See Section 6.3 for ideas about developmental spelling.)

4. Have children read their stories to you or to their peers in groups. Compile the stories into a book and place the book where children can read it. Encourage children to read the book, reminding them to use what they know about print concepts when they read.

Teaching Strategy 4

Section 2.1

What Can You Show Us?

What Can You Show Us? (Richgels, Poremba, & McGee, 1996) is a strategy that uses story reading with children's exploration of text to help them increase their literacy knowledge. When children use meaningful text to discover concepts about print, they are apt to be engaged in personal learning. What Can You Show Us? allows teachers to reinforce children's discoveries and guide them into learning about books, words, and print.

DIRECTIONS

1. Select a Big Book to read to the children or write a dictated story on the chalkboard or on chart paper. Preview the story by telling the children that there is a new story on the chalkboard or on the easel. Tell them to look at the story during the day.

2. After children have had time to look at the story, direct their attention to the text by asking them to talk with each other about what they see. Then point out the title of the story, the author's name, and the cover illustration.

3. Before reading the story, ask the children, "What Can You Show Us?" Invite a child to come to the front and show the class something about the text. After the first child has identified something about the story, have other children repeat the process. Children may identify letters, words, or pictures, or they may tell the other children something about the book. Encourage all responses.

4. Read the story to the children. Then reinforce what the children noticed by repeating things they have said. For example, if a child points to the title of the story *Where the Wild Things Are* (Sendak, 1963), point to the title and repeat it. If a child has pointed to a letter, have the children identify that letter in other words or on other pages of the story. If there is a concept that you want the children to notice, an exclamation point, for example, tell children that you also have noticed something. Show children the element you want to introduce.

5. Tell children that there are many things about stories that they can notice on their own. Have the story available so that children can look at it after you have finished the lesson. Repeat this strategy often until children become familiar with concepts related to books.

Ideas and Activities

1. Sit with a small group of children. Hand little books to each of the children. Explain that the spines of books are on the left and that books open from the right. Have children identify their left hand. You might do this by showing them that the thumb and index finger on their left hand form an L shape. Have them place the spine of the book in the curve of their left thumb and index finger. Then have them open the book.

2. Explain that when you read a book you turn pages from right to left. After children have placed a book with the spine to the left, have them practice turning pages of the book. Encourage them to turn one page at a time. Show children that each page is different and that they will need to look at each page when reading.

3. Give children books to read. Tell them that most books begin with a word. Have them identify the first word in the book. Then explain that books have an ending word. Have children identify the last word in the book.

4. Help children identify the top and bottom of books by giving them picture books. Arrange several picture books on a table. Ask children to pick up a book and open it to a picture. Tell them that they should be able to identify the subject of the picture. Have them tell you what the picture shows. Explain that when a book is held correctly, they will be able to tell what the picture is about.

5. Gather together paper, pencils, and crayons. Staple the paper so that it is in book form. Sit with a small group of children. Explain that you will be showing the children how to write a book. Have one child dictate a title. Show children where to place the title on the cover of the book. Then open the book to the first page and have another child dictate a sentence. Write the sentence on the first page. Show children where the sentence belongs and discuss where they could draw a picture. Continue writing several sentences. Show children how to turn the pages and to write the book from beginning to end. Then have children illustrate the pages. When the book is complete, read it to the children.

6. Print children's names on index cards and show one of them to the children. Point to a child's first name, say it, and then point to the child's last name and say it. Show the children the space that separates the first and last names by pointing to them. Tell the children that there are two words on the card. Frame each word with your hands. Have children frame their first name and then their last name on their index cards. Give each child the index card with his or her name on it.

7. Have children dictate a story or use a sentence from a Big Book. Write the sentence on heavy paper or tagboard. Read the sentence aloud. Then cut the sentence apart at each word. Have children put the words together and place them in a pocket chart to make up the sentence. Read the sentence together, noting how the words make up a sentence.

8. Write a sentence on the chalkboard or on chart paper. Make word cards that match the words in the sentence. Give the word cards to several children. Ask children to find the word in the sentence that matches their word card. Tell children that they have a word and that the words together make up a sentence. Point to the beginning capital letter and the ending punctuation mark. Then have children read the entire sentence.

9. Read books to children several times each day. With each reading, remind children of one of the concepts about print.

10. Read a story to the children. Write all of the words from a sentence in the story on sentence strips. Then cut them apart so that each word and punctuation mark is separate. Have each child hold one of the words or punctuation cards. Have children rearrange themselves to make the sentence.

Literacy Knowledge

11. Explain that after each word there should be a space to show where the word stops and the next word begins. Use a book to show children how spaces are used between words in stories. Explain that spaces between words should be the same size. Have children write their own stories. Their writing will probably use developmental spelling. After children write, have them place their index finger or a pencil after each word to determine whether they have included spaces in their writing.

12. Practice counting words (Cunningham, 2000). Give children 10 counters (plastic disks, paper squares, raisins, or anything similar) in a paper cup. Start by counting some familiar objects in the room such as bulletin boards, doors, or plants. Have children place one of their counters on their desks as you point to each object. Be sure children return their counters to their cups at the end of each count. Then tell children that you can also count words by putting down a counter for each word as it is said. Model the process with the sentence "Today is Tuesday." First, say the sentence naturally. Then say the sentence slowly, pausing after each word, so children can put down a counter for each word. Ask children how many words you said. Proceed to other sentences, capitalizing on children's interests. As children begin to understand that words can be counted, invite them to offer their own sentences. They should say the sentence twice, once in the normal way and then one word at a time.

13. When reading from a Big Book or from sentences on the chalkboard, move your hand from left to right underneath the print. Explain that when reading you need to read the words at the left first, then read to the right one word at a time. Show children how to move to the next line of print. Slowly show children how to track print. After you have modeled the left to right progression of print, help children track their own reading from left to right by guiding their hands as they read. Encourage young children to read with a moving hand until they no longer need to physically track words.

14. Write a sentence on the chalkboard or on chart paper. Read the sentence to the children, moving your hand under the words as you read. Explain that the sentence is made up of words. Read the sentence slowly. Then have the children clap their hands one time for each word you say.

Home School Connections: Experiences with Print

📖 Reading with your children provides them with experiences to learn how print works. Read one or more books with your children every day—bedtime is a favorite time for many children and parents. When you read, move your hand under the print to show your child which direction to read. Discuss what you read using questions such the ones that follow.

> What would you do if you were the main character?
> What was your favorite part of the story?
> Which picture is your favorite?

📖 Write Language Experience Stories together with your child. Have your child tell you a story. Write the story down as closely as you can to the child's original words. As you write, show your child which direction to write and how to make spaces between words. Have the child illustrate the story. Read the story together frequently.

📖 Have paper, crayons, markers, and pencils available to your child at all times. Encourage your child to write and illustrate stories, knowing that these experiences will build knowledge about print concepts. Praise your child for all attempts to write.

From Jerry L. Johns, Susan Davis Lenski, and Laurie Elish-Piper, *Teaching Beginning Readers: Linking Assessment and Instruction* (2nd ed.). Copyright © 2002 by Kendall/Hunt Publishing Company (1-800-247-3458, ext. 5). May be reproduced for noncommercial educational purposes.

Selected Resources
PRINT CONCEPTS

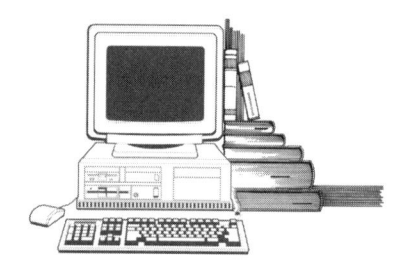

Picture Books

Baker, J. (1991). *Window*. New York: Greenwillow.

Collington, P. (1995). *The tooth fairy*. New York: Knopf.

Eastman, P.D. (1960). *Are you my mother?* New York: Random House.

Keats, E.J. (1962). *The snowy day*. New York: Viking.

Rohmann, E. (1994). *Time flies*. New York: Crown.

Sendak, M. (1963). *Where the wild things are*. New York: Harper and Row.

Sis, P. (1992). *Ocean world*. New York: Greenwillow.

Wilson, A. (1999). *Magpie magic*. New York: Dial

Media and Technology

Electro Dog CD-ROM (words for children to match as they read).
UPDATA (800-882-2844)

Lion King Animated Storybook CD-ROM (interactive story of Lion King).
UPDATA (800-882-2844)

Stickybear's Reading Room CD-ROM (bilingual program with activities in word matching and word finding).
UPDATA (800-882-2844)

The Little Turtle CD-ROM (interactive story with audiovisual effects).
UPDATA (800-882-2844)

Professional Resources

Clay, M.M. (1985). *The early detection of reading difficulties* (3rd ed.). Portsmouth, NH: Heinemann.

Gandini, L., & Edwards, C.P. (2001). *Bambini: The Italian approach to infant/toddler care*. New York: Teachers College Press.

Holdaway, D. (1979). *The foundations of literacy*. Sydney: Ashton Scholastic.

McGee, L.M., & Richgels, D.J. (1999). *Literacy's beginnings: Supporting young readers and writers* (3rd ed.). Boston: Allyn and Bacon.

From Jerry L. Johns, Susan Davis Lenski, and Laurie Elish-Piper, *Teaching Beginning Readers: Linking Assessment and Instruction* (2nd ed.). Copyright © 2002 by Kendall/Hunt Publishing Company (1-800-247-3458, ext. 5). May be reproduced for noncommercial educational purposes.

2.2 Sense of Story

> **Goal** To help children develop a sense of story.
> **Assessment Strategy 2** Retelling a Story, page 119

BACKGROUND

Young children need to develop background knowledge about how stories are structured and what characteristics and components stories possess. This knowledge is important to emergent readers because it allows them to anticipate and understand stories and how they work. A sense of story provides children with a framework for understanding the stories that are read to them and the stories they read to themselves (Lukens, 1995).

Children who come to school with many home reading experiences typically possess a good sense of story because of the many stories that have been read to them by their families or caregivers. Children who have not been read to on a regular basis prior to coming to school will need to be immersed in stories and reading experiences so they too can develop a sense of story (Edwards, 1986).

Story selections for emergent readers should focus on simple stories with related illustrations and large, clear print. Story sharing should be an interactive process with many opportunities for children to discuss, ask questions, and note observations about the stories (Salinger, 1999). If you share stories with children on a daily basis in the classroom, you will notice that children will develop an understanding of the characteristics and components of stories as well as an interest in reading.

Teaching Strategy 1

Section 2.2

Simple Story Elements

The Simple Story Elements strategy helps children verbalize what they know about how stories are structured. This strategy focuses on the places, people and animals, and things that happen in a story (Johns & Lenski, 2001). This strategy will help children develop a foundation about the components all stories possess. After children understand this strategy, story mapping and other story element activities can be introduced.

DIRECTIONS

1. Select a familiar children's book with a clear, simple story line. A familiar story such as a fairy tale works well when introducing this strategy. If possible, select a story that all or at least most of the children already know.
2. Ask the children to tell you what they know or remember about the story. List these ideas on the chalkboard.

3. After the children have had a chance to share their ideas, group their responses into the following three columns on the chalkboard: places, people and animals, and things that happen. For example, if you were using *The Three Little Pigs,* the children might list the following ideas.

Places	People and Animals	Things That Happen
in the woods	three little pigs	Wolf blows down houses.
pigs' houses	Big Bad Wolf	

4. Explain to the children that all stories include information on the places, people and animals, and things that happen in the story. Go on to discuss that a story must have all of these parts.

5. Read the familiar story to the children. Ask them to listen carefully to see if the ideas listed on the chalkboard are correct or if changes need to be made. For example, if you were using *The Three Little Pigs,* the revised list might contain the ideas listed below.

Places	People and Animals	Things that Happen
in the woods	three little pigs	Wolf blows down straw house.
straw house	Big Bad Wolf	Wolf blows down wood house.
wood house		Wolf can't blow down brick house.
brick house		

6. Ask children to make suggestions about ideas that need to be added, removed, or changed. Be sure to ask children to support and explain their responses.

7. Repeat this strategy with other stories, including stories that are new to children.

Teaching Strategy 2

Section 2.2

Plot Relationships Chart

The Plot Relationships Chart helps children understand and identify the major plot elements in fictional stories. This strategy uses the clue words *Somebody, Wanted, But,* and *So* to help children develop an understanding of how the main character, goal, problem, and solution of a story fit together (Schmidt & Buckley, 1991).

DIRECTIONS

1. Select a children's book that has clear plot elements: main character, goal, problem, and solution.
2. Read the story aloud to the children. Provide time for the children to discuss the story and their reactions to it.
3. Place a blank copy of the Plot Relationships Chart on the chalkboard, an overhead transparency, or a piece of chart paper. A sample chart is provided below.

Plot Relationships Chart

Somebody	Wanted	But	So

62   Chapter Two

4. Tell the children they will be using the chart to learn about the important parts of stories and how they fit together.
5. Guide the children through identifying the main character of the story by asking them, "Who is the important *Somebody* that the story is about?" Discuss the children's responses and, when agreement is reached, write the main character's name in the *Somebody* column on the chart.
6. Use this pattern to guide the children through identifying and discussing the other plot elements.
7. Explain to children that all stories have these important parts. Provide additional opportunities to work with the Plot Relationships Chart and other stories. A modification of the Plot Relationships Chart is the Plot Relationships Frame. A sample frame is provided below.

_____ wanted _____
            Somebody

but _____ so _____ .

Plot Relationships Chart

Somebody	Wanted	But	So

_____ wanted
(Somebody)

_____

but _____

so _____ .

From Jerry L. Johns, Susan Davis Lenski, and Laurie Elish-Piper, *Teaching Beginning Readers: Linking Assessment and Instruction* (2nd ed.). Copyright © 2002 by Kendall/Hunt Publishing Company (1-800-247-3458, ext. 5). May be reproduced for noncommercial educational purposes.

Teaching Strategy 3

Section 2.2

Story Star

The Story Star is a variation of a story map. Story maps provide visual representations of the major elements in a story. Story maps help children see and understand how the elements of a story fit together so they can understand what they are reading. There are many variations of story maps that can be used to help children develop an understanding of story elements, but those that have a simple format and focus on a limited number of elements are most appropriate for emergent and beginning readers. The Story Star is a very basic type of story map that is appropriate for use with young children.

DIRECTIONS

1. Select a children's book with a simple story line and clear story elements: main character, setting, events, problem, and solution.
2. Introduce the book to the children and invite them to make predictions about the book based on its title and cover illustration.
3. Read the book aloud to the children. Provide time for them to discuss the story and their personal reactions to it.
4. Display a blank Story Star on the chalkboard, an overhead transparency, or a piece of chart paper. Explain to the children that you will use the Story Star to identify the important parts of the story. A sample Story Star is provided below.

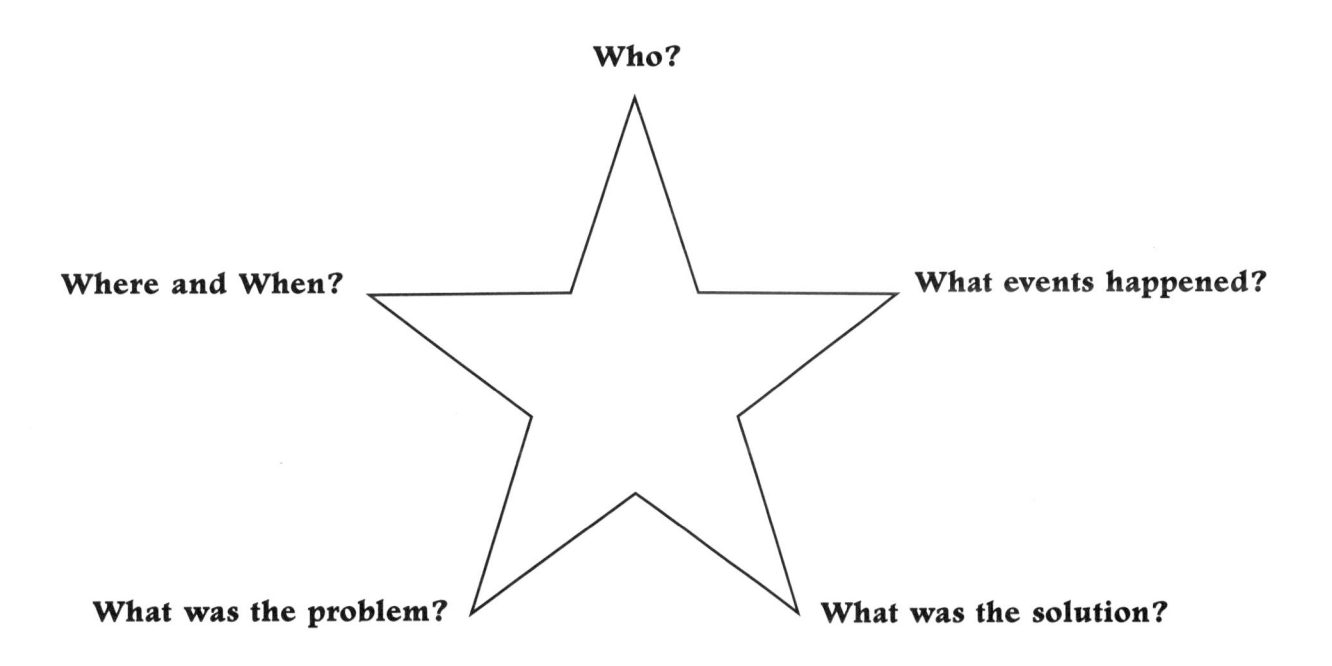

Who?

Where and When?   **What events happened?**

What was the problem?   **What was the solution?**

5. Begin with the main character from the story and ask the children, "Who was the story about?" Discuss their responses and explanations. Write the main character's name on the Story Star. If desired, a picture of the main character can also be added to this part of the Story Star.

Literacy Knowledge   65

Story Star

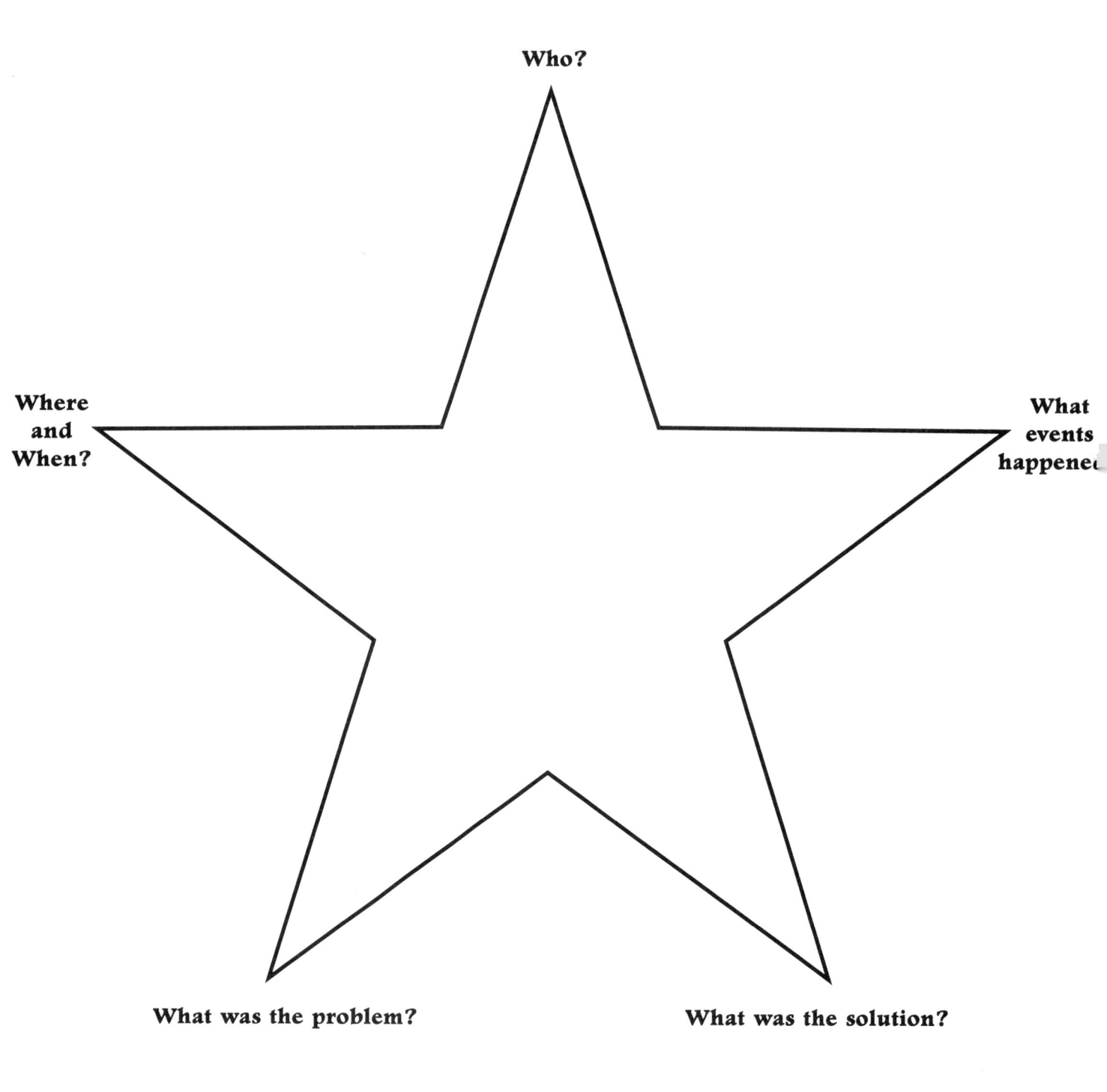

Who?

Where and When?

What events happened?

What was the problem?

What was the solution?

From Jerry L. Johns, Susan Davis Lenski, and Laurie Elish-Piper, *Teaching Beginning Readers: Linking Assessment and Instruction* (2nd ed.). Copyright © 2002 by Kendall/Hunt Publishing Company (1-800-247-3458, ext. 5). May be reproduced for noncommercial educational purposes.

Teaching Strategy 4

Story Faces

Section 2.2

Story Faces (Staal, 2000) are adaptations of story mapping that incorporate visual cues to help children remember the elements of story structure. Story Faces organize story elements with a graphic using two eyes, a nose, and a mouth. This graphic prompts children to remember each of the components of a story.

DIRECTIONS

1. Use one of the two Story Faces, the happy Story Face or the unhappy Story Face, or draw your own based on the examples that follow. The eyes should be circles with the terms *setting* and *characters* printed in them. The nose represents the *problem*, and the mouth represents the *events*.

2. Read a story to the children that has a clear setting, plot, and characters. Write the words *setting*, *plot*, and *characters* on an overhead transparency or on the chalkboard. Explain that the setting is the time and place of the story, the plot consists of a problem and events in a sequence, and the main characters are who the story is about. Remind children that characters can be animals or people.

3. Tell children to listen for the setting, plot, and main characters as you read the story to them.

4. Duplicate one of the Story Faces that follow and distribute it to children. Choose the happy face if the story is a cheerful one or the unhappy face if the story is sad.

5. An example from *Lost in the Museum* (1979) by Miriam Cohen follows.

    What is the word in the left eye on this face? (Setting) Do you remember what the setting is? (Time or place of the story) What is the setting of the story *Lost in the Museum*? Write it in the circle for the left eye. Let's add some more details for eyelashes.

    Write the names of the main characters from the story in the right eye. Add some details for eyelashes.

    What problem did the main characters have? Write it in the place for the nose.

    What happened in the story? Let's write the events in the circles that make up the mouth.

    How did the story end? That idea should be in the last circle for the mouth where it says *Solution*.

Tips for English Language Learners

Story structures are culturally developed and defined, so children from some cultures will not be familiar with stories as we know them. If children from other cultures have a difficult time understanding the structure of stories, provide lots of practice using Teaching Strategy 1 (Simple Story Elements) and Teaching Strategy 3 (Story Star). Allow children who have difficulty developing a sense of story to work in collaborative groups until they feel confident enough to work independently.

Literacy Knowledge

Happy Story Face

Name_____ Date_____

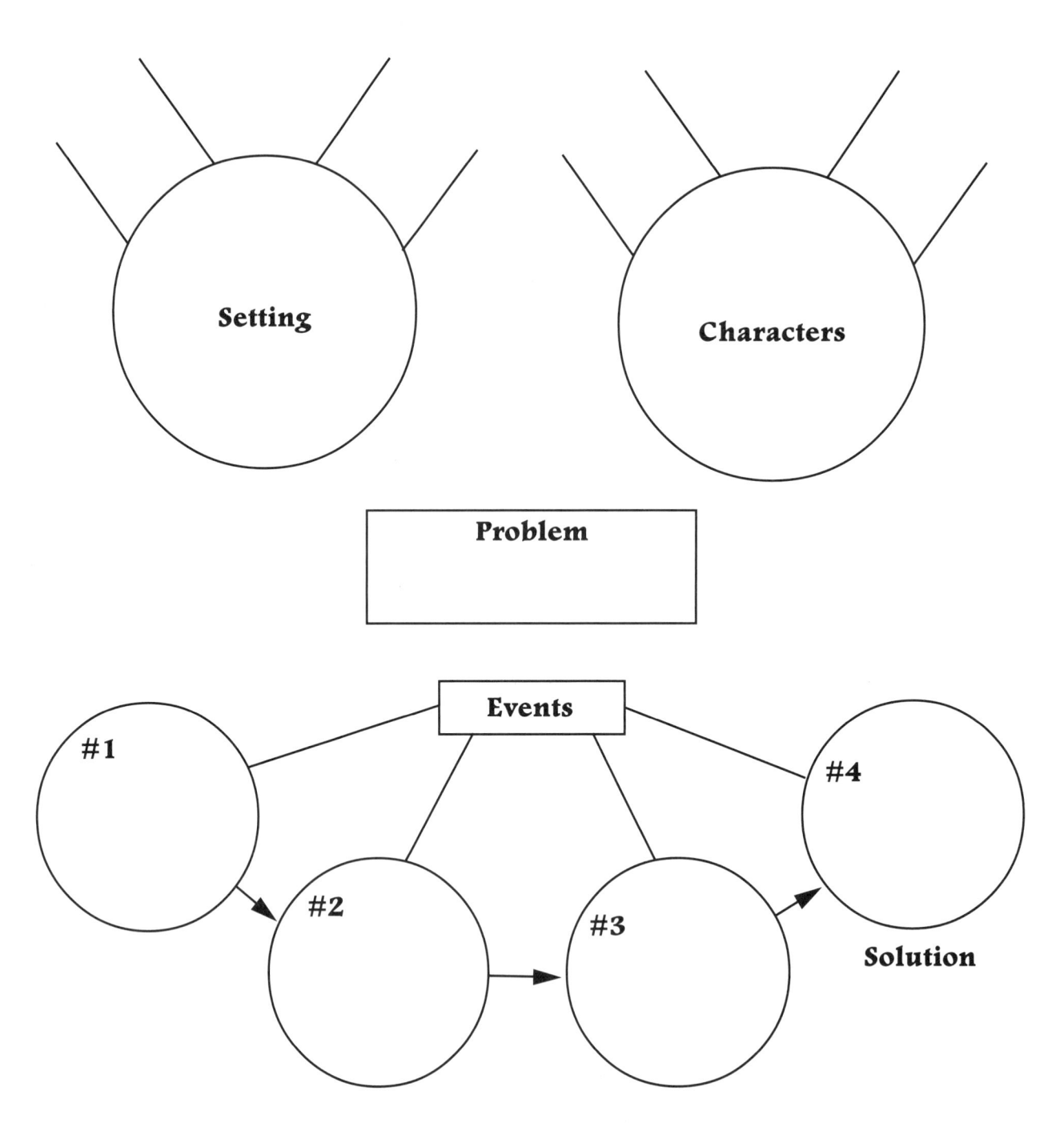

Setting

Characters

Problem

Events

#1

#2

#3

#4

Solution

From Jerry L. Johns, Susan Davis Lenski, and Laurie Elish-Piper, *Teaching Beginning Readers: Linking Assessment and Instruction* (2nd ed.). Copyright © 2002 by Kendall/Hunt Publishing Company (1-800-247-3458, ext. 5). May be reproduced for noncommercial educational purposes.

Unhappy Story Face

Name _____ Date _____

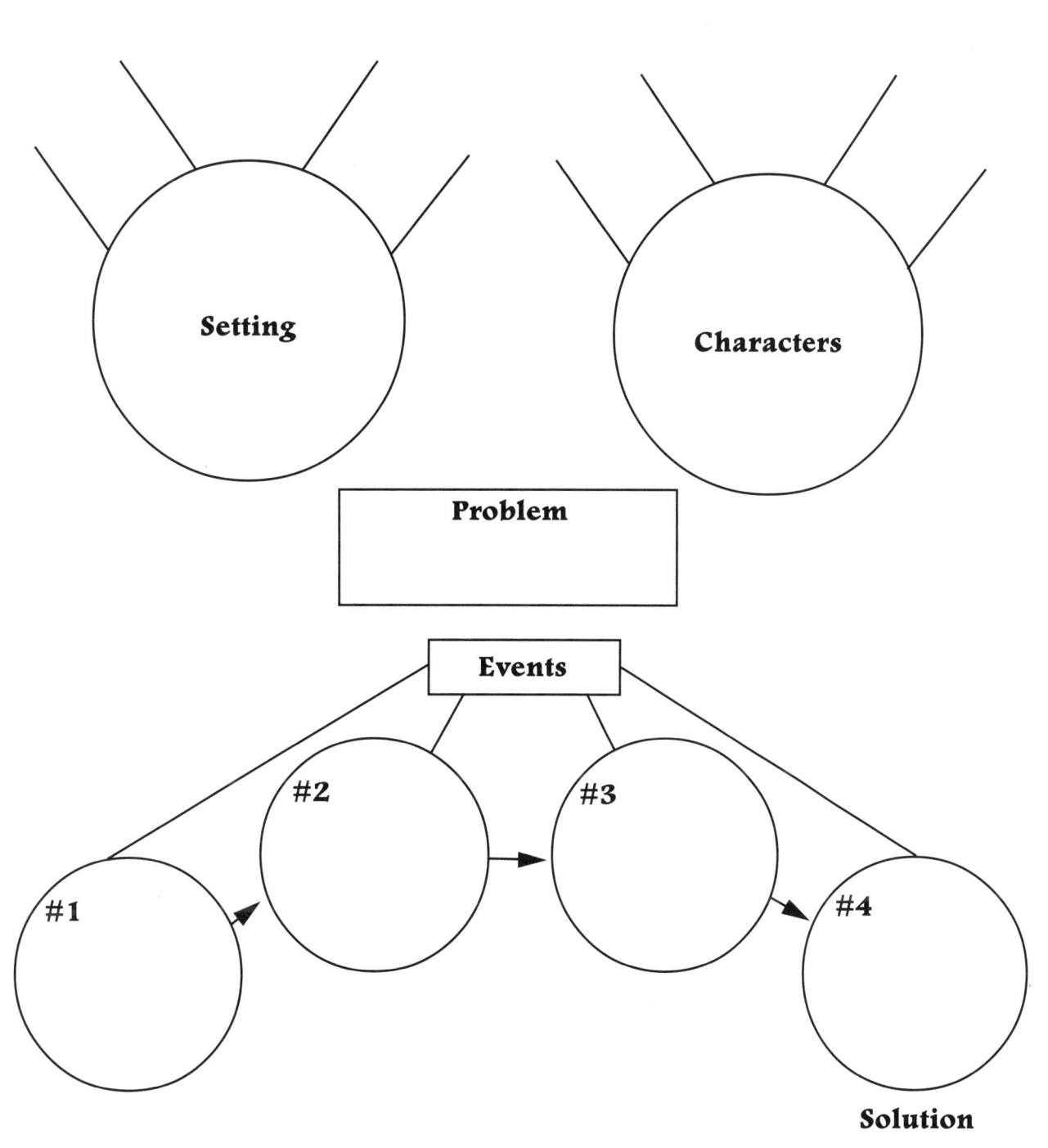

Setting

Characters

Problem

Events

#1

#2

#3

#4

Solution

From Jerry L. Johns, Susan Davis Lenski, and Laurie Elish-Piper, *Teaching Beginning Readers: Linking Assessment and Instruction* (2nd ed.). Copyright © 2002 by Kendall/Hunt Publishing Company (1-800-247-3458, ext. 5). May be reproduced for noncommercial educational purposes.

Ideas and Activities

1. Read to children on a daily basis. Expose them to a variety of good stories. During and after story reading activities, provide time for children to ask questions, note observations, and discuss the stories. Place books you have read to the children in the classroom library so they can read and look at the books during their free time.

2. Use storytelling to expose children to stories and to develop a sense of story through oral language. Select a simple story and collect several props to help you tell the story. Provide discussion time after telling the story. Encourage the children to retell the story to a classmate.

3. After reading a story with the children, invite small groups of children to retell the story using simple props, puppets, or a felt board. Place these materials in a classroom literacy center so children can engage in retelling activities during center time or their free time.

4. Have children complete simple story boards for the important elements of stories. For example, divide a piece of construction paper into four equal sections. Label the sections *Who, When, Where,* and *What*. Ask the children to draw and label *Who* the story was about, *When* the story took place, *Where* the story happened, and *What* the important events in the story were. Provide time for children to share and discuss their story boards. A sample story board format is provided below.

Who?	When?
Where?	What?

5. Invite children to use creative dramatics to act out favorite stories. If possible, supply simple props and costumes for children to use in their story dramas. Provide time for children to share their story dramas with other children.

6. Have children illustrate major events from a story. These illustrations can then be sequenced to match the events in the story. Stories such as Eric Carle's *The Very Hungry Caterpillar* (1969) work well for this type of story sequencing activity.

7. Provide access to a well-stocked classroom library so children can look at and read books on a daily basis. Schedule a daily time for children to read and discuss self-selected books.

8. Use wordless picture books to engage children in talking about the story and discussing the important components of the story. For a list of wordless picture books with clear, simple story lines, see Selected Resources: Sense of Story (page 72).

9. Encourage parents to read stories to and with their children on a daily basis. Provide access to appropriate books by sharing books from the classroom and school libraries.

Home School Connections

Stories

- When your children are watching television, ask them what the setting is for the story or who the main characters are. Remind children that television shows have some of the same elements that books have.

- Encourage your children to tell stories to their siblings. Remind children to organize their stories in a sequence of events.

- Read to your child every day.

From Jerry L. Johns, Susan Davis Lenski, and Laurie Elish-Piper, *Teaching Beginning Readers: Linking Assessment and Instruction* (2nd ed.). Copyright © 2002 by Kendall/Hunt Publishing Company (1-800-247-3458, ext. 5). May be reproduced for noncommercial educational purposes.

Selected Resources
SENSE OF STORY

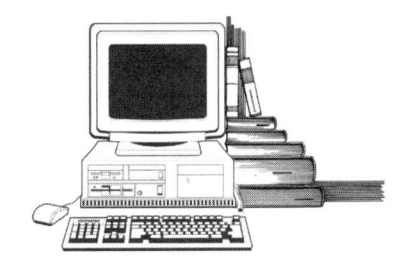

Picture Books

Bang, M. (1980). *The grey lady and the strawberry snatcher.* New York: Four Winds.

Carle, E. (1995). *The very lonely firefly.* New York: Philomel.

Cronin, D. (2000). *Click, Clack, Moo: Cows that type.* New York: Simon & Shuster.

Day, A. (1995). *Carl's birthday.* New York: Farrar Straus Giroux.

DePaola, T. (1981). *Pancakes for breakfast.* New York: Harcourt.

Ormerod, J. (1981). *Sunshine.* Wooster, OH: Lathrop.

Turkle, B. (1976). *Deep in the forest.* New York: Dutton.

Media and Technology

Goldilocks and the Three Bears CD-ROM (interactive storybook with comprehension activities).
UPDATA (800-882-2844)

Talking Classic Tales CD-ROM (interactive stories with sound effects and animation).
UPDATA (800-882-2844)

The Cat Came Back CD-ROM (interactive storybook).
Sanctuary Woods (415-578-6340)

Professional Resources

Brooks, E. (1996). *Just-right books for beginning readers: Leveled booklists and strategies.* New York: Scholastic Professional Books.

Opitz, M. (1998). *Getting the most from predictable books: Strategies and activities for teaching with more than 75 favorite children's books.* New York: Scholastic Professional Books.

Santa, C. (1999). *Early steps: Learning from a reader.* Dubuque, IA: Kendall/Hunt.

Tarlow, E. (1987). *Teaching story elements with favorite books: Creative and engaging activities to explore character, plot, setting, and theme that work with any book.* New York: Scholastic Professional Books.

From Jerry L. Johns, Susan Davis Lenski, and Laurie Elish-Piper, *Teaching Beginning Readers: Linking Assessment and Instruction* (2nd ed.). Copyright © 2002 by Kendall/Hunt Publishing Company (1-800-247-3458, ext. 5). May be reproduced for noncommercial educational purposes.

2.3 Informational Text Structures

> **Goal** To develop an understanding of informational text structures.
> **Assessment Strategy 3** Informational Text Retelling, page 121

BACKGROUND

Children in the primary grades read mainly fictional texts in school, but teachers are becoming increasingly aware of the need for young children to experience informational texts (Yopp & Yopp, 2000). Informational texts are organized differently from fictional texts, so they are unfamiliar to many children. Informational texts are organized in five patterns: description, sequence, comparison, cause-effect, and problem-solution. The patterns of description and sequence are the most commonly used patterns for informational texts young children might read and, therefore, should be taught in school. A variety of strategies, ideas, activities, and assessments follows.

Teaching Strategy 1

Section 2.3

Graphic Organizers

Graphic Organizers are visual representations of text. They can be drawn in any number of ways that depict the organization of the story.

DIRECTIONS

1. Identify a piece of informational text for children to read or to hear such as *Elephant* by Mary Hoffman (1986).
2. Determine whether the book could be represented by a graphic organizer that depicts description or sequence. A copy of each graphic organizer follows at the end of this strategy.
3. Duplicate and distribute copies of the graphic organizer to each student. Then remind children, as in the example below, that nonfictional texts are organized differently from fictional texts.

   You remember how stories are organized. They have settings, characters, a sequence of events, and a solution. These stories are called fiction. Some books don't have these elements because they are not stories. They are books that give us information rather than tell a story.

   You can remember the difference by thinking of stories you have heard at bedtime. Bedtime stories are often made up stories with settings, characters, and plots. When you are told how to build a kite, it's *explaining* something. That's like an informational book. It explains something rather than telling a story.

Literacy Knowledge 73

Informational books won't have a plot. Instead, they will have a main point and details that explain that point, or they will tell you how to do something. When we read the book *Elephants*, listen for the main point of the book and the details.

4. Read the book aloud or have children read individual copies of the book.
5. Have children identify the main point of the book. Write it in the center of the circle as in the following example.

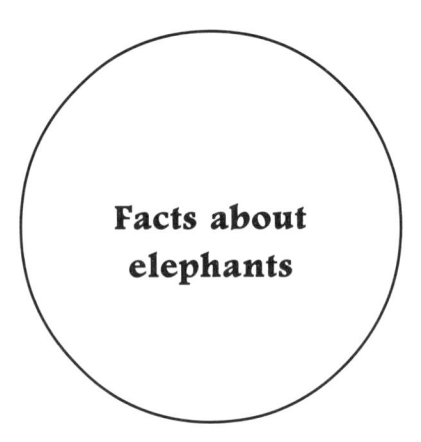

Facts about elephants

6. Ask children to brainstorm the details that they learned in the book. List the details on the spokes that radiate out from the center of the circle as in the example that follows.

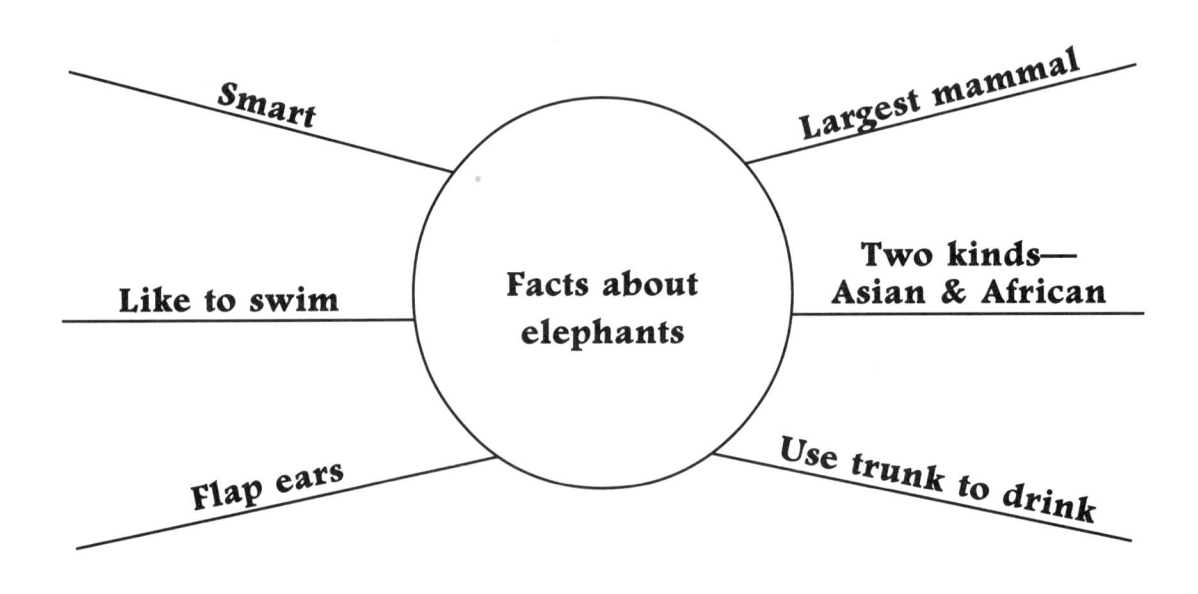

Facts about elephants
- Smart
- Largest mammal
- Like to swim
- Two kinds—Asian & African
- Flap ears
- Use trunk to drink

7. Tell children that they have completed a "picture" of the organization of the book *Elephant*. Remind children that this type of book is different from stories that they read.
8. Use a future lesson to model different organizations of informational text.

74   Chapter Two

Graphic Organizer
Informational Text: Description

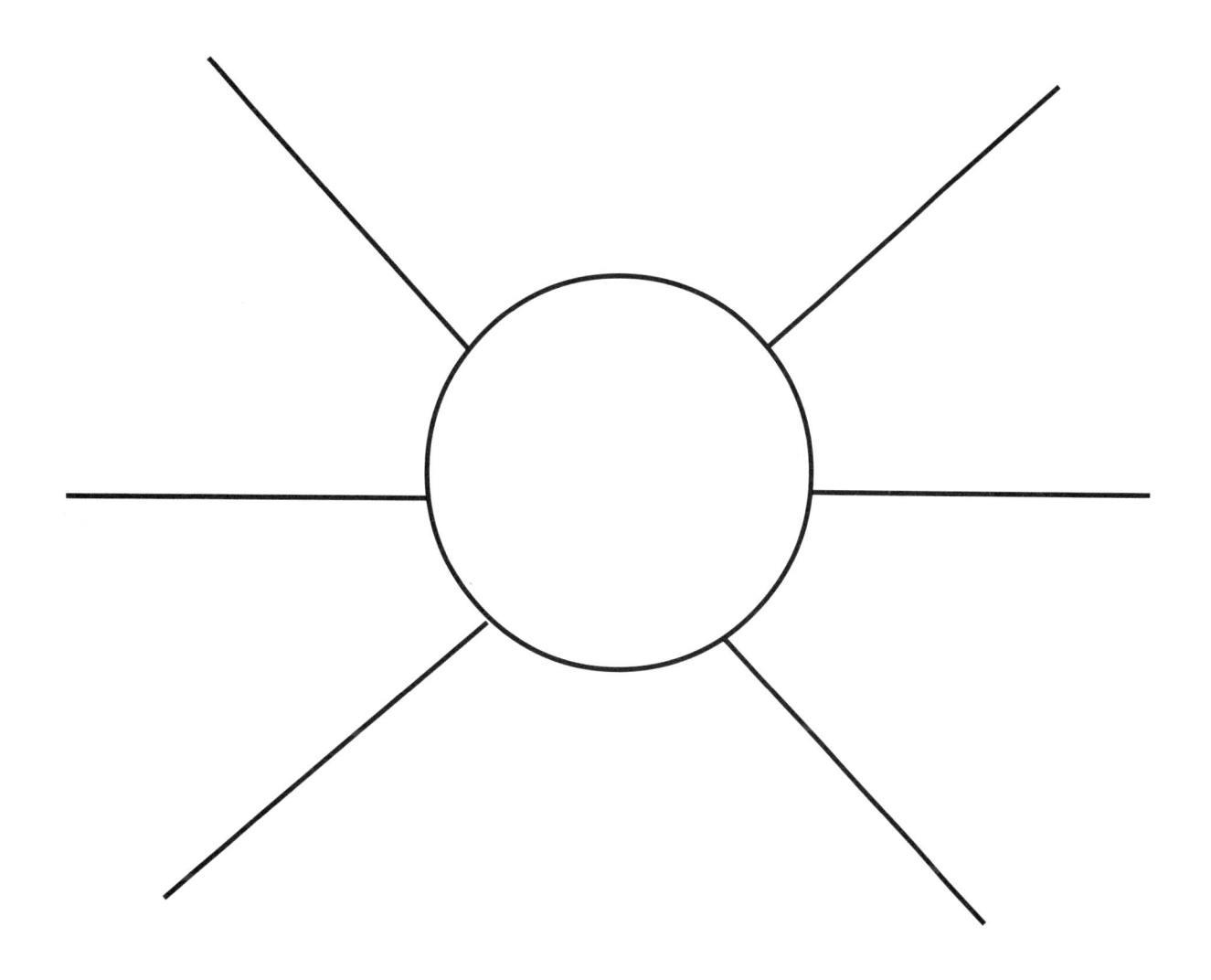

From Jerry L. Johns, Susan Davis Lenski, and Laurie Elish-Piper, *Teaching Beginning Readers: Linking Assessment and Instruction* (2nd ed.). Copyright © 2002 by Kendall/Hunt Publishing Company (1-800-247-3458, ext. 5). May be reproduced for noncommercial educational purposes.

Graphic Organizer
Informational Text: Sequence

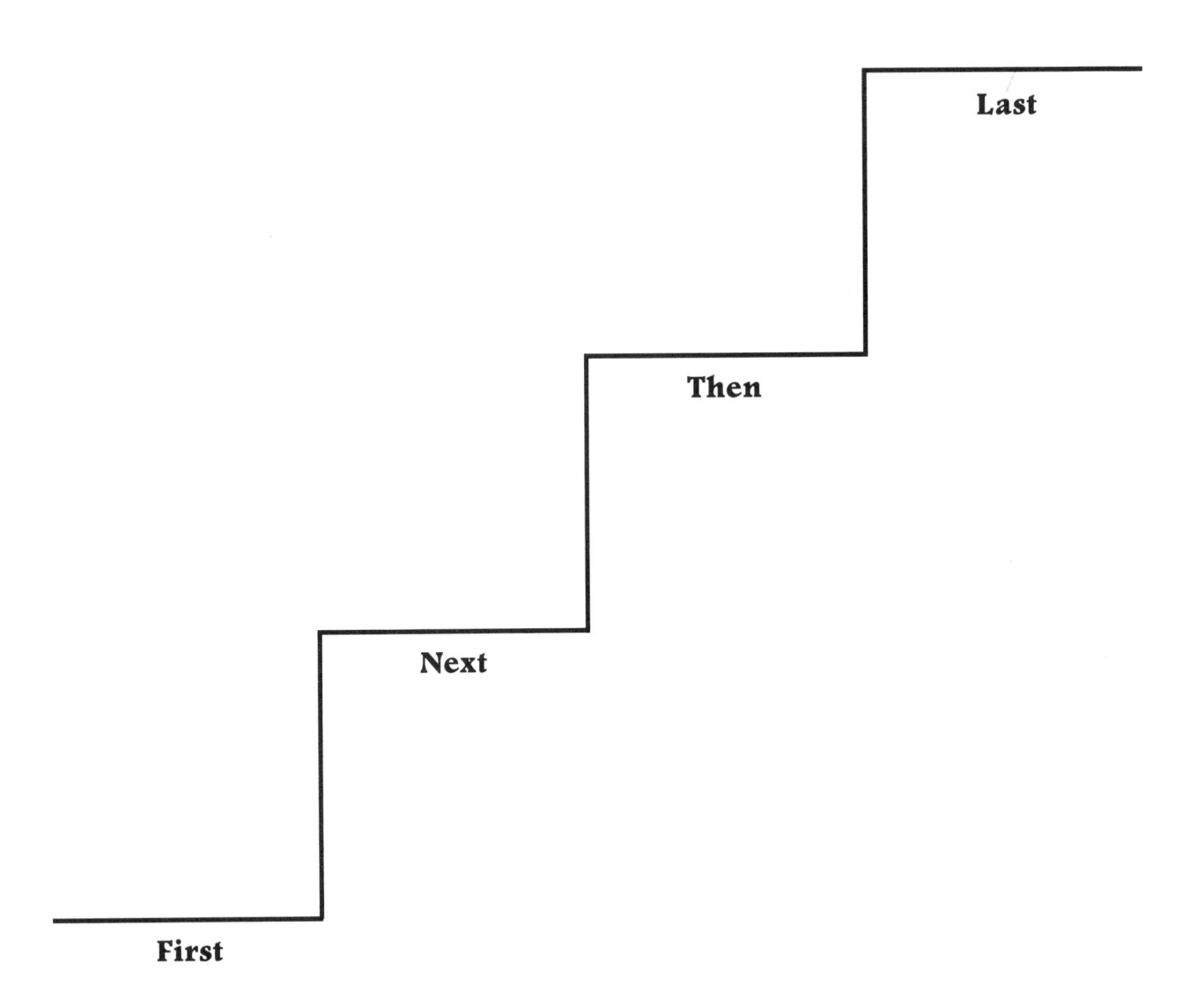

Last

Then

Next

First

From Jerry L. Johns, Susan Davis Lenski, and Laurie Elish-Piper, *Teaching Beginning Readers: Linking Assessment and Instruction* (2nd ed.). Copyright © 2002 by Kendall/Hunt Publishing Company (1-800-247-3458, ext. 5). May be reproduced for noncommercial educational purposes.

Teaching Strategy 2

Section 2.3

Expository Frames

Expository Frames are another method to teach children how informational text is organized. An Expository Frame synthesizes an entire text in a few sentences that mirror the organizational pattern of the whole text. The sentences in an Expository Frame have blanks for children to fill in specific details.

DIRECTIONS

1. Choose an informational text for children to read or to hear such as *Rain Forest Babies* (1996) by Kathy Darling.
2. Read the book to children or have children read text sets in small groups. Remind children to look for the way the text is organized.
3. Ask children to discuss the organizational pattern of the book. Remind children that informational text is organized differently from stories and that the book will not have a setting, characters, and a plot. They might say something like the following.

    The book begins with a map of the rain forests of the world. Then it describes 14 different animals, taking 2 pages for each animal. Each animal is pictured with a description. After the animals are described, the book ends with one page of general information about the rain forest.

4. Develop an Expository Frame to reinforce the pattern of the text. An example for *Rain Forest Babies* follows.

Rain Forest Babies

The rain forest spans the earth near the _____.

In every location, animal babies are born. Three of the types of animals that live in the rain forest are

_____, _____,

and _____. The babies live in

either the canopy, the understory, or the _____

of the rain forest. The number of rain forests is shrinking because the trees are being cut down.

Literacy Knowledge 77

> **Teaching Strategy 3**

Section 2.3

Scrambled Text

The Scrambled Text strategy helps focus children's attention on the organizational pattern of the text by having them recreate the text. The Scrambled Text strategy can be used with fictional stories as well as informational texts.

DIRECTIONS

1. Select an informational book that has a clear organizational pattern. Read the book to children or have them read copies of the text in small groups. Remind children to look for the organizational pattern of the text while reading.

2. List the main points of the story on chart paper or on index cards. Tell children that you are writing each of the book's main points in the order that they occurred in the book. The following example uses the book *So You Want to Be President* by Judith St. George (2000).

   The President lives in the While House.
   The President has a swimming pool, a bowling alley, and a movie theater.
   The President always has lots of homework.
   People get mad at the President.
   It's hard to be elected President.

3. Scramble the ideas from the story so that they are not listed in the order that they were written. Tell children the following.

   "You can see how this book is organized by looking at the ideas from the book that I have written. For example, the book told us that the President lives in the White House, and then it described the kinds of fun things the President has in his house. Informational books sometimes describe things from general ideas to specific ones as is the case in this example. Rearrange the items in this list so they match the way the book was written."

4. Check the children's lists to determine whether they have remembered the book's organization. It may take more than one attempt for some children to arrange the list correctly.

Tips for English Language Learners

Children who do not speak English as their first language may have difficulty reading informational text. English Language Learners master content vocabulary, such as that used in informational text, more slowly than they learn "playground language." You might think that an English Language Learner is fluent in English because he or she is able to converse with his or her classmates. However, this child may have little understanding when reading informational text. To scaffold English Language Learners' instruction, have them read informational text with a partner and provide them with visuals or concrete objects when appropriate.

> **Teaching Strategy 4**

Section 2.3

Expository Writing

Children learn text organization by participating in writing activities, so provide frequent opportunities for children to write expository text. Expository text is the writing term used for informational text. When children participate in expository writing, they often use a text pattern common in informational texts: description. Typically, expository writing begins with a main idea, includes several details, and ends with a concluding sentence.

DIRECTIONS

1. Write the phrase *expository writing* on the chalkboard or on an overhead transparency. Tell children that they will be participating in a different type of writing activity: expository writing. Remind children that they have heard you read many books that are written as expository writing. Mention one or more informational books that you have read to them.

2. Tell children that expository writing is different from story writing—that it *explains* something rather than tells a story. Explain the way expository writing is organized by using the following or similar words.

    "Sometimes when we write, we don't tell a story, we *explain* or *describe* something. When we *explain* or *describe*, we write differently; we begin with a big idea and then write details."

3. Write a short paragraph on the chalkboard illustrating the main idea-detail organization or use the following example.

    You can find many different animals in the rain forest that you won't find anywhere else on earth. One of the most colorful of these animals is a bird: a macaw. Macaws are bright blue, yellow, red, and green. They live in trees in the rain forest. Another animal that lives in the rain forest is the monkey. Monkeys have long tails which they use to swing from branches in the high trees. The animals in the rain forest are fascinating.

4. Identify the main idea and details of your paragraph and write them in the proper places on an umbrella illustration as is shown in the example.

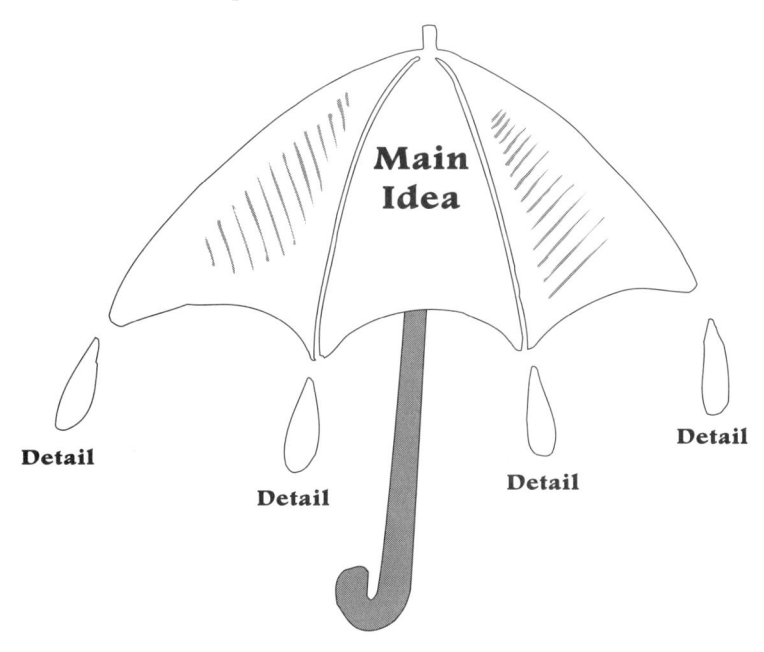

Literacy Knowledge

5. Give children a writing topic that relates to a book you have read or to your curriculum and brainstorm main ideas with your children. For example, some main ideas about rain forest animals could be the following.

> Rain forest animals are varied and colorful.
>
> Many rain forest animals are becoming extinct.
>
> Rain forest animals need a hot, humid environment.

6. Duplicate and distribute the umbrella handout that follows. Have children choose a main idea statement. Write that statement in the center of the umbrella.

7. Discuss details that match the main ideas that the children selected. Tell children to label the raindrops with the details.

8. Have children write a short paragraph beginning with their main idea and then add details. Remind children that this type of writing is expository writing.

9. Tell children that when they write expository text they use the main idea-detail organizational pattern.

Expository Writing Graphic Organizer

Name _____ Date _____

_____

_____

_____

_____

_____

From Jerry L. Johns, Susan Davis Lenski, and Laurie Elish-Piper, *Teaching Beginning Readers: Linking Assessment and Instruction* (2nd ed.). Copyright © 2002 by Kendall/Hunt Publishing Company (1-800-247-3458, ext. 5). May be reproduced for noncommercial educational purposes.

Literacy Knowledge 81

Ideas and Activities

1. Encourage children to read informational texts by giving book talks about informational books. A book talk is a one-to-two-minute "commercial" about a book. After the book talk, display the books in a book center so that children can read them during independent reading time.

2. Read informational picture books to children frequently. Before reading, remind children that the book you are reading does not have a plot but that it describes or explains something.

3. Encourage children to embed "how to" stories in traditional stories in their speaking and writing. For example, a child talking or writing about a family camping trip could describe how they put up their tent. Tell children that including "how to" sections provides readers with information inside a story.

4. Tell children that some television programs and movies are informational rather than fictional. Have children brainstorm a list of television programs that they typically watch. Have children predict which type of programs they watch more frequently. Write the names of the programs on cards that can be placed on a chart. Give children the names of two categories: fictional programs and informational programs. Have children sort the cards into the two categories. Discuss the differences between the types of television programs.

5. Pair fictional texts with informational texts to read aloud to children. Select books that are of similar topics such as *Owl Moon* by Jane Yolen and *All About Owls* by Jim Arnosky. Read one book in the morning and one in the afternoon. Discuss books with children and compare how the books were alike and different (Taberski, 2000).

6. Use a content area word wall to help familiarize children with words found in informational texts (Bean, 2001). To create a content area word wall, identify five words that will be found in informational texts the children will be reading in the next week. For example, if you're going to read *Birds* by Gallimard Jeunesse, you might select the words *beak*, *prey*, *feathers*, *nests*, and *grubs*. Print the five words on colorful paper and display them in the room. At least once a day, read the words aloud with children, having children clap and chant each letter of each word. For example, say the word beak and then say each letter, B-E-A-K. At the end of the week read the book aloud to children.

Informational Material

Home School Connections

- Broaden your child's literacy knowledge by including informational books in your child's bedtime reading. Informational books "explain" something or "tell" about something. Books that present facts about animals, for instance, are informational texts. Another popular type of informational book is a how-to book such as a book on crafts, cooking, projects, and experiments. Many young children like to read books that provide information, so try to alternate stories with informational books.

- Encourage your child to write an informational alphabet book using a familiar theme. For example, if your child plays soccer, you could start "A is for athlete. B is for ball." Continue through the alphabet, encouraging your child to write something for each letter. Your assistance, and a bit of creativity, may be necessary for some of the letters.

From Jerry L. Johns, Susan Davis Lenski, and Laurie Elish-Piper, *Teaching Beginning Readers: Linking Assessment and Instruction* (2nd ed.). Copyright © 2002 by Kendall/Hunt Publishing Company (1-800-247-3458, ext. 5). May be reproduced for noncommercial educational purposes.

Selected Resources
INFORMATIONAL TEXT STRUCTURES

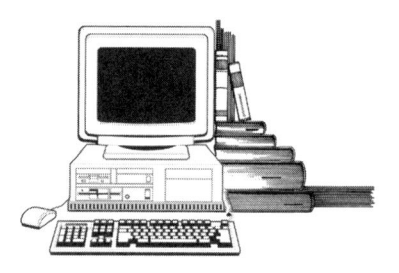

Informational books

Carlstron, N.W. (1997). *Raven and river*. Boston: Little, Brown.

Harrison, D.L. (2001). *Caves: Mysteries beneath our feet*. Honesdale, PA: Boyds Mill Press.

Morris, A. (1992). *Houses and homes*. New York: Lathrop, Lee and Shaperd.

Myers, J. (2001). *How dogs came from wolves*. Honesdale, PA: Boyds Mill Press.

Waldman, N. (2001). *They came from the Bronx: How the buffalo were saved from extinction*. Honesdale, PA: Boyds Mill Press.

Watts, B. (1985). *Butterfly and caterpillar*. Morristown, NJ: Silver Burdett.

Videotapes

American history for children. Dramatizations of historical events.

Animal life for children. Describes animal basics.

Bug city. Describes bug food, habitats, and social behavior.

Physical science for children. Demonstrates scientific principles.

Plant life for children. Uncovers facts about plant and plant growth.

Space science for children. Answers to questions about space.

Science as inquiry for children. Explores principles of investigation and observation to solve problems.

Professional Resources

Bamford, R., & Kristo, J. (1999). *Checking out nonfiction K–8: Good Choices for best learning*. Norwood, MA: Christopher-Gordon.

Newbridge Publishers. *www.newbridgeonline.com*

Sundance Publishers. *www.sundancepub.com*

Rigby Publishers. *www.rigbypub.com*

From Jerry L. Johns, Susan Davis Lenski, and Laurie Elish-Piper, *Teaching Beginning Readers: Linking Assessment and Instruction* (2nd ed.). Copyright © 2002 by Kendall/Hunt Publishing Company (1-800-247-3458, ext. 5). May be reproduced for noncommercial educational purposes.

2.4 Assessments of Literacy Knowledge

Assessment Strategy 1   Print Concepts   86

   Pull-out booklet: Friends   89
   Friends Record Sheet   101
   Pull-out booklet: Animals   105
   Animals Record Sheet   117

Assessment Strategy 2   Retelling a Story   119

   Narrative Retelling Record Sheet   120

Assessment Strategy 3   Informational Text Retelling   121

   Informational Text Retelling Record Sheet   122

Goal To assess the child's literacy knowlege.

BACKGROUND

You can assess children's literacy knowledge through ongoing, informal observations during day-to-day classroom activities. However, sometimes in classroom situations you can't be sure how well certain children understand how print works. You may want to assess these children individually through an Assessment of Print Concepts, story retelling, or informational retelling. Harp (2000) suggests that you can use this type of assessment to verify your observations in the classroom. After you have reached conclusions about the child's literacy knowledge, you can tailor your instructional emphasis to meet the child's needs.

Assessment Strategy 1

Section 2.4

Print Concepts

Overview	The Print Concepts assessment measures how well a child knows the components of a book. Children need to have adequate book handling skills before they will be able to read independently. For example, if a child doesn't understand that print is read from left to right, reading will be impossible. You will find two types of Assessment of Print Concepts: one that includes a short text and one you can use with your choice of books. Both methods measure how well a child understands how books are read.
Materials Needed	1. The book *Friends* (p. 89) or *Animals* (p. 105) 2. A pencil 3. A copy of the Print Concepts Record Sheet (pp. 101 or 117) that corresponds to the form selected for use
Procedures	1. Tear out one of the short books, *Friends* or *Animals*, that follow. Use a simple binding for the book. 2. Decide which book you want to use. Some teachers like to use Form 1 at the beginning of the year and Form 2 later in the year. 3. Show the book to the child. Say, "I'd like you to show me some of the things you know about reading. You won't have to read." Query the child with the statements on Form 1 or Form 2 as you read the book to the child. 4. Circle a plus (+) if the child gives the correct response and a minus (–) if the child gives an incorrect response. Total correct responses.
Scoring and Interpretation	Score the Print Concepts assessment by totaling the number of correct responses on the Record Sheet and by determining which types of questions were correct or incorrect. In addition, use the Qualitative Judgments of Print Concepts Record Sheet (p. 102 or p. 118) to interpret the assessment. First, determine the child's engagement with the task. Decide how engaged the child was and place an X on the continuum from low engagement to high engagement. If the child scored low in this area, see Chapter 1 for ideas on ways to increase the child's motivation to read. Then use the child's scores on the assessment to decide how well the child understands print directionality, punctuation, uppercase and lowercase letters, knowledge of letters, knowledge of words, and ability to frame a sentence. There is no magic number that will tell you whether the child is secure in these areas or insecure. However, if a child misses even one of the questions, you should continue instruction in that area.

Additional Ways of Assessing Print Concepts

1. You can informally assess print concepts by watching children "read" during independent reading time. Notice whether the child holds the book rightside-up, whether pages are turned from right to left, and whether the child turns each page. If a child does not handle books with understanding, continue instruction in print concepts.
2. You can also assess print concepts in a one-on-one situation using a child's choice of books. To assess print concepts, ask the following prompts.
   - Show me how to hold this book so I can read it.
   - Show me the front cover.
   - Show me the back cover.
   - Where would I begin reading this book?
   - Where are the words?
   - Where are the pictures?
   - Show me one word.
   - Show me the end of the book.

> **Note:**
>
> Remove and bind the following *Friends* booklet for use with Form 1 of the Print Concepts Assessment (Section 2.4).

Friends

by Dorie Cannon & Cheryl Mangione

It is Saturday.

Dog and Cat have been waiting all week for this day.

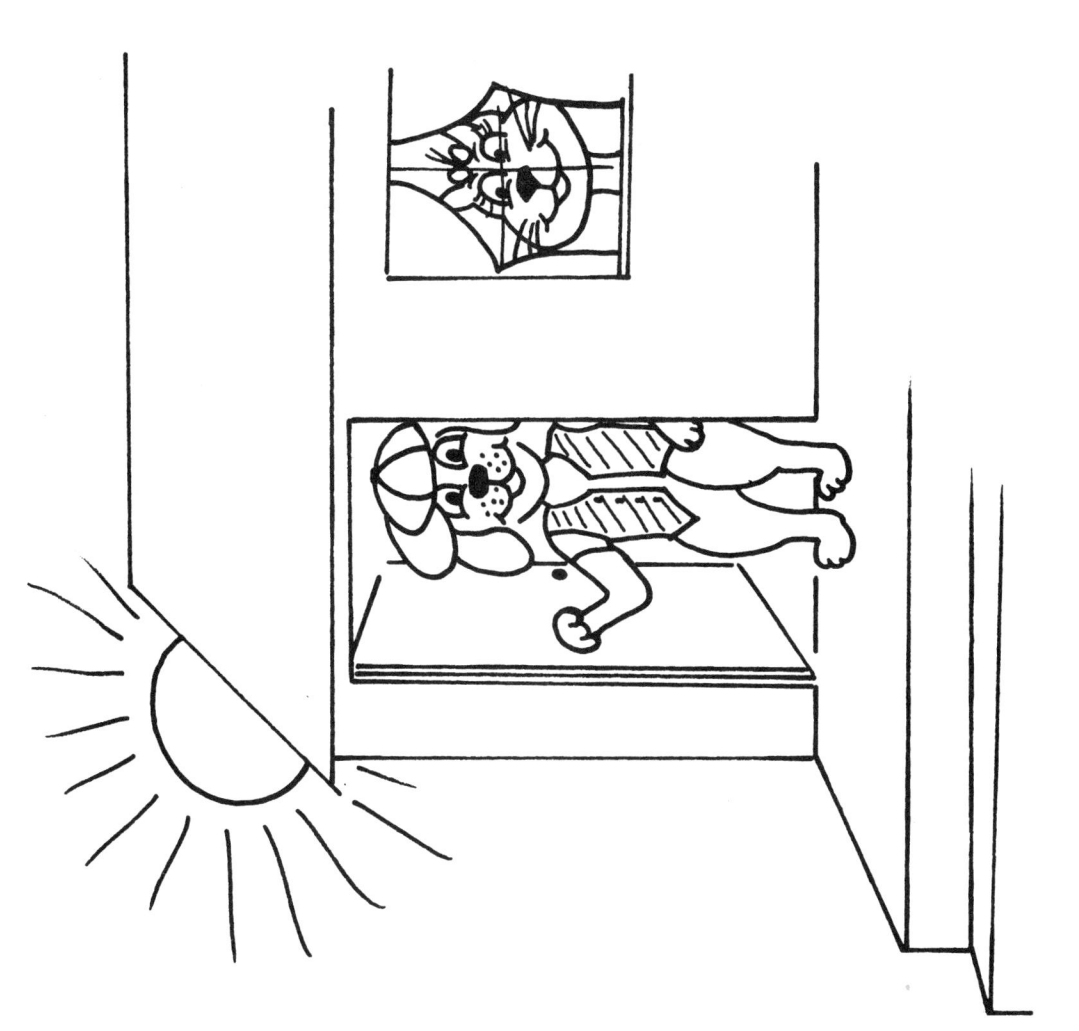

First they go running.

It makes them feel good.

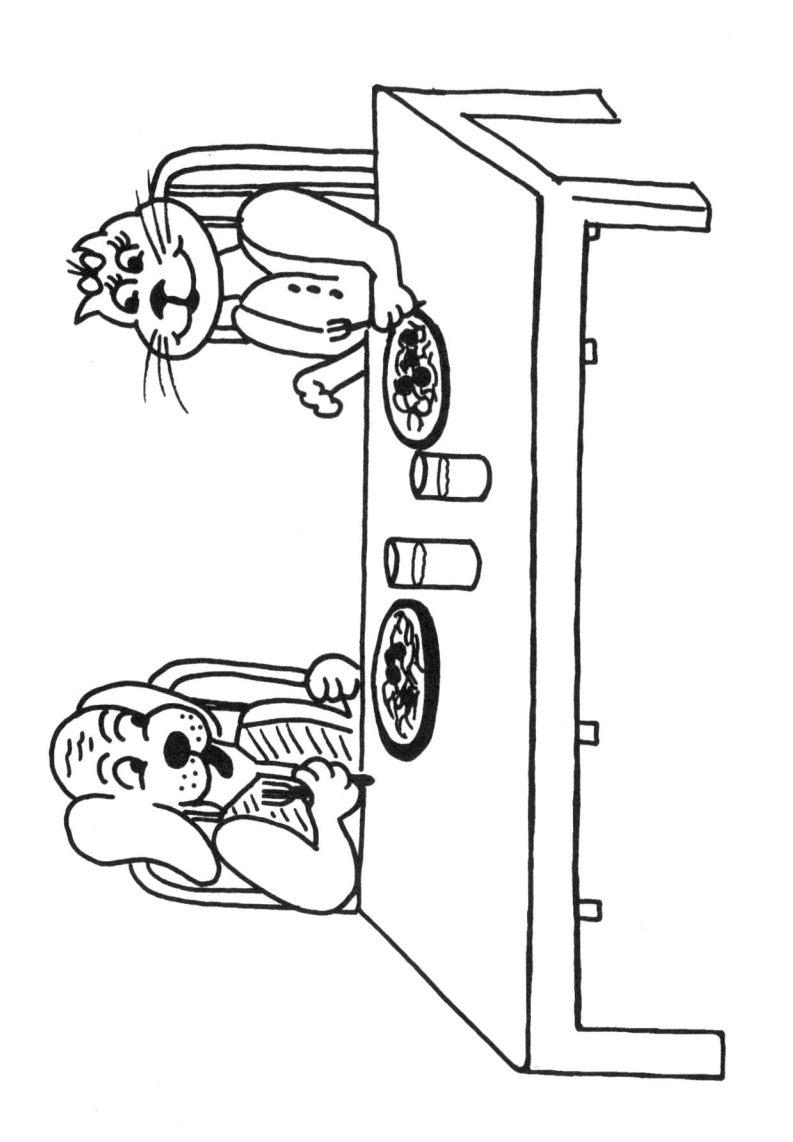

Wow, are they hungry now!

Dog and Cat go
to the park.
They like riding
their bikes.

They play ball.

This is fun!

Cat says, "Where can we read? Let me see.

How about under that tree?"

"Great idea," says Dog.

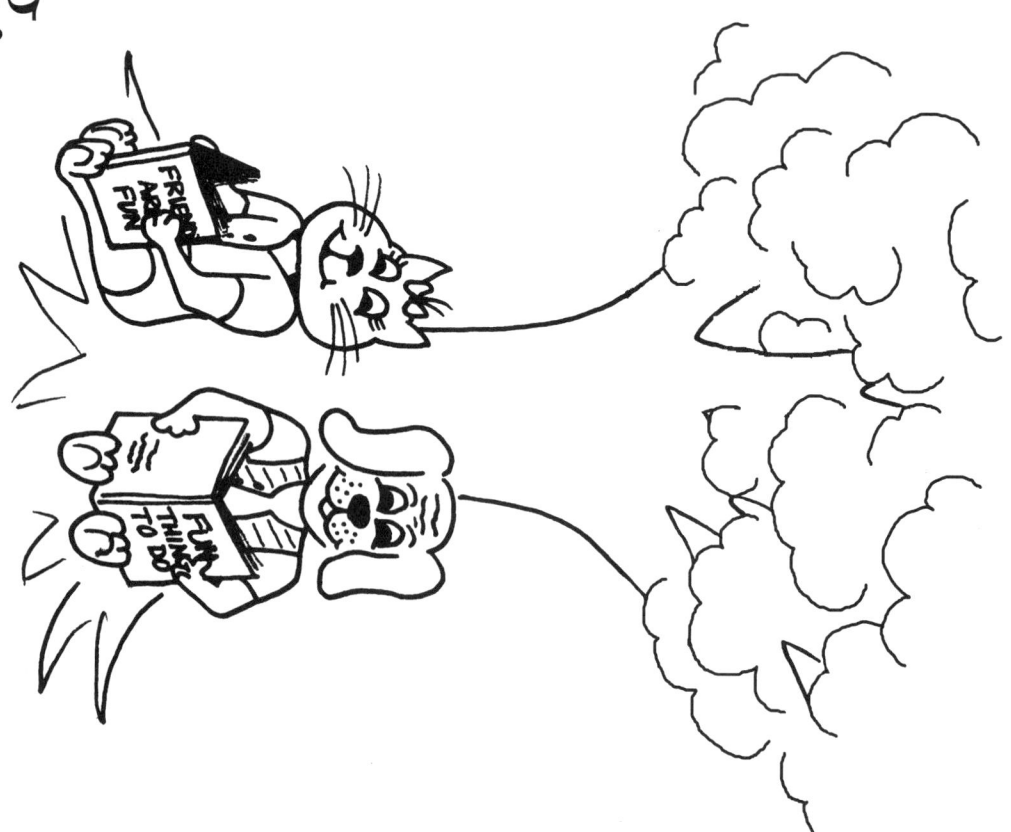

Cat and Dog sing.

They laugh.

Being friends is a lot of fun.

It is time to go home now.

It has been
a long day.

Dog and Cat are
very tired.

They are so happy!

The two friends
dream about what
will happen
tomorrow.

RECORD SHEET

Form 1

2.4 Print Concepts—"Friends"

Name_____ Date_____

PAGE

	+	−	1. Hand the book to the child and say, "Show me the front of this book."
1	+	−	2. Say, "Point to where I should start reading." *Read page 1.*
2	+	−	3. Ask, "Which way should I go?" Check for knowledge of left to right. *Read first line of page 2.*
2/3	+	−	4. Ask, "Where should I go after that?" Check for knowledge of a return sweep to the left. *Read rest of page 2 and page 3.*
3	+	−	5. On page 3, point to the comma and ask, "What's this or what's this for?"
4	+	−	6. *Read text on page 4.* Point to a period and ask, "What's this or what's this for?"
5	+	−	7. *Read text on page 5.* Point to the exclamation mark and ask, "What's this or what's this for?"
6	+	−	8. *Read text on page 6.* Point to the question mark and ask, "What's this or what's this for?"
6	+	−	9. Point to a lowercase letter *(w, g, c)* and say, "Find a capital letter like this, find an uppercase letter like this, or find the big one like this."
7	+	−	10. *Read text on page 7.* Say, "Show me one letter." (Two 3" × 5" cards may be useful for items 10–19.)
	+	−	11. Say, "Show me two letters."
	+	−	12. Say, "Show me only one word."
	+	−	13. Say, "Show me two words."
	+	−	14. Say, "Show me the first letter of a word."
	+	−	15. Say, "Show me the last letter of a word."
	+	−	16. Say, "Show me a long word."
	+	−	17. Say, "Show me a short word."
	+	−	18. Say, "Show me a sentence."
8/9	+	−	19. *Read text on pages 8 and 9.* Point to a capital letter *(I, D, T)* and say, "Find a small letter like this or find a lowercase letter like this."
10	+	−	20. *Read text on page 10.* Close the book and hand it to the child with the back cover showing and say, "Show me the title or show me the name of the book."

☐ Total Correct

From Jerry L. Johns, Susan Davis Lenski, and Laurie Elish-Piper, *Teaching Beginning Readers: Linking Assessment and Instruction* (2nd ed.). Copyright © 2002 by Kendall/Hunt Publishing Company (1-800-247-3458, ext. 5). May be reproduced for noncommercial educational purposes.

RECORD SHEET

Qualitative Judgments of Print Concepts

Name _____ Date _____

	Not Evident Low Seldom Weak Poor	Some	Evident High Always Strong Excellent
Overall engagement	├──────┼──────┼──────┼──────┤		
Understanding of print directionality	├──────┼──────┼──────┼──────┤		
Knowledge of punctuation	├──────┼──────┼──────┼──────┤		
Correspondence of uppercase and lowercase letters	├──────┼──────┼──────┼──────┤		
Knowledge of letter and letters	├──────┼──────┼──────┼──────┤		
Knowledge of word and words	├──────┼──────┼──────┼──────┤		
Ability to frame a sentence	├──────┼──────┼──────┼──────┤		

Observations, Comments, Notes, and Insights

From Jerry L. Johns, Susan Davis Lenski, and Laurie Elish-Piper, *Teaching Beginning Readers: Linking Assessment and Instruction* (2nd ed.). Copyright © 2002 by Kendall/Hunt Publishing Company (1-800-247-3458, ext. 5). May be reproduced for noncommercial educational purposes.

Note:

Remove and bind the following *Animals* booklet for use with Form 2 of the Print Concepts Assessment (Section 2.4).

Animals

by Dorie Cannon

From Jerry L. Johns, Susan Davis Lenski, and Laurie Elish-Piper, *Teaching Beginning Readers: Linking Assessment and Instruction* (2nd ed.). Copyright © 2002 by Kendall/Hunt Publishing Company (1-800-247-3458, ext. 5). May be reproduced for noncommercial educational purposes.

I love animals.

They eat, sleep,

and play

every day.

Just like me!

Cats sleep a lot.
They play with
string and eat
fish. I like their
soft fur.

Dogs eat bones,

run, and bark.

They sleep in a bed.

I sleep in a bed, too!

Fish swim, sleep, and eat in the water. I like their pretty colors.

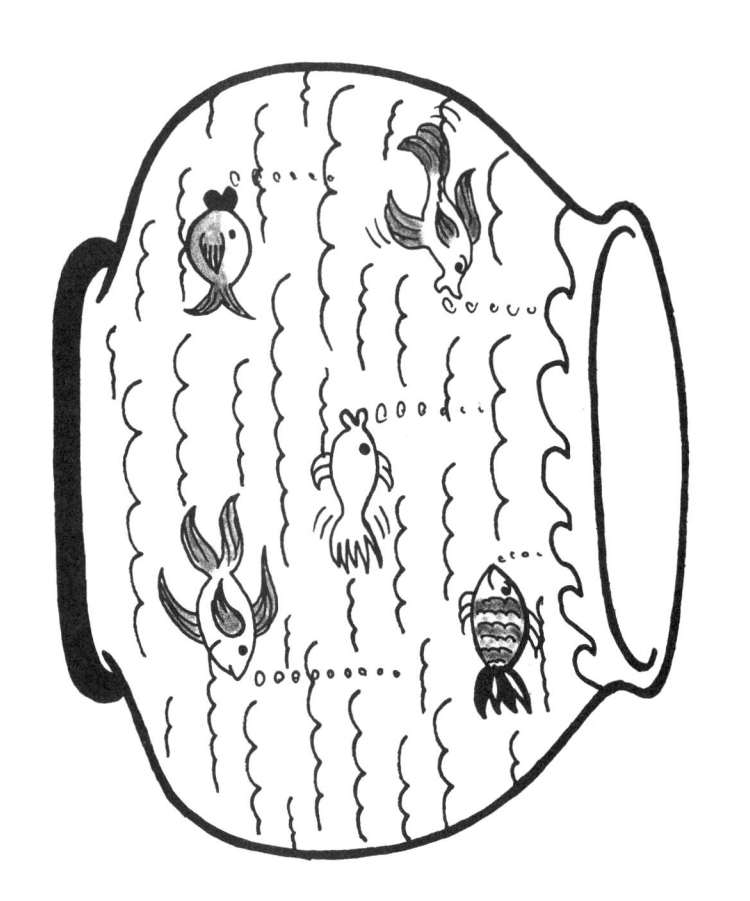

Bears eat fish and sleep in caves. They scratch their backs on trees. Ouch! That would hurt.

Elephants roll in mud
and eat tree bark

They lie on the
ground to sleep.

How do they do that?

Monkeys play
and sleep in trees.
They eat bananas.
I eat bananas too!

Birds love to fly.
They eat seeds
and sleep in nests.
There's a big
nest in my tree.

Rabbits eat plants.

They hop and sleep in underground nests. I can hop like a rabbit.

I love animals very much. Someday I will work in a zoo.

RECORD SHEET

Form 2

2.4 Print Concepts —"Animals"

Name _____ Date _____

PAGE

	+ –	1. Hand the book to the child and say, "Show me the front of this book."
1	+ –	2. Say, "Point to where I should start reading." *Read page 1.*
2	+ –	3. Ask, "Which way should I go?" Check for knowledge of left to right. *Read first line of page 2.*
2/3	+ –	4. Ask, "Where should I go after that?" Check for knowledge of a return sweep to the left. *Read rest of page 2 and page 3.*
3	+ –	5. On page 3, point to the comma and ask, "What's this or what's this for?"
4	+ –	6. *Read text on page 4.* Point to a period and ask, "What's this or what's this for?"
5	+ –	7. *Read text on page 5.* Point to the exclamation mark and ask, "What's this or what's this for?"
6	+ –	8. *Read text on page 6.* Point to the question mark and ask, "What's this or what's this for?"
6	+ –	9. Point to a lowercase letter *(w, g, c)* and say, "Find a capital letter like this, find an uppercase letter like this, or find the big one like this."
7	+ –	10. *Read text on page 7.* Say, "Show me one letter." (Two 3" × 5" cards may be useful for items 10–19.)
	+ –	11. Say, "Show me two letters."
	+ –	12. Say, "Show me only one word."
	+ –	13. Say, "Show me two words."
	+ –	14. Say, "Show me the first letter of a word."
	+ –	15. Say, "Show me the last letter of a word."
	+ –	16. Say, "Show me a long word."
	+ –	17. Say, "Show me a short word."
	+ –	18. Say, "Show me a sentence."
8/9	+ –	19. *Read text on pages 8 and 9.* Point to a capital letter *(B, p. 8 and R, I, p. 9)* and say, "Find a small letter like this or find a lowercase letter like this."
10	+ –	20. *Read text on page 10.* Close the book and hand it to the child with the back cover showing and say, "Show me the title or show me the name of the book."

☐ Total Correct

From Jerry L. Johns, Susan Davis Lenski, and Laurie Elish-Piper, *Teaching Beginning Readers: Linking Assessment and Instruction* (2nd ed.). Copyright © 2002 by Kendall/Hunt Publishing Company (1-800-247-3458, ext. 5). May be reproduced for noncommercial educational purposes.

RECORD SHEET

Qualitative Judgments of Print Concepts

Name _____ Date _____

	Not Evident Low Seldom Weak Poor	Some	Evident High Always Strong Excellent
Overall engagement	├────┼────┼────┼────┤		
Understanding of print directionality	├────┼────┼────┼────┤		
Knowledge of punctuation	├────┼────┼────┼────┤		
Correspondence of uppercase and lowercase letters	├────┼────┼────┼────┤		
Knowledge of letter and letters	├────┼────┼────┼────┤		
Knowledge of word and words	├────┼────┼────┼────┤		
Ability to frame a sentence	├────┼────┼────┼────┤		

Observations, Comments, Notes, and Insights

From Jerry L. Johns, Susan Davis Lenski, and Laurie Elish-Piper, *Teaching Beginning Readers: Linking Assessment and Instruction* (2nd ed.). Copyright © 2002 by Kendall/Hunt Publishing Company (1-800-247-3458, ext. 5). May be reproduced for noncommercial educational purposes.

Assessment Strategy 2

Retelling a Story

Section 2.4

Overview	You can get a good sense of children's knowledge of story structures by their story retelling. Children who have a developed sense of story will be able to retell stories using story grammar, but those who are unclear about story structure will tell unrelated details. Children's retelling of stories can let you know whether they need more instruction in story structure.
Materials Needed	1. An age-appropriate story that is new to the child 2. A copy of the Narrative Retelling Record Sheet (p. 120)
Procedures	1. Choose a short book that is new for the child. The book should have an obvious plot with named characters. You may choose to use props or puppets with the story if you think visual aids could help the child. 2. Before reading the book say, "I'm going to read a story to you. After I am finished reading, I will ask you to tell me the story as if you were telling it to someone who has not read the story. As you listen, try to remember as much of the story as you can." 3. Read the book aloud to the child. 4. After you have read the book say, "Now tell me as much of the story as you can." If the child hesitates, ask probing questions such as "What was the story about?" or "Who was in the story?" or "What happened next?" You may want to tape-record the retelling for future reference.
Scoring and Interpretation	Use the Narrative Retelling Record Sheet to record how well the child understands narrative story structure and the rubric for a score. If a child scores below a 4, you should continue to teach story structure explicitly. Have the child participate in another retelling within a short time for a second assessment. Some stories are easier for a child to retell than others, and a second retelling may provide different information.

Literacy Knowledge 119

RECORD SHEET

Narrative Retelling

Name_____ Date_____

Name of text _____

CHECK ALL THAT APPLY.

_____ Identifies setting of story.

_____ Identifies main characters.

_____ Identifies problem of story.

_____ Identifies sequence of events.

_____ Identifies solution to problem.

RUBRIC FOR NARRATIVE TEXT RETELLING

4   Child correctly retells story using the setting, names of characters, events as they occurred in the story, the problem, and the solution. Events are described thoroughly and events are in correct sequence.

3   Child correctly identifies setting and some of the characters although without exact names, tells the events in sequence, identifies the story's problem and solution. There are some errors in retelling, but most details are accurate.

2   Child identifies the setting and characters and gives some information about the plot. Details may be minimal.

1   Child identifies few story elements correctly.

Assessment Strategy 3

Section 2.4

Informational Text Retelling

Overview	Children have a more difficult time understanding the organizational patterns of informational text than stories, but you can assess how well children are learning the pattern of informational text by retellings. An informational text retelling is similar to a story retelling—only the type of text is different. Children who have a good understanding of informational text patterns will be able to retell the text using them, but those who are unclear about the text pattern will most likely relate a list of details. Informational text retellings can inform you of children's progress, and you can tailor your instruction to meet their needs.
Materials Needed	1. An age-appropriate informational text that is new to the child 2. Copy of the Informational Text Retelling Record Sheet (p. 122)
Procedures	1. Choose a short informational book that is new for the child. The book should have a clear text pattern such as main idea-detail or steps in a process. 2. Before reading the book say, "I'm going to read a book to you. After I am finished reading, I will ask you to tell me what occurred in the book as if you were telling it to someone who has not heard it. As you listen, try to remember as much of the book as you can." 3. Read the book aloud to the child. 4. After you have read the book say: "Now tell me as much of the book as you can." If the child hesitates, ask probing questions such as "What is the book about?" or "What happened first?" You may want to tape-record the retelling for future reference.
Scoring and Interpretation	Use the Informational Text Retelling Record Sheet to record how well the child understands informational text structure. The rubric can be used for a quantitative score. If a child scores below a 4, you should continue to explicitly teach text structure. Have the child participate in another retelling within a short time for a second assessment. Some books are easier for a particular child to retell than others are, and a second retelling may provide different information.

Literacy Knowledge 121

RECORD SHEET

Informational Text Retelling

Name _____ Date _____

Name of Text _____

CHECK ONE

_____ Text is at child's reading level.

_____ Text is above child's reading level.

CHECK ONE

_____ All important facts are recalled.

_____ Most of the important facts are recalled.

_____ Some of the important facts are recalled.

CHECK ALL THAT APPLY

_____ Supporting ideas are recalled.

_____ Ideas are recalled in logical order.

_____ Child used pictures, charts, and graphs.

_____ Child recalled important conclusions.

_____ Child made appropriate inferences.

Adapted from B. Harp (2000). *The handbook of literacy assessment and evaluation* (2nd ed.). Norwood, MA: Christopher-Gordon.

From Jerry L. Johns, Susan Davis Lenski, and Laurie Elish-Piper, *Teaching Beginning Readers: Linking Assessment and Instruction* (2nd ed.). Copyright © 2002 by Kendall/Hunt Publishing Company (1-800-247-3458, ext. 5). May be reproduced for noncommercial educational purposes.

RUBRIC FOR INFORMATIONAL TEXT RETELLING

4   Child fully explains the main points and supporting details.

3   Child provides the main points and supporting details but does not explain them fully.

2   Child explains most of the main points but is not completely accurate. Child provides some, but not all, details.

1   Child does not correctly identify the main points or supporting details. Retelling is mostly inaccurate.

Additional Ways to Assess Informational Text Structure

Retellings are the best way to assess text structure, but you can administer retellings in several different ways.

1. You can read the book to the child, as is detailed in the directions.
2. You can have the child read the book independently.
3. You can have the child give an oral retelling, but you can also have the child write a retelling.
4. You can have the child draw pictures as a retelling.

Whichever way you administer a retelling, the checklist and rubric apply.

CHAPTER 3

Letters and Sounds

OVERVIEW

Children learning to read are faced with books containing text. That text is composed of letters that make up words. Sounds can be associated with the letters and letter combinations to help decode or pronounce words that are not known at sight. The ability to pronounce words is a primary and critically important task for children in the beginning stages of reading. Although there has been debate and controversy about methods of beginning reading instruction over the years, there appears to be growing agreement that children profit from instruction in associating sounds with letters and letter combinations. This instruction is referred to as phonics. Associated with phonics instruction are knowledge of letters, auditory discrimination, and phonemic awareness. This chapter contains various strategies for helping students learn to associate letters with sounds as well as ways to help them learn related skills. Strategies for assessment are included at the end of the chapter so you can assess areas of interest and target instruction to children's needs. Beginning on the next page are answers to some questions that will help you to better understand phonics and phonemic awareness.

Is learning the alphabet important for reading?

In a word, yes. Children "need to recognize letters and their distinguishing features in order to work effectively with print; learning the names of the letters is also very useful" (Graves, Juel, & Graves, 2001, p. 99). Over the years, reading professionals have generally accepted that children's knowledge of letters of the alphabet is an early predictor of later reading success (Walsh, Price, & Gillingham, 1988). It has also been recognized that alphabet knowledge is generally a result of a literacy-rich environment where children have played with alphabet blocks and/or magnetic letters within a broader context of being read to and engaging in many natural and meaningful activities related to print. The fact that these experiences generally occur in the preschool years stresses the important role that parents play in their children's acquisition of literacy.

What is meant by the alphabetic principle?

Simply stated, children learning to read must develop an understanding of how sounds are represented by the letters of the alphabet. Stanovich (2000) notes that "this principle may be induced; it may be acquired through direct instruction; it may be acquired along with or after the buildup of a visually based sight vocabulary—but it must be acquired if a child is to progress successfully in reading" (p. 162). When phonics is taught, the alphabetic principle is developed.

I've been hearing a lot about phonemic awareness. What is it?

Phonemic awareness (PA) refers to the child's ability to focus on and manipulate phonemes in spoken words. Phonemes are the smallest units of spoken language, so phonemic awareness is the ability to manipulate these small units of sound. There are over 40 phonemes in English. Some of the phonemic awareness tasks include phoneme isolation (Tell me the first sound in *make*, phoneme blending (What word is /k/ /ī/ /t/?), and phoneme deletion (What is *fill* without the/f/?). "The theoretical and practical importance of phonological [or phonemic] awareness for the beginning reader relies not only on logic but also on the results of several decades of empirical research" (Snow, Burns, & Griffin, 1998, p. 54). In a review of the research related to PA and reading achievement, the analysis revealed that PA training produced positive effects on both word reading and comprehension (National Reading Panel, 2000).

Phonics seems to come and go. What's the latest on phonics?

As you probably know, phonics is a way of teaching beginning reading that stresses grapheme-phoneme relationships. Graphemes are letters and phonemes are sounds, so phonics is associating letters and sounds to help pronounce words. Effective reading programs have always had a phonics component. In more recent years, it has become clear that systematic phonics instruction "makes a bigger contribution to children's growth in reading than alternative programs providing unsystematic or no phonics instruction" (National Reading Panel, 2000, p. 2–92). There is not one right way that systematic phonics is taught; however, common characteristics include explicit instruction and a planned sequence of introducing the grapheme-phoneme relationships.

Why is phonics important in reading?

When most children come to school, they have a speaking vocabulary that numbers in the thousands of words. They can use and understand many different words, but these same children are typically able to recognize at sight only a small fraction of words in print. If children are taught to associate the sounds with the letters, they have a way to decode or pronounce words. Many of the words used in beginning reading instruction are probably familiar to children (because they have used them in daily conversations), and phonics provides a way for children to unlock or decode the words in print. When this process occurs, the child is likely to be able to relate the written word to a word already spoken or heard and construct a meaning from the text. As you can see, using sound-symbol relationships is one of the important cueing systems in reading.

3.1 Alphabet Knowledge

> **Goal** To help children learn the names of the letters of the alphabet.
> **Assessment Strategy 1** Alphabet Knowledge, page 168

BACKGROUND

Children learn much about reading through oral language activities. They learn the sounds of the language and how words form sentences. Children can even read some familiar words before learning the individual letters of the alphabet. As children learn about written language, they learn that language is made up of sounds, words, and sentences. Consider the young child who can identify a stop sign without knowing the names of the individual letters. Environmental print such as a stop sign is familiar to children. When children see words repeatedly, they can learn the words, even though they don't know the names of the letters in the words.

As children learn about the nature of language, however, they need to be directed to learn the names of the letters of the alphabet and to distinguish one letter from another. Learning the names of the letters of the alphabet is a developmental process. Letter names have little meaning to children before they possess some knowledge about language (Morrow, 2001).

Children need to know the letters of the alphabet to become independent readers (Ehri, 1987). As children progress beyond becoming aware of the sounds of language, such as rhyming words, they need to be able to distinguish among the letters so that they can learn how to read unknown words. It is unrealistic to think that a young reader could learn enough sight words to be able to read a new story. Therefore, children need to learn that words are made up of letters, and they need to learn the names of the letters of the alphabet.

There are many approaches to teaching the alphabet. Some teachers introduce a letter a week throughout the school year. Others teach letters in the context of words and stories. There is not one right way to teach the alphabet, although some experts believe that teaching the letters of the alphabet in context is more meaningful for children (Morrow, 2001). The following teaching strategies, activities, and ideas will assist your teaching the letters of the alphabet.

Teaching Strategy 1

Section 3.1

Alphabet Song

The Alphabet Song has been used in many homes and classrooms for years. It is a song known by many children and is a very natural and meaningful way to help children learn the alphabet.

1. Secure a recording of the Alphabet Song. You may know it is sung to the tune of *Twinkle, Twinkle, Little Star*. Tell children that you will help them learn the Alphabet Song. A number of children may say that they already know it, so encourage them to sing along.

2. Sing the Alphabet Song and encourage children who know the song to teach it to other children. Children can be asked to stand when the letter that begins their first (or last) name is sung.

3. Because the Alphabet Song is learned by repeated singing, make the connection to the printed letters above the chalkboard or on a wall chart. Point to the letters as the song is sung and then invite a child to point to the letters with you.

4. Make individual alphabet cards and randomly pass them out to children. Sing the Alphabet Song slowly and have a child stand as that letter is sung.

5. Distribute an alphabet card to each child and have the children line up as the Alphabet Song is sung slowly.

6. Have children sing the Alphabet Song in those few moments while waiting for the bell to excuse the class or at other times where there is a minute available before an activity begins.

7. Share the book *Letters and Sounds* by R. Wells (2001). Included with the book is an audiotape containing the Alphabet Song and other activities.

Teaching Strategy 2

Section 3.1

Using Alphabet Books

Alphabet books are books that have letters arranged in sequential order from A through Z. There are many attractive alphabet books available on a large number of topics (see Johns & Lenski, 2001). Reading alphabet books to children helps them become familiar with the names of the letters in alphabetical order. Alphabet books also provide a wide range of words that start with each letter in the alphabet, which helps children learn how to associate a letter with a number of words.

DIRECTIONS

1. Choose an alphabet book to read to children. Most libraries have a large collection of alphabet books. A short list of alphabet books can be found in the Selected Resources: Alphabet Knowledge (page 134). For a more complete listing of over 100 alphabet books, refer to Appendix B in Johns and Lenski (2001).

2. Show the children the cover of the book and read the title to them. Tell them that this book will have the letters of the alphabet and that it will be about a specific topic. Tell them what the topic of the book is. For example, *Alphabears* (Hague, 1984) is a book that shows different bears with names that begin with the letters of the alphabet in alphabetical order.

3. Before reading, invite children to recite the letters of the alphabet with you.

4. Read the alphabet book, making note of any special features. Point out that each page has a letter of the alphabet in alphabetical order.

5. After reading the book, have children recite the letters of the alphabet in order. Provide assistance as needed.

6. After reading the book several times, have children read along with you.

7. Tape-record the book and place the book and the tape in a listening center for children to listen to during free time.

Tips for English Language Learners

- Help children learn to recognize the letters in their names. Relate these letters to the alphabet in your classroom.

- As you sing the Alphabet Song, pair a child learning English with another child who already knows the song.

- Send home a recording of the Alphabet Song and an easy-to-use tape recorder. Encourage the child and his or her parents to sing along.

- Obtain simple alphabet books containing familiar illustrations that the child is likely to recognize. Invite the child to take the book home and share it. Simple and clear illustrations can also help the child learn words.

Teaching Strategy 3

Section 3.1

Letter Actions

Young children tend to be very active, so the strategy Letter Actions (Cunningham, 2000) has great appeal for most children. The strategy Letter Actions entails identifying an action word that begins with a specific letter and associating that letter with the action. When children are able to associate an action with the name of a letter, they more readily learn the letters of the alphabet.

DIRECTIONS

1. Identify the name of a letter that you want to teach. Write the name of a letter on one side of a large index card.

2. For each letter, think of an action that students could perform in your classroom or outside. List the action on the reverse side of the index card. For example, if you wanted to teach the letter *n*, you could write *nod* on the reverse side of the card.

3. Show students the side of the card that has the name of the letter written on it. Say the name of the letter. Have the children repeat the letter name.

4. Tell students that they will be performing an action that begins with that letter. Show them the side of the card with the action written on it. Read the action.

5. Have the children perform the action while saying the name of the letter. Reinforce the association by repeating the same action card more than once.

6. After the children have learned several letters and actions, have a child choose a card and lead the class in performing the action.

7. The following is a sample list of actions that can be used in conjunction with Letter Actions.

argue	fall	kick	paint	unbend
bounce	gallop	laugh	quack	vacuum
catch	hop	march	run	walk
dance	itch	nod	sit	xylophone (play)
eat	jump	open	talk	yawn
				zip

Teaching Strategy 4

Section 3.1

Identifying Letters

Children need to learn the letters of the alphabet in proper order, and they also need to learn how to identify letters in the context of words. Some children will have difficulty making the link from saying the letters of the alphabet to identifying letters in combination with other letters to form words. To help them learn letters in the context of words, point out letters in Big Books, the Morning Message, or their names. Guiding children to identify letters in print will help them learn how to read.

DIRECTIONS

1. Choose a story, Morning Message, or one of the children's names to teach children how to identify letters. The story can be one that you read to the children, a dictated story, or a Big Book with which the children are familiar. Be sure the material is large enough for all children to see.

2. Read the story, message, or name aloud to the children. Then have the children read it with you.

3. Place letter cards on the table in front of you. Have a child choose a letter from the stack.

4. Have the child identify the letter. If the letter is a *d*, for example, the child should say *d*.

5. Ask the children to locate any letter in the story that matches the letter chosen by the child. In this case, children should look for the letter *d*. Have one child at a time come up to point out examples of the letter in the story. If the story does not have that particular letter, the child should replace the letter in the stack and choose another letter.

6. Repeat until most of the letters of the alphabet have been chosen.

Ideas and Activities

1. Create an alphabet center in your classroom. Stock the center with plastic letters for word building, letters to trace, alphabet puzzles and games, alphabet books, alphabet stamps, and alphabet flash cards. Allow children time to use the materials in the center on a regular basis.

2. Place a layer of sand in a small container. Have children trace the letters of the alphabet in the sand.

3. Play Letter Bingo. Give each child a card filled with letters of the alphabet and markers to cover the letters. Call a letter and hold up a card with the letter on it. Have children find the letter on their Bingo cards. The first child to cover a row gets Bingo.

4. Create an alphabet path on the floor of your room. Write each letter of the alphabet on a large piece of construction paper. Laminate the pieces of paper, randomly arrange them around your room, and tape them to the floor. Have students walk on the alphabet path saying the letters of the alphabet as they walk.

5. Distribute alphabet cards to each child. Give each child one card. Call out a letter. Ask the child holding that letter to stand and repeat the name of the letter. Then ask children to say a word that begins with that letter.

6. Provide the children with letter snacks. As you introduce a letter, give children a snack whose name begins with that letter. For example, when you teach the letter *a*, provide each child with a piece of apple.

7. Place a handful of alphabet cereal on a napkin on each child's desk. Have students sort the cereal letters in alphabetical order. Give children plain round or square cereal to mark the place of letters that are not in the cereal pile. Tell children that if they have more than one of the same letter, they should place the duplicate letters in a row.

8. Write the name of a letter on the chalkboard with a wet sponge or paintbrush. Have children call out the name of the letter before the water evaporates and the letter disappears. Children can also practice writing particular letters with a wet sponge or paintbrush.

9. Distribute copies of newspapers or pages from magazines to each child. Identify a letter and have children circle the letter wherever they find it on a particular part of the page.

10. Give children a journal that has a letter of the alphabet on each page. After introducing a letter, have children practice writing the letter on that page. Have children frequently page through the book saying the letters of the alphabet.

11. Spell out a child's name with letter cards or plastic letters. Use all uppercase letters. Have the child use lowercase letters to match the uppercase letters. Scramble the top row and have the child unscramble the letters to form the correct spelling of the name.

12. Create letter posters by brainstorming words that start with a specific letter. After introducing a letter, have children think of words that start with that letter. If children are unable to correctly identify words beginning with that letter, provide several words for them. Write the words with different color markers or crayons. Display the posters in the classroom or bind them into a class alphabet book.

13. Place a set of five to seven pairs of alphabet cards face down on a table. You should have two cards for each letter. Have children turn over two cards at a time saying the names of the letters. If the cards match, children keep them. If the cards do not match, have children replace the cards. The object is to match pairs of alphabet cards.

Alphabet Books

Home School Connections

- Share alphabet books with your children and talk about the pictures and words. Then make an alphabet book with your child. A meaningful way to begin is with your child's name.

- Create a list of as many words as possible. Photographs and illustrations from magazines may also be used. If a complete alphabet book is made, arrange the letters in the order of the alphabet.

From Jerry L. Johns, Susan Davis Lenski, and Laurie Elish-Piper, *Teaching Beginning Readers: Linking Assessment and Instruction* (2nd ed.). Copyright © 2002 by Kendall/Hunt Publishing Company (1-800-247-3458, ext. 5). May be reproduced for noncommercial educational purposes.

Selected Resources
ALPHABET KNOWLEDGE

Alphabet Books

Agard, J. (1989). *The calypso alphabet*. New York: Henry Holt.

Aylesworth, J. (1992). *Old black fly*. New York: Henry Holt.

Azarian, M. (2000). *A gardener's alphabet*. Boston: Houghton Mifflin.

Base, G. (1986). *Animalia*. New York: Harry N. Abrams.

Calmenson, S. (1994). *It begins with an A*. New York: Hyperion.

Ehlert, L. (1989). *Eating the alphabet: Fruits and vegetables from A to Z*. San Diego: Harcourt.

Esposito, L. (2001). *My first ABC lift-the-flap board book*. New York: Dorling Kindersley.

Hague, K. (1984). *Alphabears: An ABC book*. New York: Henry Holt.

Lear, E. (1992). *A was once an apple*. Cambridge, MA: Candlewick Press.

Lester, M. (2001). *A is for salad*. New York: Putnam & Grosset.

Lobel, A. (1994). *Away from home*. New York: Greenwillow.

Murphy, C. (1997). *Alphabet magic*. New York: Simon & Schuster.

Palolotta, J. (1990). *The frog alphabet book*. Chicago: Children's Press.

Park, J. (1995). *My first alphabet*. New York: Oxford Children's Press.

Preller, J. (1997). *NBA action from A to Z*. New York: Scholastic.

Shannon, G. (1996). *Tomorrow's alphabet*. New York: Greenwillow.

Viorst, J. (1994). *The alphabet from Z to A*. New York: Atheneum.

Media and Technology

Animal Alphabet CD-ROM (cartoon animation of alphabet).
UPDATA (800-882-2844)

Curious George Learns the Alphabet CD-ROM (animated letters with Curious George).
UPDATA (800-882-2844)

Letters of the Alphabet Program (Big Books, audiotapes, alphabet strips).
Phoenix Learning Resources (800-221-1274)

The Big Bug Alphabet Book CD-ROM (children learn the ABCs at a circus).
UPDATA (800-882-2844)

Professional Resources

Cunningham, P.M., & Allington, R.L. (1999). *Classrooms that work: They all can read and write* (2nd ed.). New York: Longman.

Scholastic (2001). *AlphaTales teaching guide*. New York: Scholastic Professional Books.

Sorrow, B.H., & Lumpkin, B.S. (1996). *CD-ROMs for librarians and educators: A guide to over 800 instructional resources* (2nd ed.). Jefferson, NC: McFarland.

From Jerry L. Johns, Susan Davis Lenski, and Laurie Elish-Piper, *Teaching Beginning Readers: Linking Assessment and Instruction* (2nd ed.). Copyright © 2002 by Kendall/Hunt Publishing Company (1-800-247-3458, ext. 5). May be reproduced for noncommercial educational purposes.

3.2 Phonemic Awareness

> **Goal** To help children become aware of the sounds in spoken words.
> **Assessment Strategy 2** Rhyme Detection, page 174
> **Assessment Strategy 3** Phoneme Segmentation, page 177
> **Assessment Strategy 4** Phoneme Deletion and Substitution, page 180

BACKGROUND

Phonemic awareness is the ability to segment and manipulate sounds in words. Children who have phonemic awareness skills are able to recognize when words rhyme, can hear isolated sounds of words, can segment words into their sounds, and can blend the sounds together into words. Phonemic awareness is strongly related to success in reading and is a powerful predictor of reading achievement (Adams, 1990; National Reading Panel, 2000). In order to benefit from phonics instruction, students require a basic level of phonemic awareness. However, some children do not naturally learn how sounds form words.

Because phonemic awareness is the ability to hear the sounds in words, phonemic awareness activities generally should precede formal instruction in phonics. Children who are unable to identify words that rhyme, for example, may be hindered in learning the sound-symbol relationships that are a foundation of phonics instruction. In addition, children who do not understand that words are made up of sounds can often profit from instruction in phonemic awareness.

Researchers Schatschneider, Francis, Foorman, Fletcher, and Mehta (1999) identified a hierarchy of phonemic awareness skills. Based on this study, a review by Stahl (2001), and our work with teachers, the following list of skills is arranged in order from easy (1) to difficult (6).

1. Rhyming as a foundation for phonemic awareness tasks
2. Identifying the names of pictures beginning with the same first sound
3. Blending onset-rime units (e.g., /t/ *in*) into words (e.g., *tin*)
4. Blending sounds (phonemes) into words
5. Deleting a sound (phoneme) and saying the word that remains
6. Segmenting words into sounds (phonemes)

The activities that are necessary to teach children how to become aware of the sounds in language may not seem like real teaching. Instead, they may just seem like fun. However, these types of activities are appropriate and necessary for children to learn how to decode words and read independently. When you provide children with instruction in phonemic awareness skills, they will most likely improve their ability to hear sounds in words, which is a foundation for later reading development (Gillam & van Kleeck, 1996).

The teaching strategies, activities, and ideas that follow emphasize oral language activities that support phonemic awareness. As you teach children how to hear the sounds in our language, you should be aware of children's progress. Through informal assessment, you can judge whether children are able to hear sounds and rhymes. As you notice children's proficiency in hearing rhymes, sounds in isolation, and blended sounds, teach transition strategies that emphasize sounds but begin to introduce letters. Be sure that your phonemic awareness instruction is appropriate to children's level of literacy development. After you introduce letters with phonemic awareness activities, you can start the teaching of phonics so that children will begin to associate letters with sounds.

Teaching Strategy 1

Section 3.2

I Spy Rhymes

One of the foundational skills for establishing how language works is the ability to identify rhyming words. Being able to hear word rhymes helps children develop an understanding that word families can represent the same sound in different words. The strategy I Spy Rhymes helps children listen for and identify rhyming words.

DIRECTIONS

1. Read a book or poem aloud that contains several rhyming words. Tell children that they should be listening for words that rhyme. Remind children that rhyming words will sound alike. Say a rhyming word pair such as *bike* and *like*. Tell children that *bike* and *like* rhyme because they have the same ending sound.

2. Reread the story or poem. Draw children's attention to the words that rhyme.

3. Read a second story or poem. Tell children that when they hear a rhyming word pair, they should stand and say, "I spy _____ and _____." The children should say the rhyming word pair as in "I spy *bike* and *like*."

4. Most stories or poems that you read will have several different rhyming words. Allow children to say all of the rhymes. If they miss some, reread the story or poem emphasizing the rhymes that were not heard.

5. Repeat the activity several times each week until the children are able to identify rhyming words.

Teaching Strategy 2

Section 3.2

First Sounds

The First Sounds strategy helps children identify pictures that begin with the same sounds. It is one of the easier phoneme awareness tasks, and children find it fun. First Sounds will help children understand that words have sounds as well as meanings (National Reading Panel, 2000). Using pictures also makes the task more concrete for beginning readers.

DIRECTIONS

1. Obtain three objects. Two of the objects should begin with the same sound. For example, use a bag, a bat that is used to play ball, and a toy car. Make pictures of these objects.

2. Tell children that you want them to use their eyes and ears for this activity. Have them look at the bag and tell you what it is. Ask children to listen to the first sound in the word *bag*. Stress the beginning sound as you say *bbbag*. Be sure children understand the task. You could also have children note how they form their lips to say the word.

3. Hold up the toy car and have children name it. Then ask them to listen to the first sound as you say the word emphasizing the first sound. Repeat the instruction in step 2.

4. Hold up the two objects and have the children name each object. Then ask, "Do the words begin with the same first sound?" Say the words slowly, stressing the first sound in each word. Then say something

like, "You must have listened carefully. The two words do not begin with the same sound." If necessary, have the children note how they formed their mouths to say each word.

5. Hold up the bat and ask children to name it. Have them listen to the first sound as you slowly say *bbbat*. Then invite children to close their eyes and listen carefully as you say two words (e.g., bat and bag). Ask, "Do *bat* and *bag* begin with the same first sound? Raise your hand if they do." Reinforce correct responses and then hold up both objects, name them, and say that they begin with the same first sound.

6. Then select the toy car and ask the children to name it. Compare it to the first sound of bag and help children realize that the two words begin with different first sounds. Repeat this process with the car and the bat.

7. Place the three objects on a table along with the pictures of the objects. Relate the pictures to the objects and then use the pictures to review first sounds in the words. Have the children decide which pictures begin with the same first sound. The remaining picture (car) is "out" because it does not begin with the same first sound as the other two words.

8. Extend the lesson by using other pictures or objects in the classroom (e.g., book, desk, boy) to help solidify the concept of first sounds in words.

9. To provide additional teaching or practice opportunities, enlarge the pictures that follow. In each row of pictures, two of them begin with the same sound.

Letters and Sounds 139

140 Chapter Three

Letters and Sounds 141

Tips for English Language Learners

- When selecting pictures to use for instruction, try to find those that will be common to the experiences of English Language Learners. You could also ask the child to name the picture in his or her language and then compare it to the English word to determine if the words begin with the same first sound.

- Some English Language Learners may find it difficult to make or hear some of the sounds in English. For example, native speakers of Spanish may have problems with the sounds for *b, d, h, j, m, n, r, t, th, v, w,* and *y*. Speakers of Cantonese may have difficulty with the sounds associated with *th, s, n,* and *r* (Johns & Lenski, 2001). Be patient and supportive as children learn some of the unique sounds in English.

Teaching Strategy 3

Section 3.2

Sound Boxes

Sound Boxes help children segment the sounds in a word. Sound Boxes were originally developed by Elkonin (1973) and can be used to help young children develop phonemic awareness. When children use Sound Boxes, they learn that words are made up of phonemes, or sounds, and that most words contain more than one sound.

DIRECTIONS

1. Select words that are familiar to children. Prepare cards with simple illustrations along with a matrix that contains a box for each sound in the word. Note that the boxes represent each sound, not necessarily each letter. Secure sufficient counters (plastic chips, pennies, or beans) for each child. An example of a picture with sound boxes follows.

2. Slowly say the word represented by the picture and push the counters one sound at a time into the boxes. Model the process a second time. Invite the children to say the word as you move the counters. For example, if you are using the sound box for the word duck, say the word and then the sounds as in this example: "Duck. /d/ /u/ /k/." As you say the first sound, /d/, move a counter into the first box. Then say /u/ and move a second counter into the second box. Finally, say the sound /k/ and move the counter into the third box. Remember to say the sounds, not the letters, of the word.

3. Provide another example and begin to transfer the responsibility of identifying the sounds to the children. Encourage children to identify the picture and to pronounce the word carefully and deliberately. The goal is to emphasize each sound without distorting the word and to put a counter in each box while saying each sound.

4. After children have learned how to use sound boxes, eliminate the boxes below the pictures and have children move the sound counters to the bottom of the picture.

5. Pictures with sound boxes are provided on pages 144–145 for additional teaching examples or practice activities.

Teaching Strategy 4

Section 3.2

Put It Together

Children who are able to sound out words successfully are usually able to blend the sounds associated with the letters into a word. Blending sounds is one of the components of phonemic awareness and is an important skill for beginning readers (Ericson & Juliebo, 1998). The strategy Put It Together helps children learn how to blend sounds into words.

DIRECTIONS

1. Explain that you will be saying a word by its sounds. If you have a puppet available, say that the puppet only likes to say whole words. Tell children that you will be saying the sounds of the word and that the puppet will say the whole word.

2. Tell children to listen carefully as you say the sounds of the word. Then say the sounds of a word such as /l/ /u/ /n/ /ch/ for the word *lunch*. Have the children put the word together by blending the sounds into a whole word. If the children say the word correctly, have the puppet repeat the word.

3. After children are able to blend sounds, try the strategy with other words.

144   Chapter Three

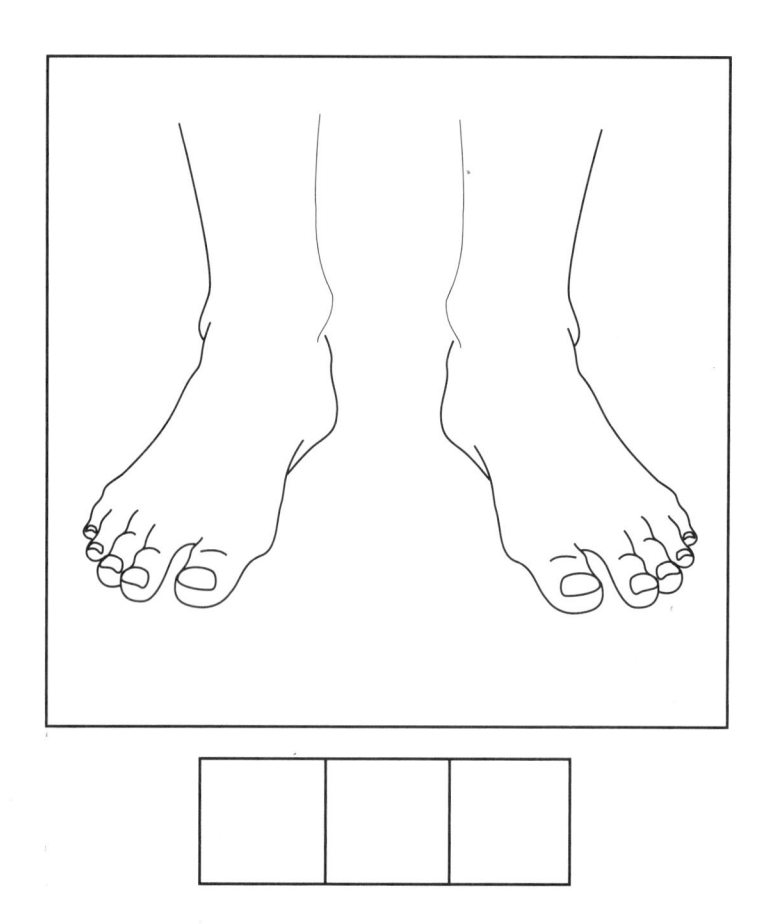

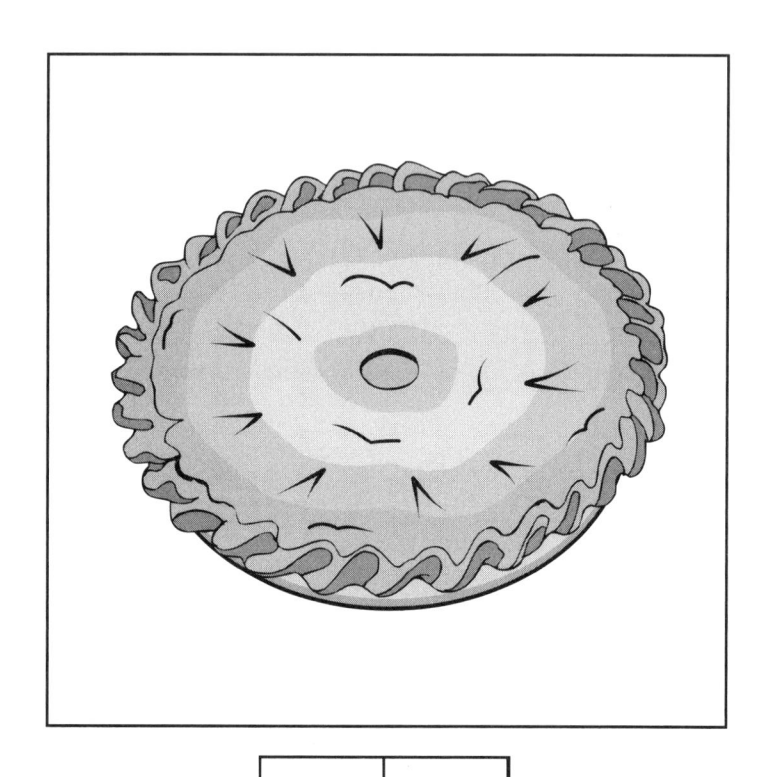

Letters and Sounds 145

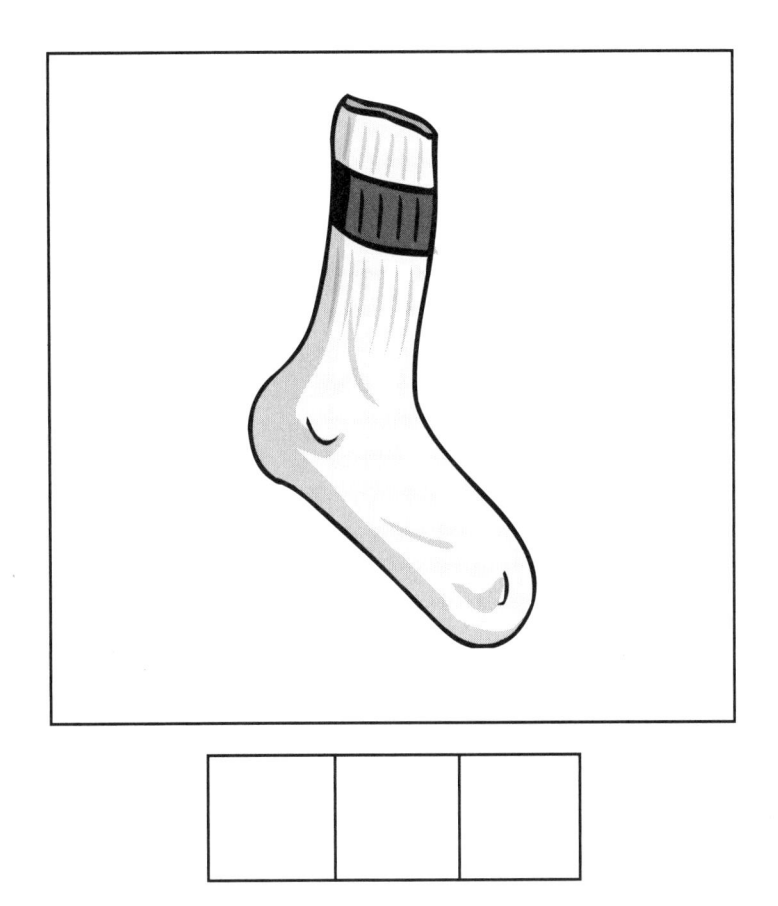

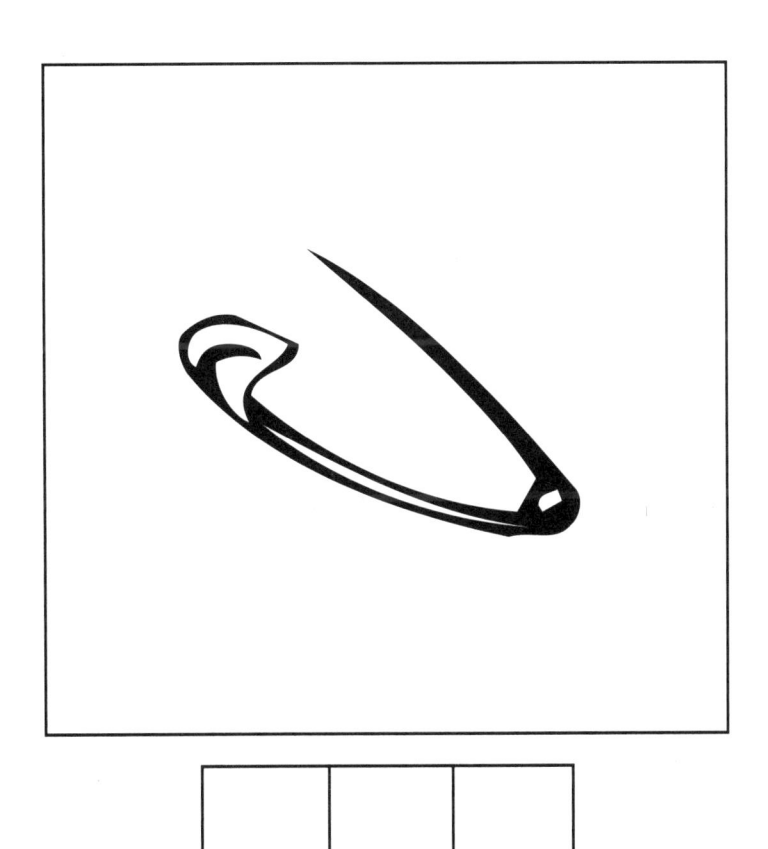

> **Teaching Strategy 5**

Section 3.2

Break and Make

Another phonemic awareness component is the ability to manipulate sounds by substituting one sound for another in a word. The strategy Break and Make gives children practice making new words from an initial word and hearing the difference between the words. Children are asked to break up a word and make a new word. As children break and make words, they hear the sounds in word families. You can use letter tiles with the Break and Make strategy if the children are ready to begin the transition from hearing sounds in words to understanding that the sounds they hear are associated with letters. In this activity, however, emphasize sound substitution, not the letter-sound correspondence.

DIRECTIONS

1. Identify a word from a word family that has easily identifiable sounds. (You can find word families in Appendix B.) Write the word on the chalkboard, a piece of chart paper, or an overhead transparency. Then form the word with manipulatives such as letter cards or tiles. Display the word for the children.

2. Read the word aloud. Say the word slowly and deliberately. Then have the children say the word with you. Repeat the word several times.

3. Tell children that you will make a new word from the first word by changing one letter. Break the word apart by moving the letter cards or tiles. Replace a letter from the word. For example, if your first word was *book* and you changed the first letter to *l*, you would have the word *look*. If the first word was *can* and you changed the last letter to *t*, the new word would be *cat*. Say the words as you change them. Have the children say the new words with you. Explain that some words are different only in one sound and that children need to listen to words carefully to distinguish between the sounds in words.

4. Invite children to participate in the Break and Make strategy using various word families.

Ideas and Activities to Develop Rhyme

1. Read rhyming books or nursery rhymes to children every day. Reread many of the children's favorites several times. As children become familiar with specific rhymes, have them say the rhymes along with you as you read. From time to time, stop reading before the last word in a rhyming line and have children supply the rhyming word.

2. Call on children whose names have many rhyming words such as *Mike* and *Pam*. Say a word that rhymes with one of the names. Have children repeat the word along with the name that rhymes with it as in *Mike* and *spike*.

3. Tell children that you are going to say three rhyming words. Say three words that rhyme such as *run, fun,* and *bun*. Tell children that you want them to listen carefully to the words and then think of more words that rhyme with the words that you said. For example, children could say the words *sun* and *spun*. If children make up a word, tell them that they need to think of words that everyone knows. Repeat this activity several times each week with different rhyming words.

4. Help children hear the difference between words that rhyme and words that do not rhyme. Say three words, two of which rhyme. For example, say *sail, mail,* and *made*. Have children say the three words with you. Then ask children which two words rhyme.

5. Sing or chant songs that contain rhyming words. Some songs that work well are *Five Little Monkeys, The Wheels on the Bus, The Name Game, A Hunting We Will Go, This Old Man,* and *The Ants Go Marching*. Sing or chant songs several times a day. After singing, point out some of the rhyming words.

6. Have a group of children act out their favorite nursery rhyme. Have the other children guess the name of the rhyme. Then have all of the children say the rhyme aloud.

7. Say a word that has many rhyming words such as *day*. Have children brainstorm words that rhyme with the original word such as *may, say, ray,* and *pay*. When possible, have children draw pictures of several of the words that rhyme with the original word.

8. Have children create silly rhyming names for characters in their favorite books or for their pets. For example, Clifford the Big Red Dog could be named Bifford. Encourage children to have fun with rhymes.

9. Have children sit in a circle. Say a rhyming word such as *spin*. Throw a soft ball to one of the children. The child who catches the ball should say a word that rhymes with *spin* such as *win*. That child should toss the ball to another child or back to you. The person who has the ball should think of another rhyme. Continue until no one can think of additional words that rhyme with the original word. Then begin with a new word.

10. Gather various objects whose names rhyme. Place the objects in a bag and have a child pick an object without looking. A second child also picks an object and decides if the names of the objects rhyme. If they rhyme, two new children are chosen. If the words do not rhyme, another child picks an object and decides if it rhymes with either of the words. Continue the process until all objects have been paired correctly.

11. Provide pictures and/or objects that rhyme and have children sort them into groups that rhyme. Begin, if possible, with actual objects.

12. Read a rhyming couplet and have children supply the missing word.

    If you are *bad*, mom will be _____ .

    If you see a *bee*, get me a cup of _____ .

    I saw a *rat;* you saw a _____ .

Letters and Sounds

Ideas and Activities for Sound Blending

1. Tell the children that you are thinking of an animal. Give them a sound clue, segmenting each of the sounds of the word and saying the sounds slowly and deliberately. If the animal is a wolf, for example, say the sounds /w/ /o/ /l/ /f/. Ask children to blend the sounds together to tell you the name of the animal. Then repeat the process with the name of another animal.

2. Read a rhyming book to the children. Choose a pair of rhyming words, segment the words between the onset and rime, and have the children blend the words together.

3. Collect pictures from magazines that have a subject that is identifiable to children. For example, a picture of a dog would be one that children could identify. Cut the picture into the number of sounds in the word. For example, cut the picture of the dog into three pieces. Have children put the picture puzzle together saying the sounds of the subject of the picture.

4. Tell children that you will be saying the sounds of a word and they will need to guess the word and draw a picture of it. Give children paper and crayons. Then say a word that can easily be drawn such as *bat*. Say the sounds in the word *bat*, /b/ /a/ /t/. Have children draw a bat. Repeat this activity with other words.

5. When you have an extra minute between activities or when your class is lining up to leave the room, say the sounds of a word that you have used during class. If you have been discussing wind in a lesson on the weather, for example, say the sounds /w/ /i/ /n/ /d/. Have the children blend the sounds to form the word *wind*.

6. Sing or chant songs that could be adapted as a blending activity. For example, adapt the song *Bingo* (Ericson & Juliebo, 1998). Sing or chant the song using the sounds of the child's name. Then repeat the name you used in the song. Tell children that the sounds can be put together to make a name. Repeat with another child's name. An example of the song follows.

    There was a teacher

    who had a student

    And Maria was her name

    /M/ /ar/ /i/ /a/, /M/ /ar/ /i/ /a/, /M/ /ar/ /i/ /a/

    And Maria was her name.

7. Say word parts of compound words such as *base* and *ball* for *baseball*. Have two children stand in front of the room. Tell the children that baseball has two word parts. Have the first child say the first word, *base*, and the second child say the second word, *ball*. Tell children that some words have two words in them and that they should listen for words within other words.

8. Place several objects in a bag or a box. Select one object. Say the name of the object and say, "I see a carrot." Say the word in its syllables or individual sounds. Have the children blend the sounds of the word together and say the word.

9. Take a large rubber band and stretch it. Tell children that you want them to stretch a word. Say a word slowly as you stretch the rubber band. Then have children pretend to stretch a rubber band as they stretch words with you.

Ideas and Activities for Sound Isolation

1. Say a child's name. Have the children repeat the name with you clapping the number of syllables. For example, say the name *Kristen*. Clap two times, one for each syllable. Say the names of other children who have two-syllable names. Have children clap with you as you say the names. Repeat with names of one syllable, three syllables, and so on.

2. Ask children to listen to you saying three words: *kite, kitten,* and *Ken.* Tell children that these words begin with the same sound, the sound /k/. Tell children that you will be saying three more words and that they should listen for the beginning sound. Say three more words and have children tell you the sound that they hear. As children become proficient at hearing beginning sounds, repeat the activity using ending sounds.

3. Tell children that you will be saying a sound and that they should think of as many words that begin (or end) with that sound as they can. Say a sound (not a letter) such as /s/ for the letter *s*. Have children think of words that begin with that sound.

4. Say words that have parts that are the same or different such as the words *ball* and *tall*. Have children say the words with you. Ask children which parts of the words are the same and which parts are different. Guide children to understand that the sounds /b/ and /t/ are different but the sound /all/ is the same in both words. Repeat using other pairs of words.

5. Read books of rhymes to children. After reading, say two of the rhyming words. Have children say the rhyming words with you several times. After children have said the rhymes, ask them which of the sounds are alike in the rhymes and which are different.

6. Sing the song "What's the Sound?" to the tune of "Old MacDonald Had a Farm" (Yopp, 1992). Use different sounds each time you sing the song. An example of a verse follows.

    What's the sound that starts these words:

    baby, ball, and bed?

    /b/ is the sound that starts these words:

    baby, ball, and bed.

    With a /b/ /b/ here, and a /b/ /b/ there,

    here a /b/, there a /b/, everywhere a /b/ /b/.

    /b/ is the sound that starts these words:

    baby, ball, and bed.

Ideas and Activities for Sound Substitution

1. Have children select a sound of the day, such as the sound /m/, and then say each of their names with that sound in place of the first sound (Yopp, 1992). Children should say Mina for Gina, Merry for Jerry, and so on.

2. Write the letters of the alphabet on large index cards and place them on a table. Say a word such as *turtle*. Have a child choose a letter from the stack on the table. Say the word *turtle*, beginning with the letter sound the child has chosen. Enjoy the fun of creating nonsense words. Repeat the activity with a new letter sound.

3. Have children create a page for a picture book with words that rhyme. For example, say the word *clown* and have children draw a picture of a *clown*. Then say the word *town* and have children draw a picture of a *town*. Repeat with other rhyming words as in *down* and *frown*. Have children read their books of rhyming words. Point out that the rhyming words have different beginning sounds but the same ending sounds. Create other pages with different rhyming words.

4. Play a consonant riddle game. Say a word such as bunny. Then present the riddle by saying, "What rhymes with bunny but starts with an /f/?" Have children guess what the word is. Other words to use are hat-cat, sun-fun, dish-fish, moo-zoo, fat-hat, meet-feet, and wish-dish.

5. Tell children that you want them to listen to the sounds in the words that you say. Tell them that you'll be switching one of the sounds. Say a pair of words with one sound switched. You might switch the beginning consonants as in *hill* and *Bill*, you might switch the vowels such as *ball* and *bell*, or you might switch the ending sounds as in *game* and *gate*. After saying the new words, have the children say them with you. Continue with several pairs of words.

6. Tell children that you will be singing a song that they know but that you will be changing some of the words (Yopp, 1992). Write a section of a song on the chalkboard or an overhead transparency. Sing or chant the song as it was written. Then suggest a new sound to use to sing the song. Sing the song with the new sound. Repeat with additional verses. The following song is sung to the tune of *Someone's in the Kitchen with Dinah*.

   I have a song that we can sing
   I have a song I know.
   I have a song that we can sing
   Strumming on the old banjo.

   Fe-Fi-Fiddly-i-o
   Fe-Fi-Fiddly-i-o
   Fe-Fi-Fiddly-i-o
   Strumming on the old banjo.

   Ke-Ki-Kiddly-i-o
   Ke-Ki-Kiddly-i-o
   Ke-Ki-Kiddly-i-o
   Strumming on the old banjo.

Home School Connections

Rhymes

📖 Help your child enjoy and play with language. Share nursery rhymes and poetry. There are many books that contain common rhymes that can be purchased or checked out from a public library. Share the poems and rhymes with your child and encourage him or her to supply a word that rhymes.

📖 As children become interested in words, they sometimes begin to rhyme and even create nonsense words. Encourage this type of word play. Some of the Dr. Seuss books help foster language play and the manipulation of sounds in words.

📖 Look through picture books with your child. As you talk about a picture, ask questions that help promote greater awareness of language. For example, "Do tree and bee rhyme? Do tree and bee begin with the same first sound? What word would we have if I take the first sound off bee and add the sound 'sss'?" Use these types of questions when they fit the book. Don't overdo the questioning. You want your child to have an enjoyable experience with the book.

From Jerry L. Johns, Susan Davis Lenski, and Laurie Elish-Piper, *Teaching Beginning Readers: Linking Assessment and Instruction* (2nd ed.). Copyright © 2002 by Kendall/Hunt Publishing Company (1-800-247-3458, ext. 5). May be reproduced for noncommercial educational purposes.

Letters and Sounds   151

Selected Resources
PHONEMIC AWARENESS

Books of Nursery Rhymes

dePaola, T. (1985). *Tomie dePaola's Mother Goose.* New York: Putnam.

Lansky, B. (1993). *The new adventures of Mother Goose: Gentle rhymes for happy times.* Deerhaven, MN: Meadowbrook.

Lobel, A. (1986). *The Random House book of Mother Goose.* New York: Random House.

Prelutsky, J. (1986). *Read-aloud rhymes for the very young.* New York: Alfred A. Knopf.

Simon, C. (1999). *Mother Goose's basket full of rhymes.* New York: Little Simon.

Watson, C. (1971). *Father Fox's penny rhymes.* New York: Thomas Y. Crowell.

Media and Technology

A Silly, Noisy House CD-ROM (animated toy box with sound effects, songs, and rhymes).
UPDATA (800-882-2844)

Allie's Playhouse CD-ROM (learning activities including 16 sing-along nursery rhymes).
UPDATA (800-882-2844)

Children's Treasury of Stories, Nursery Rhymes, and Songs CD-ROM (interactive multimedia collection of stories, nursery rhymes, and songs).
UPDATA (800-882-2844)

Phonemic Awareness Activities for 6- & 7-Year Olds (Simple activities parents or teachers can do to help children develop skills related to rhyming, blending, and segmenting words).
http://www.iusd.k12.ca.us/parent resources/phonemicawareness67.htm

Professional Resources

Adams, M.J., Foorman, B.R., Lundberg, I., & Beeler, T. (1998). *Phonemic awareness in young children: A classroom curriculum.* Baltimore, MD: Paul H. Brookes.

Dowell, R.I. (1992). *Let's talk: Performance rhymes.* Terre Haute, IN: Pollyanna Productions.

Ericson, L., & Juliebo, M.F. (1998). *The phonological awareness handbook for kindergarten and primary teachers.* Newark, DE: International Reading Association.

Gunning, T.G. (2000). *Phonological awareness and primary phonics.* Boston: Allyn and Bacon.

Fitzpatrick, J. (1997). *Phonemic awareness: Playing with sounds to strengthen beginning reading skills.* Cypress, CA: Creative Teaching Press.

Lynch, J. (1998). *Easy lessons for teaching word families.* New York: Scholastic.

Yopp, H.R. (1995). Read-aloud books for developing phonemic awareness: An annotated bibliography. *The Reading Teacher, 48,* 538–542.

Yopp, H.K., & Yopp, R.H. (1997). *Oo-pples and Boo-noo-noos: Songs and activities for phonemic awareness.* Orlando, FL: Harcourt Brace.

From Jerry L. Johns, Susan Davis Lenski, and Laurie Elish-Piper, *Teaching Beginning Readers: Linking Assessment and Instruction* (2nd ed.). Copyright © 2002 by Kendall/Hunt Publishing Company (1-800-247-3458, ext. 5). May be reproduced for noncommercial educational purposes.

3.3 Phonics

> **Goal** To help children develop phonics skills.
> **Assessment Strategy 5** Auditory Discrimination, page 184
> **Assessment Strategy 6** Phonics: Consonants, page 187
> **Assessment Strategy 7** Decoding, page 199

BACKGROUND

Reading is a complex process, and children use many tools and techniques to construct meaning. Phonics is one of the cueing systems that children use when they encounter unknown words. The other cueing systems focus on semantics (meaning) and syntax (structure of language). Effective readers use these cueing systems flexibly and in combination as they attempt to construct meaning from printed materials. While phonics is an important part of beginning reading instruction, it is not the only component (Cunningham, 2000). Within a sound reading program, teachers provide instruction in each of the various components of word identification: structural analysis, use of context, sight vocabulary, and phonics.

Phonics is not a method of teaching reading (Heilman, 1998); rather, it is an important tool for decoding unfamiliar words and making sense of what is read. Many different teaching methods and approaches include instruction on phonics. What these methods and approaches have in common is their focus on teaching children the letter-sound associations in our language (Strickland, 1998). Because approximately 84% of the words in the English language are phonetically regular, instruction in phonics is essential in helping beginning readers break the code and make sense of reading (Anderson, Hiebert, Scott, & Wilkinson, 1985).

Adams (2001, pp. 67–68) also notes that "a serious goal of any responsible program of beginning reading instruction" is to ensure children's grasp of the basics of phonics. According to the National Reading Panel (2000), those basics involve the systematic teaching of a prespecified set of letter-sound relationships. What seems to be important is the teaching of phonics in an intentional and systematic manner in kindergarten and first grade.

The following teaching strategies and activities offer a wide variety of suggestions for helping beginning readers develop phonics skills. Some of the strategies and activities provide explicit instruction of phonics, and other ideas focus on more contextualized approaches to phonics instruction. By using a variety of systematic approaches and strategies, you will be able to help children develop the phonics skills necessary to progress in reading.

Teaching Strategy 1

Section 3.3

Explicit Phonics

Explicit Phonics focuses on teaching phonics one element at a time, building systematically from individual elements to larger pieces of text. Children first learn letters and sounds, then blend words, and then read these components in connected text. Some children who have difficulty learning from more indirect methods benefit from the explicit nature of this type of phonics instruction (Adams, 1990).

DIRECTIONS

1. Select a letter, digraph, or other phonic element to be taught.
2. Present the phonic element by writing the letters that represent it on the chalkboard (e.g., sh).
3. Tell the children, "The letters *sh* stand for the /sh/ sound."
4. Ask the children to make the /sh/ sound as you point to the letters.
5. Have the children write the letters *sh* on their papers. Ask them to say the sound as they point to the letters.
6. Present the children with several words that contain the target phonic element. Have the children sound out the words and say them together. Emphasize the target phonic element. For example, you might use the following words for the /sh/ sound.

    shoe
    sheep
    she

7. This type of lesson can be extended to include writing sentences for the words, reading the words in other materials, or playing a word game.
8. Guidelines for teaching phonics appear on the following page.

Guidelines for TEACHING PHONICS

General Guidelines

- Teach common consonant sounds first.
- Teach short vowel sounds before long vowel sounds.
- Teach consonants and short vowels in combination so words can be made as soon as possible.
- Use a sequence in which the most words can be generated. Teach higher-frequency, sound-spelling relationships before less-frequent ones.
- Progress from simple to more complex sound-spellings.
- Time spent on phonics instruction should be 10 to 15 minutes daily (Gunning, 2000).

Recommended Phonic Skills for Grades K-2

Kindergarten
phonemic awareness
alphabet recognition
consonants

Grade 1
phonemic awareness
blending and word building
short vowels (CVC pattern)
consonants
final e (CVCe pattern)
long vowel digraphs (ai, ay, ae, ee, oa, ow, etc.)
consonant clusters (br, cl, st, etc.)
other vowels such as oo, ou, ow, oi, oy

Grade 2
grade 1 skills review
more complex vowel spellings (ough)
structural analysis (compound words, common prefixes, common suffixes)
multisyllable words

From Jerry L. Johns, Susan Davis Lenski, and Laurie Elish-Piper, *Teaching Beginning Readers: Linking Assessment and Instruction* (2nd ed.). Copyright © 2002 by Kendall/Hunt Publishing Company (1-800-247-3458, ext. 5). May be reproduced for noncommercial educational purposes.

> **Teaching Strategy 2**

Section 3.3

Making Words

Making Words is a hands-on phonics strategy that helps children see patterns in words as they manipulate letter cards or tiles (Cunningham & Hall, 1998). This strategy helps children understand letter and sound associations as they work with word families or onsets and rimes. An onset is the beginning part of a word that comes before the vowel. For example, in the word *cat*, the onset is *c*. A rime is the part of the word from the vowel to the end. For example, in the word *cat*, the rime is *at*. Rimes are sometimes referred to as phonograms, spelling patterns, or word families. In the Making Words strategy, children manipulate letter cards or tiles to build words that start out small and get longer as the lesson progresses. Typically, a Making Words lesson focuses on one or more rimes or spelling patterns that the children are learning. Refer to Appendix B for a list of rimes or word families. For lists of words and sample lessons for the Making Words strategy, consult Cunningham and Hall (1998).

DIRECTIONS

1. Choose the word that will be the longest word made in the lesson (e.g., splash).
2. Make a list of other words that can be made using the letters in the word *splash*. Arrange these words to show how changing letter order or adding a new letter can form a new word. An example follows.

    a
    Al
    as
    has
    ash
    lash
    splash

3. Select the words you will include in your lesson. Consider the patterns and words that can be made by rearranging letters in a previous word. Proper nouns can be included to help children learn about using capital letters correctly.
4. Make letter cards on large index cards for each letter needed for the lesson. Write each word for the lesson on a small index card. Place the large letter cards in a pocket chart.
5. Make individual letter cards for each child. This can be done by writing letters on index cards or small squares of paper. Letter tiles can also be used.
6. Distribute a set of letters to each child. Provide a few minutes for the children to explore the letters and words they can make with their letter cards.
7. Say, "Use two letters to make the word *as*. I am *as* tall *as* Bill."
8. Pause for a moment while the children make the word with their letter cards. Ask for a volunteer to come to the front of the class and make the word using the large letter cards in the pocket chart. Provide time for the children to self-check the words they made.
9. Say, "Add one letter and make the word *has*. He *has* a pet dog."
10. Ask for a volunteer to make the word in the pocket chart. Have children self-check their own words.
11. Continue the lesson using the same steps with the other words.
12. When you have used all of the words on your list except the last word (splash), challenge the children by saying, "See what word you can make using all of your letters."

Letters and Sounds

Teaching Strategy 3

Section 3.3

Whole~Part~Whole Phonics

Whole-Part-Whole Phonics focuses on teaching phonics within the context of meaningful text. This approach allows children to see the use of phonics skills in real reading situations. Typically, a Big Book is used as the focus of this strategy.

DIRECTIONS

1. Select a story or Big Book that contains a phonic element you want to emphasize. For example, you might use the Big Book *I Went Walking* (Williams, 1989) to teach the initial /w/ sound.
2. Read the story aloud to the children. Discuss the story.
3. Write several sentences from the story or Big Book that contain words with the target phonic element. For example, you might show the children the following sentence and question.

   I went walking.
   What did you see?

4. Read the sentences to the children. Invite the children to reread the sentences with you.
5. Point out the words with the target phonic element. Ask the children to read these words with you. For example, you might draw the children's attention to the following words.

   went
   walking

6. Ask the children to figure out what these words have in common. Lead the children to discover that the words contain the same beginning letter and sound.
7. Ask the children to brainstorm other words that have the target letter and sound.
8. Reread the sentences containing the target words.
9. Return to the story or Big Book and ask the children to read along with you as you reread the story.

Tips for English Language Learners

Peregoy and Boyle (2001) note that although there is little research on phonics instruction for English Language Learners, several principles developed for native English speakers should apply to teaching phonics to English Language Learners. Those principles follow.

1. Teach spelling patterns rather than rules. Word families (see Appendix B) should be helpful for such teaching.
2. Teach phonics within a meaningful context. Teaching Strategies 3 and 4 in this section may be especially relevant.
3. Provide sufficient time for children to read and write to enhance the development of phonics skills taught.
4. Use informal assessments to help determine needed areas for instruction. Then provide responsive instruction that will lead to greater independence.

Teaching Strategy 4

Section 3.3

Phonics in Context

Phonics in Context stresses teaching target words in the context of sentences and passages. In this approach, consonants are generally not isolated but taught within the context of whole words. This approach is very common in many basal anthology programs (Gunning, 1992).

DIRECTIONS

1. Make a list of words that contain the target phonic element. Limit your list to four or five words. For example, you might teach the initial /d/ sound using the following words.

    dad
    door
    dog
    do

2. Write one sentence for each word on the chalkboard. Try to make the sentences link together to form a short story or passage. For the target words listed above, you might use the following sentences.

    My dad came home from work.
    We ran to the door.
    He had a big dog with him.
    "Do we get to keep him?" we asked.

3. Underline the target words.
4. Read the sentences aloud to the children.
5. Have the children echo read the sentences with you. To do this, you read the sentence first, and the children read the sentence immediately after you.
6. Have the children read each target word after you read it aloud.
7. Ask the children what letter or letters all of the target words have in common. Discuss their responses.
8. Say the target words again and ask the children to listen carefully to determine what sound or sounds the words have in common. Discuss their responses.
9. Ask the children to brainstorm other words that have the same sound or sounds in them. Write these words on the chalkboard.
10. Ask the children to make the sound that all of the target words contain. Then ask them what letter or letters make that sound. Invite the children to state the generalization they learned (e.g., the letter *d* makes the /d/ sound).
11. Return to the sentences and ask the children to read them chorally.

Letters and Sounds

Ideas and Activities

1. Teach common spelling patterns or rimes to the children. Use the list of rimes in the box below for this activity. Present a rime to the children and then have them list other words that use the same rime. For example, for the rime *an*, the children might list *ban, can, fan, man, pan,* and so on. Underline the rime in each word. Guide the children to notice that the words all have the same rime or spelling pattern. Post the lists in the classroom. Add new words to the lists as children discover them in their reading and writing.

   Common Rimes

ack	ain	ake	ale	all	ame	an	ank	ap	ash
at	ate	aw	ay	eat	ell	est	ice	ick	ide
ight	ill	in	ine	ing	ink	ip	ir	ock	oke
op	or	ore	uck	ug	ump	unk			

   Wylie and Durrell (1970) identified this list of 37 rimes that can be used to form over 500 primary-level words.

2. Use word sorts to guide children to sort words according to phonic elements. Write words on index cards and ask children to sort the words according to a specific phonic element such as short *a* words and long *a* words.

3. Use poetry to teach common rimes and other target phonic elements. Read the poem first for enjoyment. Then direct the children's attention to the rime or phonic element you want to teach. Ask the children to say the sound with you. Invite the children to identify words in the poem that contain the rime or sound. Make a list of the words and underline the rime or target phonic element. Brainstorm other words that also contain the rime or sound.

4. Engage the children in shared reading of Big Books or other enlarged texts such as chart stories. After reading the texts for enjoyment and meaning, direct the children's attention to specific phonic elements. Ask the children to identify words from the text that contain that element.

5. Use shared writing to model phonics strategies for children. For example, as you are writing a list in front of the class, think aloud as you use phonics strategies to spell a word. You might say, "I need to make a list of things to buy at the store. First I need to get milk. How does *milk* begin? It sounds like the beginning of *money* and *Mark*. That means I need to use the letter *m*." Continue with this pattern for the remainder of the word. Model this type of sounding out strategy frequently for children through shared writing.

6. Write letters or spelling patterns you want to review on large note cards or pieces of tagboard. Give one card to each child. Have several children stand in front of the class and ask them to sequence themselves in an order that spells a word. For example, if you gave the children *c, a,* and *t* cards, they could spell the word *cat*. Ask the children how they can change one letter and make a new word. For example, the *c* can be changed to an *h* to form *hat*, a *b* to form *bat*, and an *r* to form *rat*. Continue forming new words until you have run out of words. Then introduce a new spelling pattern or rime.

7. Write an incomplete sentence on the chalkboard, a sheet of chart paper, or an overhead transparency. For example, you might write, "I like to play _____." Then write a word that is one letter away from being correct. For example, you might write *hall*. Ask the children to change a letter to form a word that makes sense in the sentence. Have a child write the correct word *ball* in the blank. Continue this pattern with additional sentences.

8. Have children play sound bingo to practice their phonics skills. Using pieces of tagboard or large index cards as the bingo game board, divide the board into five rows and five columns. Write one letter in each box. Put the letters in different order on each card. Distribute cards and markers to each child. Use picture cards or a word list to call out words. Ask the children to listen for the beginning sound of the word. If the children's game board contains the beginning letter of the word, they should cover the letter on the game board. When a child has a vertical, horizontal, or diagonal row covered, the child must read the covered letters and their sounds to verify that he or she has bingo. Variations of this game can focus on ending sounds, vowel sounds, or blends.

9. Play sound hunt with the children. Divide the class into small groups and assign each group a letter or spelling pattern that you want to review. Then ask the children to search for objects in the classroom that contain the sound represented by the letter or spelling pattern. Have children make lists of the objects they find. Provide time for groups to share their findings.

10. Use word ladders (Blevins, 1998) to help children see how changing one letter can change a word. Draw a word ladder on the chalkboard, a piece of chart paper, or an overhead transparency. Write a word on the bottom rung of the word ladder. Say the word with the children. Ask if the children can change one letter to form a new word. Write the new word on the second rung. Continue until the ladder is full. A sample word ladder is shown below.

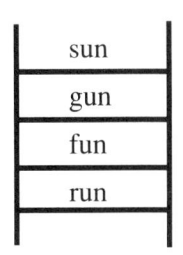

| sun |
| gun |
| fun |
| run |

11. Display a picture of an animal or object. Write its name on the chalkboard, leaving out one letter. For example, show a picture of a cat and write c __ t on the chalkboard. Ask the children what is missing. Write the missing letter in the space. Continue with other picture and word combinations. You can use this activity to focus on beginning, ending, or vowel sounds.

12. Teach children to play sound checkers to reinforce specific phonic elements. Write a word on each square of an old checkerboard. The game is played like checkers, but the children must read the words on each space they land on. If they cannot read the words correctly, they must return to their original space.

13. Use the children's names to point out similarities and differences in the way the names look and sound. Invite children to notice the sounds with which their names begin and end. For example, you might say, "Natalie's name begins with the /n/ sound. It is written with the letter *n*. Who else has a name that begins with the /n/ sound?"

14. Use children's books to teach vowel sounds. Share the book, discuss the vowel sound, and ask children to identify examples of the vowel sound. See pages 162–163 for recommended children's books for teaching short and long vowel sounds.

Children's Books with SPECIFIC SHORT VOWEL SOUNDS

Short a

Baker, K. (1999). *Sometimes*. New York: Harcourt Brace.

Cameron, A. (1994). *The cat sat on a mat*. Boston: Houghton Mifflin.

Griffith, H. (1982). *Alex and the cat*. New York: Greenwillow.

Kent, J. (1970). *The fat cat*. New York: Scholastic.

Most, B. (1980). *There's an ant in Anthony*. New York: Morrow.

Short e

Ets, M.H. (1972). *Elephant in a well*. Bergenfield, NJ: Viking.

Galdone, P. (1973). *The little red hen*. New York: Scholastic.

Lionni, L. (1994). *An extraordinary egg*. New York: Knopf.

Short i

Lankford, M.D. (1991). *Is it dark? Is it light?* New York: Knopf.

Leonard, M. (1998). *Get the ball, Slim*. Brookfield, CT: Millbrook.

McPhair, D. (1984). *Fix-it*. Bergenfield, NJ: Viking.

Sanfield, S. (1995). *Bit by bit*. East Rutherford, NJ: Viking.

Short o

Anholt, C., & Anholt, L. (1992). *All about you*. Bergenfield, NJ: Viking.

Freeman, D. (1955). *Mop top*. Bergenfield, NJ: Viking.

Hutchins, P. (1968). *Rosie's Walk*. New York: Simon & Shuster.

Seuss, Dr. (1965). *Fox in socks*. New York: Random House.

Short u

Marshall, J. (1984). *The cut-ups*. Bergenfield, NJ: Viking.

Seuss, Dr. (1982). *Hunches and bunches*. New York: Random House.

Udry, J.M. (1981). *Thump and plunk*. New York: Harper & Row.

From Jerry L. Johns, Susan Davis Lenski, and Laurie Elish-Piper, *Teaching Beginning Readers: Linking Assessment and Instruction* (2nd ed.). Copyright © 2002 by Kendall/Hunt Publishing Company (1-800-247-3458, ext. 5). May be reproduced for noncommercial educational purposes.

Children's Books with SPECIFIC LONG VOWEL SOUNDS

Long a

Aardema, V. (1981). *Bringing the rain to Kapiti Plain.* New York: Dial.

Henkes, K. (1987). *Sheila Rae, the brave.* New York: Greenwillow.

Munsch, R. (1987). *Moira's birthday.* Buffalo, NY: Firefly.

Long e

Chardiet, B., & Maccarone, G. (1992). *We scream for ice-cream.* New York: Scholastic.

Cowley, J. (1994). *The screaming mean machine.* New York: Scholastic.

Keller, H. (1983). *Ten sleepy sheep.* New York: Greenwillow.

Long i

Cameron, J. (1979). *If mice could fly.* Riverside, NJ: Atheneum.

Gelman, R. (1979). *Why can't I fly?* New York: Scholastic.

Minarik, E.E. (1978). *No fighting! No biting.* New York: Harper Collins.

Long o

Buller, J., & Schade. S. (1992). *Toad on the road.* New York: Random House.

Johnston, T. (1972). *The adventures of Mole and Troll.* East Rutherford, NJ: Viking.

Wild, M. (1994). *Going home.* New York: Scholastic.

Long u

Lobel, A. (1966). *The troll music.* New York: Harper & Row.

Segal, L. (1977). *Tell me a Trudy.* New York: Farrar, Straus & Giroux.

Slobodkin, L. (1959). *Excuse me—certainly!* New York: Vanguard Press.

From Jerry L. Johns, Susan Davis Lenski, and Laurie Elish-Piper, *Teaching Beginning Readers: Linking Assessment and Instruction* (2nd ed.). Copyright © 2002 by Kendall/Hunt Publishing Company (1-800-247-3458, ext. 5). May be reproduced for noncommercial educational purposes.

Letter Sounds

📖 Look for natural opportunities to connect sounds with letters. For example, "Who in our family has a name that begins like yours? Yes, your name (David) and dad both begin with the same sound. What other words do you know that begin like dad and David (dog, duck, door)?" Use similar activities for ending sounds.

📖 Use alphabet books to help your child associate letters with sounds. As you say a letter, invite your child to name the pictures on that page. Help your child understand that all the pictures begin with the same sound.

📖 Help your child make words with letter tiles or alphabet blocks. Use the end of a word and then place different consonant blocks at the beginning of the word to see if your child can make new words. Below are some common word endings that you can use along with consonants to make many words. Take time to help your child understand the meanings for any unknown words.

~at	~ack	~ip	~ug
bat	back	dip	bug
cat	jack	hip	dug
fat	pack	lip	hug
hat	rack	rip	jug
mat	sack	sip	mug
pat	tack	tip	plug
sat	black	zip	rug
brat	crack	chip	slug
chat	snack	flip	smug
flat	stack	grip	
that	track	ship	
	whack	skip	
		slip	
		trip	
		whip	

From Jerry L. Johns, Susan Davis Lenski, and Laurie Elish-Piper, *Teaching Beginning Readers: Linking Assessment and Instruction* (2nd ed.). Copyright © 2002 by Kendall/Hunt Publishing Company (1-800-247-3458, ext. 5). May be reproduced for noncommercial educational purposes.

Selected Resources
PHONICS

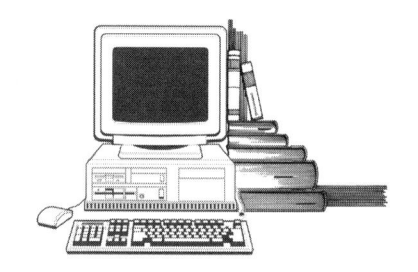

Media and Technology

Amusement Park Phonics and Reading (amusement park rides for practicing phonics skills).
T.S. Dennison (800-443-2976)

County Fair Phonics (fair games for practicing phonics skills).
T.S. Dennison (800-443-2976)

Free Phonics Worksheets (phonics worksheets that focus on vowels, consonants, blends, and other aspects of reading). http://www.schoolexpress.com

Kid Phonics (letter-sound correspondence activities using songs and a personalized dictionary).
UPDATA (800-882-2844)

Sound It Out Land (theme park games focusing on phonics and spelling).
UPDATA (800-882-2844)

Sound It Out Land 2 (theme park games focusing on consonant blends).
UPDATA (800-882-2844)

Working Phonics (84 skill-based phonics activities).
Curriculum Associates (800-225-0248)

Professional Resources

Baer, G.T. (1999). *Self-paced phonics: A text for education* (2nd ed.). Upper Saddle River, NJ: Prentice Hall.

Bear, D.R., Invernizzi, M., Templeton, S., & Johnston, F. (2000). *Words their way* (2nd ed.). Upper Saddle River, NJ: Prentice Hall.

Blevins, W. (1998). *Phonics from A to Z: A practical guide.* New York: Scholastic Professional Books.

Cunningham, P.M., & Hall, D.P. (1997). *Making more words: Multilevel, hands-on phonics and spelling activities.* Parsippany, NJ: Good Apple.

Cunningham, P.M., & Hall, D.P. (1998). *Making words: Multilevel, hands-on, developmentally appropriate spelling and phonics activities* (2nd ed.). Parsippany, NJ: Good Apple.

Cunningham, P.M. (2000). *Phonics they use* (3rd ed.). New York: Longman.

Dahl, K.L., Scharer, P.L., Lawson, L.L., & Grogan, P.R. (2001). *Rethinking phonics: Making the best teaching decisions.* Portsmouth, NH: Heinemann.

Gunning, T.G. (2000). *Phonological awareness and primary phonics.* Boston: Allyn and Bacon.

From Jerry L. Johns, Susan Davis Lenski, and Laurie Elish-Piper, *Teaching Beginning Readers: Linking Assessment and Instruction* (2nd ed.). Copyright © 2002 by Kendall/Hunt Publishing Company (1-800-247-3458, ext. 5). May be reproduced for noncommercial educational purposes.

3.4 Assessments of Alphabet Knowledge, Phonemic Awareness, and Phonics

Assessment Strategy 1		Assessment Strategy 5	
Alphabet Knowledge	168	Auditory Discrimination	184
Form 1 Child's Copy	170	Form 1 Record Sheet	185
Form 1 Record Sheet	171	Form 2 Record Sheet	186
Form 2 Child's Copy	172	**Assessment Strategy 6**	
Form 2 Record Sheet	173	Phonics: Consonants Form 1	187
Assessment Strategy 2		Form 1 Child's Copy	189
Rhyme Detection	174	Form 1 Record Sheet	191
Form 1 Record Sheet	175	Phonics: Consonants Form 2	193
Form 2 Record Sheet	176	Form 2 Child's Copy	195
Assessment Strategy 3		Form 2 Record Sheet	197
Phoneme Segmentation	177	**Assessment Strategy 7**	
Form 1 Record Sheet	178	Decoding	199
Form 2 Record Sheet	179	Form 1 Child's Copy	201
Assessment Strategy 4		Form 1 Record Sheet	202
Phoneme Deletion and		Form 1 Scoring Chart	203
Substitution	180	Form 2 Child's Copy	204
Form 1 Record Sheet	182	Form 2 Record Sheet	205
Form 2 Record Sheet	183	Form 2 Scoring Chart	206

> **Goal** To help assess children's knowledge of the alphabet, various aspects of phonemic awareness, and phonics.

BACKGROUND

There is probably no need to use all of the assessments in this section. Through your daily instruction, you can informally evaluate children's progress in the areas of alphabet knowledge, phonemic awareness, and phonics. Children's writing can also be used to give you insights into how they are using their knowledge of letter-sound associations (phonics) to help spell words. If you wish to more systematically assess one or more of the major topics in this chapter, choose the most appropriate assessment. Use it before instruction to help determine which students could profit from instruction in the area. You can also use an assessment after instruction in a specific area to help assess the effectiveness of your instruction and whether additional instruction is warranted. There are two forms of each assessment in this section to provide greater flexibility in use.

Letters and Sounds

Assessment Strategy 1

Section 3.4

Alphabet Knowledge

Overview	This assessment contains uppercase and lowercase letters of the alphabet in nonsequential order to help assess letter-naming ability. Lowercase *a* and *g* appear in both manuscript and print forms. There are two forms of the test. You may want to use Form 1 at the beginning of the year and Form 2 later in the year.
Materials Needed	1. Child's copy, either Form 1 (p. 170) or Form 2 (p. 172); two 5" × 8" cards 2. A copy of the Record Sheet that corresponds to the form selected for use, either Form 1 (p. 171) or Form 2 (p. 173)
Procedures	1. Duplicate the appropriate Record Sheet. 2. Place the alphabet page before the child. Use the 5" × 8" cards to block off everything but the line being read. If necessary, point to each letter. Say, "Here are some letters. I want to see how many you know." Encourage the child to say "pass" or "skip it" if a particular letter is not known. Stop if the child becomes frustrated or has little or no knowledge of the letters. 3. As the child responds, use the Record Sheet to note correct (+) responses. When responses are incorrect, record the actual response or *DK* (child doesn't know) above the stimulus letter. If the child self-corrects, write *s/c*; self-corrections can be made at any time. Some sample markings for the letter o are given below. | Marking	Meaning of Marking	Marking	Meaning of Marking
---	---	---	---
+ O	Identified correctly	C O	Said C for O
DK O	Don't know	C s/c O	Said C for O but self-corrected	
Scoring and Interpretation	Count the correct number of responses for the uppercase letters and the lowercase letters. Self-corrections are counted as correct. Note the scores in the boxes on the Record Sheet. Based on the number of correct responses and your observations, make a judgment about the child's alphabet knowledge. Unknown letters or incorrect responses may help form the basis for instruction. Refer to Section 3.1.

Additional Ways of Assessing Alphabet Knowledge

1. Observe the child's responses to ongoing instruction to teach the letters. Make mental notes about any particular letters that cause confusion and provide appropriate instruction. Remember that children often confuse *b, d, p,* and *q* in the early stages of reading instruction.
2. Use children's writing for indications of letters that may be confused or unknown. Provide additional instruction as needed.
3. Be alert for children whose knowledge of the alphabet appears to lag behind other children in your classroom. Use this information to help decide if special instruction may be needed.

B	T	R	Z	F	N	K
X	V	I	M	J	D	L
Y	Q	W	C	U	A	
O	H	S	E	G	P	
s	d	o	a	k	w	g
l	u	r	t	q	h	y
i	p	v	f	n	z	g
b	x	e	c	j	m	a

Form 1—Alphabet Knowledge—Child's Copy

RECORD SHEET

Form 1

Alphabet Knowledge

Name_____ Date_____

Teacher's Directions   168
Child's Copy   170

BRIEF DIRECTIONS

Present the alphabet sheet to the child. Use 5" × 8" cards to block off everything but the line being read. If necessary, point to each letter with a finger. Then say, "Here are some letters. I want to see how many you know." Place a plus (+) above correctly identified letters. Record the child's responses for incorrect letters. Total correct responses and record the score in the boxes. Note that lowercase *a* and *g* appear in both manuscript and print forms.

B	T	R	Z	F	N	K
X	V	I	M	J	D	L
Y	Q	W	C	U	A	
O	H	S	E	G	P	

☐ Total Correct

s	d	o	a	k	w	g
l	u	r	t	q	h	y
i	p	v	f	n	z	g
b	x	e	c	j	m	a

☐ Total Correct

From Jerry L. Johns, Susan Davis Lenski, and Laurie Elish-Piper, *Teaching Beginning Readers: Linking Assessment and Instruction* (2nd ed.). Copyright © 2002 by Kendall/Hunt Publishing Company (1-800-247-3458, ext. 5). May be reproduced for noncommercial educational purposes.

I	S	K	H	Q	V	L
A	G	P	J	N	D	M
T	C	Z	E	F	U	
B	O	X	Y	R	W	
r	x	z	k	t	e	y
w	q	c	g	h	m	a
i	p	s	v	d	l	j
u	o	f	b	a	n	g

Form 2—Alphabet Knowledge—Child's Copy

RECORD SHEET

Alphabet Knowledge

Form 2

Name _____ Date _____

Teacher's Directions   168
Child's Copy   172

BRIEF DIRECTIONS

Present the alphabet sheet to the child. Use 5" × 8" cards to block off everything but the line being read. If necessary, point to each letter with a finger. Then say, "Here are some letters. I want to see how many you know." Place a plus (+) above correctly identified letters. Record the child's responses for incorrect letters. Total correct responses and record the score in the boxes. Note that lowercase *a* and *g* appear in both manuscript and print forms.

I	S	K	H	Q	V	L
A	G	P	J	N	D	M
T	C	Z	E	F	U	
B	O	X	Y	R	W	

☐ Total Correct

r	x	z	k	t	e	y
w	q	c	g	h	m	a
i	p	s	v	d	l	j
u	o	f	b	a	n	g

☐ Total Correct

From Jerry L. Johns, Susan Davis Lenski, and Laurie Elish-Piper, *Teaching Beginning Readers: Linking Assessment and Instruction* (2nd ed.). Copyright © 2002 by Kendall/Hunt Publishing Company (1-800-247-3458, ext. 5). May be reproduced for noncommercial educational purposes.

Assessment Strategy 2

Section 3.4

Rhyme Detection

Overview	This assessment will help determine the child's ability to hear whether or not words rhyme. This skill is helpful in learning phonics. It is also often taught early in phonemic awareness instruction. Form 1 may be used as a pretest early in the school year. Form 2 may be used later in the year or after specific instruction in rhyming.
Materials Needed	1. A copy of the Record Sheet that corresponds to the form selected for use, either Form 1 (p. 175) or Form 2 (p. 176)
Procedures	1. Practice saying the words on the list. 2. Say the following to the child, "I want you to tell me if two words rhyme. When words sound the same at the end, they rhyme. *Hat* rhymes with *cat*. Does *look* rhyme with *book*? Yes. Does *mat* rhyme with *bat*? Yes. But not all words rhyme. *Mice* does not rhyme with *soon* because *mice* ends with *ice* and *soon* ends with *oon*. Does *cat* rhyme with *pig*? No. Does *sick* rhyme with *pick*? Yes. Now, listen carefully. I'm going to say some words, and I want you to tell me if they rhyme." 3. Say all the words distinctly but in a normal voice. 4. Place a ✓ in the appropriate column to indicate whether the child's response was correct or incorrect.
Scoring and Interpretation	Count the number of correct items and record the total on the Record Sheet. Informally judge the child's ability to detect rhymes. If the child could profit from additional instruction in rhyme detection, refer to the instructional strategies and activities in Section 3.2.

Additional Ways of Assessing Rhyme

1. Many poems and nursery rhymes provide an informal opportunity to assess the child's ability to rhyme. Note the child's ability to predict a rhyming word at the end of a line of a poem or rhyme.
2. Listen to children's language play in the classroom and on the playground. Watch for evidence of rhyming as children play a variety of games (e.g., jump rope).

RECORD SHEET

Form 1

Rhyme Detection

Teacher's Directions 174
Child's Copy None

BRIEF DIRECTIONS

Say to the child: "I want you to tell me if two words rhyme. When words sound the same at the end, they rhyme. *Hat* rhymes with *cat*. Does *look* rhyme with *book*? Yes. Does *mat* rhyme with *bat*? Yes. But not all words rhyme. *Mice* does not rhyme with *soon* because *mice* ends with *ice* and *soon* ends with *oon*. Does *cat* rhyme with *pig*? No. Does *sick* rhyme with *pick*? Yes. Now, listen carefully. I'm going to say some words, and I want you to tell me if they rhyme." Place a ✓ in the appropriate column, total correct responses, and record the score in the box.

				Correct	Incorrect
1.	bee	—	see	_____	_____
2.	tall	—	call	_____	_____
3.	jet	—	dog	_____	_____
4.	can	—	man	_____	_____
5.	him	—	gym	_____	_____
6.	hen	—	bag	_____	_____
7.	rat	—	sat	_____	_____
8.	room	—	zoom	_____	_____
9.	back	—	sing	_____	_____
10.	bake	—	rake	_____	_____

Total Correct ☐

Observations, Comments, Notes, and Insights

From Jerry L. Johns, Susan Davis Lenski, and Laurie Elish-Piper, *Teaching Beginning Readers: Linking Assessment and Instruction* (2nd ed.). Copyright © 2002 by Kendall/Hunt Publishing Company (1-800-247-3458, ext. 5). May be reproduced for noncommercial educational purposes.

RECORD SHEET

Form 2

Rhyme Detection

Name _____ Date _____

Teacher's Directions   174
Child's Copy   None

BRIEF DIRECTIONS

Say to the child: "I want you to tell me if two words rhyme. When words sound the same at the end, they rhyme. *Hat* rhymes with *cat*. Does *look* rhyme with *book*? Yes. Does *mat* rhyme with *bat*? Yes. But not all words rhyme. *Mice* does not rhyme with *soon* because *mice* ends with *ice* and *soon* ends with *oon*. Does *cat* rhyme with *pig*? No. Does *sick* rhyme with *pick*? Yes. Now, listen carefully. I'm going to say some words, and I want you to tell me if they rhyme." Place a ✓ in the appropriate column, total correct responses, and record the score in the box.

			Correct	Incorrect
1. me	—	he	_____	_____
2. ball	—	mall	_____	_____
3. hog	—	let	_____	_____
4. than	—	ran	_____	_____
5. skim	—	trim	_____	_____
6. rag	—	men	_____	_____
7. that	—	fat	_____	_____
8. green	—	broom	_____	_____
9. ring	—	sack	_____	_____
10. shake	—	bake	_____	_____

Total Correct ☐

Observations, Comments, Notes, and Insights

From Jerry L. Johns, Susan Davis Lenski, and Laurie Elish-Piper, *Teaching Beginning Readers: Linking Assessment and Instruction* (2nd ed.). Copyright © 2002 by Kendall/Hunt Publishing Company (1-800-247-3458, ext. 5). May be reproduced for noncommercial educational purposes.

Assessment Strategy 3

Section 3.4

Phoneme Segmentation

Overview	Phoneme segmentation refers to the child's ability to segment phonemes (sounds) in words. Phoneme segmentation is strongly related to success in reading and spelling acquisition. This assessment was designed for use with English-speaking kindergartners. It may also be used with older children experiencing difficulty in literacy acquisition. Two forms of the assessment are included. Use one form to help determine if the child needs instruction in phoneme segmentation. The second form can be used later to help assess the child's growth in phoneme segmentation.
Materials Needed	1. A copy of the Record Sheet that corresponds to the form selected for use, either Form 1 (p. 178) or Form 2 (p. 179)
Procedures	1. Say to the child, "Today we're going to play a word game. I'm going to say a word, and I want you to break the word apart. You are going to tell me each sound in the word in order. For example, if I say *old*, you should say /o/-/l/-/d/. Be sure to say the sounds, not the letters, in the word." 2. Then say, "Let's try a few together." The practice items are *ride, go,* and *man*. If necessary, help by segmenting the word for the child. Encourage the child to repeat the segmented sounds. 3. During practice provide feedback after each response. You can nod or say "Right" or "That's right." If the child is incorrect, correct him or her and provide the appropriate response. 4. Proceed through all of the items. Put a plus (+) beside those items that the child correctly segments. Incorrect responses may be recorded on the blank line following the item.
Scoring and Interpretation	The child's score is the number of items he or she correctly segments into all constituent phonemes. No partial credit is given. For example, *she* (item 5 on Form 1) contains two phonemes /sh/-/e/; *grew* (item 7 on Form 1) contains three phonemes /g/-/r/-/ew/; and *three* (item 4 on Form 2) contains three phonemes /th/-/r/-/ee/. If the child says letter names instead of sounds, code the response as incorrect and note the type of error on the Record Sheet. Such notes are helpful in understanding the child's literacy development. Some children may partially segment, simply repeat the stimulus item, provide nonsense responses, or give letter names. Total the number of correct responses. Place the score in the box on the Record Sheet. Then make an overall judgment of the child's phoneme segmentation abilities. A wide range of scores is likely. Yopp (1995) reported that two samples of kindergartners achieved mean scores of 11.78 and 11.39 when all 22 words were administered. The child's responses may help form a basis for instructional interventions. Refer to Section 3.2.

RECORD SHEET

Phoneme Segmentation

Form 1

Name_____ Date_____

Teacher's Directions   177
Child's Copy   None

BRIEF DIRECTIONS

Say to the child: "Today we're going to play a word game. I'm going to say a word, and I want you to break the word apart. You are going to tell me each sound in the word in order. For example, if I say *old*, you should say /o/-/l/-/d/. Be sure to say the sounds, not the letters, in the word. Let's try a few together."

PRACTICE ITEMS

ride, go, man *(Assist the child in segmenting these items as necessary.)*

TEST ITEMS

(Put a plus (+) beside those items that the child correctly segments; incorrect responses may be recorded on the blank line following the item.) The correct number of phonemes is indicated in parentheses.

1. dog (3) _____   7. grew (3) _____
2. keep (3) _____   8. that (3) _____
3. fine (3) _____   9. red (3) _____
4. no (2) _____   10. me (2) _____
5. she (2) _____   11. sat (3) _____
6. wave (3) _____

Total Correct ☐

Observations, Comments, Notes, and Insights

The author, Hallie Kay Yopp, California State University, Fullerton, grants permission for this test to be reproduced. The author acknowledges the contribution of the late Harry Singer to the development of this test. Adapted from Yopp, H.K. (1995). A test for assessing phonemic awareness in young children. *The Reading Teacher, 49,* 20–29.
From Jerry L. Johns, Susan Davis Lenski, and Laurie Elish-Piper, *Teaching Beginning Readers: Linking Assessment and Instruction.* Copyright © 2002 by Kendall/Hunt Publishing Company (1-800-247-3458, ext. 5). May be reproduced for noncommercial educational purposes.

RECORD SHEET

Phoneme Segmentation

Form 2

Name_____ Date_____

Teacher's Directions   177
Child's Copy   None

BRIEF DIRECTIONS

Say to the child: "Today we're going to play a word game. I'm going to say a word, and I want you to break the word apart. You are going to tell me each sound in the word in order. For example, if I say *old*, you should say /o/-/l/-/d/. Be sure to say the sounds, not the letters, in the word. Let's try a few together."

PRACTICE ITEMS

ride, go, man *(Assist the child in segmenting these items as necessary.)*

TEST ITEMS

(Put a plus (+) beside those items that the child correctly segments; incorrect responses may be recorded on the blank line following the item.) The correct number of phonemes is indicated in parentheses.

1. lay (2) _____
2. race (3) _____
3. zoo (2) _____
4. three (3)_____
5. job (3) _____
6. in (2)   _____
7. ice (2) _____
8. at (2)   _____
9. top (3) _____
10. by (2) _____
11. do (2) _____

Total Correct ☐

Observations, Comments, Notes, and Insights

The author, Hallie Kay Yopp, California State University, Fullerton, grants permission for this test to be reproduced. The author acknowledges the contribution of the late Harry Singer to the development of this test. Adapted from Yopp, H.K. (1995). A test for assessing phonemic awareness in young children. *The Reading Teacher, 49,* 20–29.
From Jerry L. Johns, Susan Davis Lenski, and Laurie Elish-Piper, *Teaching Beginning Readers: Linking Assessment and Instruction* (2nd ed.). Copyright © 2002 by Kendall/Hunt Publishing Company (1-800-247-3458, ext. 5). May be reproduced for noncommercial educational purposes.

Assessment Strategy 4

Section 3.4

Phoneme Deletion and Substitution

Overview	Two assessments are included in this area. Phoneme Deletion assesses the child's ability to produce a word part when the initial phoneme (sound) is deleted. Phoneme Substitution assesses the child's ability to make a new word by substituting a phoneme (sound). These phonemic awareness tasks can be assessed to determine whether children "can already perform the manipulations being taught as determined by pretests" (National Reading Panel, 2000, p. 2–31). If you assess the areas of phoneme deletion and phoneme substitution, be certain that children will be expected to make use of the two skills in your instructional program. There are two forms of each assessment. Form 1 could be used to determine if the child can already perform these phonemic awareness tasks. Form 2 could be used after instruction to help evaluate progress.
Materials Needed	1. A copy of the Record Sheet that corresponds to the form selected for administration, either Form 1 (p. 182) or Form 2 (p. 183)
Procedures	1. For Phoneme Deletion, practice the words before you administer the assessment. Then say to the child, "Listen to me say the word *fun*. I can say the word *fun* without the /f/. *Fun* without the /f/ is *un*. Now I'll say some words, and I want you to tell me what is left when the first sound is taken away." Use another example if you think it is needed. "Listen to me say the word *make*. I can say the word *make* without the /m/. *Make* without the /m/ is *ake*." 2. Use the words on the Record Sheet. The general prompt for each word is, "What is _____ without the /__/?" Place a ✓ in the appropriate column after each word. Then total the correct responses and record the score in the box. 3. For Phoneme Substitution, practice the words before you administer the assessment. Then say to the child, "Listen to the word *fun*. I can make a new word. I can take the /f/ off *fun* and put on a /r/ and make *run*. Now you say the word *car*." (Have the child say the word.) "Take the /c/ off *car* and put on a /j/ to make a new word. The new word is _____ (*jar*)." Use another example if you think it is needed. "Take the /b/ off *bunch* and put on a /l/ to make a new word. The new word is _____ (*lunch*)." 4. Use the words on the Record Sheet. Use the general prompt above. Place a ✓ in the appropriate column after each word. Then total the correct responses and record the score in the box.
Scoring and Interpretation	Count the number of correct items for each assessment administered and record the total on the Record Sheet. Informally judge the child's ability to delete and substitute phonemes. If the child could profit from additional instruction in one area or both of the areas assessed, refer to the appropriate instructional strategies and activities in Section 3.2.

Additional Ways of Assessing Phonological Awareness

1. Use ongoing instruction to make informal judgments about the child's abilities in the areas assessed as well as other areas of phonemic awareness.
2. As you read children's literature containing language play (such as rhyming words), you can judge by the responses which children seem to be learning how sounds make up words.
3. A number of commercially published tests are available. Consult resources such as Salvia and Ysseldyke (2001) or Gillet and Temple (2000).

RECORD SHEET

Form 1

Phoneme Deletion and Substitution

Name_____ Date_____

Teacher's Directions   180
Child's Copy   None

BRIEF DIRECTIONS: PHONEME DELETION

Say to the child, "Listen to me say the word *fun*. I can say the word *fun* without the /f/. *Fun* without the /f/ is *un*. Now I'll say some words, and I want you to tell me what is left when the first sound is taken away." Use another example if you think it is needed. "Listen to me say the word *make*. I can say the word *make* without the /m/. *Make* without the /m/ is *ake*."

Use the words on the Record Sheet. The general prompt for each word is, "What is _____ without the /__/?" Place a ✓ in the appropriate column after each word. Then total the correct responses and record the score in the box.

			Correct	Incorrect
1.	dad without /d/	ad	_____	_____
2.	cheek without /ch/	eek	_____	_____
3.	sock without /s/	ock	_____	_____
4.	fin without /f/	in	_____	_____
5.	nose without /n/	ose	_____	_____

Total Correct ☐

BRIEF DIRECTIONS: PHONEME SUBSTITUTION

Say to the child, "Listen to the word *fun*. I can make a new word. I can take the /f/ off *fun* and put on a /r/ and make *run*. Now you say the word *car*." (Have the child say the word.) "Take the /c/ off *car* and put on a /j/ to make a new word. The new word is _____ (jar)." Use another example if you think it is needed. "Take the /b/ off *bunch* and put on a /l/ to make a new word. The new word is _____ (lunch)."

Use the words on the Record Sheet. Use the general prompt above. Place a ✓ in the appropriate column after each word. Then total the correct responses and record the score in the box.

			Correct	Incorrect
1.	/m/ off mad and put on an /s/	sad	_____	_____
2.	/f/ off fish and put on a /d/	dish	_____	_____
3.	/b/ off bell and put on a /f/	fell	_____	_____
4.	/p/ off pup and put on a /c/	cup	_____	_____
5.	/s/ off seed and put on a /w/	weed	_____	_____

Total Correct ☐

From Jerry L. Johns, Susan Davis Lenski, and Laurie Elish-Piper, *Teaching Beginning Readers: Linking Assessment and Instruction* (2nd ed.). Copyright © 2002 by Kendall/Hunt Publishing Company (1-800-247-3458, ext. 5). May be reproduced for noncommercial educational purposes.

RECORD SHEET

Form 2

Phoneme Deletion and Substitution

Name _____ Date _____

Teacher's Directions   180
Child's Copy   None

BRIEF DIRECTIONS: PHONEME DELETION

Say to the child, "Listen to me say the word *fun*. I can say the word *fun* without the /f/. *Fun* without the /f/ is *un*. Now I'll say some words, and I want you to tell me what is left when the first sound is taken away." Use another example if you think it is needed. "Listen to me say the word *make*. I can say the word *make* without the /m/. *Make* without the /m/ is *ake*."

Use the words on the Record Sheet. The general prompt for each word is, "What is _____ without the /__/?" Place a ✓ in the appropriate column after each word. Then total the correct responses and record the score in the box.

			Correct	Incorrect
1.	team without /t/	eam	_____	_____
2.	made without /m/	ade	_____	_____
3.	sat without /s/	at	_____	_____
4.	race without /r/	ace	_____	_____
5.	leg without /l/	eg	_____	_____

Total Correct ☐

BRIEF DIRECTIONS: PHONEME SUBSTITUTION

Say to the child, "Listen to the word *fun*. I can make a new word. I can take the /f/ off *fun* and put on a /r/ and make *run*. Now you say the word *car*." (Have the child say the word.) "Take the /c/ off *car* and put on a /j/ to make a new word. The new word is _____ (*jar*)." Use another example if you think it is needed. "Take the /b/ off *bunch* and put on a /l/ to make a new word. The new word is _____ (*lunch*)."

Use the words on the Record Sheet. Use the general prompt above. Place a ✓ mark in the appropriate column after each word. Then total the correct responses and record the score in the box.

			Correct	Incorrect
1.	/c/ off cat and put on an /f/	fat	_____	_____
2.	/s/ off sing and put on a /w/	wing	_____	_____
3.	/r/ off red and put on a /b/	bed	_____	_____
4.	/d/ off duck and put on a /l/	luck	_____	_____
5.	/p/ off pack and put on a /b/	back	_____	_____

Total Correct ☐

From Jerry L. Johns, Susan Davis Lenski, and Laurie Elish-Piper, *Teaching Beginning Readers: Linking Assessment and Instruction* (2nd ed.). Copyright © 2002 by Kendall/Hunt Publishing Company (1-800-247-3458, ext. 5). May be reproduced for noncommercial educational purposes.

Assessment Strategy 5

Auditory Discrimination

Section 3.4

Overview	Auditory Discrimination will help evaluate the child's ability to distinguish between words that differ in one phoneme (sound). Children typically engage in auditory discrimination activities as part of initial instruction in phonics. Two forms are available so one form can be a pretest and the second form could be used as a posttest.
Materials Needed	1. A copy of the Record Sheet that corresponds to the form selected for use, either Form 1 (p. 185) or Form 2 (p. 186)
Procedures	1. Practice the words on the list, saying them clearly in a normal voice. 2. Do not rush the child during the assessment. 3. If the child misses a pair of items or asks for one to be repeated, move on to the next item and return to any such items at the conclusion of the test. If the child responds correctly, give credit. 4. Face the child away from you and say: "Listen to the words I am about to say: *fair-far*. Do they sound exactly the same or are they different? (For young children, the teacher may prefer the words "alike" and "not alike" in place of the words "same" and "different.") Yes, they are different. Listen to these two words: *cap-cap*. Are they the same or different? Now I am going to read you pairs of words. I want you to tell me if they are the same or different. Do you understand what you are to do? Please turn your back to me and listen very carefully." 5. Say all the words distinctly but in a normal voice. 6. Mark + for correct responses and – for incorrect responses.
Scoring and Interpretation	Note the number of correct "same" and "different" responses and enter the total on the Record Sheet. Based on the error scores, make a judgment about the child's auditory discrimination ability. A child who misses two or more of the "same" pairs may not have understood the concepts "same" and "different." Such results may mean that the test was not valid. Areas of concern can be strengthened by the instructional strategies and activities in Section 3.2.

184   Chapter Three

RECORD SHEET — Form 1

Auditory Discrimination

Name _____ Date _____

Teacher's Directions   184
Child's Copy   None

				Same	Different
1.	though	—	show		☐
2.	moss	—	moth		☐
3.	jump	—	jump	☐	
4.	luck	—	lock		☐
5.	sing	—	sing	☐	
6.	light	—	sight		☐
7.	set	—	sit		☐
8.	rap	—	rack		☐
9.	bed	—	bad		☐
10.	sit	—	sick		☐
11.	duck	—	duck	☐	
12.	can	—	tan		☐

Total Correct ☐

Observations, Comments, Notes, and Insights

From Jerry L. Johns, Susan Davis Lenski, and Laurie Elish-Piper, *Teaching Beginning Readers: Linking Assessment and Instruction* (2nd ed.). Copyright © 2002 by Kendall/Hunt Publishing Company (1-800-247-3458, ext. 5). May be reproduced for noncommercial educational purposes.

RECORD SHEET

Auditory Discrimination

Form 2

Name_____ Date_____

Teacher's Directions   184
Child's Copy   None

			Same	Different
1. debt	—	get		☐
2. tick	—	tip		☐
3. touch	—	touch	☐	
4. disk	—	desk		☐
5. mall	—	mall	☐	
6. came	—	tame		☐
7. sew	—	saw		☐
8. lass	—	laugh		☐
9. duck	—	dock		☐
10. mud	—	mug		☐
11. thing	—	thing	☐	
12. nice	—	mice		☐

Total Correct ☐

Observations, Comments, Notes, and Insights

From Jerry L. Johns, Susan Davis Lenski, and Laurie Elish-Piper, *Teaching Beginning Readers: Linking Assessment and Instruction* (2nd ed.). Copyright © 2002 by Kendall/Hunt Publishing Company (1-800-247-3458, ext. 5). May be reproduced for noncommercial educational purposes.

Assessment Strategy 6

Phonics: Consonants

Section 3.4
Form 1

Overview	This strategy will help assess the child's knowledge of the beginning and ending sounds of words. The tasks are of the recognition (not writing) type for beginning sounds and ending sounds. Two forms are included for use as a pretest and posttest. In addition, you could use only a portion of the assessment (e.g., initial sounds or final sounds) to help evaluate your instruction.
Materials Needed	1. The child's pages in this book containing the pictures and letters for Form 1 (pp. 189–190) 2. Two 5" × 8" cards 3. A copy of the Record Sheet for Form 1 (pp. 191–192)
Procedures	**Part 1 (p. 189 in Form 1)** 1. Show the child the page containing the pictures and letters. Cover everything but the first row of pictures. 2. Point to the pictures and say, "Look at the pictures and tell me what they are." If the child does not say *ball, cat, leg,* and *wagon,* say the correct words. Be sure the child knows the names of the pictures before continuing. 3. Then say, "I will say a word, and I want you to point to the picture that begins with the same beginning sound as the word I say." Then say the words one at a time and circle the child's responses on the Record Sheet. The correct responses are in bold type. The words for Form 1 are *came, wolf, box, look,* and *went.* After the last word, cover the pictures with one of the 5" × 8" cards. **Part 2 (p. 189 in Form 1)** 4. Cover the letters except the first row (*o, x, d, n, k*). Then say, "I will say a word. I want you to point to the letter that you hear at the beginning of the word I say. Be sure to listen for the sound at the beginning of the word." Then say the word and circle the child's response on the appropriate page of the Record Sheet. The correct response is in bold type. Then cover the line of letters, expose a new line of letters, and say the next word. If necessary, repeat the basic instruction: "Point to the letter you hear at the beginning of _____." The words for Form 1 are *duck, hand, kitten, mouse,* and *table.*

Letters and Sounds

Part 3 (p. 190 in Form 1)

5. Cover everything but the picture of the sun and the row of letters following it. Say, "Now I want you to name the picture and then point to the letter that begins the first sound of the picture. What's this picture? Good, now point to the letter that begins the first sound of the picture." Circle the child's response on the Record Sheet. The correct response is in bold type. Continue to the next item. If the child does not say the correct name for the picture, say the correct word and repeat the directions: "Point to the letter that begins the first sound of the picture." Continue giving the remaining items in a similar fashion. The pictures for Form 1 are *sun, fish, giraffe, net,* and *pen*.

Part 4 (p. 189 in Form 1)

6. Return to the top of the page and cover everything but the first row of pictures. Then say, "You probably remember the names of these pictures. Please say them for me."

7. Then say, "This time I want you to listen to the ending sound of the word I say. Then I want you to point to the picture with the same ending sound as the word I say." Say the words one at a time and circle the child's responses on the Record Sheet. The correct responses are in bold type. The words for Form 1 are *flat, pen, bag, street,* and *tall*. The basic direction is, "Point to the picture that ends with the same ending sound as _____." When the last item is completed, cover the pictures with one of the 5" × 8" cards.

8. Then cover the letters except for the first line. Say, "I will say a word. I want you to point to the letter that has the same ending sound as the word I say." The basic direction is, "Point to the letter that ends with the same sound as _____." Then say the word and circle the child's response on the Record Sheet. The correct response is in bold type. Then cover that line of letters, expose a new line of letters, and say the next word. If necessary repeat the basic instruction. The words for Form 1 are *duck, band, went, house,* and *win*.

Scoring and Interpretation	1. Count the number of initial sounds recognized and record the total on the Record Sheet. 2. Count the number of ending sounds recognized and record the total on the Record Sheet. Informally judge the child's recognition of initial and final sounds. If the child's initial and final phonic skills need to be strengthened, refer to the instructional strategies and activities in Section 3.3.

188 Chapter Three

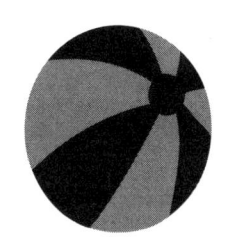

o   x   d   n   k

n   d   a   g   h

f   k   r   x   t

m   s   p   t   h

l   v   t   j   n

Form 1 — Phonics: Consonants — Child's Copy

m   s   r   o   g

h   y   f   b   c

f   k   g   s   t

w   c   r   d   n

r   h   j   n   p

Form 1 — Phonics: Consonants — Child's Copy

RECORD SHEET

Form 1

Phonics: Consonants

Name _____ Date _____

Teacher's Directions   187–188
Child's Copy   189–190

INITIAL CONSONANT SOUND RECOGNITION

Part 1
1. came	ball	**cat**	leg	wagon
2. wolf	ball	cat	leg	**wagon**
3. box	**ball**	cat	leg	wagon
4. look	ball	cat	**leg**	wagon
5. went	ball	cat	leg	**wagon**

Part 2
6. duck	o	x	**d**	n	k
7. hand	n	d	a	g	**h**
8. kitten	f	**k**	r	x	t
9. mouse	**m**	s	p	t	h
10. table	l	v	**t**	j	n

Part 3
11. sun	m	**s**	r	o	g
12. fish	h	y	**f**	b	c
13. giraffe	f	k	**g**	s	t
14. net	w	c	r	d	**n**
15. pen	r	h	j	n	**p**

Total Correct ☐

From Jerry L. Johns, Susan Davis Lenski, and Laurie Elish-Piper, *Teaching Beginning Readers: Linking Assessment and Instruction* (2nd ed.). Copyright © 2002 by Kendall/Hunt Publishing Company (1-800-247-3458, ext. 5). May be reproduced for noncommercial educational purposes.

RECORD SHEET

Form 1

Phonics: Consonants (con't.)

Name _____ Date _____

FINAL CONSONANT SOUND RECOGNITION

Part 4

1. flat	ball	**cat**	leg	wagon
2. pen	ball	cat	leg	**wagon**
3. bag	ball	cat	**leg**	wagon
4. street	ball	**cat**	leg	wagon
5. tall	**ball**	cat	leg	wagon
6. duck	o	x	d	n	**k**
7. band	n	**d**	a	g	h
8. went	f	k	r	x	**t**
9. house	m	**s**	p	t	h
10. win	l	v	t	j	**n**

Total Correct ☐

Observations, Comments, Notes, and Insights

From Jerry L. Johns, Susan Davis Lenski, and Laurie Elish-Piper, *Teaching Beginning Readers: Linking Assessment and Instruction* (2nd ed.). Copyright © 2002 by Kendall/Hunt Publishing Company (1-800-247-3458, ext. 5). May be reproduced for noncommercial educational purposes.

Assessment Strategy 6

Phonics: Consonants

Section 3.4
Form 2

Overview	Consonant phonic elements will help assess the child's knowledge of the beginning and ending sounds of words. The tasks are of the recognition (not writing) type for beginning sounds and ending sounds. Two forms are included for use as a pretest and posttest. In addition, you could use only a portion of the assessment (e.g., initial sounds or final sounds) to help evaluate your instruction.
Materials Needed	1. The child's pages in this book containing the pictures and letters for Form 2 (pp. 195–196) 2. Two 5" × 8" cards 3. A copy of the Record Sheet (pp. 197–198)
Procedures	**Part 1 (p. 195 in Form 2)** 1. Show the child the page containing the pictures and letters. Cover everything but the first row of pictures. 2. Point to the pictures and say, "Look at the pictures and tell me what they are." If the child does not say *ball, cat, leg,* and *wagon,* say the correct words. Be sure the child knows the names of the pictures before continuing. 3. Then say, "I will say a word, and I want you to point to the picture that begins with the same beginning sound as the word I say." Then say the words one at a time and circle the child's responses on the Record Sheet. The correct responses are in bold type. The words for Form 2 are *coat, wood, book, leaf,* and *wet.* After the last word, cover the pictures with one of the 5"× 8" cards. **Part 2 (p. 195 in Form 2)** 4. Cover the letters except the first row (*o, x, d, n, k*). Then say, "I will say a word. I want you to point to the letter that you hear at the beginning of the word I say. Be sure to listen for the sound at the beginning of the word." Then say the word and circle the child's response on the Record Sheet. The correct response is in bold type. Then cover the line of letters, expose a new line of letters, and say the next word. If necessary, repeat the basic instruction: "Point to the letter you hear at the beginning of _____." The words for Form 2 are *door, head, keep, mother,* and *toy.*

Letters and Sounds

Part 3 (p. 196 in Form 2)

5. Cover everything but the picture of the man (Form 2) and the row of letters following it. Say, "Now I want you to name the picture and then point to the letter that begins the first sound of the picture. What's this picture? Good, now point to the letter that begins the first sound of the picture." Circle the child's response on the Record Sheet. The correct response is in bold type. Continue to the next item. If the child does not say the correct name for the picture, say the correct word and repeat the directions: "Point to the letter that begins the first sound of the picture." Continue giving the remaining items in a similar fashion. The pictures for Form 2 are *man, fork, giraffe, nose,* and *pencil.*

Part 4 (p. 195 in Form 2)

6. Return to the top of the page and cover everything but the first row of pictures. Then say, "You probably remember the names of these pictures. Please say them for me."

7. Then say, "This time I want you to listen to the ending sound of the word I say. Then I want you to point to the picture with the same ending sound as the word I say." Say the words one at a time and circle the child's responses on the Record Sheet. The correct responses are in bold type. The words for Form 2 are *hat, hen, log, feet,* and *call.* The basic direction is, "Point to the picture that ends with the same ending sound as _____." When the last item is completed, cover the pictures with one of the 5" × 8" cards.

8. Then cover the letters except for the first line. Say, "I will say a word. I want you to point to the letter that has the same ending sound as the word I say." The basic direction is, "Point to the letter that ends with the same sound as _____." Then say the word and circle the child's response on the Record Sheet. The correct response is in bold type. Then cover that line of letters, expose a new line of letters, and say the next word. If necessary, repeat the basic instruction. The words for Form 2 are *truck, land, bend, mouse* and *pin.*

Scoring and Interpretation	1. Count the number of initial sounds recognized and record the total on the Record Sheet.
	2. Count the number of ending sounds recognized and record the total on the Record Sheet.
	Informally judge the child's recognition of initial and final sounds. If the child's initial and final phonic skills need to be strengthened, refer to the instructional strategies and activities in Section 3.3.

o   x   d   n   k

n   d   a   g   h

f   k   r   x   t

m   s   p   t   h

l   v   t   j   n

Form 2—Phonics: Consonants—Child's Copy

m   s   r   o   g

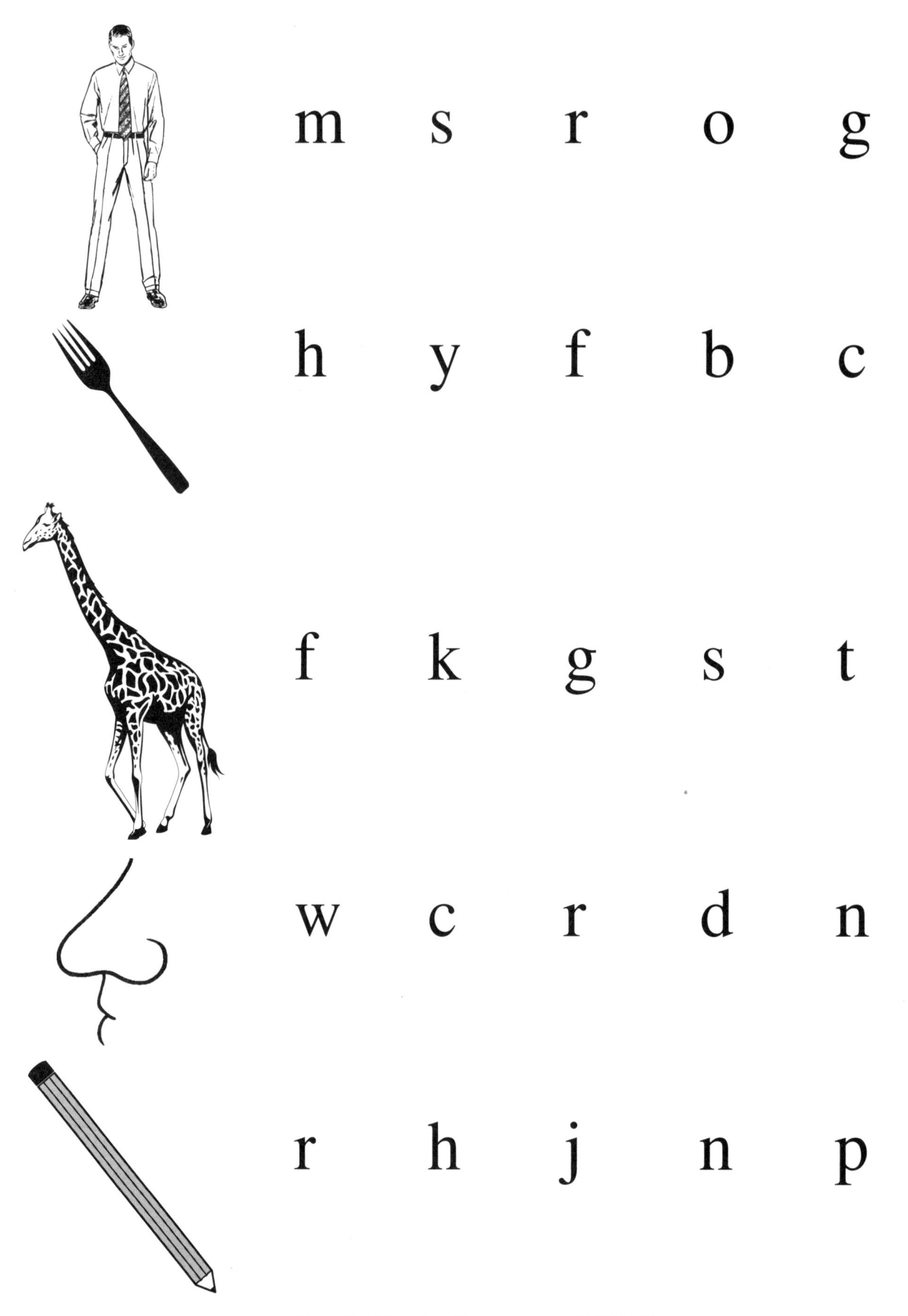

h   y   f   b   c

f   k   g   s   t

w   c   r   d   n

r   h   j   n   p

Form 2—Phonics: Consonants—Child's Copy

RECORD SHEET

Phonics: Consonants

Form 2

Name_____ Date_____

Teacher's Directions   193–194
Child's Copy   195–196

INITIAL CONSONANT SOUND RECOGNITION

Part 1

1. coat	ball	**cat**	leg	wagon
2. wood	ball	cat	leg	**wagon**
3. book	**ball**	cat	leg	wagon
4. leaf	ball	cat	**leg**	wagon
5. wet	ball	cat	leg	**wagon**

Part 2

6. door	o	x	**d**	n	k
7. head	n	d	a	g	**h**
8. keep	f	**k**	r	x	t
9. mother	**m**	s	p	t	h
10. toy	l	v	**t**	j	n

Part 3

11. man	**m**	s	r	o	g
12. fork	h	y	**f**	b	c
13. giraffe	f	k	**g**	s	t
14. nose	w	c	r	d	**n**
15. pencil	r	h	j	n	**p**

Total Correct ☐

From Jerry L. Johns, Susan Davis Lenski, and Laurie Elish-Piper, *Teaching Beginning Readers: Linking Assessment and Instruction* (2nd ed.). Copyright © 2002 by Kendall/Hunt Publishing Company (1-800-247-3458, ext. 5). May be reproduced for noncommercial educational purposes.

RECORD SHEET

Phonics: Consonants (con't.)

Form 2

Name _____ Date _____

FINAL CONSONANT SOUND RECOGNITION
Part 4

1. hat	ball	**cat**	leg	wagon	
2. hen	ball	cat	leg	**wagon**	
3. log	ball	cat	**leg**	wagon	
4. feet	ball	**cat**	leg	wagon	
5. call	**ball**	cat	leg	wagon	
6. truck	o	x	d	n	**k**
7. land	n	**d**	a	g	h
8. bent	f	k	r	x	**t**
9. mouse	m	**s**	p	t	h
10. pin	l	v	t	j	**n**

Total Correct ☐

Observations, Comments, Notes, and Insights

From Jerry L. Johns, Susan Davis Lenski, and Laurie Elish-Piper, *Teaching Beginning Readers: Linking Assessment and Instruction* (2nd ed.). Copyright © 2002 by Kendall/Hunt Publishing Company (1-800-247-3458, ext. 5). May be reproduced for noncommercial educational purposes.

Assessment Strategy 7

Section 3.4

Decoding

Overview	This assessment is adapted from the work of Cunningham (1990) and Duffelmeyer, Kruse, Merkley, and Fyfe (1994). It is intended to provide an easy and appealing way to assess the child's ability to decode words. It is possible to analyze the results to help determine the child's strengths and weaknesses in phonics. There are two forms of the assessment. To get an overview of the child's decoding skills, administer one of the forms and analyze the results. A more complete picture of the child's decoding will result if you administer both Form 1 and Form 2, because there will be a greater number of items upon which to base your analysis.
Materials Needed	1. The child's page in this book containing the list of names, either Form 1 (p. 201) or Form 2 (p. 204) 2. A 5" × 8" card 3. A copy of the Record Sheet that corresponds to the form selected for use, either Form 1 (p. 202) or Form 2 (p. 205) 4. A copy of the Scoring Chart selected for use that corresponds to the form selected for use, either Form 1 (p. 203) or Form 2 (p. 206)
Procedures	1. Place the list of names before the child and say something like, "I'd like you to pretend to be a teacher who must read the names of students in a class—just as I have done in our class. Do the best you can and make a guess if you're not sure." Use a 5" × 8" card to expose one name at a time and say, "Begin with this one." 2. Encourage the child to read the entire list but be sensitive to a child who may find the task too difficult or frustrating after several names. Be supportive and encouraging; however, use your professional judgment to decide whether to discontinue the assessment. 3. As the child responds, use the Record Sheet to note correct (+) responses. When responses are incorrect, write phonetic spellings (e.g., Rit for Rite, Chook for Chuck, Prostin for Preston) for names that are mispronounced.
Scoring and Interpretation	Use the child's responses on the Record Sheet along with the Scoring Chart to analyze the child's responses and gain insights into the child's strengths and weaknesses in phonics. The Scoring Chart contains eight categories to help you analyze the results. On the Record Sheet, mark the child's responses by circling the corresponding items on the Scoring Chart that are correct. Total the items for each category. Then you will have an indication of how well the child performed in relationship to the total number of items for the category. For example, if the child knows 12 of the 14 initial consonants in Form 1, you could reasonably conclude that the child knows most of the initial consonants assessed. You could also decide if the two "missed" consonants should be taught.

Letters and Sounds

If there is an area where only a few items are known, that particular area of phonics may need to be taught to the child.

Remember that identified areas of strength and weakness should be verified through ongoing instruction. There are also some categories that contain only a few items. For these categories, any possible weaknesses should be viewed as tentative.

Based on data obtained from Cunningham (1990), it is reasonable to expect children in second grade to obtain an average score of less than 50%. By fifth grade, the average child will achieve a score of greater than 90%. Another study by Dufffelmeyer, Kruse, Merkley, and Fyfe (1994) using a longer version of Cunningham's test found that the average child in second grade received a score of 63% correct. By fifth grade, the average score was 92%. Keep these percentages in mind as you interpret the results for the children. In addition, use the results to help decide which phonics skills and patterns should be taught within your curriculum.

Additional Ways of Assessing Phonics and Decoding

1. As children orally read instructional materials in the classroom, informally analyze their miscues or errors. Look for patterns of miscues and plan appropriate responsive instruction. For example, a child who has difficulty with the middle of words may have problems with certain vowels. Determine which specific vowels or vowel combinations need to be taught to the child.
2. Use the graded passages found in Section 5.4, Assessment Strategy 2. As the child reads the passages, mark any miscues made. Analyze the miscues to find patterns of specific sounds that may be unknown. Base your instruction on this type of analysis. Be open to change your instruction if additional information suggests another course of action.
3. Use an informal reading inventory (Johns, 2001) in the ways noted above to help determine the child's strengths and weaknesses in phonics. Many informal reading inventories have provisions to analyze miscues in a systematic manner to help determine instructional needs.

Bertha Murphy

Tim Cornell

Yolanda Clark

Roberta Slade

Gus Quincy

Ginger Yale

Patrick Tweed

Wendy Swain

Fred Sherwood

Dee Skidmore

Ned Westmoreland

Troy Whitlock

Thelma Sheperd

Form 1—Decoding—Child's Copy

Based on Cunningham, P. (1990) and Duffelmeyer, F.A., Kruse, A.E., Merkley, D.J., & Fyfe, S.A. (1994).

RECORD SHEET

Form 1

Decoding

Name _____ Date _____

Teacher's Directions   199–200
Child's Copy   201
Scoring Chart   203

BRIEF DIRECTIONS

Present the sheet with the names to the child. Say, "I'd like you to pretend to be a teacher who must read the names of students in a class—just as I have done in our class. Do the best that you can and make a guess if you're not sure." Use a 5" × 8" card to expose one name at a time and say, "Begin with this one." Note correct responses with a plus (+) and use phonetic spellings for names that are mispronounced. Total correct responses and record the score in the box.

	First Name	Last Name
Bertha Murphy	_____	_____
Tim Cornell	_____	_____
Yolanda Clark	_____	_____
Roberta Slade	_____	_____
Gus Quincy	_____	_____
Ginger Yale	_____	_____
Patrick Tweed	_____	_____
Wendy Swain	_____	_____
Fred Sherwood	_____	_____
Dee Skidmore	_____	_____
Ned Westmoreland	_____	_____
Troy Whitlock	_____	_____
Thelma Sheperd	_____	_____

Total Correct ☐

Based on Cunningham, P. (1990) and Duffelmeyer, F.A., Kruse, A.E., Merkley, D.J., & Fyfe, S.A. (1994).
From Jerry L. Johns, Susan Davis Lenski, and Laurie Elish-Piper, *Teaching Beginning Readers: Linking Assessment and Instruction* (2nd ed.). Copyright © 2002 by Kendall/Hunt Publishing Company (1-800-247-3458, ext. 5). May be reproduced for noncommercial educational purposes.

SCORING CHART

Scoring Chart for Decoding Assessment

Form 1

Name_____ Date_____

Name	Initial Con.	Initial Con. Blends	Con. Digraphs	Short Vowels	Long Vowels/ VC-e	Vowel Digraphs	Controlled Vowels	Schwa
Bertha Murphy	B M		th ph		y		er ur	a
Tim Cornell	T C			i e			or	
Yolanda Clark	Y	Cl		a	o		ar	a
Roberta Slade	R	Sl			o ade		er	a
Gus Quincy	G			u i	y			
Ginger Yale	G Y			i	ale		er	
Patrick Tweed	P	Tw		a, i		ee		
Wendy Swain	W	Sw		e	y	ai		
Fred Sherwood		Fr	Sh	e		oo	er	
Dee Skidmore	D	Sk		i		ee	or	
Ned Westmoreland	N W			e e			or	a
Troy Whitlock		Tr	Wh	i, o		oy		
Thelma Sheperd			Th Sh	e e			er	a
Totals	14	7	6	17	7	5	10	5

Based on Cunningham, P. (1990) and Duffelmeyer, F.A., Kruse, A.E., Merkley, D.J., & Fyfe, S.A. (1994).

From Jerry L. Johns, Susan Davis Lenski, and Laurie Elish-Piper, *Teaching Beginning Readers: Linking Assessment and Instruction* (2nd ed.). Copyright © 2002 by Kendall/Hunt Publishing Company (1-800-247-3458, ext. 5). May be reproduced for noncommercial educational purposes.

Jay Conway

Chuck Hoke

Kimberly Blake

Homer Preston

Cindy Sampson

Chester Wright

Stanley Shaw

Glen Spencer

Flo Thorton

Grace Brewster

Ron Smitherman

Vance Middleton

Bernard Pendergraph

Form 2—Decoding—Child's Copy

Based on Cunningham, P. (1990) and Duffelmeyer, F.A., Kruse, A.E., Merkley, D.J., & Fyfe, S.A. (1994).

RECORD SHEET

Form 2

Decoding

Name _____ Date _____

Teacher's Directions   199–200
Child's Copy   204
Scoring Chart   206

BRIEF DIRECTIONS

Present the sheet with the names to the child. Say, "I'd like you to pretend to be a teacher who must read the names of students in a class—just as I have done in our class. Do the best that you can and make a guess if you're not sure." Use a 5" × 8" card to expose one name at a time and say, "Begin with this one." Note correct responses with a plus (+) and use phonetic spellings for names that are mispronounced. Total correct responses and record the score in the box.

	First Name	**Last Name**
Jay Conway	_____	_____
Chuck Hoke	_____	_____
Kimberly Blake	_____	_____
Homer Preston	_____	_____
Cindy Sampson	_____	_____
Chester Wright	_____	_____
Stanley Shaw	_____	_____
Glen Spencer	_____	_____
Flo Thorton	_____	_____
Grace Brewster	_____	_____
Ron Smitherman	_____	_____
Vance Middleton	_____	_____
Bernard Pendergraph	_____	_____

Total Correct ☐

Based on Cunningham, P. (1990) and Duffelmeyer, F.A., Kruse, A.E., Merkley, D.J., & Fyfe, S.A. (1994).

From Jerry L. Johns, Susan Davis Lenski, and Laurie Elish-Piper, *Teaching Beginning Readers: Linking Assessment and Instruction* (2nd ed.). Copyright © 2002 by Kendall/Hunt Publishing Company (1-800-247-3458, ext. 5). May be reproduced for noncommercial educational purposes.

SCORING CHART

Scoring Chart for Decoding Assessment

Form 2

Name _____ Date _____

Name	Initial Con	Initial Con. Blends	Con. Digraphs	Short Vowels	Long Vowels/ VC-e	Vowel Digraphs	Controlled Vowels	Schwa
Jay Conway	J C			o		ay ay		
Chuck Hoke	H		Ch	u	oke			
Kimberly Blake	K	Bl		i	y ake		er	
Homer Preston	H	Pr		e	o		er	o
Cindy Sampson	C S			i a	y			o
Chester Wright			Ch	e	i		er	
Stanley Shaw		St	Sh	a		ey aw		
Glen Spencer		Gl Sp		e e			er	
Flo Thorton		Fl	Th		o		or	o
Grace Brewster		Gr Br			ace	ew	er	
Ron Smitherman	R	Sm	th	o i			er	a
Vance Middleton	V M			a i				o
Bernard Pendergraph	B P		ph	e, a			er, ar er	
Totals	12	9	6	16	8	5	10	5

Based on Cunningham, P. (1990) and Duffelmeyer, F.A., Kruse, A.E., Merkley, D.J., & Fyfe, S.A. (1994).

From Jerry L. Johns, Susan Davis Lenski, and Laurie Elish-Piper, *Teaching Beginning Readers: Linking Assessment and Instruction* (2nd ed.). Copyright © 2002 by Kendall/Hunt Publishing Company (1-800-247-3458, ext. 5). May be reproduced for noncommercial educational purposes.

CHAPTER 4

Fluency and Automaticity

OVERVIEW

As children grow in their reading ability, they are able to recognize many words at sight. A large sight vocabulary means that less time is devoted to decoding and other word-identification strategies. The result should be increased fluency in reading and the automatic recognition of more and more words. But there are times when words are not known at sight. When unknown words are encountered, children need to use a variety of cues to arrive rapidly at the pronunciation of the unknown word and to determine if it fits the context. This chapter contains strategies for helping children achieve greater fluency and automaticity as well as ways to help them begin to use context and strategies for cross-checking. Also included are assessment ideas so instruction can be especially focused in areas of need. Let's begin with some questions frequently asked by teachers.

What is fluency?

Fluency is reading that is smooth and conversational. Fluency pertains to both oral and silent reading. Basically, fluency means that the child does not have word-identification problems that would hinder the speed, accuracy, or comprehension of what is read (Harris & Hodges, 1995). It also means that the child reads with proper expression and groups words that belong together. The following sentence provides an example of what good phrasing looks like when a child reads it aloud (slashes indicate groupings): The spotted cat/ sat quietly/ under the tree.

What is automaticity?

When children process "information that requires little effort or attention," automaticity is being exhibited (Harris & Hodges, 1995, p. 16). Klenk and Kibby (2000) note that the term "fluency" is the same as automaticity. When children possess fluency, they are able to read smoothly, and they comprehend what they read. Even though we use both terms (fluency and automaticity) in this chapter, you can think of them as describing essentially the same thing.

Why is fluency important?

First, children who experience difficulty in reading, for the most part, are not fluent readers (Klenk & Kibby, 2000). Second, "it is generally acknowledged that fluency is a critical component of skilled reading" (National Reading Panel, 2000, p. 3-1). And third, fluency generally results in increased comprehension.

What conclusions about fluency can be drawn from research and expert opinion?

After reviewing numerous studies, the contributors to the Report of the National Reading Panel (2000) noted that fluency can be improved for both good readers and for readers who struggle. "Classroom practices that encourage repeated oral reading with feedback and guidance lead to meaningful improvements in reading expertise for students" (National Reading Panel, 2000, p. 3-3). This finding is supported by Klenk and Kibby (2000) who also reviewed fluency research and found that repeated reading was a common method of developing fluency, especially in the primary grades. They also found that teacher modeling of the text that children were about to read was another practice to promote fluency.

How can fluency be assessed?

Several procedures can be used to assess fluency. Informal reading inventories (e.g., Johns, 2001) permit you to time a child's reading and then calculate the number of words read per minute. Similar calculations can be done using materials from classroom instruction or by using running records (Clay, 1985). Informal fluency rubrics may also be used. Some of these methods will be described in this chapter so you will have multiple ways to assess a child's fluency if you desire to do so.

What are cueing systems and cross-checking?

Cueing systems refer to any of the sources of information (phonics, context, syntax, and background information) used to identify a word that is not recognized by sight. Children can use these cues in combination to pronounce a word and confirm that it is correct. This strategy is called cross-checking. For example, if a child is unable to pronounce "basket," he or she may use phonics to arrive at a pronunciation and then ask whether it makes sense in the sentence. The sentence is read and "basket" is checked in the context of the sentence to help decide if it makes sense. Using phonics and context in tandem is one example of cross-checking.

4.1 Sight Words

> **Goal** To help children learn words by sight.
> **Assessment Strategy 1** Basic Sight Vocabulary, page 246
> **Assessment Strategy 2** Common Nouns, page 252

BACKGROUND

There are two major ways that words are identified: automatically and through mediated strategies. The automatic method of word identification is referred to as sight words, and they are the focus of this section. (Mediated strategies refer to using phonics, structural analysis, and context. These strategies can help children identify words that are not known at sight so that the words can ultimately become sight words. Some of these strategies are introduced in Section 4.3.)

Knowledge of sight words is critical for fluent reading. When children know words by sight, the words are pronounced quickly and easily. A number of words in our language occur very frequently, and these words, called basic sight words, are important for children to learn at sight. Did you know that 13 words account for nearly 25% of the words children (and adults) encounter in their reading? The 13 words are listed below.

a   and   for   he   in   is   it   of   that   the   to   was   you

In addition to the 13 basic sight words, there are other word lists that contain basic sight words that children need to learn if their reading is to become fluent (Fry, Fountoukidis, & Polk, 2000; Johns & Lenski, 2001; Zeno, Ivens, Millard, & Duvvuri, 1995). Basic sight words are a necessary, but insufficient, basis for fluent reading. That is because basic sight words like those contained in the Revised Dolch List (Johns, 1981) comprise only 50% to 60% of the words children encounter in their reading. Many other words also need to be learned at sight. You will also need to teach words related to specific units of study and those found in particular books used for instruction.

Children need to learn to automatically read and write words by sight for two major reasons. First, by knowing words on sight, children can devote their attention to decoding less common words and focusing on the meaning of what they are reading and writing. Second, because a number of these words are not pronounced or spelled in predictable ways (Hiebert & Martin, 2001), decoding them can be difficult and confusing. Because children will often see these basic words in their reading and use them in their writing, they will benefit greatly from knowing basic words automatically.

The strategies for teaching, along with the ideas and activities presented in this section, offer a range of options for helping children learn to recognize words at sight so their reading can become more automatic and fluent. Easy-to-use strategies for assessing sight word knowledge are also provided at the end of this chapter.

Teaching Strategy 1

Section 4.1

Explicit Instruction

Explicit Instruction of sight words allows teachers to help children learn important sight words in an efficient manner. By providing focused instruction on targeted sight words, children can learn to read, spell, and write the words in a relatively short period of time. In addition, by directing children's attention to the use, spelling, and special features of sight words, you can make certain that children are aware of this important information about common sight words.

DIRECTIONS

1. Select several targeted sight words. Two lists of basic sight words are provided at the end of this strategy. The words on these lists should be learned at sight (automatically) by children. The words *take* and *make* will be exemplified in this lesson.

2. Say each word aloud and use it in a sentence.

    take   I will take my dog for a walk.

    make   My dad will make my favorite snack.

3. Encourage children to use each word in a sentence and then write the sentences on the chalkboard. Underline each target word.

    Help me take out the garbage.

    I would like to make a kite.

4. Discuss each word's use and special features. You might want to emphasize that the words rhyme, that they differ in only one letter, only the first letter in each word differs, and the *e* is "silent" (not pronounced).

5. Ask the children to spell each word aloud as you point to each letter. Be sure that each word is clearly written on the chalkboard. Children can also chant the spelling of each word as you point or a child points to each letter.

6. Invite children to spell the words in the air with their fingers as they orally recite the spelling of each word.

7. Have children write each word on paper and spell it aloud as they write.

8. Invite children to write each word on a note card and place it in their personal word banks. You can also have children hold up a card to indicate which of the words you say in a sentence. Some possible sentences appear below.

    I take out the ball for recess.

    Do you know how to make the toy?

    I must make my bed.

    Will you take me with you?

9. Make copies of the words so they can be placed on the Word Wall. Use a similar procedure as additional words are introduced.

Revised Dolch List

a*	could	he*	might	same	told
about*	cut	heard	more	saw	too
across	did	help	most	say	took
after	didn't	her*	much	see	toward
again	do	here	must	she*	try
all*	does	high	my	short	turn
always	done	him	near	should	two
am	don't	his*	need	show	under
an*	down	hold	never	six	up*
and*	draw	hot	next	small	upon
another	eat	how	new	so*	us
any	enough	I*	no	some*	use
are*	even	I'm	not*	soon	very
around	every	if*	now	start	walk
as*	far	in*	of*	still	want
ask	fast	into	off	stop	warm
at*	find	is*	oh	take	was*
away	first	it*	old	tell	we*
be*	five	its	on*	ten	well
because	for*	just	once	than	went
been	found	keep	one*	that*	were*
before	four	kind	only	the*	what*
began	from*	know	open	their*	when*
best	full	last	or*	them	where
better	gave	leave	other	then	which
big	get	left	our	there*	while
black	give	let	out*	these	white
blue	go	light	over	they*	who
both	going	like	own	think	why
bring	gone	little	play	this*	will
but*	good	long	put	those	with*
by*	got	look	ran	thought	work
call	green	made	read	three	would*
came	grow	make	red	through	yes
can*	had*	many	right	to*	yet
close	hard	may	round	today	you*
cold	has	me	run	together	your
come	have*	mean	said*		

*one of the 50 most common words.

The rationale and research for this list is described in Johns, J.L. (1981). The development of the revised Dolch list. *Illinois School Research and Development, 17,* 15–24. From Jerry L. Johns, Susan Davis Lenski, and Laurie Elish-Piper, *Teaching Beginning Readers: Linking Assessment and Instruction* (2nd ed.). Copyright © 2002 by Kendall/Hunt Publishing Company (1-800-247-3458, ext. 5). May be reproduced for noncommercial educational purposes.

High-Frequency Nouns

air	girl	nothing
back	group	people
book	hand	place
boy	head	road
car	home	room
children	house	school
city	man	side
day	men	table
dog	money	thing
door	morning	time
eye	mother	top
face	Mr.	town
father	Mrs.	tree
feet	name	water
friend	night	way
		year

The rationale and research for this list is described in Johns, J.L. (1981). The development of the revised Dolch list. *Illinois School Research and Development, 17,* 15–24. From Jerry L. Johns, Susan Davis Lenski, and Laurie Elish-Piper, *Teaching Beginning Readers: Linking Assessment and Instruction* (2nd ed.). Copyright © 2002 by Kendall/Hunt Publishing Company (1-800-247-3458, ext. 5). May be reproduced for noncommercial educational purposes.

Teaching Strategy 2

Section 4.1

Pattern Books

Pattern Books provide a meaningful way to teach children sight words in the context of real text. By your connecting sight word instruction and children's literature, children are able to see the words in the story, understand how they are used, and practice identifying the words in a meaningful context. The following strategy can be used with any pattern book, and it serves as an excellent introduction to teaching sight words to young children (May, 1998).

DIRECTIONS

1. Prior to beginning the lesson, select a pattern book that emphasizes the targeted sight word(s). For very young children, you will want to select one word for study. For older children, three to five different words can be targeted.
2. Prepare teacher-made charts that contain the text, but not pictures, from the book.
3. Write target word(s) on chart paper. Prepare sight word cards.
4. To teach the lesson, read the book aloud to the children. Read the book again, inviting the children to chime in when they can predict what comes next.
5. Invite the children to take turns with echo reading. For echo reading, the teacher reads a line or phrase, and then the children echo it back.
6. Provide opportunities for the children to engage in choral reading of the story. For choral reading, have a group of children read a section of text in unison. You can provide support by reading along with the children and then fading your voice at the points in the text when they are able to take on more of the reading responsibility. Use a pointer to point to each word during choral reading to help children track the words as they read them.
7. Next, have children read the text from teacher-made charts that do not contain pictures.
8. Invite children to engage in echo and choral readings of the text as described above in steps 5 and 6.
9. Next, show children the targeted sight word(s) on index cards and read them with the children.
10. Ask children to place matching word cards on the charts. Have children say each word as they match their cards with the words on the chart paper. This can be done by taping the word cards to the chart paper, using a pocket chart, or using magnets on a magnetic chalkboard.
11. After children place their word cards on the chart paper, read the entire text chorally with the children.
12. Next, place the word cards in random order and invite children to match the cards to the text on the chart paper. Have children say the words as they match them to the text.
13. Discuss the new words the children learned during the activity.
14. Have the children add the sight words to their word banks or personal Word Walls. You can also post the targeted word(s) on the classroom Word Wall.

Teaching Strategy 3

Section 4.1

Associative Learning

Associative Learning for high frequency words is a strategy designed for use with children who have difficulty learning high frequency words because the words lack meaning clues for the children. The associative learning technique helps children develop concrete associations for abstract high frequency words such as *for, of,* and *the* (Cunningham, 2000).

DIRECTIONS

1. Select one or two targeted basic sight words for this strategy, for example, *of*. Present the word by using it in a phrase accompanied by an illustration. The word should be underlined as shown in the example below.

a bowl <u>of</u> apples

2. Have children brainstorm other possible ways to use *of* in a phrase or sentence. After several oral examples have been shared, distribute index cards and invite children to make their own picture cards and label them. Ask children to write the targeted sight word using a red crayon or marker. Have children underline their word. Be ready to assist children with the spelling of the other words that are part of their phrase. Some sample cards are shown below.

a glass <u>of</u> juice    two <u>of</u> my friends

3. Provide time for children to share their picture cards with other children. The phrase cards can become part of children's word banks.

Tips for English Language Learners

- The basic sight words are abstract and difficult for many children to learn. Use plenty of oral language activities with the basic sight words. Children will use basic sight words when they speak, even if the utterance is incomplete. Use children's language to create phrase cards and illustrations to help children expand their reading vocabularies.

José <u>and</u> Mike   Cal <u>runs</u>.   Chandy <u>is</u> small.

- Label objects in the classroom using basic sight words and a noun. For example, the door to the classroom can be labeled "the brown door." Use a similar approach with other objects: a big clock, the white wall, our library, the teacher's desk, our reading corner, and so on. Link these phrases to ongoing lessons when appropriate.

Teaching Strategy 4

Section 4.1

Word Wall

The Word Wall strategy is helpful for teaching high frequency words. The words are taught to children, and then they are posted on the Word Wall for future reference. A variety of hands-on activities are also incorporated into Word Wall instruction to help children learn and remember the high frequency words (Cunningham, 2000). Typically, teachers will spend a few minutes each day teaching and reviewing new Word Wall words over the course of a week. The following directions provide suggestions for teaching Word Wall words over a period of several days.

DIRECTIONS

1. Select up to five target high frequency words to teach in a week. Word lists containing basic sight words, the children's spelling errors, and grade-level curricula are sources for words for the Word Wall.
2. Introduce each word to students by writing it on an index card and using the word in a sentence. Write the sentence on the chalkboard and underline the Word Wall word.
3. Ask children to suggest other sentences that use the Word Wall word. Discuss the meaning or use of the word.
4. Point to each letter of the word as you spell it aloud. Invite children to spell the word with you as you point to each letter.
5. Trace around the configuration of the word using another color of chalk. Discuss the shape of the word.

Fluency and Automaticity   215

6. Follow this pattern for each of the new Word Wall words. Place the index cards for the five new words on the Word Wall. Arrange the words alphabetically and use a different color of index card or ink for each new word.

7. Engage children in the Clap, Chant, and Write activity. Ask children to number a piece of scratch paper from one to five. Say each word, using it in a sentence. Ask children to write each word on their paper. Then have children clap and chant the spelling of each word as you lead the process. Ask children to correct their own spellings.

8. On another day, select five words appropriate for rhyming. Ask children to review rhymes using the Word Wall. Have children number a sheet of scratch paper from one to five. Ask them to write a Word Wall word that rhymes with the word you give to them. Give children the rhyming word and the first letter as clues. For example, you might say the word begins with *m* and rhymes with *by*. Continue this pattern for all five Word Wall words.

9. Guide children to check their own words. Ask them to say the word they wrote and to spell it aloud when you call each number and restate the clues. For example, after you say, "Number 1. The word begins with /m/ and rhymes with *by*," children should respond, "My, m-y." Continue with this pattern until all five words have been checked. Ask children to correct their work as you go through this step.

10. On another day, engage children in a cross-checking activity with the Word Wall words. Tell the children that they will need to select the Word Wall word that makes sense in a sentence and begins with a certain letter. For example, tell the children, "The word begins with *t* and fits in the sentence I went to _____ store yesterday." Continue with this pattern with all five Word Wall words.

11. Have children check their own words by reading each sentence again and restating the beginning letter of the word. Ask children to chant the word and then the spelling for each of the five Word Wall words.

12. Remind children that the Word Wall is an important resource to help them with their reading, writing, and spelling. For additional Word Wall activities, consult Cunningham (2000).

Ideas and Activities

1. Tell children that they will learn sight words best if they practice them in many different ways. Use the See, Write, Point, Say, and Spell cycle to help children practice new sight words. Guide the children through the following steps.
   - See the word in your head. Visualize what it looks like.
   - Write the word on paper; write it again using different colors; write it in different sizes; write it in the air with your finger; and write it on a friend's back using your pointing finger.
   - Point to the word and say it. Point to the word and spell it aloud, then silently.

2. Help children create personal Word Walls using file folders. Draw a grid on the file folder and label each section with a letter of the alphabet. Have children add high frequency words to their personal Word Walls. Children can use these resources at their desks or at home as they read and write (Cunningham, 2000).

3. Wordo is a variation of Bingo that focuses on practicing high frequency words (see Revised Dolch List on page 211). For young children, divide the Wordo card into 9 blocks, and for older children use 25 blocks. You will also need to supply plastic counters, beans, or other small objects to be used to cover words as the children fill in their blocks. Make a list of high frequency words to practice, write each word on an index card, and call out the words one at a time. Have the children chant the spelling of each word and cover it with a counter. The first child to cover an entire row of words is the winner of the game. Ask the winner to read the words aloud to check that the words have been called. The winner can then serve as the caller. Continue the game for several rounds to provide additional practice with the high frequency words. A sample Wordo card is shown on the next page.

Wordo

and	for	in
that	it	you
was	to	is

4. Select a children's book, poem, or chart story that contains a sight word you have been teaching. Using small sticky notes or removable correction tape, cover the sight word in the text. Present the book, poem, or story to the children. When you reach the covered word, ask the children what would make sense in the blank. Reveal the first letter of the covered word. Ask the children which of their guesses will still work. Continue this pattern until all letters of the word are revealed.

5. Play word games and puzzles such as hang-man, concentration, and go fish to provide opportunities for children to practice sight words.

6. Use the Language Experience Approach (LEA) to teach sight words in children's spoken vocabulary. The LEA is discussed in detail in Section 2.1, Teaching Strategy 2 (pages 54–55). Draw children's attention to specific sight words in the text they dictated. Have children read the sight words, spell them, and discuss the words' meanings or functions in that context.

7. Trace words in salt trays, sand trays, or shaving cream to help children get multiple opportunities to write, see, and remember sight words.

8. Wide reading of easy texts supports sight word development because children have many opportunities to see sight words used in meaningful contexts. Provide daily time for children to read from self-selected materials.

9. Make sight words in clay or play dough to allow students to feel the words and letters as they shape the clay or play dough. Ask children to point to each letter as they chant the spellings aloud. Pretzel dough or cookie dough can also be used so children can eat their baked sight words when the activity is over.

10. Go on a sight words hunt in the classroom or school. Ask children to identify target sight words as you tour the classroom or school. Discuss how the words are used and spelled. Discuss the importance of children knowing sight words in their daily lives.

11. Play the grab bag game with children to reinforce sight word knowledge. Write sight words on cards and place them in a bag. Have the children take turns selecting a card, reading it aloud, chanting the spelling, and using the word in a sentence. If the child is correct, he or she gets to keep the card. The winner has the most cards.

12. Scrambled words provide children with an opportunity to manipulate letter cards to spell high frequency words. Write words to be practiced on different colors of construction paper or index cards. Use one word per color. For each word, have the children arrange the letters in proper order, chant the spelling, read the word, and use it in a sentence.

13. Make phrase cards using common nouns and the words from the Revised Dolch List (page 211). Have children practice the phrases with a partner. A sample phrase card is shown below.

near the tree

Home School Connections

Sight Words

📖 Play scavenger hunt with your child by looking for a specific sight word in the newspaper, in "junk" mail, or as you and your child do errands in the community.

📖 Help your child master the 20 most frequently used words in the English language:

> the, of, and, to, a, in, is, that, it, was, for, you, he, on, as, are, they, with, be, his.

Six ideas are given below.

1. You can print the words on cards. Begin by showing each card to your child to see if the word is known. For words that are unknown, have your child look at the word while you say it and use it in a sentence.

2. Encourage your child to use the word in a phrase or sentence. Then you and your child can spell the word together out loud.

3. Have your child write the word on paper.

4. Many different experiences with these words will help your child learn them. As you read to your child, make the connection that some of the words in the book are the same as those on the cards. You can show your child the word on the card and connect it to the word on the page. Have your child also make these connections by showing you the words on the cards that match the words on a page of a book.

5. You can use these 20 words with a few other words to write phrases and sentences for your child to read. Be sure to use your child's name in the phrases and sentences.

6. Carry the cards with you so you can practice the words with your child when you have a minute or two. Practice over time will help your child master these very basic words.

From Jerry L. Johns, Susan Davis Lenski, and Laurie Elish-Piper, *Teaching Beginning Readers: Linking Assessment and Instruction* (2nd ed.). Copyright © 2002 by Kendall/Hunt Publishing Company (1-800-247-3458, ext. 5). May be reproduced for noncommercial educational purposes.

the	of
and	to
a	in
is	that
it	was

From Jerry L. Johns, Susan Davis Lenski, and Laurie Elish-Piper, *Teaching Beginning Readers: Linking Assessment and Instruction* (2nd ed.). Copyright © 2002 by Kendall/Hunt Publishing Company (1-800-247-3458, ext. 5). May be reproduced for noncommercial educational purposes.

for	you
he	on
as	are
they	with
be	his

From Jerry L. Johns, Susan Davis Lenski, and Laurie Elish-Piper, *Teaching Beginning Readers: Linking Assessment and Instruction* (2nd ed.). Copyright © 2002 by Kendall/Hunt Publishing Company (1-800-247-3458, ext. 5). May be reproduced for noncommercial educational purposes.

Selected Resources
SIGHT WORDS

Books for Teaching Sight Words

Baker, K. (1990). *Who is this beast?* New York: Harcourt Brace.

Cameron, A. (1994). *The cat sat on the mat.* Boston: Houghton Mifflin.

Christelow, E. (1989). *Five little monkeys jumping on the bed.* New York: Trumpet.

Dobeck, J. (1996). *Stop that!* Parsippany, NJ: Modern Curriculum Press.

Grejniec, M. (1992). *What do you like?* New York: North-South Books.

Hill, E. (1980). *Where's Spot?* New York: Putnam.

Hoberman, M.A. (1982). *A house is a house for me.* New York: Penguin.

Little Books for Early Readers (1999). Cambridge, MA: Educators Publishing Service.

Shapiro, A. (1991). *Who says that?* New York: Dutton.

Starters One and Two (2000). Crystal Lake, IL: Rigby.

Tolstoi, A. (1968). *The great big enormous turnip.* New York: Watts.

Media and Technology

Early Learning Center CD-ROM (interactive programs that teach word skills and sight words). UPDATA (800-882-2844)

Word Tales CD-ROM (word games with sound effects and music). UPDATA (800-882-2844)

Decoding Activities (detailed explanations of the activities teachers can do to help children learn to decode words). http://www.wfu.edu/~cunningh/fourblocks/blocks.html

Professional Resources

Cunningham, P.M. (2000). *Phonics they use: Words for reading and writing* (3rd ed.). New York: Longman.

Eldridge, J.L. (1995). *Teaching decoding in holistic classrooms.* Englewood Cliffs, NJ: Prentice Hall.

Fry, E.B., Fountoukidis, D.L., & Polk, J.K. (2000). *The reading teachers' book of lists* (4th ed.). Upper Saddle River, NJ: Merrill/Prentice Hall.

Holley, C. (1997). *Warming up to big books.* Bothell, WA: The Wright Group.

Johnson, P. (2000). *Making books.* Portland, ME: Stenhouse.

Mannix, D. (1996). *100 everyday words to read, write, and understand.* Austin, TX: PRO-ED.

From Jerry L. Johns, Susan Davis Lenski, and Laurie Elish-Piper, *Teaching Beginning Readers: Linking Assessment and Instruction* (2nd ed.). Copyright © 2002 by Kendall/Hunt Publishing Company (1-800-247-3458, ext. 5). May be reproduced for noncommercial educational purposes.

4.2 Fluency

> **Goal** To help children read smoothly and easily.
> **Assessment Strategy 3** Words Per Minute, page 258
> **Assessment Strategy 4** Fluency Scale Checklist, page 262

BACKGROUND

Good readers are fluent readers. "They read words accurately, rapidly, and efficiently" (National Reading Panel, 2000, p. 3-3). When you listen to children read orally, you can spot the fluent readers. Fluent readers are able to read text in a normal speaking voice with appropriate intonation and inflection. Fluent readers are able to read texts smoothly and easily using various strategies to construct meaning from print (Duffy & Roehler, 1989). They use their knowledge of word decoding, their knowledge of stories, and their knowledge of the world to understand the meaning of new texts. A goal of reading instruction in the primary grades is for students to read fluently with good comprehension.

Many times young children are not fluent readers. Think about the children you teach. Some children may be choppy readers, reading with many stops, starts, and hesitations. They may be monotonous readers who read with little or no expression. Or children may be hasty readers and race through the passage ignoring phrasing and punctuation. When children are choppy, monotonous, or hasty readers, they are not reading fluently (Wilson, 1988).

Primary-grade children need to learn how to read fluently while they are learning other reading skills. But you need to remember that developing fluency takes time and practice. While children are building fluency, they are also expanding their sight vocabulary, learning word-identification strategies, and learning how to use their background knowledge to construct meaning from new texts. As children become proficient with these reading strategies, they are able to read the words in a passage more automatically. As children read words more automatically, they can pay closer attention to reading texts smoothly and easily.

Teaching children how to read fluently also enables them to read with better comprehension. When children learn how to read in a way that mirrors spoken language, as fluent readers do, they are better able to understand the meaning of texts (Rasinski, 1989). It is important, therefore, to teach children how to read fluently as they are learning how to read. The following strategies, ideas, and activities support the teaching of fluent reading. In addition, two strategies for assessing fluency are provided at the end of this chapter.

Teaching Strategy 1

Section 4.2

Teacher~Assisted Reading (Neurological Impress Method)

For children to learn how to read fluently, they need to hear and practice fluent reading. Sometimes beginning readers can identify fluent reading, but they are unable to produce it. To help students learn how to read fluently, you can use Teacher-Assisted Reading, or the Neurological Impress Method (Heckleman, 1966).

The Neurological Impress Method is a technique in which the teacher and child simultaneously read aloud from the same book. The teacher reads slightly faster than the child in order to keep the child reading at a fluent pace. The child hears the reading and tries to read with the same pace and expression. The Neurological Impress Method is a useful strategy when you are helping one child or a small group of children improve fluency.

DIRECTIONS

1. Identify an interesting short book or passage that is below the child's reading level. You might identify several books and ask the child to choose one for the lesson.

2. Have the child sit slightly in front of you so that your voice is close to the child's ear.

3. Tell the child to follow your voice during the reading.

4. Read the material out loud with the child, but a little louder and faster than the child. Read only a short passage.

5. Run your finger under the words being read.

6. Reread the same passage several times. Drop your voice behind the child's as the child begins to read fluently. Place the child's hand on your hand so that both of you can use your fingers to follow the lines of print.

7. As the child reads, do not correct any miscues. Your goal is to help the child build fluency. You should mentally note miscues so you can work on needed word-identification strategies at another time.

8. Have the child read alone while the child follows the print with a finger. Support the child's reading as needed by saying the words aloud.

9. Read the passage with the child once more, speeding up the pace. Encourage the child to read fluently at a faster pace.

10. Use this strategy several times each week. Plan on guiding reading fluency for several months. Fluency needs to be developed over a long period of time.

Teaching Strategy 2

Section 4.2

Structured Repeated Readings

Structured Repeated Readings (Samuels, 1979) is a motivational strategy that engages children in repeated readings of text. A Reading Progress Chart helps monitor the child's growth in fluency, which results, in part, from the automatic recognition of words and the reduction of miscues. We have found this strategy to be especially effective with children who struggle in reading.

DIRECTIONS

1. Select a brief passage or story of 50 to 200 words for the child to read aloud. For beginning readers, or readers who struggle, a passage of approximately 50 words is sufficient for the first time the strategy is used. The passage should be at an appropriate level of difficulty. That means that the child should generally recognize more than 91% of the words. If the passage contains 50 words, the child should generally recognize about 46 of the words. If the child misses more than 6 words in a 50-word passage, it is probably not suitable for repeated reading.

2. Ask the child to read the passage orally. Using a copy of the passage (optional), note the child's miscues and keep track of the time (in seconds) it took the child to read the passage.

3. Ask the child to tell you something about the passage or ask a question or two. Be sure that the child is not just calling words.

4. Record the time in seconds and the number of miscues on a chart like that provided on page 226. In the example below, the child read a 45-word passage in 58 seconds and made 4 miscues. To convert seconds into rate in words per minute (WPM), multiply the number of words in the passage by 60 and then divide by the time (in seconds) it took the child to read the passage. As noted in the example below, the rate is approximately 46 words per minute (WPM).

$$
\begin{array}{r}
46 \text{ wpm} \\
58 \overline{\smash{)}2700} \\
\underline{232} \\
380 \\
\underline{348}
\end{array}
$$

5. Encourage the child to practice rereading the passage independently for a day or two. The reading can be done both orally and silently. It can also be done at home. The idea is to have the child practice the passage several times before you next meet with the child to repeat the process described in step 2.

6. Repeat the process of having the child read the passage to you. Record the time in seconds and the number of miscues on the chart under reading 2. Continue this general procedure over a period of time until a suitable rate is achieved. You can use your professional judgment to determine a suitable rate or refer to the norms for oral-reading rates provided on page 259. The chart below shows the 5 readings for a second-grade child over a 10-day period. The initial rate of 46 WPM was increased to approximately 87 WPM by the fifth reading. According to the norms provided for second graders in the spring of the year (p. 259), this child's rate is slightly below average. Use the information in the two charts on page 259 to help determine target reading rates.

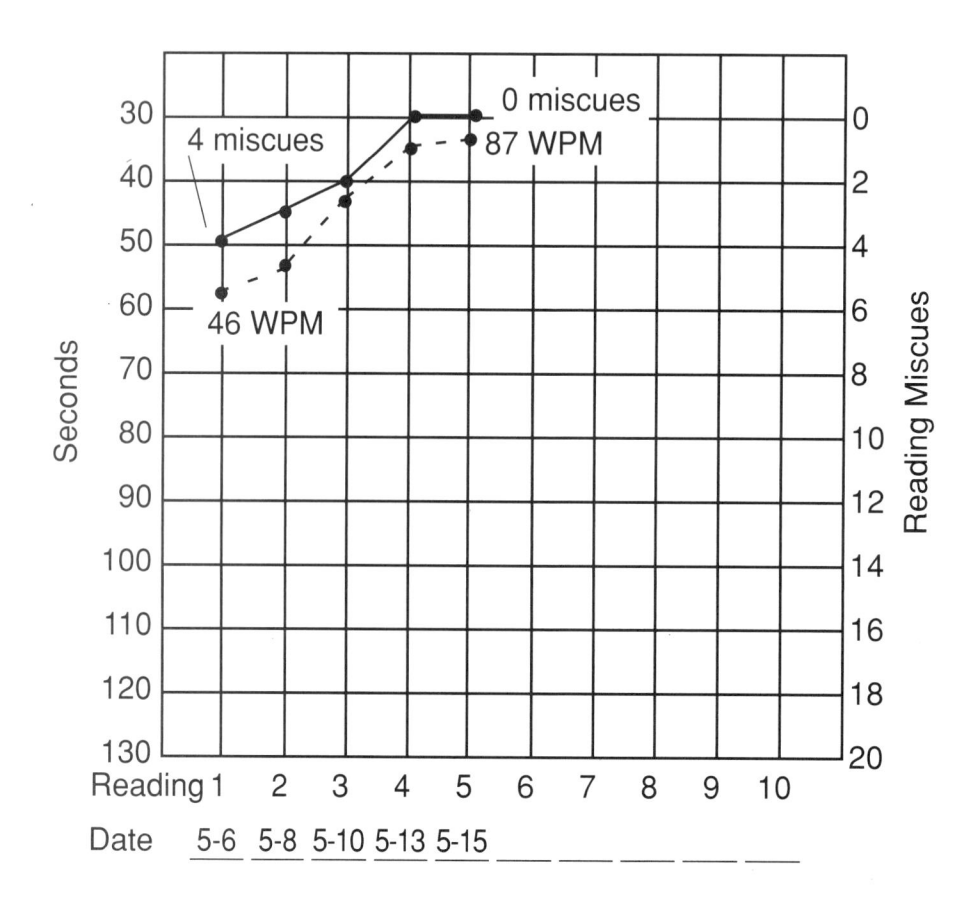

7. Repeat the strategy with a new selection. As you use the Reading Progress Chart on page 226, note that space is provided to record the date and to chart up to 10 readings. You should base the actual number of readings on the child's progress in fluency. Some children will achieve a satisfactory level of fluency after a few readings; other children may need six or seven readings. Be flexible and responsive to individual differences. The Reading Progress Chart was designed to show visible evidence of gains. Children are reinforced with the charts and are motivated to improve their rate and accuracy. The charts can be a meaningful way to gather evidence of fluency development over time with a variety of passages. As a chart is completed for a passage, it can be placed in the child's work folder or portfolio.

Reading Progress Chart for _____

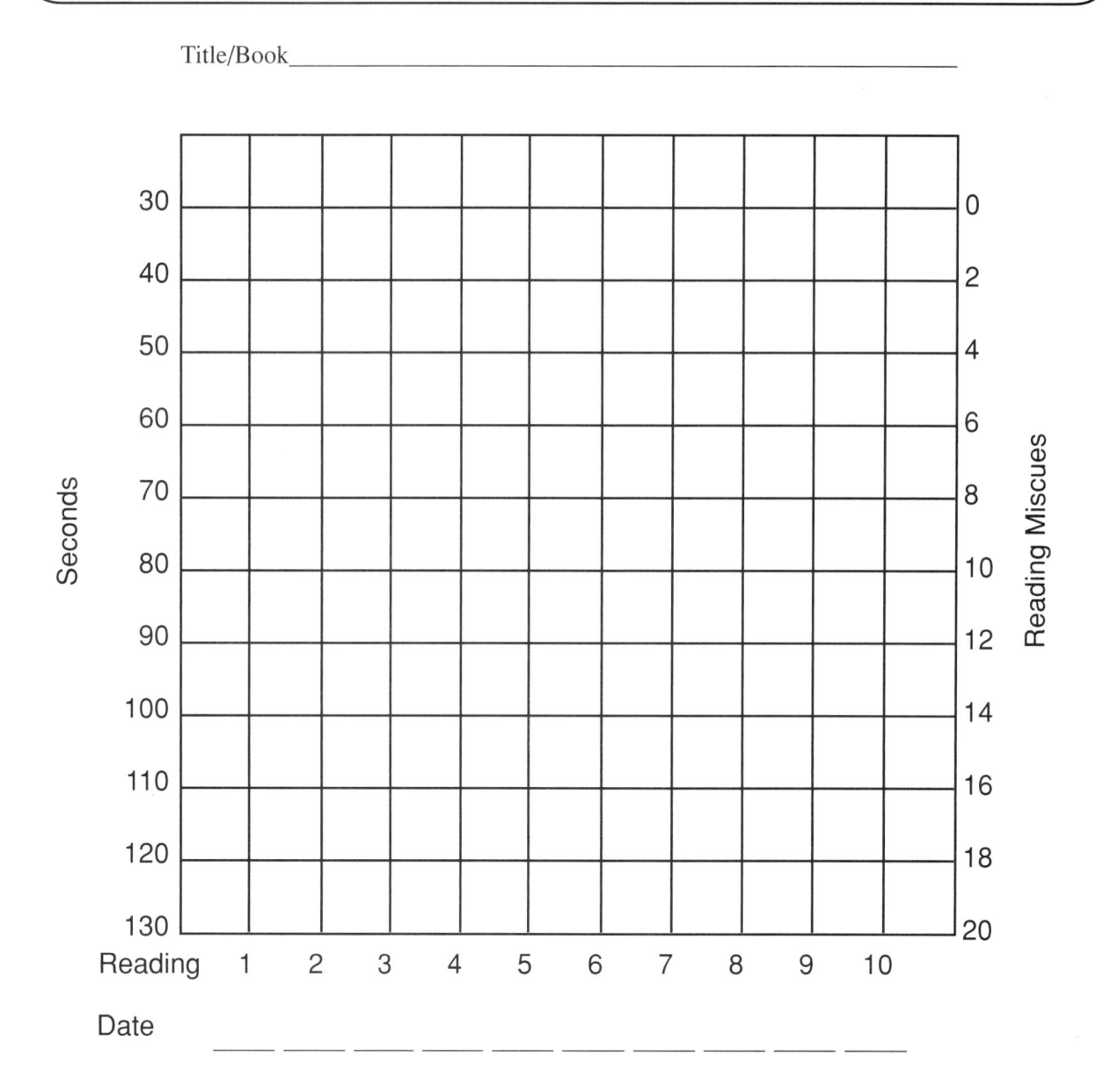

Title/Book_____

Seconds		Reading Miscues
30		0
40		2
50		4
60		6
70		8
80		10
90		12
100		14
110		16
120		18
130		20

Reading   1   2   3   4   5   6   7   8   9   10

Date ___ ___ ___ ___ ___ ___ ___ ___ ___ ___

From Jerry L. Johns, Susan Davis Lenski, and Laurie Elish-Piper, *Teaching Beginning Readers: Linking Assessment and Instruction* (2nd ed.). Copyright © 2002 by Kendall/Hunt Publishing Company (1-800-247-3458, ext. 5). May be reproduced for noncommercial educational purposes.

Teaching Strategy 3

Section 4.2

Choral Reading

Choral reading occurs when children read poetry or other short passages together or in groups. Choral reading facilitates fluency because children are able to read print along with other children. When reading in groups, children who have trouble reading fluently are carried along with the pace and expression of the other readers. All of the readers are able to read more smoothly and easily because they are able to listen to more proficient readers as they match speech and print in a smooth, steady reading pace.

DIRECTIONS

1. Identify a poem, a short book, or a passage that would be of interest to the children who will be choral reading.
2. Note words that may be new to the children or that the children may have difficulty reading. Write the words on the chalkboard or on chart paper. Read the difficult words to the class, paying special attention to sounds or patterns in the words that the children have learned.
3. Have the entire group read the passage silently.
4. Read the passage aloud or ask one of the children to read it aloud. As you read, track the print with a pointer or your hand.
5. Discuss the passage, asking children to retell the poem or story.
6. Decide on the method of choral reading. The following varieties of choral reading have been suggested by Trousdale and Harris (1993).
   - Two-part arrangement. One group of voices reads alternately with another group.
   - Soloist and chorus. One voice reads and the rest of the group joins in on the refrain.
   - Line-a-child. One child or a pair read alone. Then the next child reads the next line, and so on.
   - Increasing or decreasing volume. Voices are added or subtracted, building up to and moving away from the high point of the story.
   - Increasing or decreasing tempo. The rate of reading is increased or decreased as the passage is read.
   - Unison. The whole group reads as one.
   - Accompaniment by music, movement, or sound effects. The reading is accompanied by instruments, hand motions, or sound effects such as snapping fingers.
   - Combination. A combination of any of the above ideas.
7. Experiment with volume, tempo, and expression. Have fun.
8. Perform the choral reading for an audience. Have a leader read the title and give the first beat so the group begins together. Tape-record or videotape the performance and replay it, listening for fluent reading.

> **Teaching Strategy 4**

Section 4.2

Radio Reading

Radio Reading (Greene, 1979) helps children focus on communicating a message so it can be understood by listeners. There may be some miscues in the reading, but listeners respond to the reading by discussing it, restating the basic message, and evaluating how the message was delivered.

DIRECTIONS

1. Bring a radio to class and have children listen to it for a few minutes. You should preview a station to identify content that would be appropriate for your class. Before asking children to listen, tell them that they will discuss the message after listening.

2. After listening to the radio for a minute or two, turn it off and invite children to share what was heard. Focus on the message and clarity of what was said.

3. Relate the children's listening to the radio to the strategy called Radio Reading. Tell children that they will have an opportunity to listen to classmates read a brief selection. The material selected for reading should be a paragraph or two at an appropriate level of difficulty (e.g., at the child's instructional level where approximately 95% of the words are known). The goal is to communicate meaning.

4. Select an appropriate passage for a child to read. Stress that the goal is to communicate the meaning of the passage to the other children in the classroom. If a word is unknown during the reading, the child should merely point to the word and ask, "What is that word?" You immediately tell the child the word so the reading can proceed with limited interruption. The other children serve as listeners, and they do not have a copy of the passage.

5. After the passage is read, invite the children who were the listeners to discuss the message that was conveyed. The intent of this discussion is to confirm that an accurate message was sent and received. The reader is responsible for clearing up any confusion by the listeners by rereading selected portions of the passage. In some cases, misread words may cause confusion. In such cases, the listeners must raise questions about the clarity of the content presented. Remember that the basic goal in Radio Reading is to present a message clearly; moreover, it is the goal of the listeners to evaluate the clarity of the message and to help resolve any misunderstandings.

> **Teaching Strategy 5**

Section 4.2

Multipaired Simultaneous Oral Reading

At least once a week most primary-grade children will need to practice reading fluently. Some children are naturally fluent readers, but most are not. Most children need guidance and practice in order to read smoothly and easily. Because almost all of the children you teach will need practice reading fluently, all of the children can practice at once with Multipaired Simultaneous Oral Reading (Poe, 1986). During Multipaired Simultaneous Oral Reading, the group is divided into pairs. Each child takes turns reading to a partner. After one child reads, the partners switch roles so that all children practice reading fluently.

DIRECTIONS

1. Identify a passage of a story that would lend itself to building fluency. For older readers, select a passage from a chapter book that has dialogue in it. Write the page number of the passage on the chalkboard or on an overhead transparency.

2. Tell children that they will be reading the passage to a partner. Explain that the goal of their reading will be to read fluently with a steady pace and good expression.

3. Model reading the passage with fluency. Read the passage expressively at a pace that moves quickly.

4. Ask children to read the passage with you. If there are any challenging sections containing dialect or difficult words, help the children say the difficult words.

5. Have children choose a partner for reading or choose partners for the children. Each time you use this strategy, have children choose different partners so that no one becomes dependent on another reader. At times, have children of the same reading ability work together. At other times, pair children of differing abilities. If a pair does not work well together, ask the children to change partners.

6. Let the pairs of children set their own rules about how much each child will read—one page, one paragraph, two paragraphs, and so on—before switching to the second reader.

7. Have children read the selection aloud. Monitor the activity and provide guidance as needed.

8. When a pair finishes reading, give each child a silent activity to complete.

9. After everyone has completed the paired oral reading, discuss the children's success at reading fluently. Occasionally, have one or more than one child volunteer to read a passage to the class. Congratulate all children on learning to read more smoothly.

Tips for English Language Learners

- Prepare backpacks with a tape recorder, storybook, and audiotape of the storybook. Include a letter explaining how to use the materials in the home language of the parents. Allow the children to use the backpack at home for three to five days. Take time to teach the children how to use the tape recorder and consider color-coding the *stop, play,* and *rewind* buttons on the tape recorder. The child and parent can be encouraged to follow along in the storybook as the audiotape is played. Financial assistance to help support projects of this type may be available from school, business, community, and professional organizations. A parent may also be recruited to assist with various aspects of the backpack project.

- Encourage children to take home attractive books that they can read independently to their parents. If possible, secure books that are written in the home language as well as English. Enclose a piece of paper that parents can sign indicating that they listened to their children read. Children can also be encouraged to talk about the pictures and illustrations with their parents.

Ideas and Activities

1. Recognize that reading is a developmental process and that fluency will develop as children increase their sight vocabularies and acquire a repertoire of word-identification strategies. Children in the primary grades generally will increase fluency as they gain more experience reading.

2. Encourage the repeated readings of pattern books. Pattern books are books that have repetitive phrases like "Brown Bear, Brown Bear, what do you see?" When children read books with repetition, they quickly become familiar with the repeated phrases, making the book easier to read with fluency. See Selected Resources: Fluency (page 233) for a short list of pattern books or Appendix C in Johns and Lenski (2001) for a longer list.

3. Model good reading fluency by reading aloud to children. Occasionally point out that when you read books to the class, you are reading in a way that is similar to the spoken language children hear. Tell children that good readers try to read so that reading sounds like talking.

4. Encourage frequent reading of easy books where children recognize about 98% of the words. Children have more trouble reading fluently when they are trying to read books that are difficult for them. If a book is difficult, children have to devote attention to word identification and can't put as much effort into fluent reading. Try to have children read easy books several times each week.

5. Use flashlight reading of Big Books (Rennick & Williams, 1995). Place a Big Book on a chalkboard ledge or a tray. Tell children that you will be shining a flashlight on the words and that the children should read along with the flashlight. Move the flashlight along the sentences at a smooth, steady pace. Invite children to read the words as the flashlight shines on them.

6. Use echo reading with the class or with small groups of children. In echo reading, you read a phrase or sentence from a Big Book and the children repeat it after you. When you read, model appropriate reading pace and expression. As children repeat the phrase or sentence, they should try to "echo" your phrasing and intonation.

7. Provide opportunities for children to listen to talking books on audiotapes or to use computer programs with sound. Capitalize on children's interests when a particularly popular book is played repeatedly by allowing children to listen and read their favorite books again and again.

8. Use daily dictated stories for fluency practice. Have children dictate one or more sentences that you write on the chalkboard or on chart paper. Read the sentences to the class with expression and good phrasing. Then have the class read along with you. Tell children that you want them to read with expression.

9. Make a videotape or audiotape of yourself reading an easy book. Send the book and the tape home with the children to practice reading outside of school. You could also ask other adults who are familiar to children to participate in videotape or audiotape reading. A school principal, a head teacher, a librarian, a crossing guard, a bus driver, and a lunchroom worker are all adults that children see on a regular basis and would be good role models for reading. You may have to supervise the reading of other adults so that their reading is a good example for the children, but having a variety of reading models is worth the extra time.

10. Develop a reading pals program with older children: students in intermediate grades, middle schools, high schools, or colleges. Suggest books for the reading pals to read with your children. Ask the pals to practice reading the books several times and to aim for fluent, conversational reading. Have the reading pals read the books to your children; then have the children read along with their reading pals.

11. List common phrases on sentence strips and place them in a pocket chart. Some examples of common phrases for children in day care or schools are "in the lunchroom," "on the playground," and "to the bus." Have children practice these phrases that encourage the use of smooth, fluent reading.

12. Identify songs and poems that children enjoy. Print the songs or poems on the chalkboard or on chart paper. Read or sing them with the children. Repeat the process several times a day. Encourage children to practice independently so they can read the words fluently.

13. Have children read fluently by performing Readers' Theater scripts. Readers' Theater scripts are similar to play scripts except they do not have stage directions. Children read the lines while sitting or standing rather than acting. When asking children to perform a Readers' Theater script, assign lines; then have children read their lines several times. Children should practice their lines aloud several times. After children have practiced their lines, they can read the script for an audience.

14. Provide children with many opportunities to read to an audience. Have children identify favorite passages of books, practice them, and read them to the class. Use a small microphone to encourage fluent reading. Inexpensive microphones can be purchased at many toy stores.

Home School Connections

Reading Out Loud

📖 Encourage your child to read and reread books to you. Read along with your child at a pace that helps the child maintain reading that is reasonably smooth. Feel free to repeat sentences to help your child develop greater fluency and confidence. If the story has people or animals talking, make the dialog come alive by using different voices. Always take time to listen to your child's reading—even if your child wants to read the book again and again. Take advantage of your child's interest in rereading.

📖 Provide a good model of oral reading by reading to your child. Ask your child's teacher or a librarian for appropriate books. Reread books when asked and praise your child's efforts to read along. Enjoy the experience with your child each and every time the book is read.

From Jerry L. Johns, Susan Davis Lenski, and Laurie Elish-Piper, *Teaching Beginning Readers: Linking Assessment and Instruction* (2nd ed.). Copyright © 2002 by Kendall/Hunt Publishing Company (1-800-247-3458, ext. 5). May be reproduced for noncommercial educational purposes.

Selected Resources

FLUENCY

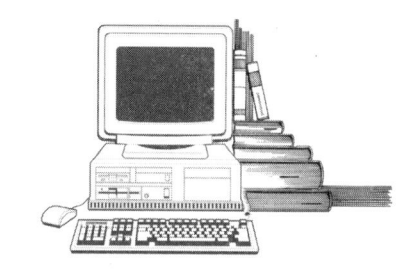

Pattern Books and Poetry

Barton, B., & Booth, D. (1995). *Mother Goose goes to school.* Portland, ME: Stenhouse.

Carle, E. (1985). *The very busy spider.* New York: Philomel.

Cowley, J. (1987). *Mrs. Wishy-Washy.* Bothell, WA: The Wright Group.

Galdone, P. (1973). *The little red hen.* New York: Scholastic.

Mandel, P. (1994). *Red cat, white cat.* New York: Henry Holt.

Martin, B. (1990). *Polar bear, polar bear, what do you hear?* New York: Holt.

McKeller, S. (2001). *Action rhymes for you and your friends.* New York: Dorling Kindersley.

Numeroff, L.J. (1991). *If you give a moose a muffin.* New York: HarperCollins.

Prelutsky, J. (Comp.) (1999). *The 20th century children's poetry treasury.* New York: Knopf.

Rosen, M. (1989). *We're going on a bear hunt.* New York: Macmillan.

Shaw, N. (1992). *Sheep out to eat.* Boston: Houghton Mifflin.

Stickland, P., & Strickland, H. (1994). *Dinosaur roar!* New York: Dutton.

Viorst, J. (1972). *Alexander and the terrible, horrible, no good, very bad day.* New York: Atheneum.

Media and Technology

Curriculum Associates Primary Reader's Theatre (four books of plays). (800-225-0248)

Failure Free Reading (talking software program). (800-542-2170)

Interactive Reading Resources (enjoyable songs on tape that tell a story). (847-658-5851)

Listening Library (books on tapes). (800-243-4504)

Reading Plus System (computer program to develop fluency). (800-732-3758)

Recorded Books, LLC (audio recorded books). (800-638-1304)

Scholastic WiggleWorks (hilarious trade books with software component). (800-325-6149)

Professional Books

Morrow, L.M. (2001). *Literacy development in the early years* (4th ed.). Boston: Allyn and Bacon.

Olson, M.W., & Homan, S.P. (Eds.). (1993). *Teacher to teacher: Strategies for the elementary classroom.* Newark, DE: International Reading Association.

Parks, B. (2000). *Read it again.* Portland, ME: Stenhouse.

From Jerry L. Johns, Susan Davis Lenski, and Laurie Elish-Piper, *Teaching Beginning Readers: Linking Assessment and Instruction* (2nd ed.). Copyright © 2002 by Kendall/Hunt Publishing Company (1-800-247-3458, ext. 5). May be reproduced for noncommercial educational purposes.

4.3 Cross~Checking

Goal To help children use various strategies to cross-check for meaning.
Assessment Strategy 5 Oral Reading Miscue Analysis, page 266

BACKGROUND

While reading, children check one kind of information against another, or cross-check, to make sense of the words (Goodman, 1965). To use cross-checking as a strategy, readers use four cues, three from print and one from their background knowledge. The cues that readers use are graphophonic (phonics) cues, semantic (context) cues, syntactic (language) cues, and background knowledge (Wilde, 2000).

When children do not recognize a word in a passage automatically, they must stop to figure it out. They can use graphophonic cues by matching sounds with letters or letter combinations; they can use semantic cues by trying to figure out what word would make sense in the sentence; they can use syntactic cues by deciding what word fits the structure and language of the sentence; and they can use their background knowledge to make sense of the sentences together. These four cues are used simultaneously so that a child can pronounce an unknown word while comprehending the passage (Rumelhart, 1985).

To use cross-checking as a strategy while they read, children need instruction on ways to use each of the language cues separately, and they also need instruction and practice using the language cues together. To know what cues children are using and what instruction they need, you will need to listen to children read on a regular basis. When you listen to children read, you will hear the types of miscues children make. Miscues are the errors children make when reading aloud. Miscues are not considered mistakes but are a window into children's reading processes (Goodman, 1965). When children make miscues, you learn which language cues they are using and which ones they need to strengthen.

For children to become proficient readers, they need a great deal of practice reading materials at their independent and instructional levels. It is through such practice that children can become competent using the four language cues. Furthermore, when children use materials that they can read easily, their reading achievement will have a greater likelihood of improving (Adams, 1990). The books children read independently need to be easy enough so that they do not miss more than one or two words per hundred. At the instructional level, students will not miss more than five or six words per hundred (Johns, 2001). When children read books that are more difficult, they have to rely more on their background knowledge and are less able to use the language cues from the print. Strategies, activities, and ideas to guide children in cross-checking follow.

> **Teaching Strategy 1**

Making Sense

Section 4.3

Children are engaged in making sense of the world. For example, they learn how different stores are arranged and where some of their favorite sections are located. They also learn routines at school and learn what to expect at recess and lunch. Reading should also make sense. In this strategy, children are given opportunities to transfer some of their knowledge of the world to reading.

DIRECTIONS

1. Choose some everyday events to which children can relate. They might include a recent field trip, a walk around the school building, or the arrangement of the lunchroom or library. Select one event, such as the lunchroom.

2. Tell children that they have lots of information in their heads that can help them in reading. Have the children close their eyes and picture their lunchroom. Invite them to think of things, people, and food. Have them try to picture their lunchroom.

3. Ask the children to open their eyes. Write a sentence on the chalkboard such as the following one.

    I saw _____ in the lunchroom.

4. Read the sentence to the class and invite students to offer words that make sense in the sentence. Many words are possible (e.g., names of people and various foods). Reinforce correct responses and suggest some additional words that may or may not make sense (e.g., elephants, chairs, plates, windows, and dad). Invite various children to explain their reasons. For example, a child may say that elephants are too big to fit in the lunchroom. Another child may note that his or her dad has never been to the lunchroom so that doesn't make sense.

5. Transfer the notion of making sense to reading. You might say something like the following. "You have information in your heads that you can use when you read. Reading should make sense. Think of words that make sense when you are reading." Then provide several more sentences and invite children to supply words that make sense or decide if the sentence makes sense. Be sure to have a child explain why a particular sentence does not make sense. Some examples follow.

    There is a _____ on the envelope.

    I like to_____.

    My teacher is wearing a _____.

    The dog said meow.

    We went to the store to buy some kangaroos.

    The game lasted over an hour.

6. Provide other opportunities for children to answer the question, "Does _____ make sense?" Have children explain their answers.

7. For older children, you might want to introduce the term *context*.

Fluency and Automaticity 235

> **Teaching Strategy 2**

Section 4.3

Predict~Sample~Confirm

As children read, they continually use the Predict-Sample-Confirm cycle (Weaver, 1994). When children come to a word they don't know, they make a prediction about the word. While making the prediction, they sample possible words based on the letters of the word, the meaning needed in the sentence, and the type of word that fits the structure of the sentence. From the sampling, children narrow their prediction to a few words. Then children decide which word to try to confirm that prediction, or they change the word. The process of Predict-Sample-Confirm is simultaneous and ongoing. Because this strategy is a key component of reading, it should be explicitly taught to children as in the following example.

DIRECTIONS

1. Tell children that you will be modeling or showing them an important strategy that they will be using as they read. Choose a story from a Big Book or a story that children can read and place it on the chalkboard or on chart paper. Cover several of the important words with tape or with sticky notes. A one-sentence example follows.

   When we went to the apple _____, we saw four types of apple trees.

2. Begin reading the story. When you come to a word that is covered, tell children that you will be making a prediction about the word. Write the word *prediction* on the chalkboard or on chart paper. Ask children for predictions for the covered word. Under the word *prediction*, write the words the children suggested. Explain that when you come to a word you don't know, you make many predictions about what the word could be.

   Predictions
   farm
   orchard
   place
   pie
   yard

3. Tell children that you will choose one of the predicted words to place in the sentence. Choose a word that is not the correct word for the sentence. For example, using the word *farm*, read the sentence to the children.

   When we went to the apple *farm*, we saw four types of apple trees.

4. Tell children that this word may make sense, but you need to confirm its accuracy by looking at the letters of the word. Uncover the first letter in the word *orchard*. Ask children if *farm* could be the correct word and invite a child to explain. Then ask children which word they think fits the sentence based on the first letter. Most children will say the correct word, *orchard*. Explain that if the word didn't fit, you would have to continue predicting more words, sampling the words, and confirming their accuracy.

5. Repeat with additional covered words. Then encourage children to try the Predict-Sample-Confirm strategy while reading independently.

Teaching Strategy 3

Section 4.3

Word Detective*

To help children use a variety of strategies to help identify unknown words, teach children to become word detectives. Basically, the Word Detective strategy helps children use three cues (sense or context, sounds or phonics, and parts or structural analysis) to help identify unknown words.

1. Introduce the notion of a word detective by dressing in a long coat and a hat and by carrying a magnifying glass. Be creative in your approach. For each of the three cues (i.e., sense, sounds, and parts), develop a visual aid similar to the illustrations below. You may also locate a plastic *brain,* a small *bell,* and a simple *puzzle*.

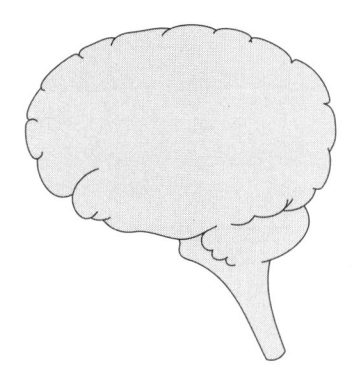

2. Decide how best to introduce the cues. It is recommended that a different cue be introduced in consecutive lessons and that activities be developed to use the cues in combination. Begin with a cue of your choice and use the basic mode of presentation that is exemplified below for the cue of sense or context.

3. Walk into the classroom dressed in detective attire. Look through your magnifying glass. Invite children to identify who you are (a detective) and what you do (solve mysteries or crimes). Then say something like the following. "You're right! I am a detective. But what you didn't know is that I'm a special kind of detective. I'm a word detective, and I can help you use cues to help figure out or identify unknown words in your reading. Here's the cue I'll share with you today." Hold up a plastic brain or enlarge the illustration of the brain above. You might also prepare a cover for a book titled *Secret Strategies for Young Word Detectives*.

4. Invite children to identify the brain and then explain how they can use their brains to be a word detective. You might say something like the following. "I use my brain when I'm reading to make sure what I read makes sense. If I come to a word I don't know, I use my brain to ask some questions." Invite students to share their ideas and lead them to understand the following strategies. Use examples as appropriate.

   - I can think about a word that would make sense.

   - I can say "blank" in place of the unknown word and read to the end of the sentence. Then I can reread the sentence and ask myself, "What word would make sense in the sentence?"

   - I can read the sentence with the word I put in and ask if it makes sense. (Possible questions might be "Does the word sound right?" or "Is this the way someone might talk?")

   - I can look at the pictures or illustrations to get an idea of what the word might be.

*Graciously shared by Joan Will, a reading coordinator in West Chicago, Illinois.

Fluency and Automaticity

5. Tell children that you have some other strategies in your secret book. In subsequent lessons, introduce strategies for sounds (phonics) and parts (structural analysis). Some of the understandings to develop are presented below. Change the statements as needed to meet your students' needs and to be consistent with your instructional program.

Sounds

- Look at the beginning of the word and make the sound. Ask, "What word begins with that sound and makes sense in the sentence?"
- Put your finger under the word and slowly say the sounds in the word. Then say the sounds faster and try to make a word you have heard before.

Parts

- Look for parts in the word that you know.
- See if the word looks like other words that you know.
- Look for two smaller words that make up the larger word.
- Separate the prefixes and/or suffixes and then try to put the pieces together.

6. Develop classroom charts with the strategies and graphics so children can refer to the cues as needed. Bookmarks with the cues can also be prepared.
7. Refer to the Word Detective strategy throughout the year and add additional strategies as they are taught.

Teaching Strategy 4

Section 4.3

Cue Questioning

As children use cross-checking, they ask themselves questions about the language cues in the sentences. Since most primary-grade children have had limited experience reading independently, they may not know the types of questions to ask. Teaching children about the kinds of questions to ask and providing them with ideas for Cue Questioning help them as they use cross-checking during reading.

DIRECTIONS

1. Identify three or four of the questions from the list on page 240 and write them on the chalkboard, a piece of chart paper, or an overhead transparency. Tell children that the questions are ones they should use as they make predictions of words while they read.

2. Ask children to take out their independent reading book and read until they come to a word that is unfamiliar. Give children several minutes to read.

3. Divide the class into groups of two or three children. Tell children that they should ask each other questions about the words. Have one child read a sentence and say "blank" in place of the unknown word. Have the other children in the group ask questions until they can figure out the missing word.

4. Repeat this strategy often using a variety of Cue Questions. Tell children that they should begin asking themselves the same questions when they read and come across an unknown word.

Tips for English Language Learners

- Children who are in various stages of learning English, like all children, will make miscues or errors when they read. Miscues are a natural part of the reading process and should be considered normal. When evaluating the significance of miscues for possible instructional intervention, do not consider dialect differences to be significant. For example, children who speak the Cantonese dialect of Chinese may add an extra syllable to the final sound in a word (e.g., *day offu* for *day off*). Speakers of Spanish may have difficulty pronouncing several English sounds: *d, b, h, m, j, n, ng, r, sh, t, the, v, w, y, z, s*-clusters and end clusters. These examples do not cover the full range of dialect differences; they merely highlight the need for you to be alert and sensitive to pronunciation differences that rarely affect comprehension, so you may ignore them.

Fluency and Automaticity

Cue Questions

Questions for Meaning Cues

✔ Did that make sense?
✔ You said _____. What does that mean?
✔ What would make sense here?
✔ What is happening in the story? Does this word make sense in the story?

Questions for Syntax Cues

✔ Did that sound right?
✔ Can you say it that way?
✔ Would it be correct to say _____?
✔ Can you think of a better word that fits?
✔ What word would sound right?

Questions for Visual Cues

✔ Did that look right?
✔ Do you know a word that looks like that?
✔ What do you notice about that word?
✔ Do you notice something familiar about that word?
✔ Do you see a part of the word you know?

Questions for Self~correction

✔ Were you right?
✔ Why did you stop?
✔ What did you notice?
✔ What else could you try?
✔ What else do you know that could help you?

Based on Clay (1993). From Jerry L. Johns, Susan Davis Lenski, and Laurie Elish-Piper, *Teaching Beginning Readers: Linking Assessment and Instruction* (2nd ed.). Copyright © 2002 by Kendall/Hunt Publishing Company (1-800-247-3458, ext. 5). May be reproduced for noncommercial educational purposes.

Ideas and Activities

1. In order for children to be able to use cross-checking strategies, they need to read materials that are at their independent and instructional reading levels. Reading levels change at different rates for different children. Therefore, make frequent assessment decisions about children's reading levels. (See Section 5.4, Assessment Strategy 2, on pages 317–319.)

2. Provide children with many opportunities to read books independently. Young children do not have attention spans that allow for long periods of reading. Therefore, provide children with five to eight minutes to read books at their own reading level at least twice a day.

3. When children read independently, they often choose books that are too difficult. Divide the books in your classroom into reading levels and mark the books with a colored sticker. For example, you might have the easiest books marked with a red sticker, the books that are closer to grade level with a blue sticker, the books at grade level with a green sticker, and the books that are above grade level with an orange sticker.

4. Young children can read many books during an independent reading period because many grade-level books are short with few words. Divide the class into groups of children who read at the same level. Provide each group of children with a small basket of books that are appropriate for the children's reading ability. Tell children that as soon as they finish reading one book they should read another one.

5. Create a strategy bookmark for children to use independently. Identify five or six questions from Cue Questioning (see Section 4.3, Teaching Strategy 4) that are most appropriate for the children. Write or print the questions as statements on a bookmark. Give a bookmark to each child in your class and have the children decorate their bookmarks. After bookmarks are decorated, laminate the bookmarks so they are more durable. Give the bookmarks back to the children and tell them that they can use the bookmarks to remind them of cross-checking strategies to use while they are reading independently. A sample bookmark is found on page 242.

6. Tell children that all readers use cross-checking as they read. Model reading an unknown passage. Read it out loud to children, thinking aloud as you come to words that you don't know. Identify the strategies you use as you read difficult passages.

7. Have children share a word they are unable to figure out and read the word in the context in which it is found. If the child is unable to share his or her strategies, model how a combination of strategies might be used to figure out the unknown word. Help children refine the effectiveness of their strategies.

8. Have children keep a log in which they record unfamiliar words, the context, and the strategies used to pronounce the words and determine their meanings. Provide opportunities for small group sharing.

9. Provide plenty of time for reading, reading, and more reading!

Home School Connections

Mistakes While Reading

When children read, they make miscues or mistakes. Mistakes are a natural part of reading. For example, a child may read *a* for *the* or *went* for *want*. When your child is reading to you, resist the temptation to correct all your child's mistakes. Instead, ask yourself, "Does the mistake make a significant change in the meaning?" If the answer is "no," ignore the miscue. You should also know that if your child makes many mistakes while reading, the material being read is probably too difficult. An easy way to judge whether the book is too difficult is to see if your child misses one or more words for every 10 words read (that's 10%). If you count mistakes and get about 10%, help your child choose an easier book.

There's more to reading than "sound it out." To help your child use a variety of skills to figure out unknown words, cut out the bookmark provided below. Help your child use it to figure out unknown words. Remember not to become overly anxious if your child makes a mistake and it does not significantly change the meaning.

What's the Word?

When I come to a word I don't know . . .

- I look at the picture.
- I think about the story.
- I look at how the word begins.
- I get my mouth ready to say the word.
- I think about a word I know that has the same sound in it.
- I see what I know in the word.
- I try a word and see if it makes sense, sounds right, and looks right.
- I go back and try again.
- I skip the word and read on.

From Jerry L. Johns, Susan Davis Lenski, and Laurie Elish-Piper, *Teaching Beginning Readers: Linking Assessment and Instruction* (2nd ed.). Copyright © 2002 by Kendall/Hunt Publishing Company (1-800-247-3458, ext. 5). May be reproduced for noncommercial educational purposes.

Selected Resources
CROSS~CHECKING

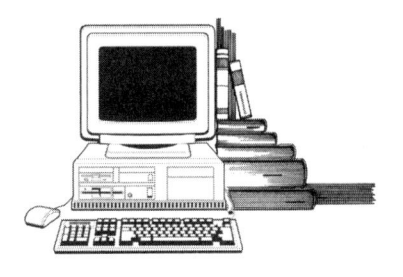

Leveled Book Series

Beginning Readers
Scholastic (800-325-6149)

Heath Little Readers
D.C. Heath (800-334-3284)

Literacy 2000
Rigby (800-822-8661)

Little Red Readers
Sundance (508-486-9201)

Ready to Read
Richard C. Owen (800-336-5588)

First Start
Troll (800-526-5289)

Learn to Read
Creative Teaching Press (714-995-7888)

Little Celebrations
Scott Foresman (800-792-0550)

Reading Corners
Dominie Press (800-232-4570)

Sunshine Books
Wright Group (800-523-2371)

Media and Technology

Discus Books CD-ROM (interactive books).
Discus Knowledge Research (800-567-4321)

Reading Blaster CD-ROM (early reading skills including reading short passages).
Davidson & Associates (800-545-7677)

Using Context Clues CD-ROM (practice software using context clues).
Computer Centerline (800-852-5802)

Professional Resources

Blachowicz, C.L.Z. (1993). C(2)QU: Modeling context use in the classroom. *The Reading Teacher, 47,* 268–269.

Clay, M.M. (1991). *Becoming literate: The construction of inner control.* Portsmouth, NH: Heinemann.

Fountas, I.C., & Pinnell, G.S. (1996). *Guided reading: Good first teaching for all children.* Portsmouth, NH: Heinemann.

Goodman, Y.M., & Marek, A.M. (1996). *Retrospective miscue analysis: Revaluing readers and reading.* Katonah, NY: Richard C. Owen.

Johnston, P. (2000). *Running records: A self-tutoring guide.* Portland, ME: Stenhouse.

Wilde, S. (2000). *Miscue analysis made easy.* Portsmouth, NH: Heinemann.

From Jerry L. Johns, Susan Davis Lenski, and Laurie Elish-Piper, *Teaching Beginning Readers: Linking Assessment and Instruction* (2nd ed.). Copyright © 2002 by Kendall/Hunt Publishing Company (1-800-247-3458, ext. 5). May be reproduced for noncommercial educational purposes.

4.4 Assessments of Sight Words, Fluency, and Cross-Checking

Assessment Strategy 1

Basic Sight Vocabulary	246
Form 1 Child's Copy	248
Form 1 Record Sheet	249
Form 2 Child's Copy	250
Form 2 Record Sheet	251

Assessment Strategy 2

Common Nouns	252
Form 1 Child's Copy	254
Form 1 Record Sheet	255
Form 2 Child's Copy	256
Form 2 Record Sheet	257

Assessment Strategy 3

Words per Minute	258
Class Record Sheet	261

Assessment Strategy 4

Fluency Scale Checklist	262
Individual Fluency Scale Record Sheet	264
Class Fluency Scale Record Sheet	265

Assessment Strategy 5

Oral Reading Miscue Analysis	266

Goal To help assess children's knowledge of basic sight words, the ability to read fluently, and the use of cross-checking strategies.

BACKGROUND

You may already have a variety of formal and informal ways to assess your children's progress in sight vocabulary, fluency, and cross-checking. If you feel the need to expand or supplement your assessment strategies, we have provided a variety of assessments that correspond to the major topics in this chapter. Use those that will help you further explore a particular area to identify what specific instruction is warranted or whether your instruction resulted in the outcomes you desired. There is no single way to use the assessments. Our goal is to provide you with easy-to-use assessments to help you evaluate or monitor children's progress in reading.

Assessment Strategy 1

Section 4.4

Basic Sight Vocabulary

Overview	The purpose of this assessment is to ascertain the child's ability to automatically identify a sample of the most common words in English. The words on the Revised Dolch List (see page 211) occur frequently in all types of printed materials. If you want to assess children's knowledge of these basic words, use one of the forms provided. The words selected for these assessments are the 50 most frequently used words in English. You could also make your own assessments by selecting other words from the Revised Dolch List if children know the basic words in these assessments. How children perform on the assessments will inform you about what words you may want to target for instruction to the entire class, small groups, or individual children.
Materials Needed	1. Child's copy, either Form 1 (p. 248) or Form 2 (p. 250) 2. A copy of the Record Sheet that corresponds to the form selected for use, either Form 1 (p. 249) or Form 2 (p. 251) 3. Two blank sheets of paper
Procedures	1. Duplicate the Record Sheet corresponding to the form selected for use. 2. Choose one form of the assessment. Cover the words with the two sheets of paper so only one word will be uncovered at a time. Place the page containing the covered words before the child. Say, "I want you to say some words for me. Let's begin with this one." 3. Move one of the blank sheets of paper below the first word and ask the child to say the word. If the child says the number, cover it up and point to the word. As the child says words, note correct responses with a plus (+) in the appropriate place on the Record Sheet. Record any incorrect responses by using the following markings (or your own system).

Marking	Meaning of Marking	Marking	Meaning of Marking
man men	Substitution	*m—* men	Partial Pronunciation
man s/c men	Self-correction	men	Repeated word
~~men~~	Omitted word	*small* ^men	Insertion
		the/small	Pause

4. Encourage the child to say "pass" or "skip it" for any unknown words. Say, "Just do the best you can." Stop the assessment if no response is given to the first four words.

246 Chapter Four

	5. Proceed through the words until the assessment is completed. If you observe anxiety, frustration, or reluctance on the part of the child, use your professional judgment to determine if the assessment should be stopped.
Scoring and Interpretation	Count the number of words pronounced correctly and record the score in the box on the Record Sheet. Self-corrections are counted as correct, but make a note about any words that were not known automatically. The intent of this assessment is to determine if the child knows the most common words in English at sight. Mispronunciations, partial words, refusals, saying "don't know," and self-corrections are evidence that the words are not known automatically. These words may become the basis for instruction using the teaching strategies described in Section 4.1. The same form of the assessment could be used after targeted instruction to note gains in basic sight word knowledge. Form 2 of the assessment could be used after the child had near mastery of the words on Form 1 or as a further assessment of the child's knowledge of the most common words in English.

1. the
2. and
3. a
4. is
5. it
6. for
7. he
8. as
9. they
10. be
11. at
12. from
13. I

14. have
15. but
16. were
17. all
18. when
19. their
20. her
21. we
22. about
23. said
24. if
25. would

Form 1—Basic Sight Vocabulary—Child's Copy

RECORD SHEET

Basic Sight Vocabulary

Form 1

Name _____ Date _____

Teacher's Directions   246
Child Copy   248

BRIEF DIRECTIONS

Present one word at a time for the child to pronounce. Say, "I want you to say some words for me. Let's begin with this one." Use a plus (+) for correct responses. Record the child's responses for incorrect words. Total correct responses and put the score in the box.

1. the _____
2. and _____
3. a _____
4. is _____
5. it _____
6. for _____
7. he _____
8. as _____
9. they _____
10. be _____
11. at _____
12. from _____
13. I _____

14. have _____
15. but _____
16. were _____
17. all _____
18. when _____
19. their _____
20. her _____
21. we _____
22. about _____
23. said _____
24. if _____
25. would _____

Total Correct ☐

From Jerry L. Johns, Susan Davis Lenski, and Laurie Elish-Piper, *Teaching Beginning Readers: Linking Assessment and Instruction* (2nd ed.). Copyright © 2002 by Kendall/Hunt Publishing Company (1-800-247-3458, ext. 5). May be reproduced for noncommercial educational purposes.

1. of
2. to
3. in
4. that
5. was
6. you
7. on
8. are
9. with
10. his
11. or
12. had
13. not

14. this
15. by
16. one
17. she
18. an
19. there
20. can
21. what
22. up
23. out
24. some
25. so

Form 2—Basic Sight Vocabulary—Child's Copy

RECORD SHEET

Basic Sight Vocabulary

Form 2

Name _____ Date _____

Teacher's Directions   246
Child Copy   250

BRIEF DIRECTIONS

Present one word at a time for the child to pronounce. Say, "I want you to say some words for me. Let's begin with this one." Use a plus (+) for correct responses. Record the child's responses for incorrect words. Total correct responses and put the score in the box.

1. of _____
2. to _____
3. in _____
4. that _____
5. was _____
6. you _____
7. on _____
8. are _____
9. with _____
10. his _____
11. or _____
12. had _____
13. not _____

14. this _____
15. by _____
16. one _____
17. she _____
18. an _____
19. there _____
20. can _____
21. what _____
22. up _____
23. out _____
24. some _____
25. so _____

Total Correct ☐

From Jerry L. Johns, Susan Davis Lenski, and Laurie Elish-Piper, *Teaching Beginning Readers: Linking Assessment and Instruction* (2nd ed.). Copyright © 2002 by Kendall/Hunt Publishing Company (1-800-247-3458, ext. 5). May be reproduced for noncommercial educational purposes.

Assessment Strategy 2

Section 4.4

Common Nouns

Overview	The purpose of this assessment is to ascertain the child's ability to identify automatically a sample of the most common nouns. There are a number of nouns that occur frequently in printed materials. The nouns in these assessments are based on the work of Johns (1975), Zeno, Ivens, Millard, & Duvvuri (1995) and Gunning's (1998) list of 500 words that occur with the highest frequency in first-grade texts and children's books that are on a first-grade level. The words selected for these assessments use some of the most common nouns in English that are likely to be among the spontaneous speaking vocabulary of children in kindergarten and first grade, appropriate to young children's interests, and related to first-grade activities. How children perform on the assessment should give you helpful indications of nouns known as well as nouns that you may want to teach. Remember that these nouns occur frequently in various types of printed materials and need to be recognized automatically if students are to become fluent readers.
Materials Needed	1. Child's copy, either Form 1 (p. 254) or Form 2 (p. 256) 2. A copy of the Record Sheet that corresponds to the form selected for use, either Form 1 (p. 255) or Form 2 (p. 257) 3. Two blank sheets of paper
Procedures	1. Duplicate the Record Sheet corresponding to the form selected for use. 2. Choose one form of the assessment. Cover the words with the two sheets of paper so only one word will be uncovered at a time. Place the page containing the words before the child. Say, "I want you to say some words for me. Let's begin with this one." 3. Move one of the blank sheets of paper below the first word and ask the child to say the word. If the child says the number, cover it up and point to the word. As the child says the words, note correct responses with a plus (+) in the appropriate place of the Record Sheet. Record any incorrect responses by using the following markings (or your own system).

Marking	Meaning of Marking	Marking	Meaning of Marking
man men	Substitution	*m—* men	Partial Pronunciation
man s/c ~~men~~	Self-correction	men	Repeated word
men	Omitted word	*small* ^men	Insertion
		the/small	Pause

252   Chapter Four

	4. Encourage the child to say "pass" or "skip it" for any unknown words. Say, "Just do the best you can." Stop the assessment if no response is given to the first four words. 5. Proceed through the words until the assessment is completed. If you observe anxiety, frustration, or reluctance on the part of the child, use your professional judgment to determine if the assessment should be stopped.
Scoring and Interpretation	Count the number of words pronounced correctly and record the score in the box on the Record Sheet. Self-corrections are counted as correct, but make a note about any words that were not known automatically. Mispronunciations, partial words, refusals, saying "don't know," and self-corrections are evidence that the words are not known automatically. These words may become the basis for instruction using the teaching strategies described in Section 4.1. The same form of the assessment could be used after targeted instruction to note gains in knowledge of common nouns. Form 2 of the assessment could be used after the child has near mastery of the words on Form 1 or as a further assessment of the child's knowledge of some of the most common nouns in English.

Additional Ways of Assessing Sight Words and Nouns

1. Observe the child's oral reading of materials being used for instruction to informally assess if the most common nouns in English are known automatically.
2. Use an informal reading inventory (Johns, 2001) or running records to help determine the number of words known at sight.
3. Observe the child's writing to note growth in the child's ability to spell the most common nouns correctly.

1. people
2. years
3. man
4. house
5. school
6. mother
7. father
8. head
9. room
10. city
11. name
12. group
13. face
14. door
15. air
16. girl
17. nothing
18. back
19. place
20. book
21. side
22. egg
23. car
24. farm
25. train

Form 1—Common Nouns—Child's Copy

RECORD SHEET

Common Nouns

Form 1

Name_____ Date_____

Teacher's Directions   252
Child Copy   254

BRIEF DIRECTIONS

Present one word at a time for the child to pronounce. Say, "I want you to say some words for me. Let's begin with this one." Use a plus (+) for correct responses. Record the child's responses for incorrect words. Total correct responses and put the score in the box.

1. people _____
2. years _____
3. man _____
4. house _____
5. school _____
6. mother _____
7. father _____
8. head _____
9. room _____
10. city _____
11. name _____
12. group _____
13. face _____

14. door _____
15. air _____
16. girl _____
17. nothing _____
18. back _____
19. place _____
20. book _____
21. side _____
22. egg _____
23. car _____
24. farm _____
25. train _____

Total Correct ☐

From Jerry L. Johns, Susan Davis Lenski, and Laurie Elish-Piper, *Teaching Beginning Readers: Linking Assessment and Instruction* (2nd ed.). Copyright © 2002 by Kendall/Hunt Publishing Company (1-800-247-3458, ext. 5). May be reproduced for noncommercial educational purposes.

1. water
2. things
3. home
4. children
5. men
6. hand
7. eye
8. night
9. money
10. day
11. feet
12. boy
13. road
14. dog
15. time
16. morning
17. friend
18. top
19. place
20. table
21. way
22. tree
23. frog
24. town
25. truck

Form 2—Common Nouns—Child's Copy

RECORD SHEET

Common Nouns

Form 2

Name _____ Date _____

Teacher's Directions   252
Child Copy   256

BRIEF DIRECTIONS

Present one word at a time for the child to pronounce. Say, "I want you to say some words for me. Let's begin with this one." Use a plus (+) for correct responses. Record the child's responses for incorrect words. Total correct responses and put the score in the box.

1. water _____
2. things _____
3. home _____
4. children _____
5. men _____
6. hand _____
7. eye _____
8. night _____
9. money _____
10. day _____
11. feet _____
12. boy _____
13. road _____

14. dog _____
15. time _____
16. morning _____
17. friend _____
18. top _____
19. place _____
20. table _____
21. way _____
22. tree _____
23. frog _____
24. town _____
25. truck _____

Total Correct ☐

From Jerry L. Johns, Susan Davis Lenski, and Laurie Elish-Piper, *Teaching Beginning Readers: Linking Assessment and Instruction* (2nd ed.). Copyright © 2002 by Kendall/Hunt Publishing Company (1-800-247-3458, ext. 5). May be reproduced for noncommercial educational purposes.

Assessment Strategy 3

Section 4.4

Words per Minute

Overview	The purpose of this assessment is to determine the child's rate of reading in words per minute. Basically, you ask the child to read new material at an appropriate level of difficulty. While the child reads, you note miscues and time the reading. Then you perform a few simple calculations to determine the child's rate of reading in words per minute. The child's rate can be compared to other students in the classroom or the norms provided on page 259. The nice thing about this assessment strategy is that it can be repeated at regular intervals using instructional materials to help gauge the child's growth in fluency.
Materials Needed	1. A reading passage at the child's instructional level (at least 95% word accuracy and 75% comprehension) 2. A copy of the passage being read 3. A stopwatch or a watch with a second hand 4. A Reading Rate Class Record Sheet (see page 261)
Procedures	1. Select a reading passage at the child's instructional level. Make a copy of the passage so that you can note any miscues the child makes. Get a stopwatch or use a watch with a second hand. 2. Present the passage to the child. Say, "I would like you to read me this passage. When you have finished reading, I'd like you to tell me about what you've read. You may begin." When the child begins reading, begin your timing. 3. Note any miscues the child makes. Use your own coding system or the one presented below.

Marking	Meaning of Marking	Marking	Meaning of Marking
man men	Substitution	*m—* men	Partial Pronunciation
man s/c men	Self-correction	men	Repeated word
~~men~~	Omitted word	*small* ^men	Insertion
		the/small	Pause

4. When the child completes the reading, note the number of seconds that elapsed. Then invite the child to tell you a bit about what was read. You might want to say, "Tell me about what you've read." You may prefer to ask a question or two to be sure that the child was not calling words without understanding the passage.

5. To determine the child's rate of reading, follow the steps below.
   *Count or estimate the number of words in the passage (e.g., 150).
   *Multiply by 60. The resulting numeral becomes the dividend (e.g., 9000).
   *Divide by the number of seconds (e.g., 100) it took the child to read the passage (e.g., 9000 ÷ 100 = 90).
   *The resulting numeral (e.g., 90) is the quotient, which is in words per minute (WPM).
6. Record the child's reading rate on the Reading Rate Class Record Sheet.

Scoring and Interpretation

There are at least three ways to interpret the results. First, you can time the child's reading at various points throughout the school year to note changes in rate of reading. Second, if you enter each child's scores on the Reading Rate Class Record Sheet, you can make informal comparisons among children. Third, there are norms for oral reading rates for first graders that have been offered by Forman and Sanders (1998). The chart below contains these rates.

Mean Oral Reading Rates for "On-Grade Level" First Graders

Month	Number of Students	Mean Accuracy	Mean Rate* (WPM)
Dec.–Jan.	1,173	95%	54
Feb.–Mar.	1,192	96%	66
April–May	1,166	96%	70

*Reported in words per minute

Hasbrouck and Tindal (1992) have published norms for grades two and three. The chart below contains these rates for several thousand students and provides words correct per minute at the 75th, 50th, and 25th percentiles for students in grades two and three for three time periods (fall, winter, and spring) of the school year. You may choose the words per minute rates in the charts for comparison purposes. Keep in mind that the figures in these charts should be used informally to help you monitor the progress of children within a particular grade and compare growth to these established standards.

Median Oral Reading Rates for Students in Grades Two and Three

Grade	Fall Percentile	Fall WCPM*	Winter WCPM	Spring WCPM
2	75	82	106	124
	50	53	78	94
	25	23	46	65
3	75	107	123	142
	50	79	93	114
	25	65	70	87

*Reported in words correct per minute

If you believe one or more of the children in your class have reading rates that warrant strengthening, consider the teaching strategies presented earlier in this chapter. Keep in mind that a limited basic sight vocabulary could be a major contributing factor to a slow rate of reading.

Fluency and Automaticity

Additional Ways of Assessing Fluency

1. Refer to the Fluency Scale Checklist on page 262.
2. Use an informal reading inventory (Johns, 2001) or running records to determine rate of reading. If running records are used, refer to the procedure described in step 5 on page 259 to calculate rate of reading.
3. Use one-minute reads. This procedure is essentially the same as Assessment Strategy 4 except that all children read for only one minute. The number of words read in one minute becomes the child's WPM.

A word of caution: Some teachers have every child in the room read the same material for one-minute reads. While this technique provides a common baseline for the data gathered, the range of reading levels in most classrooms makes this procedure less accurate for children who read above or below grade level.

READING RATE CLASS RECORD SHEET

Child	Date	WPM	Comments

From Jerry L. Johns, Susan Davis Lenski, and Laurie Elish-Piper, *Teaching Beginning Readers: Linking Assessment and Instruction* (2nd ed.). Copyright © 2002 by Kendall/Hunt Publishing Company (1-800-247-3458, ext. 5). May be reproduced for noncommercial educational purposes.

Assessment Strategy 4

Section 4.4

Fluency Scale Checklist

Overview	Many teachers informally assess the child's fluency during the course of instruction. That informal assessment may result in a mental note or a brief comment in the child's progress folder or portfolio. There are a number of fluency scales that may be used to keep the process informal but systematic. We offer a basic five-point fluency scale arranged so it can be used with an individual child or a class of children.
Materials Needed	1. Sufficient copies of the Individual Fluency Scale Record Sheet (page 264) if the scale is to be used with an individual child 2. Sufficient copies of the Class Fluency Scale Record Sheet (page 265) if the scale is to be used with the entire class
Procedures	1. Duplicate sufficient copies of the Record Sheet for the scale you intend to use. 2. Review the five levels of fluency described on the fluency scale. 3. When you decide to focus on a child's oral reading fluency, note the date on the Record Sheet and indicate the level of fluency. Use your professional judgment to arrive at a level. 4. Repeat the process from time to time or at regularly scheduled intervals. Record the date and level of fluency.
Scoring and Interpretation	The five-point informal fluency scale is not scored formally. Make numerous observations of the child's oral reading and judge the fluency. Over time, you should expect to see some improvement in fluency. If fluency for a child appears to be static compared to other children in your room, consider what in the child's reading behavior may be contributing to the situation. Then develop appropriate instructional interventions using your experience along with the strategies suggested in this chapter. Ensure that the child is given appropriate instructional materials. There may be times when a lack of fluency is actually an indication the instructional materials are too difficult for the child.

Additional Ways of Assessing Fluency

1. Use an informal reading inventory (Johns, 2001). Most informal reading inventories are designed to permit the assessment of fluency by determining rate of reading.
2. Use running records to note miscues, time the child's reading, and refer to step 5 in Assessment Strategy 3 (page 259).
3. Observe the child's oral reading and note particular behaviors that may be having a negative influence on fluency. Some of these behaviors are listed below.

    - many repetitions
    - excessive use of phonics
    - numerous unknown words
    - word-by-word reading
    - inappropriate phrasing

RECORD SHEET

Individual Fluency Scale

Child _____ Teacher _____ Grade _____

Level	Description
1	Reads almost entirely word by word; some long pauses between words
2	Reads mostly in 2- to 3-word phrases with some word by word; some evidence of punctuation
3	Reads mostly in phrases; little intonation; ignores some punctuation
4	Reads mostly in phrases; a little choppy at times; attends to punctuation
5	Reads fluently with good expression

Date	Level	Comments

Based on Cunningham & Allington (1994). From Jerry L. Johns, Susan Davis Lenski, and Laurie Elish-Piper, *Teaching Beginning Readers: Linking Assessment and Instruction* (2nd ed.). Copyright © 2002 by Kendall/Hunt Publishing Company (1-800-247-3458, ext. 5). May be reproduced for noncommercial educational purposes.

RECORD SHEET

Class Fluency Scale

Level	Description
1	Reads almost entirely word by word; some long pauses between words
2	Reads mostly in 2- to 3-word phrases with some word by word; some evidence of punctuation
3	Reads mostly in phrases; little intonation; ignores some punctuation
4	Reads mostly in phrases; a little choppy at times; attends to punctuation
5	Reads fluently with good expression

Child	Date	Level	Comments

Based on Cunningham & Allington (1994). From Jerry L. Johns, Susan Davis Lenski, and Laurie Elish-Piper, *Teaching Beginning Readers: Linking Assessment and Instruction* (2nd ed.). Copyright © 2002 by Kendall/Hunt Publishing Company (1-800-247-3458, ext. 5). May be reproduced for noncommercial educational purposes.

Assessment Strategy 5

Section 4.4

Oral Reading Miscue Analysis

Overview	When children read orally, you have the opportunity to note their miscues and make observations about their reading strategies. There are several ways to gather such information. You can use the graded passages found in Section 5.4, Assessment Strategy 2, an informal reading inventory (Johns, 2001), or instructional materials from your classroom. Oral Reading Miscue Analysis is similar to Assessment Strategy 3 (Words Per Minute) described earlier in this chapter (pages 258–259).
Materials Needed	1. Select one or more reading passages at the child's instructional level. Passages from the pre-primer through the second-grade level can be found on pages 320–335. Additional passages at these and higher levels are available in the *Basic Reading Inventory* (Johns, 2001). You can also use passages from the materials you use for instruction 2. See pages 320–335 for the copies of the passages from pre-primer through second-grade level. If you decide to use running records, you could use a blank sheet of paper and make a check mark for each word read correctly and note the specific miscues (e.g., substitutions, omissions) and other behaviors such as repetitions and word-by-word reading 3. Use a stopwatch or a watch with a second hand
Procedures	1. Invite the child to read the passage you have selected. You might say, "I would like you to read this passage to me. When you have finished reading, I'll ask you some questions (or I'd like you to tell me about what you've read)." When the child begins reading, begin timing with a stopwatch or watch with a second hand. 2. Note any miscues the child makes while reading. In addition, make notations that indicate phrasing and repetitions. Numerous marking systems are available (e.g., Burns, 2001), but you may find the one below easy to use. You may also use your own system.

Marking	Meaning of Marking	Marking	Meaning of Marking
man men	Substitution	*m—* men	Partial Pronunciation
man s/c men	Self-correction	men	Repeated word
~~men~~	Omitted word	*small* ^men	Insertion
		the/small	Pause

3. When the child finishes reading, note the number of seconds that elapsed and ask the comprehension questions or invite a retelling. The teacher's copies of the passages and questions have provisions for easy notations and record keeping.

Scoring and Interpretation

Quantitative scores for reading rate, word recognition, and comprehension can be obtained using the procedure described for Assessment Strategy 2 in Section 5.4. Because the focus of Assessment Strategy 5 is related to fluency, you should pay particular attention to reading rate and miscue analysis.

Reading rate can be determined by inserting the seconds required for reading as the divisor at the bottom of the teacher's record sheet for each graded passage. Perform the necessary division. The resulting numeral will be an estimate of the child's rate in words per minute (WPM). An example of this procedure is shown below.

$$\begin{array}{r} 85.7 \text{ WPM} \\ 70 \overline{)6000} \\ \underline{560} \\ 400 \\ \underline{350} \\ 500 \end{array}$$

For additional information, refer to Assessment Strategy 3 in this chapter. You will also find norms tables for possible use. The following questions and comments may provide assistance in formulating ideas for instruction.

- *Does the child read quite accurately but have a slow rate of reading in words per minute?* If the reading is accurate but slow, you will probably want to provide more opportunities for the child to read easy materials and participate in a variety of activities that focus on rereading. This chapter contains numerous ideas for possible use.

- *Does the child read accurately but in a word-by-word fashion?* The above ideas should be useful. In addition, you can mark phrase boundaries in passages by making light slash marks with a pencil to help the child see how to group words (e.g., the small cat/was sleeping/under the big tree). You could also model phrasing by reading aloud the passage while the child follows. Then have the child model your reading. Read-along audiotapes of favorite books and stories can also be used.

- *Does the child make a number of miscues and read fast (or slow)?* Analyze the nature of the child's miscues. Miscue analysis can be done informally to get insights into the child's general reading strategies and the impact that those strategies can have on fluency. Some of the behaviors to look for are related to the following questions. The answers to these questions suggest strategies for instruction.

- *Are the child's miscues numerous with no particular pattern?* Many miscues suggest that the reading material may be too difficult. Consider using easier materials for instruction and recreational reading.

Fluency and Automaticity   267

- *Is the child's reading generally accurate but characterized by numerous repetitions?* The repetitions may be due mostly to habit. Tape-record the child's reading and have the child listen and comment. Ask the child why he or she repeats so often. Use the child's response to help plan appropriate instruction. Also, as long as the child's comprehension is satisfactory, encourage the child to reduce the repetitions.

- *Is the child's reading characterized by sounding out many words, which reduces fluency?* The child may be overreliant on phonics. Help the child strengthen his or her sight vocabulary and teach how context can be used to help anticipate words. If phonics is the dominant mode of initial instruction, such behavior may be considered normal for some time until the child gains sight words. Be alert for children who seem to be "stuck" on phonics when other children seem to be adding words to their sight vocabularies. Remember to teach a combination of cue systems for word identification and cross-checking. Teaching Strategy 3 (Word Detective) in this chapter may be especially helpful.

- *Is the child's reading characterized by a moderate or fast rate and numerous miscues that significantly distort the meaning?* Such reading may seriously impact the child's ability to comprehend the material. You may need to use examples of the child's miscues that distort the meaning to help teach the importance of rereading when the passage doesn't make sense. Teaching the child to use phonics and context as cross-checking strategies may be helpful. Also help the child monitor whether the passage is making sense. Questions like "Am I understanding?" and "Does what I'm reading make sense?" may be used. You may also want to help the child expand his or her sight vocabulary.

- *Is the child's reading characterized by a slow rate and numerous miscues?* Such behavior may be a strong indication that the reading materials are too difficult. Use easier materials. You can also study the nature of the child's miscues to gain insights into the word-identification skills that need to be taught. You may need to teach certain consonant and vowel sounds. If many basic sight words are unknown (see the Revised Dolch List on page 211), help the child learn those words.

Additional Ways of Assessing Cross-Checking

1. Observe the child's reading to see if a variety of cues are being used (phonics, meaning, language, and background knowledge). Use evidence gathered over time to make your instruction responsive to the child's needs.
2. Invite children to share the strategies they use to identify unknown words. Their sharing can often lead to additional strategies that you will want to teach. Be sure you teach the various cueing systems.

CHAPTER 5

Storyteller Michale Gabriel

Vocabulary and Comprehension

OVERVIEW

Reading is the process of constructing meaning; therefore, teaching children to understand what they read and to respond to their reading are important goals of literacy instruction. Comprehension of text involves children connecting their prior knowledge to what they are reading in order to understand and respond to the text. Because reading is an active process, children must monitor understanding and apply fix-up strategies when comprehension is not taking place. An important dimension of understanding text is vocabulary. Vocabulary words are labels for concepts, and children must understand the meaning of key vocabulary words in order to understand what they read (Blachowicz & Fisher, 2000). While incidental word learning allows children to learn many words during their daily lives (Brett, Rothlein, & Hurley, 1996), it is important for children to be taught key vocabulary, as well as strategies for understanding new words independently. This chapter contains teaching strategies and activities for helping children understand and respond to reading. In addition, assessment strategies are also provided.

Teachers often ask important questions about how they can help children understand what they read and respond to it in meaningful ways. Some of those frequently asked questions are listed on the next page.

How do young children learn vocabulary?

Children learn vocabulary first through hearing words and connecting them to the related concepts. For example, children hear the word "helicopter" and relate it to the vehicle they have seen in the past. Once children have words in their listening and speaking vocabularies, they can connect this knowledge to the written word. When children encounter new vocabulary words in their reading for which they do not have a concept or personal experience, such connections are necessary to help them understand and remember the vocabulary words. For example, the word "rapidly" will be unfamiliar to many children, but the teacher can demonstrate how she moves "rapidly" across the room and the children can be invited to march "rapidly" around the room. The teacher can also help children make connections by discussing how the word "rapidly" is very similar to other words such as "quickly."

What does it mean to know a word?

Knowing a word can be considered on a continuum rather than an "all or nothing" proposition. Word knowledge can be divided into three main levels: no knowledge of the word, limited knowledge, and much knowledge (Dale, 1965). Multiple exposures to words are necessary for children to develop in-depth knowledge of words.

What are key factors in comprehension?

Comprehension is the process of constructing meaning from text. What this means is that each child brings his or her background knowledge and previous experiences to the text to make meaning. For example, a child who lives on a farm will likely understand a passage about cows with a different degree of comprehension than a child who lives in the city and has never had a firsthand experience with cows. It is important to note that there is not a single, correct interpretation of a story. A rich bank of background knowledge and previous experiences will greatly enhance a child's comprehension. When children come to school with limited background knowledge or experiences in certain areas, teachers can provide a variety of hands-on and vicarious experiences to assist children with comprehension. In addition, explicit instruction in various aspects of comprehension will help children understand what they read.

What is listening comprehension and how is it related to literacy development?

Listening comprehension refers to a child's ability to understand a story or passage that is read aloud to him or her. By determining a child's listening comprehension level, a teacher can determine a child's potential for growth in reading.

What does it mean to monitor understanding while reading?

When readers monitor understanding, they attend to whether the text makes sense as they read it. Because reading is the process of constructing meaning, effective readers are able to determine when they do not understand what they are reading, and they can also apply fix-up strategies to get their comprehension back on track (Pressley & Afflerbach, 1995). For example, children ask themselves, "Do I understand what I'm reading?" If they do not, they apply repair strategies such as rereading, using pictures, getting a word meaning, or asking for help (Cunningham & Allington, 1998).

5.1 Meaning Vocabulary

> **Goal** To help children learn vocabulary words.

BACKGROUND

Vocabulary knowledge is directly related to children's comprehension of text (Beck & McKeown, 1991). Vocabulary can be learned in a variety of ways, including listening, reading, instruction, and student-centered activities (Blair-Larsen & Williams, 1999). Vocabulary instruction is an important part of the curriculum, regardless of subject area. For example, in addition to learning vocabulary in conjunction with reading, children must learn key vocabulary words in math to understand important concepts. Beck and McKeown (1991) offer four principles for effective vocabulary instruction across the curriculum.

1. All approaches to teaching vocabulary are more effective than no instruction.
2. No one approach has been shown to be consistently best.
3. Multiple approaches and activities yield the best gains in vocabulary knowledge.
4. Repeated exposures to vocabulary words increase understanding.

The following strategies are designed to help children strengthen their vocabulary knowledge.

Teaching Strategy 1

Section 5.1

Preview in Context

Preteaching vocabulary enhances children's comprehension as they read. By selecting a few key vocabulary words to preteach in the context of the story or text, teachers can help children understand these words and the underlying concepts before they begin reading.

DIRECTIONS

1. Select two or three important vocabulary words children will encounter in their reading. Identify the sentences that contain these words in the text.
2. Copy the words and sentences onto an overhead transparency, chart paper, or the chalkboard.
3. Explain to the children that there are several new vocabulary words in their reading and you want them to understand what they mean before they read the story or passage.
4. Direct the children's attention to one of the words and the sentence containing it that you have written on an overhead transparency, chart paper, or chalkboard. For example, you might display the following sentence before reading a science passage on amphibians.

   A frog is an *amphibian* that lives in the water and part of the time on land.

5. Assist the children with figuring out the meaning of the word by using the context. You may need to ask questions to guide their observations and insights. For example, you might say, "What do you know about the word *amphibian* from this sentence?" The children may offer responses such as, "A frog is an amphibian," and "It lives in the water and on land."

6. Expand the children's understanding by asking questions such as, "Can you think of other animals that are like frogs that live in the water and on land?" and "What characteristics does a frog have that help him live on both land and in the water?"

Tips for English Language Learners

Provide pictures, concrete objects, or other visuals to accompany each word. Point to the appropriate visual when you read the sentence to help the English Language Learners make the connection between the visual and the English words.

Teaching Strategy 2

Section 5.1

Vocabulary Connections

Children can understand and remember new vocabulary words best when those words are connected to the children's experiences and knowledge. The Vocabulary Connections strategy introduces a new word using a synonym the children will already know.

DIRECTIONS

1. Select a key vocabulary word that is important for children to know to understand a story or passage. Identify a synonym or phrase for the word that will be familiar to the children. For example, if the vocabulary word is *rehearse*, you might select *practice* as your synonym. Ask the children, "What do you do to get ready to perform a play?"

2. Provide time for the children to share their ideas. List their ideas on an overhead transparency or the chalkboard. Discuss the connections among their ideas. For example, children may say, "I practice my lines by saying them over and over," "I learn my parts and memorize them," and "We do the play over and over until it is ready." You may respond, "Your ideas all talk about doing something over and over until you learn it very well. When you do this, you *rehearse* for the play."

3. Show the children a sentence from the story that contains the vocabulary word. Display this sentence on an overhead transparency or the chalkboard.

   We will *rehearse* for the play today after school, so we will be ready to perform on Saturday.

4. Have children turn to a partner and brainstorm sentences and situations when they could use the word *rehearse*. Provide time for sharing and write these sentences and situations on an overhead transparency or the chalkboard.

> ## Tips for English Language Learners
>
> - If the vocabulary word is an action word, invite several children to pantomime the word. This process will help English Language Learners visualize the meaning of the word.
>
> - If the vocabulary word is a concrete object, provide a visual or example or invite children to draw the object. Write the vocabulary word on a card to display with the object, visual, or drawings.

Teaching Strategy 3

Section 5.1

Word Frames

To help students fully understand important conceptual vocabulary, a Word Frame can be used (Tompkins, 2001). For maximum effectiveness, this activity should focus on a very small number of key vocabulary words rather than a long list of words. An ideal number of words for this activity is two or three. The Word Frame allows students to identify synonyms and/or examples as well as antonyms and/or nonexamples of the target vocabulary word.

DIRECTIONS

1. Select two or three key vocabulary words that are essential to understanding the unit or reading. For example, you might select the words *community* and *citizen* from your social studies book.

2. Demonstrate the procedures for completing the Word Frame using the example listed below for the word *community*.

    Community is _____. It is _____, _____, and

    _____. It is never _____ or _____.

    Community is _____.

    Explain to children that they can fill in the blanks with one word or with a phrase. A sample completed Word Frame for *community* is provided below.

    Community is <u>a neighborhood</u>. It is <u>family</u>, <u>friends</u>, and <u>neighbors</u>. It is never <u>far away</u> or <u>unfriendly</u>. Community is <u>where you live</u>.

3. Provide time for children to offer multiple responses to the Word Frame. Discuss the children's responses.

4. Present another vocabulary word to the children. Ask them to complete the Word Frame for the vocabulary word with a partner or as a whole class.

Vocabulary and Comprehension

Teaching Strategy 4

Section 5.1

Four-Square Vocabulary Grids

This strategy helps students develop personal understandings for key vocabulary words and concepts (Johns & Lenski, 2001). Students fill out a grid that contains key information about the word. To be effective, this strategy should focus on no more than two or three key vocabulary words.

DIRECTIONS

1. Draw a sample Four-Square Vocabulary Grid on the chalkboard or overhead transparency to model the process for students. Select a word they will already know. For example, if you use the word *happy*, their Four-Square Vocabulary Grid might look like this.

Word	Makes me think of . . .
Happy	Playing with friends, birthday parties, and cartoons
Meaning	**Opposite**
Glad	Sad

2. Have children fold a sheet of paper in half in length and width to form four boxes. Have them label each of the boxes using the words *Word*, *Makes me think of…*, *Meaning*, and *Opposite*. If you prefer, you can give children grids that already contain the labels. Be sure children understand the meanings of the words used for labels.

3. Give the children key words from the unit they are studying. It is important to select words they have already encountered in their reading, discussion, and activities.

4. Have children fill out the Four-Square Vocabulary Grids.

5. Provide time for children to share their grids with their peers. Discuss how and why children may have made different personal associations as part of their grids. Discuss the importance of "making new words their own" by connecting them to their life experiences.

RECORD SHEET

Four~Square Vocabulary Grids

Name _____ Date _____

Word	Makes me think of . . .
Meaning	Opposite

Word	Makes me think of . . .
Meaning	Opposite

From Jerry L. Johns, Susan Davis Lenski, and Laurie Elish-Piper, *Teaching Beginning Readers: Linking Assessment and Instruction* (2nd ed.). Copyright © 2002 by Kendall/Hunt Publishing Company (1-800-247-3458, ext. 5). May be reproduced for noncommercial educational purposes.

Vocabulary and Comprehension

Tips for English Language Learners

Modify the Four-Square Vocabulary Grid so it contains a box for the word in the child's native language, as well as a drawing related to the word. A sample Four-Square Vocabulary Grid is provided below.

Word in English	Word in Spanish
Meaning	Picture

Ideas and Activities

1. Have children keep a vocabulary box using a card file box and index cards. Instruct children to write each vocabulary word on a card and the definition or sentence on the other side. Provide time for children to review the cards independently or with a partner. Children can also take the cards home to review words with their parents or other family members.

2. Have children keep a vocabulary notebook that contains target vocabulary words with their definitions, examples, drawings, and personal associations. Encourage children to add their own vocabulary words to their notebooks. Provide time for children to discuss and compare their vocabulary notebook entries.

3. Play concentration using vocabulary words and their definitions. Have children copy a vocabulary word on each index card. Have them write definitions on other index cards. Divide the class into groups of two. Tell children to place all of the cards face down on the floor or a table. One child begins the game by selecting two cards. If the child draws a word and its definition, he or she keeps the cards and continues drawing until he or she misses. Once the child does not draw a match, the next child gets a turn. Once all of the cards have been matched, the children count the cards in their stacks to see who is the winner.

4. Play vocabulary bingo to help children practice vocabulary words they are learning. Make bingo cards with one vocabulary word in each box. Read aloud a definition or a sentence with the vocabulary word deleted. Ask children to mark the appropriate vocabulary word on their cards using pennies, beans, or plastic counters. Once a child has bingo, ask him or her to say each vocabulary word and give a definition or use it in a sentence. The child who is able to do so is the winner and becomes the caller for the next game.

5. Have children do word sorts to understand differences and commonalties among vocabulary words. Write each vocabulary word on an index card. Give each child or pair a stack of 8 to12 vocabulary words they have been studying recently. For a closed sort, ask children to sort the words into categories you provide. For an open sort, ask children to develop their own categories to divide the words. Provide time for children to share their sorts and explain their groups.

6. Use the List-Group-Label strategy (Readence & Searfoss, 1980) to activate children's background knowledge about a target vocabulary word. For example, for the word *tornado*, ask children to brainstorm words that come to mind. List these words on the chalkboard or chart paper. Next, have children group the words according to common aspects. This step can be done as a whole group or in small groups or dyads once children have learned the strategy. After the words have been grouped, ask children to label each group.

7. Share riddles with children to help them learn and understand vocabulary. For example, for the word, *sum* you might say, "I'm less than all and more than none. I add up in math like 1 + 1. What am I?" After sharing riddles with children, invite them to develop their own and share them with their peers.

Word Learning

Home School Connections

📖 Try to teach your child one new word every few days by using interesting words as you and your child talk and do daily activities. For example, instead of saying, "Are you hungry?" you could ask your child, "Are you famished?" Give your child hints about the meaning of the word so he or she can understand it. Try to use the word many times to help your child remember it. Encourage your child to use the word also.

📖 Talk about new and interesting words your child encounters while reading with you, watching television or videos, listening to the radio, using the computer, or talking with others.

📖 Encourage your child to describe the things he or she sees, hears, and experiences. For example, as you are traveling to the grocery story, ask your child to find something that has wheels. If your child says "a bus," ask him or her to describe the bus using color, size, and other descriptive words.

📖 As you are reading with your child, point out words that may be new to him or her. Discuss what they mean. After you are done reading the story, go back and make up sentences with your child to use the new words.

From Jerry L. Johns, Susan Davis Lenski, and Laurie Elish-Piper, *Teaching Beginning Readers: Linking Assessment and Instruction* (2nd ed.). Copyright © 2002 by Kendall/Hunt Publishing Company (1-800-247-3458, ext. 5). May be reproduced for noncommercial educational purposes.

Selected Resources

MEANING VOCABULARY

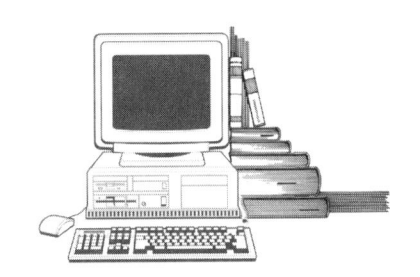

Children's Books with Interesting Language

Heller, R. (1989). *Many luscious lollipops: A book about adjectives*. New York: Grosset Dunlap.

Henkes, K. (2000). *Wemberly worried*. New York: Greenwillow.

Shannon, D. (2000). *The rain came down*. New York: Blue Sky Press.

Sierra, J. (2000). *There's a zoo in room 22*. San Diego: Gulliver Books.

Terban, M. (1987). *Mad as a wet hen and other funny idioms*. New York: Houghton Mifflin.

Tullet, H., & Tingley, M. (1999). *Night/day: A book of eye-catching opposites*. New York: Little Brown.

Media and Technology

Brain Bytes Reading Roller Coaster (word study activities in an amusement park setting). IBM/Edmark. Available from Smart Kids Software (*www.smartkidssoftware.com* or 888-881-6001).

Reading K-1 (stories, writing activities, and an interactive dictionary). School Zone. Available from Smart Kids Software (*www.smartkidssoftware.com* or 888-881-6001).

Word Explorers Deluxe (interactive vocabulary activities, including an electronic picture dictionary). Dorling Kindersley. Available from Smart Kids Software (*www.smartkidssoftware.com* or 888-881-6001).

Wacky World of Words (web site with a wide variety of word games and fun activities related to interesting words in the English language). Available at *http://www.members.home.net/teachwell/index.htm*

Reading Instructional Handbook: Vocabulary Strategies (web site with instructional strategy ideas for teaching vocabulary). Available at *http://smasd.k12.pa.us/pssa/html/Reading/rihand17.htm*

Professional Resources

Blachowicz, C., & Fisher, P. (1995). *Teaching vocabulary in all classrooms*. Upper Saddle River, NJ: Prentice Hall.

Hartill, M. (1998). *Fab vocab: 30 creative vocabulary boosting activities for kids*. New York: Scholastic.

Rasinski, T.V., Hendershot, J., Roskos, K.A., Henry, J.M., Peck, J.K., Moss, B.G., Church, B.W., Fawcett, G., Padak, N.D., & Pryor, E.G. (Eds.). (2001). *Teaching word recognition, spelling, and vocabulary: Strategies from The Reading Teacher*. Newark, DE: International Reading Association.

From Jerry L. Johns, Susan Davis Lenski, and Laurie Elish-Piper, *Teaching Beginning Readers: Linking Assessment and Instruction* (2nd ed.). Copyright © 2002 by Kendall/Hunt Publishing Company (1-800-247-3458, ext. 5). May be reproduced for noncommercial educational purposes.

5.2 Reading Comprehension

> **Goal** To help children understand what they read.
> **Assessment Strategy 1** Caption Reading, page 310
> **Assessment Strategy 2** Passage Reading, page 317
> **Assessment Strategy 3** Retelling, page 336

BACKGROUND

Reading is the process of comprehending text. As children read, they construct meaning from texts or passages. The meaning each child constructs is typically a bit different from the way other readers understand the story. That's because there is not one single, correct interpretation of any story. Comprehension is based on a number of factors, one of which is prior knowledge. As a result, no two readers will produce the same meaning from a text, and no reader's understanding of a text will exactly match what the author had in mind while writing (Goodman, 1996).

As children read, they rely on their background knowledge to make sense of the ideas and concepts of the story. Children also use their knowledge of word identification strategies to identify the words of the text. As they read, children set purposes for reading and monitor their reading progress. Finally, children summarize what they have read and apply those summaries to other situations (Flood & Lapp, 1990). The result of these mental activities is a construction of meaning of the passage.

As you can see, comprehending text is a complex thinking process. Because comprehension is so individual, children will vary in their ability to comprehend different stories. For example, children with a great interest in and knowledge about dogs may closely attend to the Clifford books and read with rich comprehension. Other children may not have that interest and may not comprehend Clifford stories as easily.

The way children apply strategies as they process text also has an impact on reading comprehension. Children who apply many strategies will probably have rich comprehension. Children who do not apply the reading strategies they have learned may not have as deep an understanding of the story. Therefore, you need to teach children how to use thinking strategies to comprehend the stories and books they read. Several teaching strategies, ideas, and activities follow that can help you teach children how to construct meaning as they read.

Teaching Strategy 1

Section 5.2

Think Aloud

Since reading comprehension is an internal act, some children have difficulty understanding what you mean when you say, "Make a prediction," or ask "What was the main idea?" Children often do not know the meaning of the language we use in schools (Johns, 1980). To help them understand the meaning of abstract strategies, conduct a Think Aloud. When you conduct a Think Aloud, children are able to understand better how to use comprehension strategies when reading.

DIRECTIONS

1. Select a passage from a story or informational article that contains a few sentences that may be difficult for the children. For example, you might select the following passage from *Earthquakes* by Franklyn M. Branley (1990).

    Large sections of the Earth's crust are always moving. Sometimes two sections push against each other. The place where they meet is called a fault (p. 16).

2. Display the passage on an overhead projector using a transparency. Read the passage aloud to the children.

3. Think aloud to model how to deal with the vocabulary word *fault*, which has another more common meaning. You may say, "The word *fault* sounds funny here. I know what fault means. It means you did something and you are responsible for it, but I don't know how fault fits with a book on earthquakes. I think I better reread the section to see if I can find clues to what fault means here." Reread the passage aloud. Think aloud by saying, "It says a fault is where they meet. Since they are talking about sections of the Earth's crust, that must be what a fault is. It sounds like a crack. I bet another word for fault is crack. I can look at the picture in the book to see if it looks like a crack."

4. Explain to children that they can use strategies such as rereading and using pictures to help them with difficult words when reading.

5. Engage in Think Alouds on a regular basis so children can understand how to use strategies in real reading situations.

6. Some important reading strategies and Think Aloud prompts are provided in the following table.

Think Alouds

Strategy	Think Aloud Prompts
Previewing	When I look over this passage, I can see . . . The pictures tell me that . . .
Accessing background knowledge	I know some things about . . . This story reminds me of . . .
Setting a purpose	I want to find out about . . . I'm reading this because . . .
Predicting	From the title I can tell . . . I think . . . will happen next because . . .
Visualizing	The picture I have in my mind is . . .
Identifying new words	If I use the other words in the sentence, this word must be . . . What parts of the word do I know?
Thinking through a confusing point	This might mean . . . I'm not sure I understand this because . . .
Checking for understanding	So far, this story is about . . . The important parts so far are . . .
Using fix-up strategies	I need to reread the part about . . . I need help with . . .
Summarizing the story	The story was about . . . The story means . . .

From Jerry L. Johns, Susan Davis Lenski, and Laurie Elish-Piper, *Teaching Beginning Readers: Linking Assessment and Instruction* (2nd ed.). Copyright © 2002 by Kendall/Hunt Publishing Company (1-800-247-3458, ext. 5). May be reproduced for noncommercial educational purposes.

Tips for English Language Learners

- Use gestures such as pointing to your head or an actual hat labeled as a thinking cap to clarify that you are sharing thoughts in your head.

- Write the name of the strategy you are using on the chalkboard and display a graphic or icon next to it to clarify its meaning. For example, for rereading, show an arrow pointing back to the beginning of the word.

Teaching Strategy 2

Section 5.2

Directed Reading-Thinking Activity (DR-TA)

The Directed Reading-Thinking Activity (DR-TA) (Stauffer, 1969) is a strategy that mirrors the thinking processes good readers use as they construct meaning from texts. The DR-TA can be applied to fiction and nonfiction. The strategy encourages making predictions and monitoring reading comprehension.

DIRECTIONS

1. Select a story or a passage to read aloud to the children. Read the title aloud. Then ask the children to predict the contents of the story by saying, "What do you think the story will be about?" Encourage children to suggest many ideas.

2. Read the first few paragraphs or pages. Stop reading after you have introduced a few ideas or events. Ask children to monitor their comprehension by saying, "What just happened in the story?" Tie in their predictions about the title of the story by asking, "Was your first prediction about the story correct?" Allow children time to think; then have them volunteer their answers. If children give a misinterpretation, you may choose to correct them, or you may decide to reread the passage and ask again.

3. After children have a clear understanding of the story thus far, encourage predictions by asking them the following question, "What do you think will happen next?" Allow children to predict many options. After each prediction, ask the follow-up question, "Why do you think so?"

4. After children have made several predictions, tell children that you will continue to read the story and that they should listen to find out if their predictions were correct.

5. Read several more paragraphs or pages. Stop once more and ask children to monitor their comprehension and to make predictions. Use the same questions you asked previously. Allow children time to discuss the story thus far and make additional predictions.

6. Read the rest of the story and ask children to retell the entire story. You may choose to have children retell the story to a partner, to you, or by writing in their journals.

Vocabulary and Comprehension

7. Repeat the DR-TA questions frequently to encourage children to ask the same questions as they read independently. Also, use the DR-TA during guided reading lessons. The basic DR-TA questions are listed below.

> ### DR-TA Questions
> What do you think the story will be about?
>
> What just happened?
>
> What do you think will happen next? Why do you think so?

Teaching Strategy 3

Section 5.2

Story Frame

A Story Frame is a summary outline of an entire story. After reading a story, children can fill in the blanks of a Story Frame to improve their comprehension (Fowler, 1982). You can create a general Story Frame as in the example below or write one specifically for a story or passage.

DIRECTIONS

1. Identify a story or a passage that has a plot that children can easily identify. Read the story aloud or have the children read it independently or with partners.

2. Encourage children to construct meaning from the story by reminding them to use comprehension monitoring strategies. For example, have them read and monitor their comprehension using the DR-TA. (See Teaching Strategy 2.) Remind them to use fix-up strategies if they lose track of the story's plot.

3. After the children have finished reading, remind them of the elements of the story. Explain that every story has a problem but that the problem might be something the main character wants done. For example, the problem in the story *Rainy Day Fun* (Palazzo, 1988) is that the children are trying to think of what they could do on a rainy day. Explain that this is the problem of the story and that events will happen through the story to solve the problem. Have children identify the solution to the problem. In *Rainy Day Fun* (Palazzo, 1988), the children decided to put on a play.

4. After children have identified the problem in the story, remind them that stories are told by events in sequential order. Have them identify the events in the story they have read.

5. Ask children to retell the story they read. Remind them to state the problem of the story, the events in the plot, and how the problem was solved. If they forget any part of the plot, direct the children to reread that portion of the story.

6. Provide children with a copy of a Story Frame. Tell them that they should fill in the blanks so that the entire paragraph tells part of the story. Children can work with a partner or independently.

7. Identify one of the children's Story Frames that correctly tells the story. Read it aloud to the children. Have children check their Story Frames to determine if they understood the story. A copy of a Story Frame is on the following page.

Story Frame

Story Title _____ Name _____

In this story, the problem starts when _____
_____.

After that, _____
_____.

Next, _____
_____.

Then, _____
_____.

The problem is finally solved when _____
_____.

The story ends _____
_____.

From Jerry L. Johns, Susan Davis Lenski, and Laurie Elish-Piper, *Teaching Beginning Readers: Linking Assessment and Instruction* (2nd ed.). Copyright © 2002 by Kendall/Hunt Publishing Company (1-800-247-3458, ext. 5). May be reproduced for noncommercial educational purposes.

Tips for English Language Learners

- Teach the Story Frame strategy to English Language Learners first with a very familiar story so they can learn how to use the strategy itself.

- Encourage English Language Learners to use pictures and writing to complete the Story Frame.

- Pair an English Language Learner with a native English-speaking student for the Story Frame strategy to provide support and collaboration.

Teaching Strategy 4

Section 5.2

Idea-Mapping

Idea-Mapping (Armbruster, 1986) is a visual picture of how ideas are organized in informational texts. As children read nonfiction or content area textbooks such as social studies or science books, they need to understand how text is organized in order to understand it fully. Idea-Maps help children identify important information, understand the relationship among the ideas, and improve their comprehension of the passages.

DIRECTIONS

1. Select a passage from an informational book such as a science text that is organized so that the main idea comes first and the details follow. An example adapted from *Whales: A First Discovery Book* (Jeunesse, Delafosse, Fuhr, & Sautai, 1991) follows.

   > There are two kinds of whales—toothed whales and baleen whales. Baleen whales have big mouths and no teeth. Instead, they have baleens. Baleens look like the teeth of a comb, hanging from the upper jaw. With their baleens, the biggest animals in the ocean catch the tiniest animals in the ocean. There are four kinds of baleen whales. They are blue whales, right whales, humpback whales, and gray whales.

2. Write the passage on the chalkboard, a piece of chart paper, or an overhead transparency. Have children read the passage independently or with a partner. After children have read the passage, ask them to tell their partner what they have learned.

3. Explain that sometimes books are not written as a story with a plot, setting, and characters but that they are providing information. Ask children to name additional informational books they have read or heard. If children do not mention school textbooks such as their science book, remind children that their science book also gives information.

4. Tell children that informational books are written in many different ways. Tell them that one of the ways authors of informational books organize their facts is by giving a main idea first, then writing details that fit the main idea. Ask children to identify the topic of the passage they have read. If they have difficulty identifying the topic, tell them that the topic in this passage is a description of a baleen whale.

5. Distribute copies of the Idea-Map. A sample Idea-Map follows.

Name _____ Date _____

Idea-Map

Main Idea:

Detail:

Detail:

Detail:

Detail:

Main Idea Sentence:

From Jerry L. Johns, Susan Davis Lenski, and Laurie Elish-Piper, *Teaching Beginning Readers: Linking Assessment and Instruction* (2nd ed.). Copyright © 2002 by Kendall/Hunt Publishing Company (1-800-247-3458, ext. 5). May be reproduced for noncommercial educational purposes.

6. Have children write the topic of the passage on the first line. The topic they write should be baleen whales.

7. Ask children what they learned about baleen whales from the passage. Tell them that even though they may know other information about baleen whales, they should identify only things they have read in this particular passage. Give children a few minutes to identify the details. Then have them write the details on the next several lines. Tell them that they do not need to fill in every line but that they should list as many details as they find in the passage.

8. Finally, have children create a sentence that combines the topic and the details. Have children reread their Idea-Map, turn it face down on their desks, and tell their partner what the passage was about. Guide children to understand that the main idea sentence should be something like the following one: Baleen whales are the four kinds of whales that eat using baleens.

9. Have children write their main idea sentence on the final line of the Idea-Map. Allow children to write different main idea sentences.

10. Repeat this activity several times, each time giving children more independence until they can use the Idea-Map on their own.

Teaching Strategy 5

Section 5.2

Making Text Connections

Children can enhance their comprehension by making connections from what they are reading to their own experiences, prior knowledge, or other texts with which they are familiar. The Making Text Connections strategy helps children understand and remember what they are reading by making it personally meaningful. This strategy works well with both fiction and informational text.

DIRECTIONS

1. Introduce the Making Text Connections strategy to students by explaining how important it is for readers to connect what they are reading to their own experiences, what they already know, and other books they have read or stories they know.

2. Select a story that the children will be able to relate to and read it aloud to them. For example, you might select *Chrysanthemum* by Kevin Henkes (1991). In this story, Chrysanthemum loves her name until the other mice at her school begin to tease her. When a very special substitute teacher tells her how much she loves her name, Chrysanthemum is thrilled and all of her schoolmates want to change their names to flowers, too.

3. Display the Making Text Connections sheet on the overhead transparency, chalkboard, or chart paper. Explain to the children that you want them to think of a connection the story has to their own lives. If the children are unsure, you may share one of your own connections such as, "When I was younger, a boy at school teased me because I was the tallest one in the class. It made me feel sad and embarrassed." Provide time for children to share their connections to self.

4. Direct the children's attention to the next column: connections to the world. Ask the children what connections they can think of between the story and something else in life and the world. If children have difficulty making a connection, you may share one of your own connections such as, "Chrysanthemum is such an interesting name. I think it is interesting to find out how people and places get their names. I learned that our town is named after the first family that lived here."

5. Direct the children's attention to the next column: connections to other texts. Ask the children what other books, stories, poems, movies, television programs, or other texts the story makes them think of. Invite them to share their reasons.
6. A blank Making Text Connections chart is provided on the next page.

Making Text Connections

Name _____ Date _____

Title _____

Text to Self	Text to World	Text to Text

From Jerry L. Johns, Susan Davis Lenski, and Laurie Elish-Piper, *Teaching Beginning Readers: Linking Assessment and Instruction* (2nd ed.). Copyright © 2002 by Kendall/Hunt Publishing Company (1-800-247-3458, ext. 5). **May be** reproduced for noncommercial educational purposes.

Tips for English Language Learners

- Invite English Language Learners to work with a partner, draw their responses and label them, or share their connections orally.

- Use a very familiar story to introduce the Making Text Connections strategy. By using such a story, English Language Learners will be able to focus their attention on identifying and verbalizing the connections rather than trying to understand a new story.

Ideas and Activities

1. Have children read a story independently. They may read silently, with a partner, or out loud. After they have finished reading the story, ask one child to begin to retell the story. Encourage the first child to retell only one or two sentences. Write the sentences on the chalkboard or on an overhead transparency. Then invite another child to continue retelling the story. Write that child's retelling and continue until the story is completed. Read the retold story aloud inviting children to read with you. Explain that after readers finish reading a passage they should retell the story to themselves to help them remember it.

2. Have children create a literature time line after reading a story. Tell children that as they are reading the story they should pay particular attention to the events in the story. After children have finished reading, have them draw a horizontal line at the center of a long piece of paper. Under the line, they should write information about the time the event took place. They may have information about days of the week, months, seasons, or years. Above the time, they can draw a picture of the event that took place. Display the literature time lines around the room.

3. Encourage children to read books in a series. After they begin a series, have children write journal entries that record the main events of the story and other particulars about the main characters. As they get to know characters that are repeated in series books, children can begin writing questions to the characters. Another child reading the same series can answer the questions.

4. Help children identify the main idea of a story. Cut passages from old books or articles that are at a variety of reading levels. Fasten the passages to index cards. On the back of each card write several possible phrases or sentences that describe the main idea. Have children read the passage, write their answers on a separate sheet of paper, and then compare them with the answers on the back of the cards.

5. Before children read a story, list several words from the passage on the chalkboard or an overhead transparency. Add other words to the list that are not included in the story. For example, if you were reading *Sam's Sandwich* (Pelham, 1990), you might include the following words: *horse, lettuce, cake, picnic, cucumber, salami, ants, swim,* and *ketchup*. Before children read the story, have them predict what words they think they will encounter as they read. Ask children for reasons for their choices. As children read, have them write down the words that they found in the text. After children read, encourage them to retell the story using the words that were part of the original list.

6. Encourage children to think deeply about characters in stories by having them create a character web. To create a character web, place the name of the character in the center of a circle. Then have children brainstorm qualities of the character. Since children often have difficulty thinking of character traits, you might also volunteer some ideas. Then write the characteristics of the story character on lines radiating out from the circle. See page 293 for a blank character web.

7. Have children act out a story after reading with a tableau (Purves, Rogers, & Soter, 1990). Tell children that they will be creating a tableau, or a frozen scene, from a story they have read. Explain that a tableau is a scene much like a photograph. A tableau captures a scene and, unlike a videotape, it does not show movement. Explain that to create a tableau children will have to discuss which event they want to portray. Then have children decide how to arrange themselves and their props so that the audience will understand the event. Have children practice creating the tableau several times before presenting it to an audience.

8. Help children form mental images as they read by asking them to describe images as they are reading. For example, if children are reading a Curious George story, have them describe what George is seeing and what George is doing. Then have them draw a picture of a scene from the story. Explain that when readers are reading, they try to picture what they are reading.

9. Encourage children to identify sequence as they read. Explain that stories have a beginning, a middle, and an end and that the events are in a specific order. To reinforce the concept of sequence, gather several comic strips that children can read independently. Cut the comic strips into their frames. Scramble the order of the frames and have children put them in order.

10. Have children write Prove-It Prompts (May, 1998). Have children identify a section in their story to predict. Before children read, have them write what they think the passage will be about. Then have them write why they think so. After that, have children read that section of the story. After children read, have them write whether their predictions were correct and what happened in the story that proved the outcome of their predictions. See page 294 for a sample Prove-It Prompts Sheet.

11. Have children complete paper bag retellings to enhance their comprehension. First, ask children to identify key items from a story, then make paper cutouts of these items, and finally put them in a paper bag they have decorated and labeled with the title of the book. Children can then do their retellings by using the items in the bag. Children can share their retellings with partners, the class, or their families.

12. Use the quilting strategy to help children identify and understand the message, moral, or theme of a story. Ask children to write the message, moral, or theme in the center of a piece of construction paper and then give examples of it from the book or their lives. Children can share their construction paper quilt blocks and assemble them into a classroom story quilt on the bulletin board or wall. A sample quilt block for *Ruby the Copycat* (Rathmann, 1997) is shown on page 295.

Character Web

Name _____ Date _____

Character

From Jerry L. Johns, Susan Davis Lenski, and Laurie Elish-Piper, *Teaching Beginning Readers: Linking Assessment and Instruction* (2nd ed.). Copyright © 2002 by Kendall/Hunt Publishing Company (1-800-247-3458, ext. 5). May be reproduced for noncommercial educational purposes.

Prove-It Prompts

Name _____ Date _____

Pages _____ to _____

BEFORE YOU READ: What do you think this section will be about?

_____

_____

_____

_____

Why do you think so?

_____

_____

_____

_____

AFTER YOU READ: Prove you were right or wrong.

_____

_____

_____

_____

From Jerry L. Johns, Susan Davis Lenski, and Laurie Elish-Piper, *Teaching Beginning Readers: Linking Assessment and Instruction* (2nd ed.). Copyright © 2002 by Kendall/Hunt Publishing Company (1-800-247-3458, ext. 5). May be reproduced for noncommercial educational purposes.

Ruby the Copycat
by Peggy Rathmann

Ruby is a great hopper.

Angela was good at lots of things.

Everyone is special and has talents.

I am a good artist.

My sister is good at singing.

Home School Connections: Sharing Books

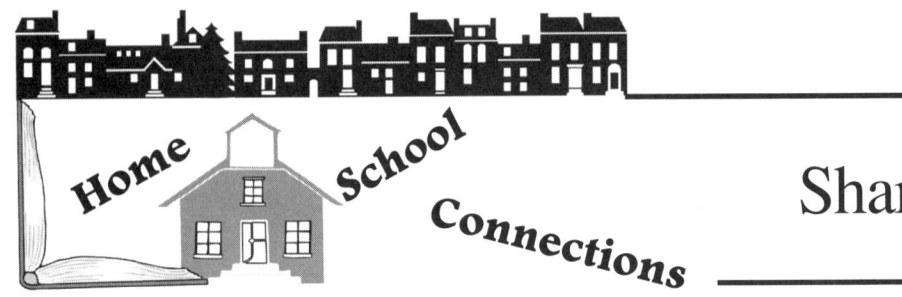

📖 Retelling a story is a great way to help your child understand and remember stories. Your child has completed a paper bag retelling activity at school. Ask your child to retell the story using the cards in the bag. Discuss the story. Sign your child's paper bag to show that you completed the activity.

📖 Reading and sharing books is a great way to help your child become a good reader. Your child's class is doing a book bag program to make connections between home and school. Please read the enclosed book with your child and complete the activities listed below. Return the book bag to school as soon as possible so it can be shared with other families.

Book Bag Program

1. Read the book with your child.
2. Talk about your favorite parts.
3. Draw something about the book in the notebook.
4. Write a sentence to explain your picture.
5. Sign your name and have your child write his or her name.
6. Return the bag, book, notebook, and crayons to school by _____.

From Jerry L. Johns, Susan Davis Lenski, and Laurie Elish-Piper, *Teaching Beginning Readers: Linking Assessment and Instruction* (2nd ed.). Copyright © 2002 by Kendall/Hunt Publishing Company (1-800-247-3458, ext. 5). May be reproduced for noncommercial educational purposes.

Selected Resources
READING COMPREHENSION

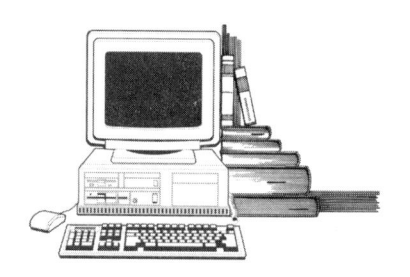

Series Books

Amelia Bedelia Series by P. Parish (New York: Scholastic).
Amelia Bedelia, Amelia Bedelia goes camping, Amelia Bedelia's family album.

Boxcar Children Series by G. C. Warner (New York: Albert Whitman).
Boxcar children: Bicycle mystery, Boxcar children: Camp-out mystery, Boxcar children: Snowbound mystery.

Cam Jansen Series by D.A. Adler (New York: Puffin).
Cam Jansen and the mystery at the monkey house, Cam Jansen and the mystery of the gold coins.

Corduroy Series by D. Freeman (New York: Viking).
Corduroy, Corduroy's party, Corduroy's toys.

Curious George Series by H.A. Rey (Boston: Houghton Mifflin).
Curious George, Curious George flies a kite, Curious George goes to the circus.

Frog and Toad Series by A. Lobel (New York: Harper & Row).
Frog and Toad are friends, Frog and Toad all year, Frog and Toad together.

Madeline Series by L. Bemelmans (New York: Puffin).
Madeline, Madeline and the gypsies, Madeline in London.

Mr. Putter and Tabby Series by C. Rylant (Orlando, FL: Harcourt Brace).
Mr. Putter and Tabby bake the cake, Mr. Putter and Tabby pour the tea.

Nate the Great Series by S.M. Weinman (New York: Dell).
Nate the Great, Nate the Great and the lost list, Nate the Great and the snowy trail.

Pee Wee Scout Series by J. Delton (New York: Dell).
Pee Wee Scouts: Cookies and crutches, Pee Wee's on first, Pee Wee's on parade.

Media and Technology

Interactive Reading Journey CD-ROM (interactive trip through stories). The Learning Company. Available from Smart Kids Software (*www.smartkidssoftware.com* or 888-881-6001).

Magic Tales (interactive folktales from around the world). Davidson. Available from Smart Kids Software (*www.smartkidssoftware.com* or 888-881-6001).

Reader Rabbit's Personalized Reading (imaginative trip through reading lessons and interactive storybooks). The Learning Company. Available from Smart Kids Software (*www.smartkidssoftware.com* or 888-881-6001).

Reader Rabbit Reading Development Library 1–4 (collections of interactive fairy tales). The Learning Company. Available from Smart Kids Software (*www.smartkidssoftware.com* or 888-881-6001).

Reading Quest with Aladdin (activities to build reading comprehension and sequencing skills). Disney. Available from Smart Kids Software (*www.smartkidssoftware.com* or 888-881-6001).

From Jerry L. Johns, Susan Davis Lenski, and Laurie Elish-Piper, *Teaching Beginning Readers: Linking Assessment and Instruction* (2nd ed.). Copyright © 2002 by Kendall/Hunt Publishing Company (1-800-247-3458, ext. 5). May be reproduced for noncommercial educational purposes.

5.3 Monitoring Reading

> **Goal** To help children monitor their reading.
> **Assessment Strategy 4** Monitoring Strategies Checklist, page 339

BACKGROUND

Effective readers monitor their reading to ensure that what they are reading makes sense. One of the keys to becoming an independent reader is the ability to identify and correct one's comprehension problems (Paris, Lipson, & Wixon, 1994). Effective readers ask themselves, "Do I understand what I'm reading?" They also make pictures in their minds, predict from the text, and ask themselves questions as they read. When effective readers detect that what they are reading does not make sense, they realize this and apply appropriate correction or "fix-up" strategies. For example, they may look at pictures, reread to clarify ideas, look up a word in a dictionary, reread for word meaning, or ask for help (Cunningham & Allington, 1998).

Metacognition, or thinking about one's own thinking processes, is an important aspect of monitoring reading (Flavell, 1977). Baker (1991) has identified specific areas that help children develop monitoring strategies for reading. Even young readers can be taught to be on the lookout for the following:

- Words they don't understand.
- Information that doesn't connect with what they already know; and
- Ideas that don't make sense.

While most young children do not automatically monitor their reading, they can be taught simple strategies to help them monitor as they read. The strategies and activities discussed below provide suggestions for teaching your students to become active readers who monitor their reading.

Teaching Strategy 1

Section 5.3

Critter

The Critter strategy helps children create a visual image to assist them with monitoring their reading (Johns & Lenski, 2001). It serves as a concrete reminder to children that they need to think while they are reading and that their reading should make sense.

DIRECTIONS

1. Draw a cartoon-like Critter and present it to the children on the chalkboard, a piece of chart paper, or an overhead transparency. A sample Critter is provided on the next page.

2. Tell children that they can use the Critter to help them think and understand as they read.

3. Ask children to visualize a Critter that they have in their heads that helps them read. Provide time for children to share their ideas.

4. Have children draw and color their Critters.

5. Guide children to develop a list of important questions the Critter can help the children ask themselves as they read. Some possible questions follow.

    - Do I understand what I am reading?
    - What do I already know about the topic?
    - How can I figure out this hard word?
    - Can I use a picture to help me?
    - Do I need to reread?
    - Should I look up the word in a dictionary?
    - Should I ask for help?

6. Laminate the children's Critters and mount them on their desks or reading folders. Post in the classroom the list of questions their Critters can prompt the children to ask themselves. Remind the children to use their Critters to help them think about and understand what they are reading.

Vocabulary and Comprehension

> **Teaching Strategy 2**

Section 5.3

Monitoring Think-Along

The Monitoring Think-Along strategy helps children understand the self-monitoring strategies that good readers use. The Monitoring Think-Along can be used to model many different self-monitoring strategies, such as making pictures in your mind, predicting what will come next, asking questions about the text, rereading to clarify ideas, rereading for word meanings, and connecting the text to personal experiences.

DIRECTIONS

1. Select a Big Book or other text that all children will be able to see. Tell children that you are going to show them some strategies that good readers use.
2. Point your index finger to your head to show that you are thinking. Tell children, "I am thinking about what this book might be about."
3. Read the title aloud and, using information from the title, make a comment such as, "That is the name of a girl. I think the story will be about her."
4. Tell the children, "Now, I'll look at the picture on the cover."
5. Make a comment using information from the cover illustration such as, "It looks like a birthday party. I think the book will be about the girl's birthday party."
6. Close your eyes, point your index finger to your head to show you are thinking, and say, "Now I'll try to make a picture in my mind of what might happen at the birthday party." Share with the children some of the things you are visualizing. For example, "I see presents, a chocolate birthday cake, balloons, and lots of children. It looks like everyone is having fun."
7. Begin to read the text aloud. After reading several sentences, stop and ask yourself a question about what you just read. For example, say, "Am I right that the book is about a birthday party? Do I need to change my prediction?" Share your answers with the children.
8. Continue reading the text, stopping periodically to model a monitoring strategy that good readers use. The list below contains possible strategies to model as part of the Monitoring Think-Along.

    Self-Monitoring Strategies

    - Make pictures in your mind.
    - Predict what will come next.
    - Ask questions about the text.
    - Reread to clarify ideas.
    - Reread for word meanings.
    - Connect the text to personal experiences.

Teaching Strategy 3

Section 5.3

Pause~Think~Retell

The Pause-Think-Retell (Robb, 1996) strategy helps children get into the habit of monitoring their comprehension while reading longer texts. This strategy focuses on having children pause at the end of a paragraph, page, or section of text, think about what they have read, and retell the important ideas to themselves. If children are unable to remember enough to retell the text to themselves, they should reread that portion of the text.

DIRECTIONS

1. Select a text that might be challenging for the children. Recopy the text onto chart paper or copy it onto overhead transparencies so all of the children will be able to see it.

2. Tell children that good readers use the Pause-Think-Retell strategy to make sure they understand what they are reading.

3. Model the strategy for children by reading the first paragraph, page, or section of text aloud. Then Pause, point to your head as you Think, and ask yourself, "Can I Retell what I just read?"

4. Retell several of the ideas from the paragraph, page, or section but leave out some important ideas.

5. Tell children, "I think I need to reread that because I can't retell all of the important ideas."

6. Reread the section aloud, emphasizing the important points. Then Pause, point to your head as you Think, and prompt yourself to Retell the important information. Tell children that because you remembered the important ideas from the section, you can go on to the next part of the text. You may also want to remind children how to distinguish among ideas; some are more important than others.

7. Continue modeling this strategy for the next paragraph, page, or section. This time, provide a complete retelling and tell children, "I remembered the important ideas so I can go on to the next part of the book."

8. Continue modeling this strategy for several paragraphs, pages, or sections.

9. Ask children to try the strategy with the next section of the text. Provide prompts such as "Stop and think," "Can you retell what you just read?" and "Did you remember all the important ideas?" to guide them through the process. If children have difficulty distinguishing between important ideas and minor details in their retellings, before conducting further retellings you may want to reteach students how to distinguish minor details from important ideas.

10. Display a poster that has the words Pause-Think-Retell on it. Remind children to use this strategy when they are reading independently.

Tips for English Language Learners

- Encourage English Language Learners to pantomime or draw parts of the retellings they have difficulty verbalizing.

- Provide props to assist English Language Learners do retellings of what they have read. Picture cards with labels can also be used to support retellings for English Language Learners.

> **Teaching Strategy 4**

Section 5.3

Monitoring Logs

Monitoring Logs allow children to gain insight into how to monitor their independent reading and which monitoring strategies work best in specific situations. When Monitoring Logs are first introduced, the teacher will take on much of the responsibility. Gradually, children will learn to complete the logs on their own.

DIRECTIONS

1. Tell students that good readers monitor their reading. Explain that monitoring means to think about and make sure you are understanding what you are reading. If you are not understanding it, you should go back and try to fix up your understanding.

2. Remind students of fix-up strategies they have learned such as rereading, using picture clues, getting a word meaning, or asking for help. List these on an overhead transparency or write them on the chalkboard or a piece of chart paper.

3. Display a transparency containing a short passage or sentence that may be confusing to the children. Read the passage aloud and think aloud to demonstrate how you handle the difficult text. For example, you could model how to use context to figure out an unknown word by using the following sentence.

    After the dog died, he felt so miserable that he thought he would never stop crying.

    You might say, "If my dog died, I'd cry a lot too. I'd feel so sad. I bet the word *miserable* means sad."

4. Place a transparency containing a page from a Monitoring Log on the overhead projector. Explain to the children that you want to keep track of what strategies you can use to monitor your reading. Fill out the log using the example you just demonstrated.

Title	Problem	What I did	Did it work?
My Dog Sport	I didn't know what miserable meant.	Used context	Yes

5. Tell children that they will be keeping Monitoring Logs. Begin using the Monitoring Logs in conjunction with guided reading groups to provide support for the children. As children begin to understand the process more fully, ask them to add one new entry to their Monitoring Logs at the end of independent reading. Provide time for children to share and discuss their Monitoring Logs with you and their peers.

Monitoring Log

Name _____ Date _____

Title	Problem	What I did	Did it work?

From Jerry L. Johns, Susan Davis Lenski, and Laurie Elish-Piper, *Teaching Beginning Readers: Linking Assessment and Instruction* (2nd ed.). Copyright © 2002 by Kendall/Hunt Publishing Company (1-800-247-3458, ext. 5). May be reproduced for noncommercial educational purposes.

Vocabulary and Comprehension

Ideas and Activities

1. Make bookmarks that include monitoring strategies and questions. Provide copies for home and school reading.

2. Develop an I-Need-Help Procedure for children when they realize their reading doesn't make sense and their strategies are not working. Have children copy the I-Need-Help Procedure on the cover of their reading folder or on a bookmark. Also display the I-Need-Help Procedure on a poster in the classroom. A sample I-Need-Help Procedure is listed in the box.

I-Need-Help Procedure

1. Think for a minute. Try to solve the problem yourself.
2. Use classroom resources to help you (monitoring log, monitoring posters, World Wall).
3. Ask three students for help.
4. Ask the teacher.

---

3. Explain to the children that good readers create pictures in their minds as they read. Read a passage aloud and ask the children to draw what they saw in their minds. Provide time for the children to share their drawings. Compare their drawings to the text. Explain that good readers create these types of pictures in their minds while they are reading. Read another passage to the children and ask them to close their eyes and visualize a picture in their minds based on the passage. Provide sharing time. Encourage children to use visualization as they read.

4. Have children use partner questioning to support the use of monitoring strategies. Divide the class into partners and have one partner serve as the questioner and the other as the reader. The reader should read a paragraph aloud, and the questioner should ask a question about how the reader monitored his or her reading. For example, the questioner may ask, "Did that make sense to you?" or "Can you retell that in your own words?" or "What did you do when you came to the hard word?" Children can refer to the list of monitoring questions from their Monitoring Logs (Teaching Strategy 4) or the strategy picture cards (Idea 5) to help them with this activity.

5. Use strategy picture cards to provide children with a visual clue regarding the monitoring strategies they can use to help them understand their reading. Post the picture cards in the classroom, provide children with their own copy for their reading folder, and send a copy home for the children and their parents to use for home reading. Sample strategy picture cards are provided on the next page.

Strategy Picture Cards

Does It Make Sense?	What Do You Already Know?
Read On.	Look at Word Parts and Letters.
Reread.	Make a Prediction. *The picture makes me think of . . .*
Make a Picture in Your Head.	Retell in Your Own Words. *In this story, the . . .*
Look at Picture Clues.	Ask for Help. **Try 3; then ask me for HELP!**

From Jerry L. Johns, Susan Davis Lenski, and Laurie Elish-Piper, *Teaching Beginning Readers: Linking Assessment and Instruction* (2nd ed.). Copyright © 2002 by Kendall/Hunt Publishing Company (1-800-247-3458, ext. 5). May be reproduced for noncommercial educational purposes.

Home School Connections

Checking Understanding

📖 Good readers use a variety of strategies to monitor their reading to make sure they understand what they are reading. Use this bookmark to prompt your child to use monitoring strategies when you are reading together. Be sure to provide at least five seconds of "thinking time" before prompting your child.

- Does it make sense?
- What do you already know?
- Look at word parts and letters.
- Make a prediction.
- Read on.
- Reread.
- Make a picture in your head.
- Look at picture clues.
- Retell in your own words.

From Jerry L. Johns, Susan Davis Lenski, and Laurie Elish-Piper, *Teaching Beginning Readers: Linking Assessment and Instruction* (2nd ed.). Copyright © 2002 by Kendall/Hunt Publishing Company (1-800-247-3458, ext. 5). May be reproduced for noncommercial educational purposes.

Home School Connections: Pause-Think-Retell

📖 Your child has learned the Pause-Think-Retell strategy at school. Please use this strategy with your child after reading a book or watching a television program. The steps are outlined in the box below.

Pause-Think-Retell

PAUSE: Stop near the middle of the story or television program.

THINK: Think what it has been about so far.

RETELL: Tell about the important parts so far.

From Jerry L. Johns, Susan Davis Lenski, and Laurie Elish-Piper, *Teaching Beginning Readers: Linking Assessment and Instruction*. Copyright © 2002 by Kendall/Hunt Publishing Company (1-800-247-3458, ext. 5). May be reproduced for noncommercial educational purposes.

Selected Resources
MONITORING READING

Big Books for Demonstrating Monitoring Reading

Cowley, J. (1983). *Meanies*. San Diego: Rigby.

Ehlert, L. (1990). *Feathers for lunch*. New York: Trumpet.

Oppenheim, J. (1994). *"Not now! said the cow."* New York: Trumpet.

Peek, M. (1985). *Mary wore her red dress*. New York: Trumpet.

Wells, R. (1985). *Hazel's amazing mother*. New York: Dial.

Williams, S. (1989). *I went walking*. New York: Trumpet.

Media and Technology

Reader Rabbit's Thinking Adventures CD-ROM (activities to build problem solving strategies and early reading strategies). The Learning Company. Available from Smart Kids Software (*www.smartkidssoftware.com* or 888-881-6001).

Reading K-1 CD-ROM (predictable stories for beginning readers). School Zone. Available from Smart Kids Software (*www.smartkidssoftware.com* or 888-881-6001).

Reading Maze CD-ROM (mazes that require thinking and reading strategies). Great Wave Surfware. Available from Smart Kids Software (*www.smartkidssoftware.com* or 888-881-6001).

Professional Resources

Baskwell, J., & Whitman, P. (1997). *Every child can read: Strategies and guidelines for helping struggling readers*. New York: Scholastic Professional Books.

Combs, M. (1996). *Developing competent readers and writers in the primary grades*. Columbus, OH: Merrill.

Robb, L. (1996). *Reading strategies that work: Teaching your students to become better readers*. New York: Scholastic Professional Books.

From Jerry L. Johns, Susan Davis Lenski, and Laurie Elish-Piper, *Teaching Beginning Readers: Linking Assessment and Instruction* (2nd ed.). Copyright © 2002 by Kendall/Hunt Publishing Company (1-800-247-3458, ext. 5). May be reproduced for noncommercial educational purposes.

5.4 Assessments of Reading Comprehension and Monitoring Reading

Assessment Strategy 1   Caption Reading   310
- Form 1 Child's Copy   311
- Form 1 Record Sheet   312
- Form 2 Child's Copy   314
- Form 2 Record Sheet   315

Assessment Strategy 2   Passage Reading   317
- Form 1 Easy Sight Word Reading Child's Copy   320
- Form 1 Easy Sight Word Reading Record Sheet   321
- Form 1 Beginning Passage Reading Child's Copy   322
- Form 1 Beginning Passage Reading Record Sheet   323
- Form 1 Grade 1 Child's Copy   324
- Form 1 Grade 1 Record Sheet   325
- Form 1 Grade 2 Child's Copy   326
- Form 1 Grade 2 Record Sheet   327
- Form 2 Easy Sight Word Reading Child's Copy   328
- Form 2 Easy Sight Word Reading Record Sheet   329
- Form 2 Beginning Passage Reading Child's Copy   330
- Form 2 Beginning Passage Reading Record Sheet   331
- Form 2 Grade 1 Child's Copy   332
- Form 2 Grade 1 Record Sheet   333
- Form 2 Grade 2 Child's Copy   334
- Form 2 Grade 2 Record Sheet   335

Assessment Strategy 3   Retelling   336
- Record Sheet   337

Assessment Strategy 4   Monitoring Strategies Checklist   339
- Record Sheet   340

Goal To assess a child's comprehension and monitoring strategies.

Vocabulary and Comprehension   309

BACKGROUND

Teachers can learn a great deal about children's understanding of vocabulary, comprehension, and use of monitoring strategies through ongoing observation, often called "kidwatching" (Goodman, 1982). At times, however, teachers want to have additional documentation about children's performance, strengths, and needs. The assessment strategies offered in this section are designed to give you useful information about children's understanding of vocabulary, comprehension, and use of monitoring strategies in real reading contexts. The results of the assessments will provide you insights about how to plan instruction to support the children in your classroom.

Assessment Strategy 1

Section 5.4

Caption Reading

Overview	Caption Reading will assess the child's ability to read a brief story with helpful picture clues. This is a helpful assessment to use with children who are just beginning to read.
Materials Needed	1. The page in this book containing the caption story, either Form 1 (p. 311) or Form 2 (p. 314) 2. A copy of the Record Sheet that corresponds to the form selected for use, either Form 1 (p. 312) or Form 2 (p. 315)
Procedures	1. Show the child the page containing the story. 2. Invite the child to look at frames of the story (pictures and text) in order as numbered. 3. Then ask the child to read the story aloud. Say, "I want you to read the story to me." As the student reads, mentally note any miscues or record them on the appropriate page of the Record Sheet. 4. If the child has difficulty reading the story, have the child listen while you read it aloud. Say, "Listen to me read the story. Then I will want you to read it to me." After your reading, invite the child to read. 5. Encourage the child to talk about the story with you.
Scoring and Interpretation	Informally note the miscues the child made, the degree of fluency, and other behaviors on the Record Sheet. If the child was able to read the captions, you can informally analyze fluency, miscues, and overall engagement with the task. If you read the story first, evaluate the degree to which the child was able to memorize and repeat the text. Be alert for how the child uses language as you talk about the story.

1

The cat sleeps.

2

The dog sleeps.

3

The bird sleeps.

4

The baby sleeps.

Form 1—Caption Reading—Child's Copy

RECORD SHEET

Form 1

Caption Reading

Name _____ Date _____

The cat sleeps.

The dog sleeps.

The bird sleeps.

The baby sleeps.

QUALITATIVE JUDGMENTS OF READING

If the child read the story, check the statement that best describes the child's reading.

_____ The child's reading is an exact match with the text.

_____ The child's reading closely matches the text.

_____ The child's reading is somewhat related to the text but is based on the illustrations.

_____ The child's reading is related mostly to the illustrations.

If you read the story first, check the statement that best describes the child's reading.

_____ The child used memory to read the text with high accuracy.

_____ The child used memory and illustrations to read the text with fair accuracy.

_____ The child did not seem to remember your reading and relied almost entirely on the illustrations to read the text.

From Jerry L. Johns, Susan Davis Lenski, and Laurie Elish-Piper, *Teaching Beginning Readers: Linking Assessment and Instruction* (2nd ed.). Copyright © 2002 by Kendall/Hunt Publishing Company (1-800-247-3458, ext. 5). May be reproduced for noncommercial educational purposes.

RECORD SHEET

Caption Reading (Continued)

Form 1

Record your overall qualitative judgment of reading with an X on the continuum located on this record sheet.

	Not Evident / Low / Seldom / Weak / Poor	Some	Evident / High / Always / Strong / Excellent

Other Reading Behaviors

Retelling

Reads left to right

Reads top to bottom

Demonstrates letter-sound relationships

Uses monitoring (rereads, corrects)

Points to correct words (if requested by you)

Engagement

Confidence as a reader

Observations, Comments, Notes, and Insights

From Jerry L. Johns, Susan Davis Lenski, and Laurie Elish-Piper, *Teaching Beginning Readers: Linking Assessment and Instruction* (2nd ed.). Copyright © 2002 by Kendall/Hunt Publishing Company (1-800-247-3458, ext. 5). May be reproduced for noncommercial educational purposes.

1

The frog sits.

2

The frog eats.

3

The frog jumps.

4

The frog swims.

Form 2—Caption Reading—Child's Copy

RECORD SHEET

Caption Reading

Form 2

Name _____ Date _____

The frog sits.

The frog eats.

The frog jumps.

The frog swims.

QUALITATIVE JUDGMENTS OF CAPTION READING

If the child read the story, check the statement that best describes the child's reading.

_____ The child's reading is an exact match with the text.

_____ The child's reading closely matches the text.

_____ The child's reading is somewhat related to the text but is based on the illustrations.

_____ The child's reading is related mostly to the illustrations.

If you read the story first, check the statement that best describes the child's reading.

_____ The child used memory to read the text with high accuracy.

_____ The child used memory and illustrations to read the text with fair accuracy.

_____ The child did not seem to remember your reading and relied almost entirely on the illustrations to read the text.

From Jerry L. Johns, Susan Davis Lenski, and Laurie Elish-Piper, *Teaching Beginning Readers: Linking Assessment and Instruction* (2nd ed.). Copyright © 2002 by Kendall/Hunt Publishing Company (1-800-247-3458, ext. 5). May be reproduced for noncommercial educational purposes.

Vocabulary and Comprehension 315

RECORD SHEET

Form 2

Caption Reading (Continued)

Record your overall qualitative judgment of reading with an X on the continuum located on this record sheet.

	Not Evident Low Seldom Weak Poor	Some	Evident High Always Strong Excellent

Other Reading Behaviors

Retelling

Reads left to right

Reads top to bottom

Demonstrates letter-sound relationships

Uses monitoring (rereads, corrects)

Points to correct words (if requested by you)

Engagement

Confidence as a reader

Observations, Comments, Notes, and Insights

From Jerry L. Johns, Susan Davis Lenski, and Laurie Elish-Piper, *Teaching Beginning Readers: Linking Assessment and Instruction* (2nd ed.). Copyright © 2002 by Kendall/Hunt Publishing Company (1-800-247-3458, ext. 5). May be reproduced for noncommercial educational purposes.

316   Chapter Five

Assessment Strategy 2

Section 5.4

Passage Reading

Overview	The Passage Reading assessment strategy is designed to give you information about a child's ability to read connected text. In addition, you can gain insights into a child's comprehension and understanding of vocabulary presented in a passage. Important information on a child's word recognition strategies (See Chapter 3) and fluency (Chapter 4, Section 4.2) can also be identified through this assessment. The four passages are based in part on Gunning's (1998) work and descriptions of beginning reading levels. The table below provides some basic information about each of the passages. | Passage	Grade Level	Reading Level Code	Words	Approximate Reading Recovery Level
---	---	---	---	---
Easy Sight Word	Pre-primer	EE	25	4–8
Beginning	Primer	E	50	9–11
Grade 1	1	E7141	100	12–20
Grade 2	2	E8224	100	—	
Materials Needed	1. The pages in this book containing the passages 2. The Record Sheet that corresponds to the passage(s) selected 3. One 5" × 8" card
Procedures	1. Duplicate the appropriate section of the Record Sheet. 2. Choose a passage that you think the child can read. Place the passage before the child and cover everything but the illustration and the title. 3. Activate the child's background knowledge by saying, "Read the title to yourself and look at the pictures. Then tell me what you think this story will be about." Informally judge the extent of the child's background knowledge and record an X along the continuum on the Record Sheet. Then say, "Read the story to me. I'll ask you to answer some questions when you are finished." As the child reads, note any miscues in the appropriate place on the Record Sheet using the following markings (or your own system). 	Marking	Meaning of Marking
man over men	Substitution
man s/c over men	Self-correction
~~men~~	Omitted word	

Vocabulary and Comprehension 317

(continued)

m — men	Partial pronunciation
<u>men</u> *small*	Repeated word
^men	Insertion

Also, note other behaviors, such as finger pointing, ignoring punctuation, engagement, and strategies used to pronounce words not known at sight. Count the *total* number of miscues or the number of *significant* (those that affect meaning) miscues. Self-corrections need not be included in counting miscues.

4. When the child has finished reading, ask the comprehension questions or invite a retelling of the story. Record a plus (+) for correct responses and a minus (–) for incorrect responses. You may also give half credit. The letter beside the comprehension questions indicates the following types of questions.

Letter	**Type of Question**
T	Topic—main idea of passage
F	Fact—specific information stated in the passage
E	Experience/Evaluation—making judgments using prior knowledge
I	Inference—putting together information from the passage that is not explicitly stated
V	Vocabulary—explaining a specific word in the passage

5. If the child was successful, present the next passage. Continue administering graded passages until the child has many word recognition miscues (i.e., frustration level) or is unable to answer more than half of the comprehension questions. If the initial passage was too difficult, try an easier passage or go back to Caption Reading.

Scoring and Interpretation

1. Use the scoring guides on the Record Sheet to evaluate word recognition and comprehension. For word recognition, count the total number of miscues or the number of significant (those that affect meaning) miscues. Record the number of miscues in the appropriate box on the Record Sheet. Then find and circle the level (Independent, Ind./Inst., Instructional, Inst./Frust, or Frustration) on the scoring guide at the bottom of the passage corresponding to the number of total or significant miscues.

2. For comprehension, count the number of comprehension questions missed and record this number in the appropriate box on the record sheet. Then find and circle the level on the scoring guide at the bottom of the questions. If retelling is used to assess comprehension, circle *excellent* for independent level, *satisfactory* for instructional level, and *unsatisfactory* for frustration level.

3. There are also areas of word recognition and comprehension at the bottom of some record sheets that you can evaluate on a scale of 1 to 3. Then make an overall qualitative judgment of the child's word recognition and comprehension abilities on the summary page of the Record Sheet.

(continued)

4. Throughout the assessment, watch for behaviors often associated with frustration: lack of expression, word-by-word reading, excessive anxiety, and so on. Note such behaviors in the margins of the Record Sheet.
5. Estimate the child's oral reading rate by timing the reading and inserting the seconds required for reading as the divisor in the formula at the bottom of the Record Sheet. Perform the necessary division. The resulting numeral will be an estimate of the child's rate in words per minute (WPM). An example of rate determination is shown below. See Johns (2001, p. 35) for further information about reading rate as well as Chapter 4.

$$115 \overline{\smash{)}6000} 52 \text{WPM}$$
$$\underline{575}$$
$$250$$
$$230$$

An informal analysis of the child's word recognition and comprehension abilities should help you identify areas for instruction.

My Dog

I have a dog.

My dog is Spark.

Spark is a big dog.

He plays ball.

I play with Spark.

Spark is a fun dog.

RECORD SHEET

Form 1

Easy Sight Word Passage Reading

Name _____ Date _____

Teacher's Directions   317–319
Child's Copy   320

Background: Low |———|———| High

My Dog

I have a dog.

My dog is Spark.

Spark is a big dog.

He plays ball.

I play with Spark.

Spark is a fun dog.

Total Miscues ☐   **Significant Miscues** ☐   **Questions Missed** ☐

EE (Pre-Primer) Activating Background:
Read the title to yourself and look at the pictures. Then tell me what you think this story will be about.

T   1. ___   What is the story mostly about?
            (a dog; Spark)

F   2. ___   What is the dog's name?
            (Spark)

F   3. ___   What does Spark do?
            (play ball)

E   4. ___   Why do you think Spark is a fun dog?
            (any logical response; because he likes to play ball)

I   5. ___   What other things might Spark like to do? (any logical response)

V   6. ___   What is a dog?
            (any logical response; an animal; a pet)

Word Recognition Scoring Guide		
Total Miscues	Level	Significant Miscues
0	Independent	0
1	Ind./Inst.	—
2	Instructional	1
—	Inst./Frust.	—
3	Frustration	2

Retelling
Excellent
Satisfactory
Unsatisfactory

WPM
)‾1500

Comprehension Scoring Guide	
Questions Missed	Level
0	Independent
1	Ind./Inst.
1½	Instructional
2	Inst./Frust.
2½+	Frustration

Qualitative Analysis of Word Identification and Comprehension
(1 = never; 2 = sometimes; 3 = always)

Word Identification				Comprehension			
Uses graphophonic information	1	2	3	Makes predictions	1	2	3
Uses semantic information	1	2	3	Seeks to construct meaning	1	2	3
Uses syntactic information	1	2	3	Understands topic and major ideas	1	2	3
Knows basic sight words automatically	1	2	3	Remembers facts or details	1	2	3
Possesses sight vocabulary	1	2	3	Evaluates ideas from passages	1	2	3
Possesses numerous strategies	1	2	3	Makes and supports appropriate inferences	1	2	3
Uses strategies flexibly	1	2	3	Stays focused on reading	1	2	3

From Jerry L. Johns, Susan Davis Lenski, and Laurie Elish-Piper, *Teaching Beginning Readers: Linking Assessment and Instruction* (2nd ed.). Copyright © 2002 by Kendall/Hunt Publishing Company (1-800-247-3458, ext. 5). May be reproduced for noncommercial educational purposes.

The Small Fish

There are two small fish. One is red and the other is blue. They live in the sea. They like to play.

One day a big green fish came to the sea. It did not want to play. It wanted to eat the small fish. The big fish was mean.

RECORD SHEET

Form 1

Beginning Passage Reading

Name _____ Date _____

Teacher's Directions   317–319
Child's Copy   322

Background: Low |—|—| High

The Small Fish

There are two small fish. One is red and the other is blue. They live in the sea. They like to play.

One day a big green fish came to the sea. It did not want to play. It wanted to eat the small fish. The big fish was mean.

E (Primer) Activating Background:
Read the title to yourself and look at the picture. Then tell me what you think this story will be about.

T 1. ___ What is this story about?
          (fish; two fish who almost got eaten by a big green fish)

F 2. ___ What size was the green fish?
          (big)

F 3. ___ What do the red fish and the blue fish like to do in the sea?
          (play)

E 4. ___ What do you think the small fish will do to get away from the green fish?
          (any logical response; swim fast)

I 5. ___ What do you think the red fish and the blue fish did when they saw the green fish? (any logical response; they swam away quickly)

V 6. ___ What does "play" mean?
          (any logical response)

Total Miscues ☐   Significant Miscues ☐   Questions Missed ☐

Word Recognition Scoring Guide		
Total Miscues	Level	Significant Miscues
0	Independent	0
1–2	Ind./Inst.	—
3	Instructional	1
4	Inst./Frust.	2
5+	Frustration	3

Retelling
Excellent
Satisfactory
Unsatisfactory
____ WPM
) 3000

Comprehension Scoring Guide	
Questions Missed	Level
0	Independent
1	Ind./Inst.
1½	Instructional
2	Inst./Frust.
2½+	Frustration

Qualitative Analysis of Word Identification and Comprehension (1 = never; 2 = sometimes; 3 = always)							
Word Identification				**Comprehension**			
Uses graphophonic information	1	2	3	Makes predictions	1	2	3
Uses semantic information	1	2	3	Seeks to construct meaning	1	2	3
Uses syntactic information	1	2	3	Understands topic and major ideas	1	2	3
Knows basic sight words automatically	1	2	3	Remembers facts or details	1	2	3
Possesses sight vocabulary	1	2	3	Evaluates ideas from passages	1	2	3
Possesses numerous strategies	1	2	3	Makes and supports appropriate inferences	1	2	3
Uses strategies flexibly	1	2	3	Stays focused on reading	1	2	3

From Jerry L. Johns, Susan Davis Lenski, and Laurie Elish-Piper, *Teaching Beginning Readers: Linking Assessment and Instruction* (2nd ed.). Copyright © 2002 by Kendall/Hunt Publishing Company (1-800-247-3458, ext. 5). May be reproduced for noncommercial educational purposes.

Paws Visits School

Fred has a big black cat. The cat is named Paws. Fred took Paws to his small school. All of the children loved Paws. They all tried to pet Paws at one time. Paws was very afraid. She jumped out of Fred's arms and ran away. Fred looked all around but could not find Paws. Fred's friend, Anne, looked under the little table. Anne saw Paws under the table. Anne ran and told Fred where she saw Paws. Paws came out when she saw Fred. Fred hugged Paws tightly. Fred took Paws home and gave her some food to eat.

RECORD SHEET

Grade 1 Passage Reading

Form 1

Name _____ Date _____

Teacher's Directions   317–319
Child's Copy   324

Background: Low |—|—| High

Paws Visits School

Fred has a big black cat. The cat is named Paws. Fred took Paws to his small school. All of the children loved Paws. They all tried to pet Paws at one time. Paws was very afraid. She jumped out of Fred's arms and ran away. Fred looked all around but could not find Paws. Fred's friend, Anne, looked under the little table. Anne saw Paws under the table. Anne ran and told Fred where she saw Paws. Paws came out when she saw Fred. Fred hugged Paws tightly. Fred took Paws home and gave her some food to eat.

E 7141 (Grade 1) Activating Background:
Read the title to yourself and look at the picture. Then tell me what you think this story will be about.

T 1. ___ What is this story about?
           (Paws; a cat; a boy who takes his cat to school)

F 2. ___ What color was the cat?
           (black)

F 3. ___ What was the cat's name?
           (Paws)

F 4. ___ Why did the cat run away?
           (she was afraid)

F 5. ___ Who helped Fred find his cat?
           (Anne)

F 6. ___ Where did Anne find Paws?
           (under the table)

I 7. ___ How do you think Anne felt when she found Paws? (any logical response; happy; excited; glad)

I 8. ___ Why do you think Fred took Paws to school? (any logical response; to show the other children)

E 9. ___ Do you think Fred will take Paws to school again? Why? (any logical response)

V 10. ___ What does "afraid" mean?
           (scared)

Total Miscues ☐   **Significant Miscues** ☐   **Questions Missed** ☐

Word Recognition Scoring Guide		
Total Miscues	Level	Significant Miscues
0–1	Independent	0–1
2–4	Ind./Inst.	2
5	Instructional	3
6–9	Inst./Frust.	4
10+	Frustration	5+

Retelling
Excellent
Satisfactory
Unsatisfactory
_____ WPM
) 6000

Comprehension Scoring Guide	
Questions Missed	Level
0–1	Independent
1½–2	Ind./Inst.
2½	Instructional
3–4½	Inst./Frust.
5+	Frustration

From Jerry L. Johns, Susan Davis Lenski, and Laurie Elish-Piper, *Teaching Beginning Readers: Linking Assessment and Instruction* (2nd ed.). Copyright © 2002 by Kendall/Hunt Publishing Company (1-800-247-3458, ext. 5). May be reproduced for noncommercial educational purposes.

The Lost Babies

It was getting dark outside. All the animal mothers were looking for their children. Mrs. Turtle found her babies near a tree. Mrs. Toad jumped in the weeds after she found her hungry children. Mrs. Fish found her babies by the rocks in the river. They were safe and happy.

Mrs. Rabbit was very scared. She could not find her babies anywhere. She was afraid that a fox might find her babies first. She looked all over the forest.

Mrs. Mouse helped Mrs. Rabbit look for her lost babies. Mrs. Mouse found them. The lost babies were safe at home.

RECORD SHEET

Form 1

Grade 2 Passage Reading

Name_____ Date_____

Teacher's Directions   317–319
Child's Copy   326

Background: Low |—|—| High

E 8224 (Grade 2) Activating Background:
Read the title to yourself and look at the picture. Then tell me what you think this story will be about.

The Lost Babies

It was getting dark outside. All the animal mothers were looking for their children. Mrs. Turtle found her babies near a tree. Mrs. Toad jumped in the weeds after she found her hungry children. Mrs. Fish found her babies by the rocks in the river. They were safe and happy.

Mrs. Rabbit was very scared. She could not find her babies anywhere. She was afraid that a fox might find her babies first. She looked all over the forest.

Mrs. Mouse helped Mrs. Rabbit look for her lost babies. Mrs. Mouse found them. The lost babies were safe at home.

T   1. ___ What is this story about?
(Mrs. Rabbit looking for her lost babies; lost babies)

F   2. ___ Where did Mrs. Turtle find her babies? (by a tree)

F   3. ___ Where were the baby fish? (by the rocks in the river)

F   4. ___ Who couldn't find her babies? (Mrs. Rabbit)

F   5. ___ What was Mrs. Rabbit afraid of? (that a fox might find her babies)

F   6. ___ Who found the baby rabbits? (Mrs. Mouse)

I   7. ___ What time of day did the story take place? Why? (any logical response; night)

I   8. ___ What do you think Mrs. Rabbit did when she heard Mrs. Mouse's news? (any logical response; went right home)

E   9. ___ Why would Mrs. Rabbit be afraid of a fox? (any logical response; it might eat her babies)

V   10. ___ What does "safe" mean? (any logical response; no danger; no harm; protection)

Total Miscues ☐   **Significant Miscues** ☐   **Questions Missed** ☐

Word Recognition Scoring Guide		
Total Miscues	Level	Significant Miscues
0–1	Independent	0–1
2–4	Ind./Inst.	2
5	Instructional	3
6–9	Inst./Frust.	4
10+	Frustration	5+

Retelling
Excellent
Satisfactory
Unsatisfactory
WPM
⟌6000

Comprehension Scoring Guide	
Questions Missed	Level
0–1	Independent
1½–2	Ind./Inst.
2½	Instructional
3–4½	Inst./Frust.
5+	Frustration

From Jerry L. Johns, Susan Davis Lenski, and Laurie Elish-Piper, *Teaching Beginning Readers: Linking Assessment and Instruction* (2nd ed.). Copyright © 2002 by Kendall/Hunt Publishing Company (1-800-247-3458, ext. 5). May be reproduced for noncommercial educational purposes.

Vocabulary and Comprehension   327

Sam Likes Books

Sam likes books.

He likes big books.

He likes small books.

He likes all kinds of books.

Sam likes to read his books at home.

RECORD SHEET

Form 2

Easy Sight Word Passage Reading

Name_____ Date_____

Teacher's Directions 317–319
Child's Copy 328

Background: Low |—|—| **High**

Sam Likes Books

Sam likes books.

He likes big books.

He likes small books.

He likes all kinds of books.

Sam likes to read his books at home.

EE (Pre-Primer) Activating Background:
Read the title to yourself and look at the pictures. Then tell me what you think this story will be about.

T 1. ____ What is the story mostly about?
           (books; Sam)

F 2. ____ Who likes books?
           (Sam)

F 3. ____ Where does Sam like to read?
           (at home)

E 4. ____ What do you think Sam reads about?
           (any logical response)

I 5. ____ Why do you think Sam likes to read?
           (any logical response; it is fun)

V 6. ____ What is a book?
           (any logical response; something you read)

Total Miscues ☐   **Significant Miscues** ☐   **Questions Missed** ☐

Word Recognition Scoring Guide		
Total Miscues	Level	Significant Miscues
0	Independent	0
1	Ind./Inst.	—
2	Instructional	1
—	Inst./Frust.	—
3	Frustration	2

Retelling
Excellent
Satisfactory
Unsatisfactory
WPM
)1500

Comprehension Scoring Guide	
Questions Missed	Level
0	Independent
1	Ind./Inst.
1½	Instructional
2	Inst./Frust.
2½+	Frustration

Qualitative Analysis of Word Identification and Comprehension						
(1 = never; 2 = sometimes; 3 = always)							
Word Identification			Comprehension		
Uses graphophonic information	1	2	3	Makes predictions	1	2	3
Uses semantic information	1	2	3	Seeks to construct meaning	1	2	3
Uses syntactic information	1	2	3	Understands topic and major ideas	1	2	3
Knows basic sight words automatically	1	2	3	Remembers facts or details	1	2	3
Possesses sight vocabulary	1	2	3	Evaluates ideas from passages	1	2	3
Possesses numerous strategies	1	2	3	Makes and supports appropriate inferences	1	2	3
Uses strategies flexibly	1	2	3	Stays focused on reading	1	2	3

From Jerry L. Johns, Susan Davis Lenski, and Laurie Elish-Piper, *Teaching Beginning Readers: Linking Assessment and Instruction* (2nd ed.). Copyright © 2002 by Kendall/Hunt Publishing Company (1-800-247-3458, ext. 5). May be reproduced for noncommercial educational purposes.

Ball Game

Bob went to a ball game with his dad.

They sat by first base. Dad got two hot

dogs and two cold drinks for lunch.

The ball player hit the ball. It came

to Bob. He caught the ball with his glove.

Bob jumped up and down. He was happy.

RECORD SHEET

Form 2

Beginning Passage Reading

Name _____ Date _____

Teacher's Directions 317–319
Child's Copy 330

Background: Low |—|—| High

Ball Game

Bob went to a ball game with his dad.

They sat by first base. Dad got two hot

dogs and two cold drinks for lunch.

The ball player hit the ball. It came

to Bob. He caught the ball with his glove.

Bob jumped up and down. He was happy.

E (Primer) Activating Background:
Read the title to yourself and look at the picture. Then tell me what you think this story will be about.

T 1. ___ What is this story about?
            (a boy and his dad at a ball game)

F 2. ___ Where did Bob and his dad sit?
            (by first base)

F 3. ___ What did they eat for lunch?
            (hot dogs and cold drinks)

E 4. ___ What do you think Bob will do with the ball he caught at the game?
            (any logical response; keep it in a safe place; show it to his friends)

I 5. ___ Why do you think Bob was happy?
            (any logical response; he caught the ball; he sat by first base)

V 6. ___ What does "glove" mean?
            (something that goes over your hand to catch balls)

Total Miscues ☐   **Significant Miscues** ☐   **Questions Missed** ☐

Word Recognition Scoring Guide		
Total Miscues	Level	Significant Miscues
0	Independent	0
1–2	Ind./Inst.	—
3	Instructional	1
4	Inst./Frust.	2
5+	Frustration	3

Retelling
Excellent
Satisfactory
Unsatisfactory
WPM
)3000

Comprehension Scoring Guide	
Questions Missed	Level
0	Independent
1	Ind./Inst.
1½	Instructional
2	Inst./Frust.
2½+	Frustration

Qualitative Analysis of Word Identification and Comprehension							
(1 = never; 2 = sometimes; 3 = always)							
Word Identification				**Comprehension**			
Uses graphophonic information	1	2	3	Makes predictions	1	2	3
Uses semantic information	1	2	3	Seeks to construct meaning	1	2	3
Uses syntactic information	1	2	3	Understands topic and major ideas	1	2	3
Knows basic sight words automatically	1	2	3	Remembers facts or details	1	2	3
Possesses sight vocabulary	1	2	3	Evaluates ideas from passages	1	2	3
Possesses numerous strategies	1	2	3	Makes and supports appropriate inferences	1	2	3
Uses strategies flexibly	1	2	3	Stays focused on reading	1	2	3

From Jerry L. Johns, Susan Davis Lenski, and Laurie Elish-Piper, *Teaching Beginning Readers: Linking Assessment and Instruction* (2nd ed.). Copyright © 2002 by Kendall/Hunt Publishing Company (1-800-247-3458, ext. 5). May be reproduced for noncommercial educational purposes.

The Pet Shop

Mike ran home quickly from school. He was in a hurry to see his mom. Mike asked, "Are you ready, mom?" Mom just smiled. She was feeding the new baby. Mike jumped up and down saying, "Let's go, mom!" When mom finished, all three of them got into the car. They drove to the pet shop.

Mike looked in all the cages. He saw some brown baby dogs. He saw cats and kittens. Mike also saw birds, hamsters, and turtles. Mike wanted to choose a small pet with only two legs. He knew he would take good care of it.

RECORD SHEET

Form 2

Grade 1 Passage Reading

Name_____ Date_____

Teacher's Directions 317–319
Child's Copy 332

Background: Low |—|—| High

The Pet Shop

Mike ran home quickly from school. He was in a hurry to see his mom. Mike asked, "Are you ready, mom?" Mom just smiled. She was feeding the new baby. Mike jumped up and down saying, "Let's go, mom!" When mom finished, all three of them got into the car. They drove to the pet shop.

Mike looked in all the cages. He saw some brown baby dogs. He saw cats and kittens. Mike also saw birds, hamsters, and turtles. Mike wanted to choose a small pet with only two legs. He knew he would take good care of it.

E 7141 (Grade 1) Activating Background:
Read the title to yourself and look at the picture. Then tell me what you think this story will be about.

T 1. ___ What is this story about?
(getting a new pet; a trip to the pet shop)

F 2. ___ How did Mike get home from school?
(he ran)

F 3. ___ Why did Mike run home from school?
(he was in a hurry to see his mom; he wanted to go to the pet shop)

F 4. ___ What was mom doing when Mike got home from school? (feeding the baby)

F 5. ___ How did Mike get to the pet shop?
(he rode in his mom's car; mom drove the car)

F 6. ___ What animals did Mike see?
(dogs, cats, kittens, birds, hamsters, turtles [any three])

I 7. ___ Which animal do you think Mike will choose to be his pet? Why?
(a bird because it has two legs)

I 8. ___ What kind of things will Mike probably have to do to take care of his new pet? (any logical response)

E 9. ___ What animal would you choose for a pet? Why? (any logical response)

V 10. ___ What are "cages"?
(a place for animals to sleep; where zoo animals live)

Total Miscues ☐   Significant Miscues ☐   Questions Missed ☐

Word Recognition Scoring Guide		
Total Miscues	Level	Significant Miscues
0–1	Independent	0–1
2–4	Ind./Inst.	2
5	Instructional	3
6–9	Inst./Frust.	4
10+	Frustration	5+

Retelling
Excellent
Satisfactory
Unsatisfactory
WPM
)‾6000

Comprehension Scoring Guide	
Questions Missed	Level
0–1	Independent
1½–2	Ind./Inst.
2½	Instructional
3–4½	Inst./Frust.
5+	Frustration

From Jerry L. Johns, Susan Davis Lenski, and Laurie Elish-Piper, *Teaching Beginning Readers: Linking Assessment and Instruction* (2nd ed.). Copyright © 2002 by Kendall/Hunt Publishing Company (1-800-247-3458, ext. 5). May be reproduced for noncommercial educational purposes.

Vocabulary and Comprehension 333

Night Time Friend

"It's time to come in the house," Mother called to Joe from the kitchen. "It's getting late and will be dark soon."

Joe did not want to go inside. He sat outside waiting for his friend. Mother watched from the window.

Joe looked up into the sky. He wondered what was taking his friend so long. Then Joe saw something black glide across the night sky. He knew it was his night time friend. Joe watched as it ate insects while flying around the garden.

In the morning, his friend would hang upside down in a cave and fall asleep.

RECORD SHEET

Grade 2 Passage Reading

Form 2

Name _____ Date _____

Teacher's Directions   317–319
Child's Copy   334

Background: Low |———|———| High

Night Time Friend

"It's time to come in the house," Mother called to Joe from the kitchen. "It's getting late and will be dark soon."

Joe did not want to go inside. He sat outside waiting for his friend. Mother watched from the window.

Joe looked up into the sky. He wondered what was taking his friend so long. Then Joe saw something black glide across the night sky. He knew it was his night time friend. Joe watched as it ate insects while flying around the garden.

In the morning, his friend would hang upside down in a cave and fall asleep.

E 8224 (Grade 2) Activating Background:
Read the title to yourself and look at the picture. Then tell me what you think this story will be about.

T 1. ___ What is this story about?
(a boy waiting for his friend)

F 2. ___ Where was Joe?
(outside; in the yard)

F 3. ___ What did Mother want Joe to do?
(come in the house)

F 4. ___ Why did Joe want to stay outside?
(he was waiting for his friend)

F 5. ___ How did Joe's friend sleep?
(upside down)

F 6. ___ What did Joe's friend eat?
(insects)

I 7. ___ What season do you think it is in this story? Why?
(any logical response)

I 8. ___ What is Joe's friend?
(a bat)

E 9. ___ Why do you think Mother wanted Joe to come inside?
(any logical response; it was time for bed; it is dangerous to be outside after dark)

V 10. ___ What does "glide" mean?
(to move smoothly)

Total Miscues ☐   **Significant Miscues** ☐   **Questions Missed** ☐

Word Recognition Scoring Guide		
Total Miscues	Level	Significant Miscues
0–1	Independent	0–1
2–4	Ind./Inst.	2
5	Instructional	3
6–9	Inst./Frust.	4
10+	Frustration	5+

Retelling
Excellent
Satisfactory
Unsatisfactory
_____ WPM
)6000

Comprehension Scoring Guide	
Questions Missed	Level
0–1	Independent
1½–2	Ind./Inst.
2½	Instructional
3–4½	Inst./Frust.
5+	Frustration

From Jerry L. Johns, Susan Davis Lenski, and Laurie Elish-Piper, *Teaching Beginning Readers: Linking Assessment and Instruction* (2nd ed.). Copyright © 2002 by Kendall/Hunt Publishing Company (1-800-247-3458, ext. 5). May be reproduced for noncommercial educational purposes.

Assessment Strategy 3

Section 5.4

Retelling

Overview	Retellings can provide a great deal of information about a child's comprehension of a story. Retelling is a learned task; therefore, you are encouraged to use some of the instructional strategies for retelling (see Section 5.2) prior to using retelling as an assessment.
Materials Needed	1. A story that is new to the child 2. Story Retelling Record Sheet (p. 337)
Procedures	1. Choose a short book that is new to the child. The book should have a clear plot with named characters. You may choose to use props or puppets with the story if you think these visual aids will support the child's retelling. 2. Before reading the book say, "I'm going to read a story to you. After I'm finished reading, I will ask you to tell me the story as if you were telling it to someone who has not read the story. As you listen, try to remember as much of the story as you can." 3. Read the book aloud to the child. 4. After you have read the book say, "Now tell me about the story as if you were telling it to someone who has not read the story." 5. If the child has difficulty getting started or adding information to the retelling, use the following prompts. • What was the story about? • Who was in the story? • Where did the story take place? • What happened next? • Can you tell me anything else about the story? 6. Use the Story Retelling Record Sheet (p. 337) to record the child's performance on the retelling. You may want to tape-record the retelling so you can analyze it more thoroughly at a later time.
Scoring and Interpretation	Record the child's retelling in the appropriate boxes on the Record Sheet. Rate each part of the retelling using a scale of 0–3 as outlined on the Story Retelling Record Sheet. If a child scores below a 12, he or she should receive additional instruction in retelling and comprehension of stories.

RECORD SHEET

Story Retelling

Name _____ Date _____

Story _____

Retelling Element	Child's Response	Score 0–3
Beginning/Setting (How and where does the story begin?)		
Characters (Who are the main characters?)		
Sequence of Major Events (What are the important things that happen in the story?)		
Problem (What was the problem in the story?)		
Solution (How was the problem solved? How did the story end?)		

Scoring: 0 = omitted or inaccurate
1 = fragmentary
2 = partial
3 = complete/detailed

From Jerry L. Johns, Susan Davis Lenski, and Laurie Elish-Piper, *Teaching Beginning Readers: Linking Assessment and Instruction* (2nd ed.). Copyright © 2002 by Kendall/Hunt Publishing Company (1-800-247-3458, ext. 5). May be reproduced for noncommercial educational purposes.

Vocabulary and Comprehension   337

Additional Ways of Assessing Comprehension

1. Modify the retelling format to match an individual child's preferred approach to learning. For example, you may ask a child to draw a retelling and then explain it to you. A child can also write a retelling or act it out.
2. Develop questions for a story. Ask the child the questions to determine if the child comprehended the story.
3. Use a Story Frame (See Section 5.2, Teaching Strategy 3) to assess if a child understood a story.

Assessment Strategy 4

Section 5.4

Monitoring Strategies Checklist

Overview	You can learn a great deal about a child's use of monitoring strategies through individual reading conferences. This assessment will help you determine which monitoring strategies a child is using when reading as well as which ones you will need to model and instruct the child on in the future.
Materials Needed	1. Appropriate book for the child (either fiction or nonfiction is acceptable) 2. Monitoring Strategies Checklist (p. 340)
Procedures	1. Select a book that is at the child's instructional level. 2. Tell the child, "I want you to read the story aloud. After you are done, I'm going to ask you what strategies you used as a reader." 3. After the child reads the story (or part of it) aloud, ask the child what he or she did before reading. Circle *yes* for the Strategies the child reports using and *no* for those the child does not use. 4. Ask the child what he or she did during reading to make sure the story made sense. Circle *yes* for the strategies the child reports using and *no* for those the child does not use. 5. Ask the child what he or she would typically do after reading the story. Circle *yes* for the strategies the child reports using and *no* for those the child does not use.
Scoring and Interpretation	Place a ✓ next to the strategies the child reports using. Also, mark any of the strategies you observed the child using that he or she did not report. Based on findings from this assessment, you can determine which monitoring strategies the student needs to learn and apply.

Vocabulary and Comprehension 339

RECORD SHEET

Monitoring Strategies Checklist

Name _____ Date _____

Book _____

Before reading did you:

Think about the title and cover?	Yes	No
Make predictions?	Yes	No
Think about what you already know about the topic?	Yes	No

During reading did you:

Ask yourself if the reading made sense?	Yes	No
Pause-Think-Retell?	Yes	No
Make pictures in your mind?	Yes	No
Use strategies to figure out hard words? If yes, what did you do?	Yes	No
Reread to help yourself understand?	Yes	No
Use pictures for clues?	Yes	No
Ask yourself questions?	Yes	No

After reading do you usually:

Retell the story?	Yes	No
Think about what you read?	Yes	No
Share what you learned with someone?	Yes	No
Think about what strategies you used to help you read?	Yes	No

From Jerry L. Johns, Susan Davis Lenski, and Laurie Elish-Piper, *Teaching Beginning Readers: Linking Assessment and Instruction* (2nd ed.). Copyright © 2002 by Kendall/Hunt Publishing Company (1-800-247-3458, ext. 5). May be reproduced for noncommercial educational purposes.

CHAPTER 6

Writing and Spelling

OVERVIEW

Children can learn and practice their literacy skills by reading and writing. As they read, children use cueing systems to figure out unknown words, and they construct meaning from text. During writing, children apply their knowledge of language to write words, and they compose text. The processes of reading and writing, therefore, mutually support each other and are further developed as children write in response to their reading.

When children respond to literature, they are building their meaning-making capabilities through their own development of meaning. Children can respond to text in a number of ways; they can respond with feelings, they can respond to the plot of the story, and they can respond to the story's message. As children respond to text through discussion and through writing, they use language to communicate their own meanings. As they talk and write, children develop their ability to use language effectively which also promotes better writing.

Another process that is supported as children read and write is the process of learning how to spell words with conventional spelling. As children read, they learn how letters form patterns to make words. During writing, children experiment with their knowledge of letters, sounds, and rules to discover how to spell new words. Spelling, therefore, is developed as children read and write. The spelling that children use as they learn how to spell conventionally is sometimes called invented spelling or developmental spelling (Gentry, 2000). Many teachers ask questions about the ways to teach writing and spelling. A selection of frequently asked questions and answers follows.

Should reading and writing be integrated or taught separately?

Most of your instruction should be based on authentic texts with real literacy purposes, so your primary means of instruction should be integrated. However, Teale and Yokota (2000) suggest that reading and writing also be taught as separate subjects. Most children need explicit instruction in reading and writing processes, so part of your instructional plan should be to teach reading and writing skills separately.

When children write, should I help them spell words or should they figure out words themselves?

Children learn how to spell by experimenting with the rules and patterns of language, so most of children's spelling should be independent. When children write, they should be encouraged to use their knowledge of letters and sounds to spell words even though their attempts may not conform to conventional spelling. You can help children spell words as they write by reinforcing the phonics and spelling rules that you have taught and by encouraging children to use resources such as Word Walls to find the conventional spelling of words.

What if a child won't write anything without knowing the spelling?

If a child is completely stumped and your assistance isn't helping, go ahead and spell the word for the child. Sometimes children lack confidence to try letter patterns and insist on "correct" spelling of all words they write. If that is the case, tell the child how to spell the troublesome words and continue to encourage the child to try spelling new words. In addition, continue to provide a classroom environment that encourages children to take risks so children will be willing to try new things and explore the spelling of words.

Parents in my district do not like the term invented spelling. What term do you recommend?

In some respects, invented spelling is an unfortunate term. Although it describes how children "invent" rules to spell words, it has been misunderstood. The important principle behind invented spelling is that children need to write in order to learn how to spell. Since young children do not know the spelling of very many words, they need opportunities to write with their own spelling. In this book we use the term developmental spelling instead of invented spelling. Others call it temporary spelling or phonic spelling. Find a term that is acceptable to the teachers, administrators, and parents in your school and use that term. Remember, the term isn't as important as the principle behind the term: children need to practice spelling by writing.

Some teachers I know do not give spelling lists or spelling tests. Should I give spelling tests to young children?

Spelling has traditionally been taught using spelling workbooks with weekly spelling tests. Teachers have found that spelling tests alone do not help children learn how to spell (Rosencrans, 1998). More importantly, you should provide children with specific instruction on how to spell new words, such as you'll find in Section 6.3. As long as you have instruction on how to learn spelling, you might occasionally use spelling tests to assess children's ability to spell words. You may also want to assess target words in the children's writing.

I teach kindergarten. Should children this young be asked to respond to stories?

Yes, children of all ages should be given the opportunity to respond to stories. If you teach young children who are unable to read and write their own responses, you can read stories aloud to the class and write their responses on a Language Chart (see Section 6.1, Teaching Strategy 1). In addition, young children can share their responses orally, through art, and by dramatization.

6.1 Responding to Literature

> **Goal** To help children learn to discuss and write about literature.

BACKGROUND

A natural extension of reading or hearing stories is to discuss or write about them. When children read or listen to stories, they form a provisional interpretation of the text. That interpretation deepens if they respond to the story in some way—through talk, writing, drama, or art. As children respond to stories, they learn that they can make their own meanings from text.

Teaching Strategy 1

Section 6.1

Language Charts

Language Charts are a useful tool for young children who cannot write independently. They are a collection of the reflections, extensions, and creations of meaning in which children talk about books and save their ideas on a large chart (Roser & Hoffman, 1995).

DIRECTIONS

1. Select a book to read aloud to the class. Some picture books that are especially thought-provoking follow; others can be found in the Selected Resources (page 353).
   - Bunting, E. (1992). *Summer wheels*. San Diego: Harcourt Brace.
   - Cronin, D. (2000). *Click, clack, moo: Cows that type*. New York: Simon & Schuster.
   - Lionni, L. (1967). *Frederick*. New York: Pantheon.
   - Viorst, J. (1971). *The tenth good thing about Barney*. New York: Atheneum.

2. Before reading, tell children that you will be asking them to respond to the story after you are finished. Be specific about the type of response that you will elicit. For example, you might have children tell you how the book made them feel, what the book reminded them of, or what they thought about a story. If you read *Click, Clack, Moo: Cows That Type*, for example, you might say, "I'm going to read you a story today that I think you will like. It's about some cows that get a typewriter. You're going to find out what the cows do with the typewriter. Do you think this story could be real? No, cows can't really type, so the story is made up. After I finish reading, we're going to talk about what you liked most about the *Click, Clack, Moo: Cows That Type*."

3. Read the story aloud to children. After reading, ask children to remember the part they liked best and to share that part.

4. Write the children's responses on a large piece of chart paper that can be displayed in the classroom. At the top of the chart write the title of the story and the names of the author and illustrator. Then write the heading "Parts we liked best." List the children's responses with their names under the heading as in the example that follows.

Click, Clack, Moo: Cows That Type
Author: Doreen Cronin
Illustrator: Betsy Lewin

Parts we liked best:

- when the cows went on strike (Samantha)
- when the farmer read the first note (Carlos)
- when the duck asked for blankets (Brett)

5. Reread the entire Language Chart with children, frequently pointing to the words as you read. Encourage children to read their own ideas independently. Emphasize that the Language Chart is a place for children to record their own thoughts about stories.

Tips for English Language Learners

When English Language Learners talk about stories, they should be allowed to discuss the stories in their native language if at all possible (Battle, 1995). Children who are learning English may have difficulty forming their ideas into English words and may have an easier time responding to the stories using their first language. Encourage young children to talk about stories with others who speak the same language. If you know the children's first language, record their ideas on the Language Chart using that language.

Teaching Strategy 2

Section 6.1

Getting the Feeling

One way to respond to literature is to identify the feelings you get from the story. Young children often have difficulty identifying feelings that go beyond mad, sad, and glad. Helping children identify feelings from stories gives them an opportunity to develop their own personal interpretations of text.

DIRECTIONS

1. Tell children that stories can make them feel lots of different ways and that responding to stories should include how they feel. Provide an example from your own adult reading as in the example that follows. "Last night I was reading *The Africa Diaries* by Dereck and Beverly Joubert (2001). (Show book to children.) As I read the book, I had lots of different feelings. First, I was totally *amazed* at the vivid photographs the authors took of elephants. Then in the chapter on lions, I was *afraid* for the authors. They put themselves in really dangerous situations. Later in the book, I was *angry* at the poachers who killed the wild animals, and, finally, I was *anxious* to see those African animals before they become extinct."

Writing and Spelling 345

2. Develop a list of emotions that children could feel from stories or use the list that follows. Over the course of several days, describe each of the emotions on the list so that children have a good idea what each emotion means.

3. Select a book to read aloud to children or have them read independently. Before reading, tell children that you will be asking them how the story made them feel and to identify the part that made them feel that way. Use your own personal example and list your feelings along with the appropriate part of the story. An example follows.

Feelings	**Part of story**
amazed	photographs of elephants
afraid	taking pictures of lions
angry	people who kill animals
anxious	to see animals before they're extinct

4. Read the selected book to the class or have them read independently. After reading is completed, ask children to think about how the story made them feel. List their feelings and the part of the story on a Language Chart (see Section 6.1, Teaching Strategy 1).

EMOTIONS

afraid
alone
amazed
angry
anxious
awful

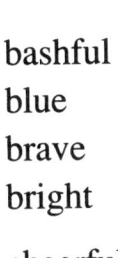

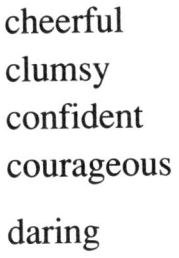

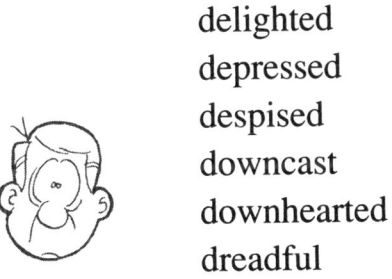

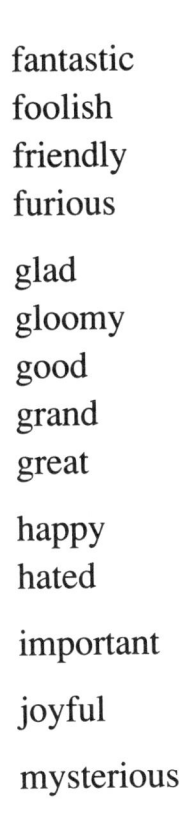

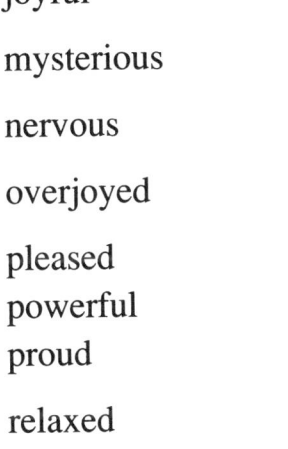

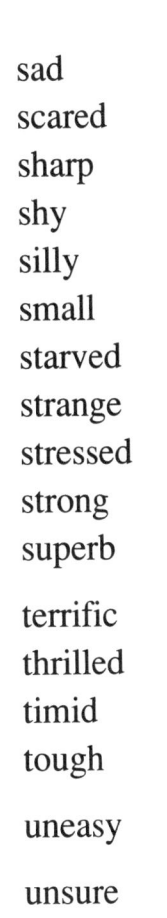

bashful
blue
brave
bright

cheerful
clumsy
confident
courageous

daring
delighted
depressed
despised
downcast
downhearted
dreadful

fantastic
foolish
friendly
furious

glad
gloomy
good
grand
great

happy
hated

important

joyful

mysterious

nervous

overjoyed

pleased
powerful
proud

relaxed

sad
scared
sharp
shy
silly
small
starved
strange
stressed
strong
superb

terrific
thrilled
timid
tough

uneasy

unsure

warm
weak
wise
wonderful
worried

From Susan Davis Lenski and Jerry L. Johns, *Improving Writing: Resources, Strategies, and Assessments.* Copyright © 2000 by Kendall/Hunt Publishing Company (1-800-247-3458, ext. 5). May be reproduced for noncommercial educational purposes.

Teaching Strategy 3

Section 6.1

Responding to Plot

Children can respond to stories in a number of ways when they react to the plot of the story (Moss, 1995). They can respond to the characters, the events in the story, and the problem. When children respond to the plot, they can even make connections to their own lives.

DIRECTIONS

1. Select a book to read to children or that children can read independently that has a clear plot and interesting characters. The plot should have an identifiable problem, events in a sequence, and a conclusion to the problem. Characters can be humans or animals, but they should be developed so that children can form an opinion.

2. Explain to children that they will be responding to the plot or the characters in the story after reading.

3. Read the book aloud or have children read independently.

4. Duplicate and distribute the response questions on page 349. Read the questions with children, explaining terms as needed.

5. Tell children that they should select one question to answer as a response to the story. Emphasize that no response is incorrect but that responses reflect individual ideas. Provide children with adequate time for writing.

6. After children have finished writing their responses, invite them to share their responses with their peers.

7. Encourage children to write responses using the Response Questions when they read on their own.

Tips for English Language Learners

In order for children to respond to text, they need to have some background knowledge about the topic or some connection to parts of the story. Children who do not speak English may have similar backgrounds to the English speakers in your classroom, or they may have very different experiences. Au (2000) reminds us that, as educators, we need to connect instruction to children's experiences rather than connecting children to instruction. Therefore, as you select books for children's responses, choose books that have themes that are familiar to all children.

Response Questions

1. Who was your favorite character? Why?

2. Was there a character you did not like? Why?

3. What was your favorite part of the story? Why?

4. Who was the hero or heroine? How do you know?

5. Who was the villain? How do you know?

6. Was there a helper? What did this character do?

7. What was the problem in the story? How was it solved?

8. What do you think is the most important thing to remember about this story?

9. Does this story remind you of any other story you have read or heard?

10. What did you think of the illustrations? Did you find anything in the pictures that was not included in the words?

Adapted from Moss, J. F. (1995). Preparing focus units with literature: Crafty foxes and authors' craft. In N. L. Roser & M. G. Martinez (Eds.), *Book talk and beyond: Children and teachers respond to literature* (pp. 53–65). Newark, DE: International Reading Association.

From Jerry L. Johns, Susan Davis Lenski, and Laurie Elish-Piper, *Teaching Beginning Readers: Linking Assessment and Instruction* (2nd ed.). Copyright © 2002 by Kendall/Hunt Publishing Company (1-800-247-3458, ext. 5). May be reproduced for noncommercial educational purposes.

> **Teaching Strategy 4**

Section 6.1

Discovering the Message

Stories have a message, or a theme, that children can identify through response (Martinez & Roser, 1995). Identifying the message of a story takes the ability to think conceptually, so very young children may have difficulty with this strategy. However, even young children should be exposed to the message of the story as they learn the different ways to respond to literature.

DIRECTIONS

1. Select a book to read to children or have children read independently something that has a clear message. A list of appropriate books follows.

   - Blume, J. (1974). *The Pain and the Great One.* New York: Dell.
   - Hutchins, P. (1968). *Rosie's walk.* New York: Aladdin.
   - Rylant, C. (1995). *Dog heaven.* New York: Simon & Schuster.
   - Sendak, M. (1963). *Where the wild things are.* New York: Harper and Row.

2. Before reading, tell children that they should listen to the story for the message. Explain that a message is a main point that the author is describing by means of a story. Provide an example similar to the following one.

   > Juan was new to Mrs. White's second grade classroom. He moved to the school from San Salvador where he had been a good student in school and an excellent soccer player. Juan didn't speak much English. He was trying to learn, but he made lots of mistakes. Some of the children in the class laughed at him, but Juan laughed right along with them. His favorite time of the day was recess where he kicked a soccer ball all by himself. One day a group of boys who had been playing kickball asked Juan to teach them how to play soccer. Juan didn't understand right away, but after the boys pantomimed kicking the soccer ball, Juan understood. Every day after that Juan and his friends played soccer with Juan teaching the boys the rules of the game—in Spanish.

3. Tell children that this story has several messages. Ask children to think about what some of the messages could be. After several minutes, have children volunteer possible messages from the story. List them on a chalkboard or on chart paper. Some messages that children could glean from the story follow.

   - Moving to a new class is difficult.
   - A good nature helps make friends.
   - Speaking different languages doesn't have to prevent friendships.
   - We can all learn from each other.

4. Tell children that this story illustrates how several messages can be discovered from the same story. Explain to children that not everyone will agree on the messages for a story but that each child can interpret the story's message in different ways.

5. Read a story to children or have them read independently. After reading, have them list the messages they discovered in the story on a Language Chart (pages 344–345).

Ideas and Activities

1. Children can respond to stories through drama. Choose a story that has a clear plot and more than one important character. Tell children that they will be acting out the story after you read it to them. Read the story to children while dramatizing the action. Then list the names of the important characters on the chalkboard or on chart paper. Ask students to volunteer for the roles. After choosing volunteers, ask them to restate the plot. If necessary, write sentences describing the plot on the chalkboard or on chart paper. Read the sentences and encourage the children to act out the story.

2. To encourage responses to literature, have children write a literary letter. A literary letter is a letter written to one of the characters in a story. Read children a story that has several important characters. Ask the class to choose one of the characters to receive a literary letter. Once a character is chosen, have children brainstorm ideas for the letter. Remind children that good letters consist of statements about the letter writer and also ask questions. Write a letter together or have children write them independently. Select children to read their letters to the class or in small groups; then bind the letters into a book.

3. Some children like to draw pictures in response to stories. After reading a story, provide children with paper, markers, crayons, and paint. Ask children to draw a picture in response to the story. Tell them that they can draw a picture about how the story makes them feel, or they can draw about events or characters in the story. After the pictures are completed, have children tell or write about their pictures. Display the pictures in the classroom.

4. For children who can write independently, have them write character journals. To write a character journal, children need to pretend to be the character and write about the character's life. Provide an example of a character journal from a story that is familiar to children such as the three little pigs. Remind children that the first little pig built his house of straw and the wolf blew it down. Then write the event from the pig's point of view as in the following example. After the children have heard the example, tell them to write a journal entry from a character's point of view.

   > I am so embarrassed! My brothers and I decided to build separate houses, and we had a bet about who could be finished first. I decided to build my house of straw because our neighbor had just mowed his field and straw was lying all over the place. I just gathered up the straw and started building my house. I was finished in no time, but before I could find my brothers to tell them I had won, a huge wolf came to the door and said he'd blow my house down. And that's exactly what he did! He blew and blew, and my house came tumbling down. I made a mad dash for it, and, luckily, I got to my brother's house before he could catch me. I'm going to have nightmares about this day for a long time, and I'll never again do anything as foolish as building a straw house.

5. Children can also respond to literature by writing to authors. You can write to any author in care of the publisher or on the author's web site. Before having children write to an author, brainstorm ideas for their letters. Remind children to be kind and to ask specific questions in their letters. Tell children they can tell the author how well they liked a book, but that they need to be polite. Model a letter to an author for children before they write.

Responding to Reading
Home School Connections

When you read to your children, give them time to respond to the story through talking or through writing. Instead of asking specific questions about the story, ask your children how they felt or what they thought about the story. Tracey (2000) suggests that you also remember four important principles when having children respond to stories.

- Choose books carefully. Make sure books are interesting to your child and worth the time to read.

- Encourage your child to talk about the book during and after reading. Any conversation about books should be encouraged.

- Help your child understand the story if necessary. While reading, ask your child what is happening in the story. If your child doesn't know, reread parts of the book.

- Praise your child for all attempts to discuss books.

From Jerry L. Johns, Susan Davis Lenski, and Laurie Elish-Piper, *Teaching Beginning Readers: Linking Assessment and Instruction* (2nd ed.). Copyright © 2002 by Kendall/Hunt Publishing Company (1-800-247-3458, ext. 5). May be reproduced for noncommercial educational purposes.

Selected Resources
RESPONDING TO LITERATURE

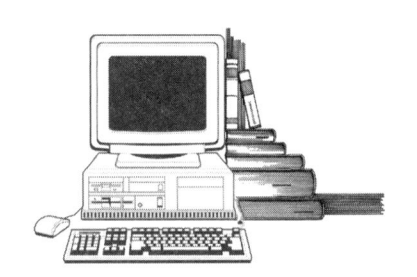

Books That Promote Conversation

Abercrombe, B. (1990). *Charlie Anderson*. New York: Simon & Schuster.

Baylor, B. (1994). *The table where rich people sit*. New York: Simon & Schuster.

Curtis, J. L. (1998). *Today I feel silly & other moods that make my day*. New York: HarperCollins.

dePaola, T. (1978). *Nana upstairs, Nana downstairs*. New York: Penguin.

Henkes, K. (1991). *Chrysanthemum*. New York: Greenwillow.

Rathman, P. (1998). *Ten minutes till bedtime*. New York: Putnam.

Tsuchiya, Y. (1988). *Faithful elephants*. Boston: Houghton Mifflin.

Williman, S. A. (1992). *Working cotton*. San Diego: Harcourt Brace.

Yolen, J. (1988). *Owl moon*. New York: Philomel.

Web Sites about Reading Response

The Johns Hopkins Guide to Literacy Theory and Criticism (discusses the history of reader response). The Johns Hopkins University Press. Available at *http://www.press.jhu.edu/books/hopkins_guide-to_literacy_theory/entries/reader-response_theory_and_criticism.html*

ERIC Clearinghouse on Reading and Communication Skills (discusses reader response in conjunction with the idea of literature appreciation). Available at *http://www.ed.gov/databases/ERIC_Digest/ed292108.html*

Reader: Essays in Reader-Oriented Theory, Criticism, and Pedagogy (semiannual publication that generates discussion on reader response ideas). Available at *http://www.hu.mtu.edu/reader*

Professional Books

Ashmore, R. A. (2001). *Promoting the gift of literacy*. Boston: Allyn and Bacon.

Gunning, T. G. (2000). *Creating literacy instruction for all children* (3rd ed.). Boston: Allyn and Bacon.

Roser, N. L., & Martinez, M. G. (Eds.). (1995). *Book talk and beyond: Children and teachers respond to literature*. Newark, DE: International Reading Association.

Strickland, D. S., & Morrow, L. M. (Eds.). (2000). *Beginning reading and writing*. Newark, DE/New York: International Reading Association/Teachers College Press.

From Jerry L. Johns, Susan Davis Lenski, and Laurie Elish-Piper, *Teaching Beginning Readers: Linking Assessment and Instruction* (2nd ed.). Copyright © 2002 by Kendall/Hunt Publishing Company (1-800-247-3458, ext. 5). May be reproduced for noncommercial educational purposes.

6.2 Writing

> **Goal** To help children express their ideas in writing.
> **Assessment Strategy 1** Writing, page 379
> **Assessment Strategy 2** Writing Rubrics, page 381
> **Assessment Strategy 3** Writing Observational Checklist, page 387

BACKGROUND

Young children learn to write as they read, write, and explore language and writing materials. Scribbles and drawings are a child's first venture into writing, and they serve as an important foundation for later writing development (Calkins, 1986). Young children need the opportunity to explore, scribble, pretend to write, invent messages, copy important words, write labels, and write messages for their own purposes (Clay, 1975). Exploration is essential for young children to develop an understanding and awareness of writing and its forms and uses. Wide reading is also an important component of early writing development because it helps children learn about language, story structure, and print conventions in meaningful contexts. Children also learn a great deal about letter-sound associations in conjunction with their attempts at writing (Strickland, 1998). As children gain more experience with writing, they begin to write in different forms and use drawing, play, and social talk in their writing (Dyson, 2001).

Writing is a process that involves children in a variety of activities. Graves (1983) describes writing as a series of recursive steps that children cycle through while writing. The steps include prewriting, drafting, revising, editing, and publishing. Because writing is a recursive process, children will not necessarily progress through each step of the process in order. Furthermore, young children may only engage in limited work with certain steps such as revising and editing.

Teachers can create classroom environments that support writing development by providing opportunities for children to write on a regular basis, to choose their own personal writing topics, to have easy access to writing materials, to engage in sharing time, to receive responses to their writing, and to engage in wide reading. The following strategies and activities provide suggestions for creating a classroom environment and program that support young children's writing development.

Teaching Strategy 1

Section 6.2

Shared Writing

Shared writing provides a framework for children and teachers to compose collaboratively. The teacher acts as the scribe and expert, and the children serve as the apprentices (Routman, 1994). In shared writing, teachers demonstrate writing conventions, think aloud regarding processes they use to write, and invite children to become actively involved in the writing process.

DIRECTIONS

1. Select a predictable story to read to the children. Read and discuss the story.
2. Explain to the children that you will be composing a new version of the story.

3. Invite the children to offer suggestions and ideas for the new version of the book. Record the children's ideas on the chalkboard, an overhead transparency, or a piece of chart paper.

4. Offer prompts to guide the children's thinking and composing. For example, you might say, "I think we need to tell what the boy does next. I will write, *Then the boy....*" Offer these prompts as necessary throughout the shared writing activity.

5. Model use of appropriate writing conventions by using a think-aloud procedure. For example, if you want children to remember to use a capital letter to begin each sentence, you might say, "I'm starting a new sentence. I need to use a capital letter here."

6. Once the children have shared their ideas, engage them in reading the new version of the story.

7. Discuss what revisions need to be made to improve the story. If necessary, use a think-aloud procedure to guide the children in discovering areas for revision and editing. For example, you might ask, "Does this make sense, or do we need to add something here?" or "What do we need to put at the end of a sentence?"

8. Make revisions to the story. Reread the story with the children.

9. Copy the final story onto chart paper and ask the children to illustrate the story. Bind the story and illustrations into a Big Book. Place the Big Book in the classroom library or encourage the children to take it home to share with their parents.

Tips for English Language Learners

Some African American children speak a nonstandard dialect of English that is often called Ebonics or Black English Vernacular. As you read the writing of children who speak a nonstandard dialect, you should consider their dialect similar to a second language. Their language is not wrong; it is just a dialect that is different from standard English. Strickland (2001) reminds us that African American children have learned the language to which they have been exposed at home and to do any differently would be quite unusual. Therefore, you should respect children's languages or dialects as you teach them how to write standard English.

Teaching Strategy 2

Section 6.2

Text Tapping

Text tapping provides a format for helping children write in a specific genre or format. Text Tapping uses children's background knowledge and previous experiences with reading and writing (Turbill, Butler, Cambourne, & Langton, 1991). Children draw on their knowledge about specific genres and language styles to help them write in various formats and styles.

DIRECTIONS

1. Select a familiar nursery rhyme such as "Jack and Jill." Read the nursery rhyme to the children. Discuss it with the children.

2. Write the nursery rhyme on the chalkboard, an overhead transparency, or a piece of chart paper. Read and reread the nursery rhyme with the children.

3. Inform the children that they will be writing their own versions of "Jack and Jill."

4. Provide a frame for "Jack and Jill" with several pieces of text deleted. For example, you may present children with the following frame.

    Jack and Jill went up the hill to fetch _____.

    Jack fell down and _____.

    And Jill came tumbling after.

5. Invite several children to share their ideas.

6. Provide time for children to complete their own versions of "Jack and Jill." Invite children to share their writing. Ask children to illustrate their writing. Display the children's writing on a bulletin board or in the classroom writing center.

7. Provide regular opportunities for children to engage in Text Tapping activities.

Tips for English Language Learners

Text Tapping is an especially good strategy for English Language Learners. Text genres are culturally developed, so children whose home language is not English may not be familiar with the patterns of text commonly found in English. Frequently hearing the text genres used in schools can help English Language Learners learn how to write.

Teaching Strategy 3

Section 6.2

Writing from Songs

Most young children love music, so songs are an ideal resource to promote children's writing (Bromley, 2000). Think of songs as a genre with which children are familiar and that you can use as the basis of a writing lesson.

DIRECTIONS

1. Choose a song that you like and that you think children will like. Several songs you can use for this activity follow.
    - Aliki. (1968). *Hush little baby*. Englewood Cliffs, NJ: Prentice Hall.
    - Allender, D. (1987). *Shake my sillies out*. New York: Crown.
    - Baer, E. (1995). *The is the way we eat our lunch: A book about children around the world*. New York: Scholastic.
    - Berry, H. (1994). *Old MacDonald had a farm*. New York: Morrow.
    - Krauss, L. (1993). *The first song ever sung*. New York: Lothrop Lee.
    - Trapani, I. (1993). *The itsy bitsy spider*. New York: Whispering Coyote.
    - Weiss, N. (1987). *If you're happy and you know it*. New York: Greenwillow.
    - Weiss, N., & Thiele, B. (1994). *What a wonderful world*. New York: Atheneum.

2. Read the lyrics of the song to children so that they can hear all of the words. Then teach the song by singing the song with children. Each of these songs has a simple melody that children can easily learn.

3. Write the lyrics on the chalkboard or on chart paper. Read the lyrics to children, pointing to each word as you read. Then have children read the words with you.

4. Tell children that you will be writing your own verses to the songs. Write the beginning of the song for children if necessary such as "This is the way we . . . ." Have children finish the sentence writing their own song lyric. Some examples follow.

   This is the way we eat our lunch.

   This is the way we learn to spell.

   This is the way we go to gym.

   This is the way we do our math.

5. Have children share their lyrics with the class. Then write several of the new lyrics on the chalkboard or on chart paper. Have children sing the song with their new lyrics.

Teaching Strategy 4

Section 6.2

Parent~Recommended Topics

Parents are a natural source of ideas for their children's writings. By asking parents to recommend topics for their child's writings, you are involving the parents in their child's schooling and you are providing children with fresh ideas for writing topics (Lenski & Johns, 2000).

DIRECTIONS

1. Tell children that you will be sending a letter to their parents asking them for some of their favorite memories to use as writing topics. Ask children to tell their parents in advance that a letter will be sent home.

2. Duplicate or adapt the following letter and send it home with the children. Give parents at least three days to think of topics before returning the letter to school. After three or four days, ask children to place their parents' letters in their writing folders.

3. For parents who cannot read English or do not complete the letter, tell children they can give the letter to a friend or to a relative. Or students may be able to translate the letter for their parents. Tell children that other options are to complete the list of topics themselves or ask another adult in the school to help the child come up with topics.

4. When children are asked to select topics for writing, have them refer to their Parent-Recommended Topics lists.

Parent Recommended Topics

Dear Parent,

In school, students often have the opportunity to choose their own topics for writing. Because you have more knowledge about your child than just about anyone else, I would like you to list five possible writing topics for your child. To identify writing topics, think for a moment about your child. Think of a funny story, a trip, or a learning experience your child will remember. Or think of the times your child got into trouble. Any of these ideas could make good topics for writing. You will love the stories your child will write about these topics.

Please list five writing topics and return this letter to school with your child in three days. If you have any questions, don't hesitate to ask your child or to call me at school.

Sincerely,

Possible Writing Topics

1. _____

2. _____

3. _____

4. _____

5. _____

From Susan Davis Lenski and Jerry L. Johns, *Improving Writing: Resources, Strategies, and Assessments*. Copyright © 2000 by Kendall/Hunt Publishing Company (1-800-247-3458, ext. 5). May be reproduced for noncommercial educational purposes.

Teaching Strategy 5

Section 6.2

Let Me Tell You About . . .

Young children can have difficulty developing an entire story in their minds. They are able to think of more details if they can tell someone else about their writing before they begin. The strategy Let Me Tell You About . . . (Lenski & Johns, 2000) gives children the opportunity to talk about their topics before writing.

DIRECTIONS

1. Tell children that they will be choosing their own topics for writing. Explain that they will be able to write about anything they want.

2. Tell children that writers often talk about their topics before they begin to write. Give an example from your own life or use the following example. "Last night I decided to write a letter to my son who is at college. I wanted to tell him about the new puppy that we bought. So I asked my husband what he thought. He thought it would be a good idea to write about what the puppy looks like but not to write about his visits to the veterinarian for puppy shots. Then my husband and I talked about how cute the puppy is and what he looked like. After our conversation, I had lots of things to write about."

3. Duplicate and distribute the list on the next page. Ask children to circle three items on the list. Explain that they will be discussing their circled items with their friends before writing.

4. Divide the class into groups of two or three children. Ask children to bring their lists to the group and to take turns discussing one idea on the list. Direct members of the group to choose an item on the list. Give the children time to discuss the topic. Have the group members discuss whether the topic would be good for a story. After the first child has found a topic, provide time for the other group members to discuss their lists.

Tips for English Language Learners

Writers generate topics for writing more easily if they have heard stories that resonate with their home lives and cultures. If you have English Language Learners in your classroom, you should consider reading books aloud that are written by authors of diverse backgrounds to which some of the children in your class can relate (Galda & Cullinan, 2000). After reading, emphasize the cultural background of the authors and discuss what the authors told their readers. A list of authors of diverse backgrounds follows.

Alma Flor Ada	Jan Spivey Gilcrist	Pat Mora
John Agard	Eloise Greenfield	Isaac Olaleye
Elaine Maria Alpin	Sheila Hamanaka	Jerrie Oughton
Olaf Baker	Gerald Hausman	Brian Pinkney
Shonto Begay	Daisaku Ikeada	Patricia Polacco
Pura Belpre	Rachel Isadora	Eileen Roe
Ashley Bryan	Nina Jaffe	Allen Say
Floyd Cooper	Hettie Jones	Jenny Stow
Martel Cruz	Frane Lessac	Joyce Carol Thomas
Pat Cummings	Ted Lewin	Janey Wong
Arthur Dorros	Gerald McDermott	Jane Yolen
Mem Fox	Patricia McKissack	

Writing and Spelling 359

Name_____ Date_____

Let Me Tell You About . . .

Please ask me about one of these ideas that I've circled.

My family

A pet

A special friend

Things I like to do

My favorite sport

A special game or toy

A time I had fun

A time I was afraid

A trip I took

My collection

From Jerry L. Johns, Susan Davis Lenski, and Laurie Elish-Piper, *Teaching Beginning Readers: Linking Assessment and Instruction* (2nd ed.). Copyright © 2002 by Kendall/Hunt Publishing Company (1-800-247-3458, ext. 5). May be reproduced for noncommercial educational purposes.

Ideas and Activities

1. Use a message board in the classroom to provide meaningful opportunities for children to draw or write to you and to their peers. Consider creating a classroom post office to encourage children to write letters to one another.

2. Provide literacy play centers that involve writing (e.g., restaurant, office, post office, and grocery story).

3. Invite children to create "All about Me" books that contain pictures, words, and sentences about themselves. Have children bind the books and share them with their classmates and parents.

4. Create a classroom writing center that contains a variety of writing materials. Provide daily time for children to visit the writing center. A list of suggested materials for a writing center follows.

   Suggested Materials for Writing Center

lined paper	stationery	ink pads
unlined paper	envelopes	interesting pictures
construction paper	children's typewriter	list of writing topics
pencils	rubber stamps	posters with steps in the writing process
markers	picture dictionaries	access to Word Wall words
pens	children's writing samples	message board
crayons	binding supplies	computer with children's word processing
note cards	letter stamps	program

5. Use a morning sign-in procedure to engage children in daily writing (Richgels, Poremba, & McGee, 1996). For example, at the beginning of the year, children may just sign their names on the sign-in sheet. As their writing develops, you may pose a question for them to answer, such as "Are you going to order hot lunch today?" As the year progresses, you may pose more complex questions that require more detailed responses.

6. Implement journal writing to provide children with meaningful opportunities to write each day. Suggestions for implementing personal journals follow.

   Suggestions for Implementing Personal Journals

   Children record and reflect on personal events and experiences. They may use writing, drawing, or a combination of the two to record their ideas. The purpose of personal journals is to engage children in personally meaningful writing. Some suggestions for implementing personal journals are shared below.

   1. Use a spiral notebook so all entries are kept together. Provide time for children to decorate the covers of their journals to establish ownership.

   2. Provide daily time for personal journal writing/drawing. Younger children will need 5 to 10 minutes, and older children will need 10 to 15 minutes for writing/drawing.

   3. While children write/draw in their journals, the teacher should write in a journal to model the importance of journaling.

   4. Encourage children to develop their own ideas for journal entries. If children are unable to think of ideas to write about, consult the list of journal prompts provided on the next page.

   5. Provide time for children to share their journals if they would like to do so.

7. Help children identify topics for their journals by using open-ended prompts that relate to the children's lives and experiences. A list of suggested journal prompts is provided below.

   Journal Prompts

   If I had three wishes . . .
   If I could trade places with the teacher . . .
   If I could trade places with the principal . . .
   I laughed so hard when . . .
   I felt so sad when . . .
   I felt so nervous when . . .
   I was so excited when . . .
   I felt so silly when . . .

   The best present I ever got . . .
   My favorite food is . . . because . . .
   My favorite book is . . . because . . .
   My favorite animal is . . . because . . .
   When I grow up, I want to . . .
   When I was little, I . . .
   If I could go anywhere I would . . .
   If I had a million dollars, I would . . .

8. Invite children to make signs, labels, and informative posters for the classroom. Post these materials in the classroom.

9. Establish a cross-age writing project with older children who will assist the younger children with writing and binding books. The older children can take dictation for younger children who are not writing on their own yet.

10. Use shared writing to send letters, thank you notes, and invitations to classroom visitors, guest speakers, parents, and school personnel. A classroom newsletter can also be written using a shared writing format.

11. Establish an author's chair so children can share their writing. A rocking chair, tall stool, or other special chair works well for this purpose. When children are ready to share their writing, they should sit in the author's chair while the other children and the teacher gather around to listen.

12. Develop an "Author of the Week" bulletin board to display and celebrate children's writing. Rotate this honor throughout the classroom during the year.

13. Invite children into writing by presenting them with wordless picture books. Ask them to dictate or write the story or a portion of the story told by the pictures. Display their stories with the book.

14. Implement a pen-pal program or e-mail key-pal program so children can exchange letters with other children or adults. Internet addresses for identifying e-mail key pals are provided in the following list.

Key-Pal Resources

http://www.siec.k12.in.us/~west/edu/keypal.htm

This site provides detailed directions and links for locating key pals for children. Internet safety tips related to key pals are also provided. By having children connect with key pals, they will practice their reading and writing skills in a meaningful way.

http://www.iwaynet.net/~jwolve/school.html#AAA

This site is the home of the School Pen Pal Exchange. Tips and connections for locating key pals are provided at this site.

15. Engage children in author studies to learn about how and why their favorite authors write. Helpful resources for implementing author studies are provided in Selected Resources: Writing.

16. Provide creative opportunities for children to publish their writing. Possible ideas for publishing children's writing are listed in the box on page 363.

Publishing Ideas for Children's Writing

Class books	Author's chair
Class Big Books	Sharing with other classrooms
Individual books	Intercom reading of children's writing
Classroom newsletter	Mailing letters, cards, and invitations
Posters	Posting children's writing on classroom
Displays in classroom writing center	or school Internet web site
Classroom bulletin boards	Displays in school library
Performances such as plays or puppet shows	Displays in classroom library

Home School Connections

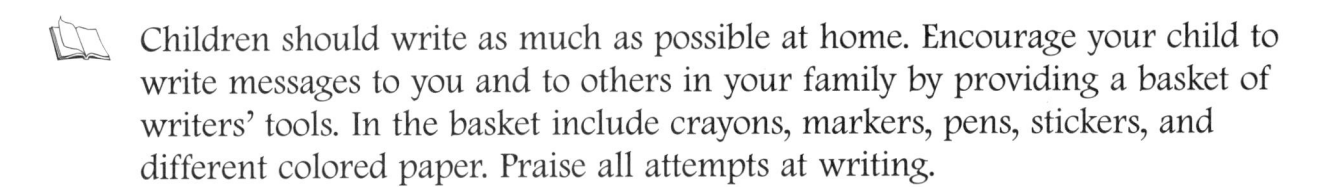

Writing at Home

📖 Children should write as much as possible at home. Encourage your child to write messages to you and to others in your family by providing a basket of writers' tools. In the basket include crayons, markers, pens, stickers, and different colored paper. Praise all attempts at writing.

📖 Let your child see you writing notes, letters, messages, and lists. If you use e-mail, let your child watch you send messages over the Internet. Your child will benefit from knowing that you use writing to communicate with others.

From Jerry L. Johns, Susan Davis Lenski, and Laurie Elish-Piper, *Teaching Beginning Readers: Linking Assessment and Instruction* (2nd ed.). Copyright © 2002 by Kendall/Hunt Publishing Company (1-800-247-3458, ext. 5). May be reproduced for noncommercial educational purposes.

Selected Resources
WRITING

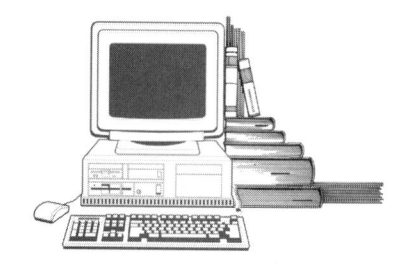

Children's Books That Invite Children to Write and Text Tap

Guarino, D. (1989). *Is your mama a llama?* New York: Scholastic.

Numeroff, L.J. (2000). *If you take a mouse to the movies.* New York: HarperCollins.

Numeroff, L.J. (1985). *If you give a mouse a cookie.* New York: Harper and Row.

Sendak, M. (1962). *Chicken soup with rice.* New York: Holt, Rinehart and Winston.

Wescott, N.B. (1988). *The lady with the alligator purse.* Boston: Little Brown.

Williams, S. (1998). *I went walking.* San Diego: Harcourt Brace.

Williams S. (1998). *Let's go visiting.* New York: Gulliver/Harcourt Brace.

Wood, A. (1984). *The napping house.* San Diego: Harcourt Brace Jovanovich.

Media and Technology

Student Publishing Center (publishes student writing). *www.sesd.sk.ca/publish.default.htm.*

Workshop CD-ROM (word processing and painting program for young children). Arkose (888-389-5500) Young Writer's Club. *www.cs.bilkent.edu.tr~david/derya/ywc.html/*

2 CD-ROM (word processing, paint program with text-to-speech features) (publishes student writing). UPDATA (800-882-2844).

Professional Resources

Graves, D. (1994). *A fresh look at writing.* Portsmouth, NH: Heinemann.

Kotch, L., & Zackman, L. (1995). *The author studies handbook.* New York: Scholastic Professional Books.

Kovacs, D., & Preller, J. (1991). *Meet the authors and illustrators* (Vol. 1). New York: Scholastic Professional Books.

Lenski, S.D., & Johns, J.L. (2000). *Improving writing: Resources, strategies, and assessments.* Dubuque, IA. Kendall/Hunt.

McCarrier, A., Pinnell, G.S., & Fountas, I.C. (2000). *Interactive writing.* Portsmouth, NH: Heinemann.

Silvey, A. (Ed.). (1995). *Children's books and their creators.* Boston: Houghton Mifflin.

Sunflower, C. (1993). *75 creative ways to publish students' writing.* New York: Scholastic Professional Books.

From Jerry L. Johns, Susan Davis Lenski, and Laurie Elish-Piper, *Teaching Beginning Readers: Linking Assessment and Instruction* (2nd ed.). Copyright © 2002 by Kendall/Hunt Publishing Company (1-800-247-3458, ext. 5). May be reproduced for noncommercial educational purposes.

6.3 Spelling

Goal To help children move from developmental spelling to conventional spelling.
Assessment Strategy 4 Developmental Spelling, page 389

BACKGROUND

Spelling words correctly is a challenge in any language, but spelling English is more difficult than spelling in many other languages. English is not a purely phonetic language, so words are not always spelled the way they sound. There are, however, rules, patterns, and relationships that govern the spelling of many words. As children learn these rules, they often use invented, or developmental, spelling.

Developmental spelling is a child's own way of spelling a word. When young children write, they create or invent their own spellings of words (Read, 1986). For example, when young children write *I love you*, they may spell the words using what they know about language at that time. The word love is often spelled, *L*, *lv*, or *luv* by young children. This developmental spelling is part of the learning process that children go through as they become conventional spellers.

Developmental spelling is an important part of a child's literacy development. As children experiment with spelling, they systematically develop their own spelling rules (Richgels, 2001). These "invented" spelling rules help children communicate through writing as they are learning the rules of conventional spelling.

The goal of spelling programs is to give young children practice spelling words and to help them become conventional spellers as soon as possible. There are many teaching strategies, ideas, activities, and assessments that help children become conventional spellers. A number of them are described in this section.

Teaching Strategy 1

Section 6.3

Have-a-Go

The Have-a-Go Strategy was adapted by Routman (1994) from a spelling strategy used in Australia. Have-a-Go encourages children to identify words that they have written with developmental spelling and to learn how to write those words with conventional spelling. The process children use with the Have-a-Go strategy mirrors the thinking processes writers use as they write with conventional spelling. Writers first spell a word using the best information they have available, determine whether the word is spelled correctly, or try various letter patterns until the word looks correct. Have-a-Go is an ideal strategy for children using developmental spelling or for children who spell most words correctly.

DIRECTIONS

1. Have children write a story using the best spelling they can. Encourage children to spell words using the letters and sounds that they know, even if the word is not spelled correctly.

2. After children have finished writing, distribute Have-a-Go sheets similar to the example on page 368.

3. Ask children to identify three words from their story that they think might not be spelled with conventional spelling. In the first column, have children write the words the way they spelled them in their writing. Move about the group and look at the words the children have selected. Place a checkmark (✓) above each letter that is correct in the words the children have written. An example follows.

Have-a-Go Spelling

Original Spelling	First Try	Second Try	Conventional Spelling
✓ ✓ feed			
✓✓ ✓ gonna			
✓✓✓ spais			

4. Have children try to spell the word in the second column, writing the letters that were correct and trying other letter combinations for the word. Move about the group and place checkmarks (✓✓) above the letters in the first try that are correct. If the word is not spelled correctly, have children try to spell the word a second time. If children do not spell the word correctly the second time, write the conventional spelling in the last column. For words that are spelled correctly, congratulate children on spelling with conventional spelling and have them write the word again in the last column. An example follows.

Have-a-Go Spelling

Original Spelling	First Try	Second Try	Conventional Spelling
feed	✓✓ ✓✓✓ freend	✓✓✓✓✓ frend	friend
gonna	✓✓✓ ✓✓ gon to	✓✓✓✓✓ ✓✓ going to	going to
spais	✓✓✓ spas	✓✓✓ ✓ spase	space

5. Have children write the words they have chosen in their spelling dictionary, in a spelling journal, or on a piece of paper for the Word Wall. Tell children that they should try to spell those words with conventional spelling in their writing.

Writing and Spelling 367

Have~a~Go

Name _____ Date _____

Original Spelling	First Try	Second Try	Conventional Spelling

From Jerry L. Johns, Susan Davis Lenski, and Laurie Elish-Piper, *Teaching Beginning Readers: Linking Assessment and Instruction* (2nd ed.). Copyright © 2002 by Kendall/Hunt Publishing Company (1-800-247-3458, ext. 5). May be reproduced for noncommercial educational purposes.

Tips for English Language Learners

Children whose home language has similarities to English can use what they know about their own language to spell words. For example, Spanish contains many of the same cognates as English. Remind children to use what they know about their own language, if possible, as they try to spell words in English. A short list of Spanish-English cognates follows.

English word	Spanish word
baby	bebé
class	clase
color	color
family	familia
flower	flor
number	número
television	televisión

Teaching Strategy 2

Section 6.3

Directed Spelling Thinking Activity (DSTA)

The Directed Spelling Thinking Activity (DSTA) (Zutell, 1996) is a strategy that helps children understand some of the patterns in the spelling of words. The underlying belief supporting the DSTA is that children learn how to spell not by memorizing the spelling of words but by learning the concepts of how letters are combined to form words. For example, the concept behind the spelling of the word *bite* is that a word with a long vowel often has a silent *e* at the end of the word. There are other generalizations for long vowels, of course, and children who learn many of the concepts that govern spelling will be able to use these concepts to spell words correctly.

DIRECTIONS

1. Gather a small group of children who have nearly the same spelling ability.
2. Identify words and word patterns that these children may be using but have not mastered. For example, you may find that children do not add a second consonant when adding *-ing* to a word such as *running*.
3. Select a set of 15 to 20 words that have the word pattern that the children need to learn or that are in contrast to the word pattern. In the example of the word *running*, a contrasting word would be *jumping*. When adding *-ing* to the word *jump*, you do not need to double the consonant.
4. Give the children a spelling test on the list of words. Most likely, some of the children will miss several of the words.
5. Identify several words that most of the children spelled incorrectly. Ask the children why they spelled the words as they did and why they thought the words were spelled that way. Allow several minutes for discussion.
6. Using the pattern, show children how to spell the words correctly. After showing two or three examples, encourage children to use the pattern for other words on the list.
7. After children understand the pattern, give them letter cards for two or three of the words on the list. Say one word at a time giving children time to make the words from letter cards.
8. Have children write the words and the word pattern in their spelling journals.

Teaching Strategy 3

Section 6.3

Spelling Workshop

Many teachers have implemented reading and writing workshops in their classrooms. The principles behind using a workshop approach toward reading and writing also hold true for spelling (Gentry & Gillet, 1993). Spelling workshops are based on the belief that, if children are in control of their learning, they will become more motivated to learn. Spelling workshops can motivate children to learn how to spell and to use conventional spelling in their writing.

DIRECTIONS

1. Have children select their own words to study for a week. These words may be selected from their writing, or they may be words that the children want to learn how to spell. Children in the primary grades should select from four to nine words for the week.

2. After children have selected words to study, add one or two words to their lists that are connected to topics or themes about which the children will be learning that week.

3. Have children list their spelling words in a spelling book or journal.

4. Conduct a focus lesson about ways to learn spelling words. You might introduce various spelling strategies from the Ideas and Activities section.

5. Introduce or review the look-cover-write-check strategy. Have children look at one spelling word at a time, cover the word, and write it on a piece of paper or on a slate. After children have written one word, have them check the correct spelling with their spelling list. If they have spelled the word incorrectly, they should practice writing the word correctly.

6. Have children give each other a final spelling test. Although there are disadvantages to having children give a test, the advantages outweigh the disadvantages for most children. Having children give each other the test frees the teacher from having to give multiple spelling tests. It also makes the children more responsible for their own work. Finally, it gives young readers the opportunity to read a classmate's list of words.

7. Tell children that the words they have chosen and learned should be written correctly in their writing. Encourage children to use their individual spelling lists as they write.

Teaching Strategy 4

Section 6.3

That Reminds Me . . .

That Reminds Me . . . (Rosencrans, 1998) is a spelling strategy that helps children apply spelling patterns to words through self-questioning. This strategy is especially useful for students who are moving toward conventional spelling.

DIRECTIONS

1. Develop a list of words that children do not already know how to spell but that have familiar parts in them. An example of a list that could be appropriate for a first- or second-grade child follows.

    running
    jumping
    skipping
    playing

2. Tell children that they can use their knowledge of spelling to spell new words by asking themselves questions. Write the following questions on a chalkboard or on chart paper.

    Does my new word remind me of another word I already know?
    Is the new word like a word I have written before?
    Do I remember any spelling rules that fit this word?

3. Demonstrate how to use the questions with the list of words you have developed. Write a sentence on the chalkboard or on chart paper using one of the words, such as "When I was playing in the soccer game, I was _____ as fast as I could to make a goal."

4. When you come to the targeted word, model how you could use That Reminds Me questions as in the following example. "As I was writing this sentence, I used my knowledge of spelling, the words on the word wall, and my personal spelling dictionary to spell all of the words. When I came to the word *running*, I realized that I didn't know how to spell it. *Running* isn't on the Word Wall, and it's not in my personal spelling dictionary. So I asked myself the That Reminds Me questions.

    First, I asked whether *running* reminded me of a word I already know. It does. It reminds me of *run* because that's part of the word. I know how to spell *run* because I know that *run* has the consonant-vowel-consonant (CVC) pattern. But I'm not sure of the word *running*. Then I asked myself whether *running* is like a word I have written before. It kind of reminds me of the word *skipping* because *skipping* has a CVC word in it. I wrote *skipping* in my story yesterday when I wrote about the things I like to do at recess. I remember that I had used a new rule when I wrote *skipping*—I had to double the final consonant. Since *running* reminds me of *skipping*, I'll try the rule of doubling the final consonant to spell my new word."

5. Tell children that good spellers use what they know about words and spelling rules to spell words. Emphasize that while they are learning spelling rules, they will not spell every word with conventional spelling, but that they will be continuing to learn how to spell better.

Tips for English Language Learners

The home language of some students is more phonetic than English is. Children who have learned some sounds and letters in their first language may be surprised that English sounds and letters do not match as often as words in their home language. (For example, Spanish is a highly phonetic language.) As English Language Learners use the That Reminds Me strategy, remind them that the spelling rules of English may be very different from the spelling rules of their home language.

Ideas and Activities

1. Develop a Words-for-Free Chart. Choose five or six words that children frequently use but spell incorrectly. Write the words on a chart and post it on the wall. Add one or two words to the chart each week. As children write or try to spell words, remind them to look on the Words-for-Free Chart.

2. Encourage children to create their own personal spelling dictionary. Have children self-select spelling words that they have learned how to spell. Ask children to review frequently the words they have selected.

3. Use sentences with lined blanks to enhance children's use of spelling strategies (Snowball, 1997). Identify words that children want to learn to spell. Choose one of the words. Write a sentence using the word, but leave a blank where the word would fit. For example, write *The _____ forest is the home of many birds.* Ask children to guess which word would fit in the blank. Have children try to spell the missing word by using spelling strategies such as sounding, thinking of word patterns, and using memory. After children have correctly spelled the word, use word patterns to spell similar words. For example, the word that fits the sentence, *rain*, has several rhyming words: *Spain, main, pain.*

4. Read rhyming books to children. Words that rhyme often have the same spelling pattern. Point out the words that have similar spelling. Have children practice the new spelling words by writing them in their spelling dictionaries.

5. Help children analyze spelling patterns by giving them word clues (Gaskin, Ehri, Cress, O'Hara, & Donnelly, 1997). Identify a spelling word to teach. Write the word on a large index card. On the back of the index card, list spelling clues. Spelling clues are listed below.

   - The word has _____ sounds.
   - The word has _____ letters.
   - The vowel makes the same sound that you hear in _____.
   - The word begins with the same letter as the word _____.
   - The spelling pattern of the word is _____.

   Say the word and give one clue at a time until children have spelled the word. After children are familiar with the game, develop Word Clue Cards for children to use during independent learning time.

6. Provide children with the opportunity to make their spelling words or word families with letters cut from sandpaper, textured wallpaper, or felt. (See Appendix B for word families.) After they have made the words, have them trace the letters with their hands to get the feel of the spelling.

7. Create a spelling center for your classroom (Gentry, 1998). Include the following items in the spelling center: several books that have repeated spelling patterns, charts of previously taught words, reusable game mats and letter tiles, erasable markers, letter cards, writing journals, student dictionaries, paper, and gold stars. Display on a chart target words that you want children to learn to spell. Have children look for the target words in their writing journals. Tell them to circle all the target words they have found. For every circled word that is spelled correctly, reward children with a gold star. Have children find the words in other books in the spelling center. Then have children practice spelling target words with letter tiles, markers, or letter cards.

8. Play Back Spelling. Have children choose a word from their list of spelling words or from the words on the Word Wall. Have the children get in groups of two. Have one child "write" the spelling word with a finger on the back of the other child. The second child should try to guess the word. Then tell the children to change roles so that the first child can write a spelling word on the back of the second child.

9. Have children try to memorize the spelling of words. Identify a word that you want children to spell. Write the word on a large index card. Tell children that you will show them the word for five seconds and then ask them to write the word. Show children the spelling words and count silently to five. Then ask children to write the word on the chalkboard, a slate, or a piece of paper. After children are finished writing, show them the spelling word again. Ask children to compare the word they wrote with the correct spelling. Repeat using the same word if necessary or use a new word.

10. Play Spelling Bingo. Give each child a card filled with spelling words and markers to cover the words. Call a word and hold up a card with the word on it. Have children find the word on their Bingo cards. The first child to cover a row gets Bingo.

11. Play Spelling Concentration. Place a set of five to seven pairs of spelling words face down on a table. You should have two cards for each word. Have children turn over two cards at a time. If the cards match, children keep them and spell the words without looking at them. If the cards do not match, have children replace the cards. The object is to match pairs of spelling words.

12. Reinforce the spelling of words children have learned with the following game. Have children form a circle. Say a spelling word that children have learned. Point to a child to say the word. Ask the child to the right of the first child to say the first letter in the word. The next child says the next letter and so on until the word is spelled. If a child says an incorrect letter, quietly say the correct letter and give the child a chance to say the next one. Repeat with several spelling words.

13. Play the following game to practice spelling words. Identify 10 to 12 spelling words that children need to learn. Write the letters of each word on individual index cards or use preprinted letter cards. Scramble the letters of all of the words face down on a table. Have the children line up as in a relay race. Say one spelling word. The first child in the line should walk quickly to the table, find the first letter, turn it over, place the letter on the ledge of the chalkboard, and walk back to the line. The second child should find the second letter and so on until the word is spelled. Repeat with all of the spelling words.

14. Create a Word Wall in your classroom (Cunningham, 2000). Identify key words that you want children to spell correctly. You may choose words that are frequently misspelled such as *they*, or you may want to include words from your science or social studies lessons. Write the words on large pieces of paper and hang them on the wall. Tell children that these words are a part of the Word Wall and that they should refer to the Word Wall when they have questions about the spelling of a word. Review the spelling of three or four words every day. It takes several teaching lessons for most children to remember how to spell some of the difficult words in English.

Home School Connections

Spelling

Spelling is learned through writing. As your children write at home, encourage them to use their knowledge of letters, sounds, and rules to spell words the way you do. If your children ask you for help with spelling, gently encourage them to use what they know to help spell words. Praise all efforts, even if words are not spelled conventionally.

Selected Resources

SPELLING

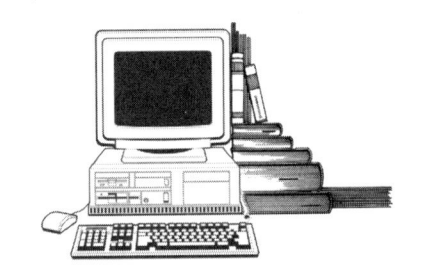

Children's Books with Repeated Word Patterns

Baillie, M. (2001). *Nose to toes.* Honesdale, PA: Boyds Mill Press.

Brown, M.W. (1993). *Four fur feet.* New York: Doubleday.

Bunting, E. (1994). *Flower garden.* San Diego: Harcourt Brace.

Cole, J. (1989). *Anna Banana: 101 jump rope rhymes.* New York: William Morrow.

Deming, A.G. (1994). *Who's tapping at my window?* New York: Penguin.

Fleming, D. (1993). *In the small, small pond.* New York: Henry Holt.

Gelman, R.G. (1984). *The biggest sandwich ever.* New York: Scholastic.

Lewison, W. (1992). *Buzz said the bee.* New York: Scholastic.

Ochs, C.P. (1991). *Moose on the loose.* Minneapolis: Carolrhoda Books.

Seuss, Dr. (1965). *Fox in socks.* New York: Random House.

Weatherford, C.B. (2001). *Sidewalk chalk.* Honesdale, PA: Boyds Mill Press.

Williams, S. (1998). *I went walking.* New York: Harcourt Brace.

Media and Technology

Reader Rabbit 1 CD-ROM (letter recognition and spelling activities).
UPDATA (800-882-2844)

Reading Blaster: Invasion of the Word Snatchers CD-ROM (spelling activities and tips for parents and teachers).
UPDATA (800-882-2844)

Spellbound CD-ROM (digitized spoken words with spelling activities).
UPDATA (800-882-2844)

The Reading Carnival CD-ROM (spelling games and reading puzzles).
UPDATA (800-882-2844)

Professional Resources

Bear, D.R., Invernizzi, M., Templeton, S., & Johnson, F. (2000). *Words their way: Word study for phonics, vocabulary and spelling* (2nd ed.). Upper Saddle River, NJ: Prentice Hall/Merrill.

Bolton, F., & Snowball, D. (1993). *Teaching spelling: A practical resource.* Portsmouth, NH: Heinemann.

Gentry, J.R., & Gillet, J.W. (1993). *Teaching kids to spell.* Portsmouth, NH: Heinemann.

Rosencrans, G. (1998). *The spelling book.* Newark, DE: International Reading Association.

From Jerry L. Johns, Susan Davis Lenski, and Laurie Elish-Piper, *Teaching Beginning Readers: Linking Assessment and Instruction* (2nd ed.). Copyright © 2002 by Kendall/Hunt Publishing Company (1-800-247-3458, ext. 5). May be reproduced for noncommercial educational purposes.

6.4 Assessments of Writing and Spelling

Assessment Strategy 1   Writing   379
   Writing Record Sheet   380

Assessment Strategy 2   Writing Rubrics   381
   Kindergarten Writing Rubric   382
   First-Grade Writing Rubric   383
   Second-Grade Writing Rubric   384
   Student Record Sheet   386

Assessment Strategy 3   Writing Observational Checklist   387
   Record Sheet   388

Assessment Strategy 4   Developmental Spelling   389
   Developmental Spelling Scoring Chart   390
   Child's Copy   391

Goal To assess child's ability to write and spell words, sentences, and stories.

BACKGROUND

Writing and spelling abilities can only be assessed by having the child write or by observing a child write. You can have the child write lists, sentences, or stories. To assess writing ability you can use samples of writing, observational checklists, and/or writing rubrics.

Spelling development can be assessed by comparing a child's spelling to the stages young children typically move through as they progress to conventional spelling. There are several stage theories that have been developed, but the most common is Gentry's stages of spelling development (Gentry, 1981). The stages are listed below.

- **Precommunicative spelling**
  Children string letters, numbers, scribbles, and forms together but do not associate the marks with any letter sounds (e.g., *ggh4kesos* for *puppy*).

- **Semiphonetic spelling**
  Children begin to represent letter sounds in words with the appropriate letters. They may have one or two letters correct in a word (e.g., *DG* for *dog*).

- **Phonetic spelling**
  Children spell words as they sound (e.g., *sokar* for *soccer*).
- **Transitional spelling**
  Children use a high percentage of correctly spelled words and the remaining words are spelled using some type of spelling generalization (e.g., *afternewn* for *afternoon*).
- **Conventional spelling**
  Children apply the basic rules of English to spelling and correctly spell 90% of the words they write.

Assessment Strategy 1

Section 6.4

Writing

Overview	In the Writing assessment, the child is asked to demonstrate his or her ability to write words, letters, and sentences.
Materials Needed	1. A pencil or pen 2. Paper (lined and unlined) 3. Record Sheet (p. 380)
Procedures	1. Give the child lined and unlined paper and a pencil or pen. If possible, have choices of paper and writing instruments. 2. Depending on the child's age or ability, you may want to give separate directions for each task: "Write some letters for me." Then say, "How many words can you write?" Finally "Write a sentence." For an older child, you could say, "I'd like you to write some letters, words, and sentences." Be patient and encouraging. You might ask the child to begin by writing his or her first name. If there is some success, try the last name. 3. After the child has finished, invite him or her to share what was written. Make mental notes or jot down your ideas. 4. For children who say "I can't write," you might want to ask them to use "kid writing" or to print an X. Continue with a few other letters and perhaps names and numbers that the student may know. You might also suggest general categories of words: pets, colors, foods, and things you can do.
Scoring and Interpretation	Informally evaluate the child's writing using the areas on the Record Sheet that follows. Record an **X** on the continuum that represents your overall judgment. Compare the results of the child's writing to the progress of children at the same developmental stage.

RECORD SHEET

Writing

Name _____ Date _____

	Not Evident Low Seldom Weak Poor	Some	Evident High Always Strong Excellent

Directionality

Left to right |—————|—————|—————|—————|

Top to bottom |—————|—————|—————|—————|

Child's Name

Knowledge of first (F) and last (L) name |—————|—————|—————|—————|

Letter-Sound Relationships

Represents sounds heard at word beginnings |—————|—————|—————|—————|

Represents sounds heard at word endings |—————|—————|—————|—————|

Represents sounds heard in word middles |—————|—————|—————|—————|

Uses vowels |—————|—————|—————|—————|

Writing Conventions

Use of word boundaries |—————|—————|—————|—————|

Use of punctuation |—————|—————|—————|—————|

Writing (check one)

_____ Scribbles or "cursivelike" scribbles

_____ Letter-like formations

_____ Repeated letters, numbers, words

_____ Variety of letters, numbers, words

Overall Message Intent (check one)

_____ Child indicated no message intent or did not communicate a message.

_____ Child talked about but did not read or pretend to read what was written.

_____ Child was able to read what was written.

Teacher could make sense of writing independently.   yes   no

From Jerry L. Johns, Susan Davis Lenski, and Laurie Elish-Piper, *Teaching Beginning Readers: Linking Assessment and Instruction* (2nd ed.). Copyright © 2002 by Kendall/Hunt Publishing Company (1-800-247-3458, ext. 5). May be reproduced for noncommercial educational purposes.

Assessment Strategy 2

Section 6.4

Writing Rubrics

Overview	Writing can be assessed using writing rubrics. Rubrics can be used to evaluate an individual piece of writing in one or more areas. Effective rubrics tend to be specific to grade and/or ability levels. The best rubrics are those you create yourself that fit your particular class and your writing standards. The rubrics that follow were developed for kindergarten, first-grade, and second-grade children. Use or adapt the rubrics to fit your teaching situation.
Materials Needed	1. A grade appropriate Writing Rubric (pp. 382–385) 2. A pencil 3. Samples of children's writing
Procedures	1. Duplicate the appropriate number of copies of the rubrics, one for each piece of writing you will be assessing. 2. Tell the children: "Today I'm going to assess your writing in several areas. The areas include (list the rubric's criteria). As you write today, remember that your writing will be graded in these areas." 3. Collect the children's writings and score them by circling a number in each area of assessment. If you believe the writing falls between two scores, either assign a higher score or a lower score consistently.
Scoring and Interpretation	Set cutoff points that identify pieces of writing that meet your class or grade standards, are below standards, or exceed standards. The score on a piece of writing will reflect whether a child's writing meets your grade-level expectations. Or use the scoring that is at the end of each rubric. If the scoring doesn't fit your ideas of grade-level standards, adjust the scores as needed. Score several pieces of writing with the rubric over time. List the child's scores on a continuum to determine whether growth is occurring, or use the Class Writing Record Sheet to record several children's scores.

Kindergarten Writing Rubric

	1	2	3	4
Content	Picture and writing do not match	N/A	N/A	Writing matches picture
	Uses random scribbles	Uses letter-like symbols	Uses conventional letters with some sound/symbol relationships	Uses conventional letters with readable sound/symbol relationships
Oral Expression	Unnatural language patterns	Mixture of natural and unnatural language	Natural language for the most part	Natural language throughout
Conventions	Random scribbles	Letters unclear	Lowercase or uppercase letters throughout	Mixture of lowercase and uppercase letters
	N/A	No attempt at spaces between words	Attempt at spaces between words	Spaces between words Attempt at end marks
Total Score				

Scoring

11–12 Exceeds Standards
8–10 Meets Standards
less than 8 Does Not Meet Standards

From Jerry L. Johns, Susan Davis Lenski, and Laurie Elish-Piper, *Teaching Beginning Readers: Linking Assessment and Instruction* (2nd ed.). Copyright © 2002 by Kendall/Hunt Publishing Company (1-800-247-3458, ext. 5). May be reproduced for noncommercial educational purposes.

First~Grade Writing Rubric

Content	1	2	3	4
	Of little interest	Mildly interesting	Somewhat interesting	Interesting
	No details or examples	A few details or examples	Some details or examples	Many details or examples
Organization	**1**	**2**	**3**	**4**
	Topic is not clear	Topic is evident but not clear	Paper stays on topic with one or two exceptions	Paper stays on topic
	No evident beginning, middle, and end	Beginning, middle, and end attempted	Beginning, middle, and end are evident but not clear	Paper has a clear beginning, middle, and end
Fluency	**1**	**2**	**3**	**4**
	Unnatural language patterns	Patterned or stilted language	Some natural and some patterned language	Paper is written in natural, not patterned, language
Conventions	**1**	**2**	**3**	**4**
	Little evidence of conventional spelling	Conventional spelling attempted	Many words (50%) are spelled with conventional spelling	Spelling is nearly conventional (80% of the words used)
	Little evidence of correct conventions • capital letters • ending marks • spaces between words	Correct conventions evident but not used throughout the paper • capital letters • ending marks • spaces between words	Conventions are generally correct with some errors • capital letters • ending marks • spaces between words	Convention use is consistent but not perfect • capital letters • ending marks • spaces between words
Total Score				

Scoring

10–12	Exceeds Standards
7–9	Meets Standards
less than 7	Does Not Meet Standards

From Jerry L. Johns, Susan Davis Lenski, and Laurie Elish-Piper, *Teaching Beginning Readers: Linking Assessment and Instruction* (2nd ed.). Copyright © 2002 by Kendall/Hunt Publishing Company (1-800-247-3458, ext. 5). May be reproduced for noncommercial educational purposes.

Second-Grade Writing Rubric

Content	1	2	3	4
	Of little interest	Mildly interesting	Fairly interesting	Captures reader's interest
	No specific descriptions or examples	Few specific descriptions or examples	Some specific descriptions or examples	Several vivid descriptions or examples
	(Narrative) Does not express emotions or feelings	(Narrative) Some emotions or feelings expressed	(Narrative) Expresses emotions or feelings but not effectively	(Narrative) Effectively expresses emotions or feelings
Organization	**1**	**2**	**3**	**4**
	Topic is not clear	Topic is evident but not clear	Stays on topic with one or two exceptions	Stays on topic
	No evident beginning, middle, and end	Partially written beginning, middle, and end	Beginning, middle, and end are evident but not clear	Has a clear beginning, middle, and end

From Jerry L. Johns, Susan Davis Lenski, and Laurie Elish-Piper, *Teaching Beginning Readers: Linking Assessment and Instruction* (2nd ed.). Copyright © 2002 by Kendall/Hunt Publishing Company (1-800-247-3458, ext. 5). May be reproduced for noncommercial educational purposes.

Second-Grade Writing Rubric (continued)

Fluency	1	2	3	4
	Sentences are choppy or run-on	More choppy or run-on sentences than sentence fluency	Some sentence fluency but not throughout the paper	Sentences flow from one to another
	Sentences do not vary	Little variation in sentence length	Some variation in sentence length	Sentences vary in length
	Few or no transitions	Some transitions	Transitions evident but may not fit the context	Transitions between sentences are natural
Conventions	**1**	**2**	**3**	**4**
	Little evidence of conventional spelling	Conventional spelling evident (50%) but not used throughout	Most words (75%) are spelled conventionally	Spelling is conventional (90% of the words used)
	Little evidence of correct conventions • capital letters • ending marks	Correct conventions evident but not used throughout the paper • capital letters • ending marks	Conventions are generally correct with some errors • capital letters • ending marks	Convention use is consistent but not perfect • capital letters • ending marks • subject-verb agreement • paragraph form
Total Score				

Scoring
10–12   Exceeds Standards
7–9   Meets Standards
less than 7   Does Not Meet Standards

From Jerry L. Johns, Susan Davis Lenski, and Laurie Elish-Piper, *Teaching Beginning Readers: Linking Assessment and Instruction* (2nd ed.). Copyright © 2002 by Kendall/Hunt Publishing Company (1-800-247-3458, ext. 5). May be reproduced for noncommercial educational purposes.

RECORD SHEET

Student Writing Record

Name _____

	Does not meet standards	**Meets standards**	**Exceeds standards**
Title of paper and date			

From Jerry L. Johns, Susan Davis Lenski, and Laurie Elish-Piper, *Teaching Beginning Readers: Linking Assessment and Instruction* (2nd ed.). Copyright © 2002 by Kendall/Hunt Publishing Company (1-800-247-3458, ext. 5). May be reproduced for noncommercial educational purposes.

Assessment Strategy 3

Section 6.4

Writing Observational Checklist

Overview	Writing can be assessed using an observational checklist as well as by analyzing writing samples. At times observing children writing can give more information than their written product. In general, an observational checklist assesses process as well as product.
Materials Needed	1. The Writing Observational Checklist Record Sheet (p. 388). 2. A pencil
Procedures	1. Duplicate the appropriate number of copies of the Record Sheet, one for each student you will be assessing. If you use the Writing Observational Checklist Record Sheet with your entire class, you should assess only four or five students at a time. 2. Tell the children: "Today I'm going to watch you write. I won't be writing myself, nor will I conduct writing conferences. I'll be walking around, taking notes, and asking you questions as you write. I'll try not to disturb your writing." 3. Observe and take notes of four or five students during any one writing period. As you observe, if you are unsure of a child's development, ask appropriate questions. Some examples follow. If you are not sure whether a child is a confident writer, ask, "How do you feel about yourself as a writer?" If you don't know whether a child is able to generate topics, ask, "How did you think of the topic of your writing? Is that difficult for you?"
Scoring and Interpretation	Writing can be evaluated on a continuum similar to spelling development (Harp, 2000). Children who exhibit most of the behaviors on the Writing Observational Checklist Record Sheet would be considered to be beginning writers. If children are unable to accomplish the items on the Writing Observational Checklist Record Sheet, you should tailor your instruction to meet their needs. If you checked all of the items, you should continue to stress the writing process and provide children many opportunities to write.

RECORD SHEET

Writing Observational Checklist

Name_____

In the spaces to the right, record the date you observed one of these behaviors. Write additional comments under each item.

	Date	Date	Date

1. Is a confident writer.

2. Is able to generate topics.

3. Writes on a variety of topics.

4. Understands the purposes for writing.

5. Is beginning to make corrections when writing.

6. Knows that writing can be read by others.

7. Can select pieces for publication.

8. Is able to use a word processing program.

From Jerry L. Johns, Susan Davis Lenski, and Laurie Elish-Piper, *Teaching Beginning Readers: Linking Assessment and Instruction* (2nd ed.). Copyright © 2002 by Kendall/Hunt Publishing Company (1-800-247-3458, ext. 5). May be reproduced for noncommercial educational purposes.

Assessment Strategy 4

Section 6.4

Developmental Spelling

Overview	Developmental spelling refers to the stages of spelling that children go through prior to conventional spelling. Developmental spelling provides windows into children's thinking about letter-sound relationships. This assessment consists of challenging words that most emergent readers and writers cannot spell. For this reason, it requires them to use their knowledge of letter-sound relationships to spell the words they hear. The children's spellings are not scored as correct or incorrect; rather, they are analyzed by using a developmental scale. This assessment can be administered individually, to a small group, or to an entire class of children.
Materials Needed	1. The child's page in this book (p. 391). 2. The Developmental Spelling Stage Scoring Chart (p. 390)

Procedures	1. Duplicate the appropriate number of copies of the child's page in this book (p. 391) along with the Developmental Spelling Stage Scoring Chart (p. 390).
	2. Tell the child(ren), "Today we are going to spell some words. Some of the words will be hard but don't worry. Just spell them the best you can by making good guesses about the sounds and letters you hear in the words."
	3. Distribute the child's copy to each child taking the assessment.
	4. Dictate the list of 10 words. After saying each word, use it in a simple sentence. For example, for the first word in the list (drop), say, "drop . . . Do not drop the dish when you dry it." Continue through the entire list of words. Repeat words and sentences, as necessary.
	    1. drop 6. mess
	    2. faster 7. packed
	    3. liked 8. make
	    4. back 9. earn
	    5. monster 10. greet

Scoring and Interpretation	The child's general developmental spelling stage is determined by analyzing the child's spelling for each word on the list and then identifying the stage that appears most frequently. Follow these steps when analyzing the child's developmental spelling. 1. Look at the child's spelling for each word on the list. Analyze the child's spelling using the Developmental Spelling Stage Scoring Chart. The child's spelling may not match exactly, but it should be the best match on the chart.

Writing and Spelling   389

(continued)

2. Write the appropriate developmental spelling stage label (e.g., precommunicative, semiphonetic, etc.) next to each of the 10 words on the child's copy.
3. To determine the child's general developmental spelling stage, look for the label that appears most frequently.

Developmental Spelling Stage Scoring Chart

Precommunicative (Pre.)	Semiphonetic (Semi.)	Phonetic (Phon.)	Transitional (Trans.)	Conventional (Conv.)
1. random letters or symbols	dp	dop	dropp	drop
2. random letters or symbols	ft	fasr	fastr	faster
3. random letters or symbols	lt	likt	licked	liked
4. random letters or symbols	bk	bak	backe	back
5. random letters or symbols	mtr	mostr	monstur	monster
6. random letters or symbols	ms	mss	mes	mess
7. random letters or symbols	pt	pkt	paked	packed
8. random letters or symbols	mk	mak	macke	make
9. random letters or symbols	en	ern	earnn	earn
10. random letters or symbols	gt	gret	grete	greet

4. Circle the child's developmental spelling stage for each word.

   1. drop   Precommunicative   Semiphonetic   Phonetic   Transitional   Conventional

   2. faster   Precommunicative   Semiphonetic   Phonetic   Transitional   Conventional

   3. liked   Precommunicative   Semiphonetic   Phonetic   Transitional   Conventional

   4. back   Precommunicative   Semiphonetic   Phonetic   Transitional   Conventional

   5. monster Precommunicative   Semiphonetic   Phonetic   Transitional   Conventional

   6. mess   Precommunicative   Semiphonetic   Phonetic   Transitional   Conventional

   7. packed   Precommunicative   Semiphonetic   Phonetic   Transitional   Conventional

   8. make   Precommunicative   Semiphonetic   Phonetic   Transitional   Conventional

   9. earn   Precommunicative   Semiphonetic   Phonetic   Transitional   Conventional

   10. greet   Precommunicative   Semiphonetic   Phonetic   Transitional   Conventional

General Developmental Spelling Stage (Check One)

☐ Precommunicative ☐ Semiphonetic ☐ Phonetic ☐ Transitional ☐ Conventional

From Jerry L. Johns, Susan Davis Lenski, and Laurie Elish-Piper, *Teaching Beginning Readers: Linking Assessment and Instruction* (2nd ed.). Copyright © 2002 by Kendall/Hunt Publishing Company (1-800-247-3458, ext. 5). May be reproduced for noncommercial educational purposes.

Child's Name _____

Stage

1. _____ _____

2. _____ _____

3. _____ _____

4. _____ _____

5. _____ _____

6. _____ _____

7. _____ _____

8. _____ _____

9. _____ _____

10. _____ _____

Developmental Spelling—Child's Copy

From Jerry L. Johns, Susan Davis Lenski, and Laurie Elish-Piper, *Teaching Beginning Readers: Linking Assessment and Instruction* (2nd ed.). Copyright © 2002 by Kendall/Hunt Publishing Company (1-800-247-3458, ext. 5). May be reproduced for noncommercial educational purposes.

Additional Ways of Assessing Writing and Spelling

1. You can informally assess a child's spelling using the child's writing. Collect four or five pieces of writing and look for spelling patterns. Refer to the Developmental Stages of Spelling to identify the child's spelling stage.

2. Some teachers use standardized tests to assess children's writing development. Standardized tests typically measure how well children can identify correct conventions in writing. Although these tests give some information about writing, they should not replace authentic writing samples.

Appendices

Appendix A
Professional Organizations and Agencies

Appendix B
Word Families

Appendix A

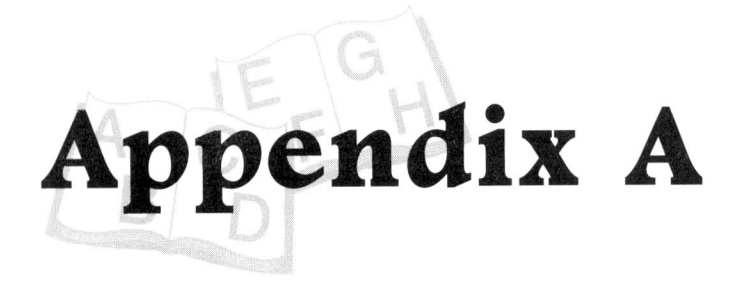

PROFESSIONAL ORGANIZATIONS AND AGENCIES

Association for Supervision and Curriculum Development (ASCD)
1250 Pitt
Alexandria, VA 22314
1-800-933-ASCD
http://www.ascd.org

Association of Childhood International
17904 Georgia Ave.
Suite 215
Olney, MD 20832
1-800-423-3563
http://www.udel.edu/bateman/acei/index.html

Center for the Improvement of Early Reading Achievement (CIERA)
University of Michigan School of Education
610 University Ave., Rm. 1600 SEB
Ann Arbor, MI 48109-1259
1-734-647-6940
http://www.ciera.org

Children's Book Council
568 Broadway, Suite 404
New York, NY 10012
1-212-966-1990
http://www.cbcbooks.org

Council for Exceptional Children (CEC)
1920 Association Dr.
Reston, VA 22091
1-888-CEC-SPED
http://cec.sped.org

International Reading Association (IRA)
800 Barksdale Rd.
P.O. Box 8139
Newark, DE 19714
1-800-336-READ
http://www.reading.org

National Association of the Education of Young Children (NAEYC)
1509 16th St., NW
Washington, DC 20036-1426
1-800-424-2460
http://www.naeyc.org

National Council of Teachers of English
1111 Kenyon Rd.
Urbana, IL 61801
1-800-369-6283
http://www.ncte.org

From Jerry L. Johns, Susan Davis Lenski, and Laurie Elish-Piper, *Teaching Beginning Readers: Linking Assessment and Instruction* (2nd ed.). Copyright © 2002 by Kendall/Hunt Publishing Company (1-800-247-3458, ext. 5). May be reproduced for noncommercial educational purposes.

Appendix B

WORD FAMILIES

Short a Sounds

~ab	~ack	~ad	~ag	~am	~amp	~an	~and
cab	back	ad	bag	am	camp	an	and
dab	hack	bad	gag	dam	damp	ban	band
gab	jack	cad	hag	ham	lamp	can	hand
jab	pack	dad	nag	jam	champ	fan	land
lab	rack	fad	rag	clam	clamp	man	sand
nab	sack	had	sag	cram	cramp	pan	gland
tab	tack	lad	tag	slam	stamp	ran	grand
blab	black	mad	wag	swam	tramp	tan	stand
slab	slack	pad	brag			van	strand
crab	crack	sad	drag			clan	
drab	track	clad	flag			plan	
grab	shack	glad	shag			scan	
scab	whack	shad	snag			span	
stab	smack		stag			than	
	snack						
	stack						

~ang	~ank	~ap	~ash	~ast	~at	~atch
bang	bank	cap	ash	cast	at	catch
fang	rank	gap	bash	fast	bat	hatch
gang	sank	lap	cash	last	cat	latch
hang	tank	map	dash	mast	fat	match
rang	yank	nap	gash	past	hat	patch
sang	blank	rap	hash	vast	mat	thatch
tang	clank	sap	lash	blast	pat	
clang	plank	tap	mash		sat	
slang	crank	chap	rash		vat	
	drank	clap	sash		brat	
	frank	flap	clash		chat	
	spank	slap	crash		flat	
	thank	snap	smash		slat	
		trap	stash		scat	
			trash		that	

From Jerry L. Johns, Susan Davis Lenski, and Laurie Elish-Piper, *Teaching Beginning Readers: Linking Assessment and Instruction* (2nd ed.). Copyright © 2002 by Kendall/Hunt Publishing Company (1-800-247-3458, ext. 5). May be reproduced for noncommercial educational purposes.

Short e Sounds

~eck	~ed	~eg	~ell	~en	~end	~ent
deck	bed	beg	bell	den	end	bent
heck	fed	keg	dell	hen	bend	dent
neck	led	leg	fell	men	lend	lent
peck	red	peg	sell	pen	mend	rent
check	wed		tell	ten	send	sent
speck	bled		well	glen	blend	tent
	fled		yell	then	spend	went
	sled		quell	when	trend	spent
	shed		shell			
	sped		smell			
			spell			
			swell			

~ess	~est	~et
less	best	bet
mess	nest	get
bless	pest	jet
chess	rest	let
dress	vest	met
	west	net
	chest	pet
	crest	set
	quest	wet
		vet
		fret

From Jerry L. Johns, Susan Davis Lenski, and Laurie Elish-Piper, *Teaching Beginning Readers: Linking Assessment and Instruction* (2nd ed.). Copyright © 2002 by Kendall/Hunt Publishing Company (1-800-247-3458, ext. 5). May be reproduced for noncommercial educational purposes.

Short i Sounds

~ib	~ick	~id	~ift	~ig	~ill	~im
bib	kick	bid	gift	big	bill	dim
fib	lick	did	lift	dig	fill	him
rib	nick	hid	rift	fig	gill	rim
crib	pick	kid	sift	jig	hill	skim
	sick	lid	drift	pig	kill	slim
	tick	rid	shift	rig	mill	swim
	wick	grid	swift	wig	pill	trim
	brick	skid		brig	rill	whim
	trick	slid		swig	sill	
	chick				till	
	thick				will	
	click				chill	
	flick				drill	
	slick				grill	
	quick				quill	
	stick				spill	

~in	~ing	~ink	~ip	~ish	~it	~itch
in	bing	ink	dip	dish	it	itch
bin	ring	pink	hip	fish	bit	ditch
din	sing	sink	lip	wish	fit	pitch
fin	wing	wink	nip	swish	hit	witch
kin	bring	blink	rip		kit	stitch
pin	fling	slink	sip		lit	switch
sin	sting	stink	tip		pit	
tin	swing	think	yip		sit	
win	thing		zip		wit	
chin			chip		grit	
shin			ship		mitt	
thin			whip		quit	
grin			flip		slit	
skin			slip		skit	
spin			grip		spit	
twin			trip		twit	
			quip			
			skip			
			snip			

From Jerry L. Johns, Susan Davis Lenski, and Laurie Elish-Piper, *Teaching Beginning Readers: Linking Assessment and Instruction* (2nd ed.). Copyright © 2002 by Kendall/Hunt Publishing Company (1-800-247-3458, ext. 5). May be reproduced for noncommercial educational purposes.

Short o Sounds

~ob	~ock	~od	~og	~ong	~ot
cob	cock	cod	bog	bong	cot
fob	dock	hod	cog	gong	dot
gob	hock	nod	dog	long	got
job	lock	pod	fog	song	hot
rob	mock	rod	hog	tong	not
mob	pock	sod	jog	wrong	pot
sob	rock	clod	log	strong	rot
blob	sock	plod	clog		blot
slob	tock	shod	frog		clot
snob	clock		smog		plot
	flock				slot
	crock				shot
	frock				spot
	shock				trot
	smock				
	stock				

From Jerry L. Johns, Susan Davis Lenski, and Laurie Elish-Piper, *Teaching Beginning Readers: Linking Assessment and Instruction* (2nd ed.). Copyright © 2002 by Kendall/Hunt Publishing Company (1-800-247-3458, ext. 5). May be reproduced for noncommercial educational purposes.

Short u Sounds

~ub	~uck	~ud	~uff	~ug	~ull	~um
cub	buck	bud	buff	bug	cull	bum
dub	duck	cud	cuff	dug	dull	gum
hub	luck	mud	huff	hug	gull	hum
nub	muck	stud	muff	jug	hull	mum
pub	puck	thud	puff	lug	lull	rum
rub	suck		bluff	mug	mull	sum
sub	tuck		gruff	pug	null	glum
tub	chuck		stuff	rug	skull	slum
club	shuck			tug		drum
grub	cluck			chug		scum
stub	pluck			thug		chum
	stuck			plug		
				slug		
				smug		

~ump	~un	~unch	~ung	~unk	~up	~ush
bump	bun	bunch	dung	bunk	up	gush
dump	fun	lunch	hung	dunk	cup	hush
hump	gun	punch	lung	hunk	pup	lush
jump	nun	brunch	rung	junk	sup	mush
lump	pun	crunch	sung	sunk		rush
pump	run		clung	chunk		blush
clump	sun		flung	drunk		flush
plump	shun		stung	flunk		plush
slump	spun		swung	skunk		slush
stump	stun					brush
thump						crush
						shush

~ust	~ut
bust	but
dust	cut
just	gut
must	hut
rust	jut
crust	nut
	rut
	shut

From Jerry L. Johns, Susan Davis Lenski, and Laurie Elish-Piper, *Teaching Beginning Readers: Linking Assessment and Instruction* (2nd ed.). Copyright © 2002 by Kendall/Hunt Publishing Company (1-800-247-3458, ext. 5). May be reproduced for noncommercial educational purposes.

Long a Sounds

~ace	~ade	~age	~aid	~ail	~ain	~ale	~ame
ace	fade	age	aid	ail	gain	ale	came
face	jade	cage	laid	bail	main	dale	dame
lace	lade	page	maid	fail	pain	hale	fame
mace	made	rage	paid	hail	rain	kale	game
pace	wade	sage	raid	jail	vain	male	lame
race	blade	wage	braid	mail	brain	pale	name
brace	glade	stage		nail	drain	sale	same
place	grade			pail	grain	tale	tame
space	trade			rail	train	vale	blame
	shade			sail	chain	scale	flame
	spade			tail	plain	shale	frame
				wail	slain	stale	shame
				frail	stain	whale	
				quail			
				snail			
				trail			

~ane	~ape	~aste	~ate	~ave	~ay	~aze
cane	ape	baste	ate	cave	bay	daze
lane	cape	haste	date	gave	day	gaze
mane	gape	paste	fate	nave	gay	haze
pane	nape	taste	gate	pave	hay	maze
sane	tape	chaste	hate	rave	jay	blaze
vane	drape		late	save	lay	glaze
wane	grape		rate	brave	nay	graze
crane	shape		sate	crave	pay	
			crate	grave	ray	
			grate	shave	say	
			plate	slave	way	
			skate		clay	
			slate		play	
			state		fray	
					tray	
					stay	
					sway	

From Jerry L. Johns, Susan Davis Lenski, and Laurie Elish-Piper, *Teaching Beginning Readers: Linking Assessment and Instruction* (2nd ed.). Copyright © 2002 by Kendall/Hunt Publishing Company (1-800-247-3458, ext. 5). May be reproduced for noncommercial educational purposes.

Long e Sounds

~e	~ea	~each	~ead	~eak	~eal	~eam
be	pea	each	bead	beak	deal	beam
he	sea	beach	lead	leak	heal	ream
me	tea	peach	read	peak	meal	seam
we	flea	reach	plead	weak	peal	team
she	plea	teach		bleak	real	cream
		bleach		freak	seal	dream
				speak	veal	gleam
					zeal	
					steal	

~ean	~eat	~ee	~eed	~eek	~eel	~een
bean	eat	bee	deed	leek	eel	keen
dean	beat	fee	feed	meek	feel	seen
lean	feat	see	heed	peek	heel	teen
mean	heat	tee	need	reek	keel	green
wean	meat	wee	seed	seek	peel	queen
clean	neat	free	weed	week	reel	sheen
glean	peat	tree	bleed	cheek		
	seat	glee	breed	creek		
	cheat	thee	creed	sleek		
	cleat	three	freed			
	pleat		greed			
	treat		speed			
	wheat		steed			
			tweed			

~eep	~eet
beep	beet
deep	fleet
jeep	meet
keep	greet
peep	sheet
seep	sleet
weep	sweet
creep	tweet
sheep	
steep	
sweep	

From Jerry L. Johns, Susan Davis Lenski, and Laurie Elish-Piper, *Teaching Beginning Readers: Linking Assessment and Instruction* (2nd ed.). Copyright © 2002 by Kendall/Hunt Publishing Company (1-800-247-3458, ext. 5). May be reproduced for noncommercial educational purposes.

Long i Sounds

~ice	~ide	~ie	~ife	~igh	~ight	~ike
lice	bide	die	knife	high	bright	bike
mice	hide	lie	life	nigh	fight	dike
nice	ride	pie	rife	sigh	flight	hike
rice	side	tie	wife	thigh	fright	like
vice	tide	vie			light	mike
slice	wide				might	pike
spice	bride				night	spike
twice	glide				plight	
	slide				right	
					sight	
					slight	
					tight	

~ild	~ile	~ime	~ind	~ine	~ipe	~ire
mild	file	dime	bind	dine	pipe	ire
wild	mile	lime	find	fine	ripe	dire
child	pile	time	hind	line	wipe	fire
	rile	chime	kind	mine	gripe	hire
	tile	crime	mind	nine	swipe	mire
	vile	grime	rind	pine		sire
	smile	slime	wind	tine		tire
	while		blind	vine		wire
			grind	shine		
				spine		
				swine		
				thine		
				twine		
				whine		

~ite	~ive
bite	dive
kite	five
mite	hive
site	live
quite	chive
spite	drive
white	

From Jerry L. Johns, Susan Davis Lenski, and Laurie Elish-Piper, *Teaching Beginning Readers: Linking Assessment and Instruction* (2nd ed.). Copyright © 2002 by Kendall/Hunt Publishing Company (1-800-247-3458, ext. 5). May be reproduced for noncommercial educational purposes.

Long o Sounds

~o	~oad	~oam	~oan	~oast	~oat	~obe
go	goad	foam	loan	boast	oat	lobe
no	load	loam	moan	coast	boat	robe
so	road	roam	roan	roast	coat	globe
	toad		groan	toast	goat	
					moat	
					bloat	
					float	
					gloat	

~ode	~oe	~oke	~old	~ole	~olt	~ome
ode	doe	coke	old	dole	bolt	dome
bode	foe	joke	bold	hole	colt	gnome
code	hoe	poke	cold	mole	dolt	home
mode	toe	woke	fold	pole	jolt	Nome
rode	woe	yoke	gold	role	volt	
		bloke	hold	stole		
		choke	mold			
		smoke	sold			
		spoke	told			

~one	~ope	~ose	~ost	~ote	~ow
bone	cope	hose	ghost	note	bow
cone	dope	nose	host	rote	low
lone	hope	pose	most	tote	mow
pone	mope	rose	post	vote	row
tone	rope	chose		quote	sow
zone	scope	those			tow
shone	slope	close			blow
stone					flow
					glow
					slow
					crow
					grow
					show
					snow

Long u Sounds

~use	~ute
use	cute
fuse	mute
muse	flute

From Jerry L. Johns, Susan Davis Lenski, and Laurie Elish-Piper, *Teaching Beginning Readers: Linking Assessment and Instruction* (2nd ed.). Copyright © 2002 by Kendall/Hunt Publishing Company (1-800-247-3458, ext. 5). May be reproduced for noncommercial educational purposes.

References

Adams, M.J. (1990). *Beginning to read: Thinking and learning about print.* Cambridge, MA: MIT Press.

Adams, M.J. (2001). Alphabetic anxiety and explicit, systematic phonics instruction: A cognitive science perspective. In S.B. Neuman & D.K. Dickinson (Eds.), *Handbook of early literacy research* (pp. 66–80). New York: Guilford.

Anderson, R.C. (1994). Role of reader's schema in comprehension, learning, and memory. In R.B. Ruddell, M.R. Ruddell, & H. Singer (Eds.), *Theoretical models and processes of reading* (4th ed.) (pp. 469–482). Newark, DE: International Reading Association.

Anderson, R.C., Hiebert, E.H., Scott, J.A., & Wilkinson, I.A.G. (1985). *Becoming a nation of readers: The report of the Commission on Reading.* Champaign, IL: The National Academy of Education.

Armbruster, B.B. (1986, December). *Using frames to organize expository text.* Paper presented at the National Reading Conference, Austin, TX.

Au, K.H. (1998). Constructivist approaches, phonics, and the literacy learning of students of diverse backgrounds. In T. Shanahan & F.V. Rodriguez-Brown (Eds.), *47th Yearbook of the National Reading Conference* (pp. 1–21). Chicago: National Reading Conference.

Au, K.H. (2000). Literacy instruction for young children of diverse backgrounds. In D.S. Strickland & L.M. Morrow (Eds.), *Beginning reading and writing* (pp. 35–45). Newark, DE/New York: International Reading Association/Teachers College Press.

Baker, L. (1991). Metacognition, reading, and science education. In C.M. Santa & D.E. Alvermann (Eds.), *Science learning: Processes and applications* (pp. 2–13). Newark, DE: International Reading Association.

Battle, J. (1995). Collaborative story talk in a bilingual kindergarten. In N.L. Roser & M.G. Martinez (Eds.), *Book talk and beyond: Children and teachers respond to literature* (pp. 157–167). Newark, DE: International Reading Association.

Bean, K. (2001). Using a content area word wall. *Illinois Reading Council Journal, 28,* 62–64.

Beck, I., & McKeown, M. (1991). Conditions of vocabulary acquisition. In R. Barr, M.L. Kamil, P. Mosenthal, & P.D. Pearson (Eds.), *Handbook of reading research* (Vol. II) (pp. 789–814). White Plains, NY: Longman.

Blachowicz, C., & Fisher, P. (2000). Vocabulary instruction. In M.L. Kamil, P.B. Mosenthal, P.D. Pearson, & R. Barr (Eds.), *Handbook of reading research* (Vol. III) (pp. 503–523). Mahwah, NJ: Erlbaum.

Blair-Larsen, S.M., & Williams, K.A. (Eds.). (1999). *The balanced reading program: Helping all students achieve success.* Newark, DE: International Reading Association.

Blevins, W. (1998). *Phonics from A to Z: A practical guide.* New York: Scholastic Professional Books.

Branley, F.M. (1990). *Earthquakes.* New York: Trumpet.

Brett, A., Rothlein, L., & Hurley, M. (1996). Vocabulary acquisition from listening to stories and explanations of target words. *Elementary School Journal, 96,* 415–422.

Bromley, K. (2000). Teaching young children to be writers. In D.S. Strickland & L.M. Morrow (Eds.), *Beginning reading and writing* (pp. 111–120). Newark, DE/New York: International Reading Association/Teachers College Press.

Burns, B. (2001). *Guided reading: A how-to for all grades.* Arlington Heights, IL: Skylight.

Calkins, L. (1986). *The art of teaching writing.* Portsmouth, NH: Heinemann.

Carle, E. (1969). *The very hungry caterpillar.* Cleveland, OH: Collins-World.

Carle, E. (1996). *Little Cloud.* New York: Scholastic.

Chomsky, N. (1968). *Language and mind.* New York: Harcourt Brace Jovanovich.

Clay, M.M. (1975). *What did I write? Beginning writing behavior.* Exeter, NH: Heinemann.

Clay, M.M. (1985). *The early detection of reading difficulties* (3rd ed.). Portsmouth, NH: Heinemann.

Clay, M.M. (1993). *Reading Recovery: A guidebook for teachers in training.* Portsmouth, NH: Heinemann.

Clay, M.M. (1998). *By different paths to common outcomes.* York, ME: Stenhouse.

Cochrane, D., Cochrane, D., Scalena, D., & Buchanan, E. (1988). *Reading, writing, and caring.* Katonah, NY: Richard C. Owen.

Cohen, M. (1979). *Lost in the museum.* New York: Bantam Doubleday Dell.

Cunningham, P.M. (1990). The Names Test: A quick assessment of decoding ability. *The Reading Teacher, 44,* 124–129.

Cunningham, P.M. (2000). *Phonics they use: Words for reading and writing* (3rd ed.). New York: Longman.

Cunningham, P.M., & Allington, R.L. (1994). *Classrooms that work: They can* all *read and write.* New York: Longman.

Cunningham, P.M., & Allington, R.L. (1998*). Classrooms that work: They can* all *read and write* (2nd ed.). New York: HarperCollins.

Cunningham, P.M., & Hall, D.P. (1994). *Making words: Multilevel, hands-on, developmentally appropriate spelling and phonics activities.* Parsippany, NJ: Good Apple.

Cunningham, P.M., & Hall, D.P. (1998). *Making words: Multilevel, hands-on, developmentally appropriate spelling and phonics activities* (2nd ed.). Parsippany, NJ: Good Apple.

Dale, E. (1965). Vocabulary measurement: Techniques and major findings. *Elementary English, 42,* 82–88.

Darling, K. (1996). *Rain forest babies.* New York: Scholastic.

Duffelmeyer, F.A., Kruse, A.E., Merkley, D.J., & Fyfe, S.A. (1994). Further validation and enhancement of the Names Test. *The Reading Teacher, 48,* 118–129.

Duffy, G.G., & Roehler, L.R. (1989). *Improving classroom reading instruction* (2nd ed.). New York: Random House.

Duke, N. (2000). 3.6 minutes per day: The scarcity of informational texts in first grade. *Reading Research Quarterly, 35,* 202–224.

Dyson, A.H. (2001). Writing and children's symbolic repertoires: Development unhinged. In S.B. Neuman & D.K. Dickinson (Eds.), *Handbook of early literacy research* (pp. 126–141). New York: Guilford.

Edwards, P.A. (1986). *Parents as partners in reading.* Chicago: Children's Press.

Ehri, L.C. (1987). Learning to read and spell words. *Journal of Reading Behavior, 19,* 5–31.

Elkonin, D.B. (1973). USSR. In J. Downing (Ed.), *Comparative reading: Cross-national studies of behavior and processes in reading and writing* (pp. 551–579). New York: Macmillan.

Ericson, L., & Juliebo, M.F. (1998). *The phonological awareness handbook for kindergarten and primary teachers.* Newark, DE: International Reading Association.

Flavell, J.H. (1977). *Cognitive development.* Englewood Cliffs, NJ: Prentice-Hall.

Flood, J., & Lapp, D. (1990). Reading comprehension for at-risk readers: Research-based practices that can make a difference. *Journal of Reading, 33,* 490–496.

Forman, J., & Sanders, M.E. (1998). *Project Leap first grade norming study: 1993–1998.* Unpublished Manuscript.

Fowler, G.L. (1982). Developing comprehension skills in primary students through the use of story frames. *The Reading Teacher, 36,* 176–179.

Fry, E.B., Fountoukidis, D.L., & Polk, J.K. (2000). *The reading teacher's book of lists* (4th ed.). Upper Saddle River, NJ: Merrill/Prentice Hall.

Galda, L., & Cullinan, B.E. (2000). Reading aloud from culturally diverse literature. In D.S. Strickland & L.M. Morrow (Eds.), *Beginning reading and writing* (pp. 134–142). Newark, DE/New York: International Reading Association/Teachers College Press.

Gaskins, I.W., Ehri, L.C., Cress, C., O'Hara, C., & Donnelly, K. (1997). Analyzing words. *Language Arts, 74,* 172–192.

Gentry, J.R. (1981). Learning to spell developmentally. *The Reading Teacher, 34,* 378–381.

Gentry, J.R. (1998). Spelling strategies. *Instructor, 107,* 40.

Gentry, J.R. (2000). A retrospective on invented spelling and a look forward. *The Reading Teacher, 54,* 318–332.

Gentry, J.R., & Gillet, J.W. (1993). *Teaching kids to spell.* Portsmouth, NH: Heinemann.

Gillam, R.B., & van Kleeck, A. (1996). Phonological awareness training and short-term working memory: Clinical implications. *Language Disorders, 17,* 72–81.

Gillet, J.W., & Temple, C. (2000). *Understanding reading problems: Assessment and instruction* (5th ed.). New York: Longman.

Goodman, K.S. (1965). A linguistic study of cues and miscues in reading. *Elementary English, 42,* 639–643.

Goodman, K.S. (1996). *On reading.* Portsmouth, NH: Heinemann.

Goodman, Y.M. (1982). Kidwatching: Evaluating written language development. *Australian Journal of Reading, 5,* 120–128.

Graves, D. (1983). *Writing: Teachers and children at work.* Exeter, NH: Heinemann.

Graves, M.F., Juel, C., & Graves, B.B. (2001). *Teaching reading in the 21st century* (2nd ed.). Boston: Allyn and Bacon.

Greene, F. (1979). Radio reading. In C. Pennock (Ed.), *Reading comprehension at four linguistic levels* (pp. 104–107). Newark, DE: International Reading Association.

Gunning, T.G. (1992). *Creating reading instruction for all children.* Boston: Allyn and Bacon.

Gunning, T.G. (1998). *Best books for beginning reading.* Boston: Allyn and Bacon.

Gunning, T.G. (2000). *Phonological awareness and primary phonics.* Boston: Allyn and Bacon.

Guthrie, J.T., & Wigfield, A. (2000). Engagement and motivation in reading. In M.L. Kamil, P.B. Mosenthal, P.D. Pearson, & R. Barr (Eds.), *Handbook of reading research* (Vol. III) (pp. 403–422). White Plains, NY: Longman.

Hague, K. (1984). *Alphabears.* New York: Holt.

Harp, B. (2000). *The handbook of literacy assessment and evaluation* (2nd ed.). Norwood, MA: Christopher-Gordon.

Harris, T.L., & Hodges, R.E. (1995). *The literacy dictionary: The vocabulary of reading and writing.* Newark, DE: International Reading Association.

Hasbrouck, J.E., & Tindal, G. (1992). Curriculum-based oral reading fluency norms for students in grades 2 through 5. *Teaching Exceptional Children, 24,* 41–44.

Heckleman, R.G. (1966). Using the neurological impress method of remedial reading instruction. *Academic Therapy Quarterly, 1,* 235–239.

Heilman, A.W. (1998). *Phonics in proper perspective* (8th ed.). Upper Saddle River, NJ: Merrill Prentice Hall.

Henkes, K. (1991). *Chrysanthemum.* New York: Greenwillow.

Henkes, K. (1996). *Lily's purple plastic purse.* New York: Greenwillow.

Hiebert, E.H., & Martin, L.A. (2001). The texts of beginning reading instruction. In S.B. Neuman & D.K. Dickinson (Eds.), *Handbook of early literacy research* (pp. 361–375). New York: Guilford.

Hoffman, M. (1986). *Elephant.* Austin, TX: Steck-Vaughn.

International Reading Association and National Association for the Education of Young Children (1998). *Learning to read and write: Developmentally appropriate practices for young children.* Newark, DE: Author.

Jeunesse, G., Delafosse, C., Fuhr, U., & Sautai, R. (1991). *Whales: A first discovery book.* New York: Scholastic.

Johns, J.L. (1975). The Dolch list of common nouns—A comparison. *The Reading Teacher, 28,* 338–340.

Johns, J.L. (1980). First graders' concepts about print. *Reading Research Quarterly, 15,* 529–549.

Johns, J.L. (1981). The development of the Revised Dolch List. *Illinois School Research and Development, 17,* 15–24.

Johns, J.L. (2001). *Basic reading inventory* (8th ed.). Dubuque, IA: Kendall/Hunt.

Johns, J.L., & Lenski, S.D. (2001). *Improving reading: Strategies and resources* (3rd ed.). Dubuque, IA: Kendall/Hunt.

Joubert, D., & Joubert, B. (2001). *The Africa diaries.* Washington, DC: National Geographic.

Klenk, L., & Kibby, M.L. (2000). Re-mediating reading difficulties: Appraising the past, reconciling the present, constructing the future. In M.L. Kamil, P.B. Mosenthal, P.D. Pearson, & R. Barr (Eds.), *Handbook of reading research* (Vol. III) (pp. 667–690). Mahwah, NJ: Erlbaum.

Lenski, S.D., & Johns, J.L. (2000). *Improving writing: Resources, strategies, and assessments.* Dubuque, IA: Kendall/Hunt.

Lukens, R.J. (1995). *A critical handbook of children's literature* (5th ed.). Glenview, IL: Scott, Foresman.

Macon, J., & Macon, J. (1991). Knowledge chart. In J.M. Macon, D. Bewell, & M.E. Vogt (Eds.), *Responses to literature: Grades K–8* (pp. 13–14). Newark, DE: International Reading Association.

Martinez, M.G., & Roser, N.L. (1995). The books make a difference in story talk. In N.L. Roser & M.G. Martinez (Eds.), *Book talk and beyond: Children and teachers respond to literature* (pp. 32–41). Newark, DE: International Reading Association.

May, F.B. (1998). *Reading as communication: To help children write and read* (5th ed.). Upper Saddle River, NJ: Merrill.

McGee, L.M., & Richgels, D.J. (2000). *Literacy's beginnings: Supporting young readers and writers* (3rd ed.). Needham Heights, MA: Allyn and Bacon.

McKenna, M.C., & Kear, D.J. (1990). Measuring attitude toward reading: A new tool for teachers. *The Reading Teacher, 43*, 626–639.

Mooney, M.E. (1990). *Reading to, with, and by children*. Katonah, NY: Richard C. Owen.

Morrow, L.M. (2001). *Literacy development in the early years: Helping children read and write* (4th ed.). Boston: Allyn and Bacon.

Morrow, L.M., & Gambrell, L.B. (2001). Literature-based instruction in the early years. In S.B. Neuman & D.K. Dickinson (Eds.), *Handbook of early literacy research* (pp. 348–360). New York: Guilford.

Moss, J.F. (1995). Preparing focus units with literature: Crafty foxes and authors' craft. In N.L. Roser & M.G. Martinez (Eds.), *Book talk and beyond: Children and teachers respond to literature* (pp. 53–65). Newark, DE: International Reading Association.

National Council of Teachers of English/International Reading Association (1996). *Standards for the English language arts*. Urbana, IL/Newark, DE: Author.

National Reading Panel. (2000). *Teaching children to read: An evidence-based assessment of the scientific research literature on reading and its implications for reading instruction*. Washington, DC: National Institute of Child Health & Human Development.

Ogle, D. (1986). K-W-L: A teaching model that develops active reading of expository text. *The Reading Teacher, 38*, 564–570.

Palazzo, J. (1988). *Rainy day fun*. Mahwah, NJ: Troll.

Paris, S.G., Lipson, M.Y., & Wixon, K.G. (1994). Becoming a strategic reader. In R.B. Ruddell, M.R. Ruddell, & H. Singer (Eds.), *Theoretical models and processes of reading* (4th ed.) (pp. 788–810). Newark, DE: International Reading Association.

Pelham, D. (1990). *Sam's sandwich*. New York: Dutton.

Peregoy, S.F., & Boyle, O.F. (2001). *Reading, writing, & learning in ESL* (3rd ed.). New York: Longman.

Poe, V.L. (1986). Using multipared simultaneous oral reading. *The Reading Teacher, 40*, 239–240.

Pressley, M., & Afflerbach, P. (1995). *Verbal protocols of reading: The nature of constructively responsive reading*. Hillsdale, NJ: Erlbaum.

Pressley, M., Allington, R.L., Wharton-McDonald, R., Block, C.C., & Morrow, L.M. (2001). *Learning to read: Lessons from exemplary first-grade classrooms*. New York: Guilford.

Purves, A.C., Rogers, T., & Soter, A.O. (1990). *How porcupines make love II: Teaching a response-centered literature curriculum*. White Plains, NY: Longman.

Rasinski, T.V. (1989). Fluency for everyone: Incorporating fluency instruction in the classroom. *The Reading Teacher, 42*, 690–693.

Rasinski, T.V., & Padak, N.D. (1999). *Holistic reading strategies: Teaching children who find reading difficult* (2nd ed.). Columbus, OH: Merrill.

Rathmann, P. (1997). *Ruby the Copycat*. New York: Scholastic.

Read, C.C. (1986). *Children's creative spelling*. London: Routledge & Kegan Paul.

Readence, J.E., & Searfoss, L.W. (1980). Teaching strategies for vocabulary development. *English Journal, 67*, 43–46.

Rennick, L.W., & Williams, K.M. (1995). Flashlight reading: Making the reading process concrete. *The Reading Teacher, 49*, 174.

Richgels, D.J. (2001). Invented spelling, phonemic awareness, and reading and writing instruction. In S.B. Neuman & D.K. Dickinson (Eds.), *Handbook of early literacy research* (pp. 142–155). New York: Guilford.

Richgels, D.J., Poremba, K.J., & McGee, L.M. (1996). Kindergartners talk about print: Phonemic awareness in meaningful contexts. *The Reading Teacher, 49,* 632–642.

Robb, L. (1996). *Reading strategies that work: Teaching your students to become better readers.* New York: Scholastic.

Rosencrans, G. (1998). *The spelling book: Teaching children how to spell, not what to spell.* Newark, DE: International Reading Association.

Roser, N.L., & Hoffman, J.V. (1995). Language charts: A record of story time talk. In N.L. Roser & M.G. Martinez (Eds.), *Book talk and beyond: Children and teachers respond to literature* (pp. 80–89). Newark, DE: International Reading Association.

Routman, R. (1994). *Invitations: Changing as teachers and learners K–12.* Portsmouth, NH: Heinemann.

Rumelhart, D.E. (1985). Toward an interactive model of reading. In H. Singer & R.B. Ruddell (Eds.), *Theoretical models and processes of reading* (3rd ed.) (pp. 722–750). Newark, DE: International Reading Association.

Salinger, T.S. (1999). *Literacy for young children* (3rd ed.). Columbus, OH: Merrill.

Salvia, J., & Ysseldyke, J.E. (2001). *Assessment* (8th ed.). Boston: Houghton Mifflin.

Samuels, S.J. (1979). The method of repeated readings. *The Reading Teacher, 32,* 403–408.

Schatschneider, C., Francis, D., Foorman, B., Fletcher, J., & Mehta, P. (1999). The dimensionality of phonological awareness: An application of item response theory. *Journal of Educational Psychology, 91,* 439–449.

Schmidt, B., & Buckley, M. (1991). Plot relationships chart. In J.M. Macon, D. Bewell, & M. Vogt (Eds.), *Responses to literature: Grades K–8* (pp. 7–8). Newark, DE: International Reading Association.

Sendak, M. (1963). *Where the wild things are.* New York: Harper and Row.

Snow, C.E., Burns, S.M, & Griffin, P. (Eds.). (1998). *Preventing reading difficulties in young children.* Washington, DC: National Academy Press.

Snowball, D. (1997). Use sentences with word blanks to pump spelling strategies. *Instructor, 101,* 22–23.

St. George, J. (2000). *So you want to be president.* New York: Philomel.

Staal, L.A. (2000). The Story Face: An adaptation of story mapping that incorporates visualization and discovery learning to enhance reading and writing. *The Reading Teacher, 54,* 26–31.

Stahl, S.A. (2001). Teaching phonics and phonological awareness. In S.B. Neuman & D.K. Dickinson (Eds.), *Handbook of early literacy research* (pp. 333–347). New York: Guilford.

Stanovich, K.E. (2000). *Progress in understanding reading: Scientific foundations and new frontiers.* New York: Guilford.

Stauffer, R.G. (1969). *Teaching reading as a thinking process.* New York: Harper & Row.

Stauffer, R.G. (1970). *The language experience approach to the teaching of reading.* New York: Harper & Row.

Stein, N.L., & Glenn, C.G. (1979). An analysis of story comprehension in elementary school children. In R.O. Freedle (Ed.), *New directions in discourse processing* (pp. 53–120). Norwood, NJ: Ablex.

Strickland, D.S. (1998). *Teaching phonics today: A primer for educators.* Newark, DE: International Reading Association.

Strickland, D.S. (2001). Early intervention for African American children considered to be at risk. In S.B. Neuman & D.K. Dickinson (Eds.), *Handbook of early literacy research* (pp. 322–332). New York: Guilford.

Sulzby, E., & Teale, W. (1991). Emergent literacy. In R. Barr, M.L. Kamil, P. Mosenthal, & P.D. Pearson (Eds.), *Handbook of reading research* (Vol. II) (pp. 727–757). New York: Longman.

Sweeney, J. (1996). *Me on the map.* New York: Dragonfly Books.

Taberski, S. (2000). *On solid ground: Strategies for teaching reading K–3.* Portsmouth, NH: Heinemann.

Taylor, D. (1983). *Family literacy: Young children learning to read and write.* Exeter, NH: Heinemann.

Teale, W.H., & Sulzby, E. (1989). Emerging literacy: New perspectives. In D.S. Strickland & L.M. Morrow (Eds.), *Emerging literacy: Young children learn to read and write* (pp. 1–15). Newark, DE: International Reading Association.

Teale, W.H., & Yokota, J. (2000). Beginning reading and writing: Perspectives on instruction. In D.S. Strickland & L.M. Morrow (Eds.), *Beginning reading and writing* (pp. 3–21). Newark, DE/New York: International Reading Association/Teachers College Press.

Tompkins, G. (2001). *Literacy for the 21st century: A balanced approach* (2nd ed.). Columbus, OH: Prentice-Hall.

Tracey, D.H. (2000). Enhancing literacy growth through home-school connections. In D.S. Strickland & L.M. Morrow (Eds.), *Beginning reading and writing* (pp. 46–57). Newark, DE/New York: International Reading Association/Teachers College Press.

Trousdale, A., & Harris, V. (1993). Interactive storytelling: Scaffolding children's early narratives. *Language Arts, 67,* 164–173.

Turbill, J., Butler, A., Cambourne, B., & Langton, G. (1991). *Frameworks course notebook.* Stanley, NY: Wayne Finger Lakes Board of Cooperative Educational Services.

Walsh, D., Price, G., & Gillingham, M. (1988). The critical but transitory importance of letter naming. *Reading Research Quarterly, 23,* 108–122.

Watson, R. (2001). Literacy and oral language: Implications for early literacy acquisition. In S.B. Neuman & D.K. Dickinson (Eds.), *Handbook of early literacy research* (pp. 43–53). New York: Guilford.

Weaver, C.A. (1994). *Reading process and practice.* Portsmouth, NH: Heinemann.

Wells, R. (2001). *Letters and sounds.* New York: Puffin.

Wilde, S. (2000). *Miscue analysis made easy: Building on student strengths.* Portsmouth, NH: Heinemann.

Williams, S. (1989). *I went walking.* New York: Trumpet.

Wilson, P.T. (1988). *Let's think about reading and reading instruction: A primer for tutors and teachers.* Dubuque, IA: Kendall/Hunt.

Wylie, R., & Durrell, D.D. (1970). Teaching vowels through phonograms. *Elementary English, 47,* 787–791.

Yopp, H.K. (1992). Developing phonemic awareness in young children. *The Reading Teacher, 49,* 20–29.

Yopp, H.K. (1995). A test for assessing phonemic awareness in young children. *The Reading Teacher, 45,* 696–703.

Yopp, R.H., & Yopp, H.K. (2000). Sharing informational text with young children. *The Reading Teacher, 53,* 410–419.

Zeno, S.M., Ivens, S.H., Millard, R.T., & Duvvuri, R. (1995). *The educator's word frequency guide.* Brewster, NY: Touchstone Applied Science.

Zutell, J. (1996). The directed spelling thinking activity (DSTA): Providing an effective balance in word study instruction. *The Reading Teacher, 50,* 98–108.

Index

Italicized entries refer to Strategies and titles of books.

A

Access to reading material
    background knowledge and, 19
    classroom environment and, 8–9
    sense of story and, 70
African Diaries, The, 345–346
All About Owls, 82
Alphabears, 129
Alphabet Knowledge, 168–173
Alphabet recognition/knowledge
    Alphabet Knowledge, 168–173
    Alphabet Song, 128–129
    further ideas/activities, 132
    home-schooled children and, 164
    Identifying Letters, 131
    importance of, 126–127
    Letter Actions, 130
    phonics instruction and, 125–127
    Using Alphabet Books, 129–130
Alphabet Song, 128–129–
Animals, 105–116
Arnosky, Jim, 82
Art/artwork. *See* Illustrations
Assessments
    Alphabet Knowledge, 168–173
    Auditory Discrimination, 184–186
    Basic Sight Vocabulary, 246–251
    Caption Reading, 310–316
    Common Nouns, 252–257
    Decoding, 199–206
    Developmental Spelling, 389–392
    Elementary Reading Attitude Survey, 38–46
    of fluency, 208, 260
    Fluency Scale Checklist, 262–265
    Interviews About Reading, 30–34
    Monitoring Strategies Checklist, 339–340
    News about Me, 35–37
    Oral Reading Miscue Analysis, 266–268
    Phoneme Deletion and Substitution, 180–183
    Phoneme Segmentation, 177–179
    Phonics: Consonants, 187–198
    of print concepts, 86–87, 100–102, 117–118
    by retelling of stories, 119–123
    Rhyme Detection, 174–176
    Words per Minute, 258–261
    Writing, 379–380
    Writing Observational Checklist, 387
    writing/spelling discussion and, 377–378
Associative Learning, 214–215
Attitudes of children and literacy, 2
Audio books, 10
Auditory Discrimination, 184–186

B

Background knowledge of children
    Brainstorming and, 16–17
    building of, 13
    comprehension of text and, 288–291
    development of, 18–20
    emergent literacy development and, 2
    English Language Learners and, 348
    Knowledge Chart and, 15–16
    sense of story and, 61
    vocabulary meaning and, 272–273
Basic Sight Vocabulary, 246–251
Big Books, 53, 57–58, 158, 160
Bilingualism, 4. *See also* English Language Learners
Birds, 82
Black English Vernacular, 355
Blume, J., 350
Book Boxes, 14–15
Book talks
    informational text structures and, 82
    literature genres and, 9
Bookmarks, 306
Brainstorming, 16–17
Brainstorming, 26
Branley, Franklyn M., 281
Break and Make, 144–146
Bunting, E., 344

C

Cannon, Dorie, 89, 105
Caption Reading, 310–316
Carle, Eric, 53, 70
Choral Reading, 227
Classroom environments
   alphabet centers/displays and, 132
   classroom libraries, 10
   development of motivation and, 3
   discovery centers and, 19–20
   literacy displays and, 362–363
   literacy play centers, 9
   possible displays for, 8
   storytelling and, 26
   writing/spelling centers and, 372–373
Click, Clack, Moo: Cows That Type, 344–345
Cohen, Miriam, 67
Common Nouns, 252–257
Communication skills
   assessment of attitudes/interests and, 47
   game of telephone and, 26
   Language Experience Approach (LEA) and, 54–55
Comprehension of text. *See also* Monitoring reading
   Caption Reading (assessment), 310–316
   Directed Reading~Thinking Activity (DR~TA), 283–284
   discussion, 269–270, 280
   English Language Learners and, 286, 291
   further ideas/activities, 291–294, 297
   home-schooled children and, 296
   Idea~Mapping, 286–288
   Making Text Connections, 288–291
   Passage Reading (assessment discussion), 317–320
   Passage Reading (assessment of beginning sight word), 323–324, 331–332
   Passage Reading (assessment of easy sight word), 321–322
   Passage Reading (assessment of easy sight word), 329–330
   Passage Reading (assessment of Grade 1 sight word), 325–326, 333–334
   Passage Reading (assessment of Grade 2 sight word), 327–328, 335
   Retelling (assessment), 336–337
   Story Frame, 284–286
   Think Aloud, 281–283
Conventional spelling, 378
Critter, 298–299

Cronin, Doreen, 344
Cross-checking
   Cue Questioning, 239–240
   discussion, 234
   example of, 208
   further ideas/activities, 241
   home-schooled children and, 242
   Making Sense, 235
   Predict~Sample~Confirm, 236
   Word Detective, 237–238
Cue Questioning, 239–240
Cueing systems, 208

D

Darling, Kathy, 77
Decoding, 199–206
Developmental Spelling (assessment), 389–392
Directed Reading~Thinking Activity (DR~TA), 283–284
Directed Spelling Thinking Activity (DSTA), 369
Direction of reading, 55–57
Discovering the Message, 350
Discussions
   after reading, 17
   open-ended questions and, 26
Displays. *See* Classroom environments
Dog Heaven, 350
Dolch list of sight words, 211
Dramatics
   comprehension of text and, 292
   fluency and, 231
   literature responses and, 351
   monitoring reading and, 301
   phonemic awareness (PA) and, 147
   sense of story and, 70
   use of, 26
   writing/spelling and, 363

E

Earthquakes, 281
Ebonics, 355
Elementary Reading Attitude Survey, 38–46
Elephant, 73–74
English Language Learners (ELL)
   alphabet knowledge for, 130
   book boxes and, 15
   brainstorming tips for, 17
   comprehension of text and, 283, 286, 291
   cross-checking and, 239

favorite books of, 6
fluency and, 229
informational text structures and, 78
learning methods and, 4
literature responses and, 345
monitoring reading and, 301
phonemic awareness (PA) and, 142
phonics instruction and, 158
print concepts and, 54–55
sense of story and, 67
sight word learning and, 215
storytelling and, 5, 25
Text Tapping and, 356
vocabulary meaning and, 272–273
word cards for, 24
writing/spelling and, 354–355, 359–360, 368, 371
Environments. *See* Classroom environments
Evaluations. *See* Assessments
Expand~a~Sentence, 24
Explicit Instruction, 210–212
Explicit Phonics, 155
Expository Frames, 77
Expository Writing, 79–81

F

Favorite Book Show and Tell, 5–7
Felt boards, 26
Fiction. *See also* Informational text structures
informational text structures and, 82
Plot Relationships Chart and, 62–64
structure of, 49
Field trips, 18, 21
First Sounds, 137–142
Fluency
assessment of, 260
Choral Reading, 227
definition, 207–208
discussion, 222
English Language Learners and, 228–229
Fluency Scale Checklist, 262–265
further ideas/activities, 230–231
home-schooled children and, 232
Radio Reading, 228
Structured Repeated Readings, 223–226
Teacher~Assisted Reading, 222–223
Writing Rubrics (assessment), 381–382
Fluency Scale Checklist, 262–265
Four~Square Vocabulary Grids, 274–276
Frederick, 344
Friends, 89–100

G

Games/puzzles
cross-checking and, 237
sight word learning and, 216–217
vocabulary meaning and, 277
writing/spelling and, 373
Garfield and *Elementary Reading Attitude Survey*, 38–46
Genres of literature
book choices for reading aloud and, 26
book talks and, 9
Getting the Feeling, 345–347
Grapheme-phoneme relationships. *See* Phonics
Graphic Organizers, 73–76
Guest speakers, 18

H

Have~a~Go, 366–368
Henkes, Kevin, 5
Hoffman, Mary, 73
Home-schooled children
alphabet knowledge and, 133
comprehension of text and, 296
cross-checking and, 242
fluency and, 232
informational text structures and, 83
literature responses and, 352
monitoring reading and, 306
open-ended questions and, 27
phonemic awareness (PA) and, 151
phonics instruction and, 164
print concepts and, 59
reading programs and, 8
reading programs for, 8
reading/writing hints for, 11
sense of story and, 71
sight word learning and, 218–220
storytelling and, 27
vocabulary meaning and, 278
writing/spelling and, 364, 374
Hutchins, P., 350

I

I Spy Rhymes, 137
I Went Walking, 158
Idea~Mapping, 286–288
Identifying Letters, 131
Illustrations
artistic responses to literature and, 9

background knowledge and, 19
Favorite Book Show and Tell and, 7
home-schooled children and, 11
literature responses and, 351
picture walks and, 5
Predicting with Pictures and, 17
sight word learning and, 217
storytelling and, 26
use in writing of, 4
Independent reading
  comprehension of text and, 291
  cross-checking and, 241
Informational text structures
  Expository Frames and, 77
  Expository Writing and, 79–81
  further ideas/activities, 82
  Graphic Organizers and, 73–76
  home-schooled children and, 83
  phonics instruction and, 125–127
  Scrambled Text and, 78
Interests of children and literacy, 2
Interviews About Reading. See Assessments
Invented spelling, 343
Isolation of sound. See Sound isolation

J

Jackdaws, 18
Jeunesse, Gallimard, 82
Joubert, Beverly, 345
Joubert, Dereck, 345
Journals, 361–362. See also Writing

K

K-W-L charts, 18–19
Knowledge Chart, 15–16

L

Language Charts, 344–345
Language development, 50
Language Experience Approach (LEA), 54–55
Learning about Print Through Writing, 55–56
Learning methods, 4, 9. See also Print concepts; Sense of story
Let Me Tell You About...., 359–360
Letter Actions, 130
Letters and Sounds, 129
Libraries
  background knowledge and, 21

creation in classroom of, 10
home-schooled children and, 11
Lily's Purple Plastic Purse, 5
Lionni, L., 344
List-Group-Label strategy, 277
Listening comprehension. See Comprehension of text
Literacy. See also Literature responses
  attitudes of children and, 2
  desire for, 3
  listening comprehension and, 270
  play centers for, 9
  writing/spelling and, 341–343
Literacy play centers
  further ideas/activities, 361
  writing/spelling and, 372
Literature responses
  Discovering the Message, 350
  English Language Learners and, 346
  further ideas/activities, 351
  Getting the Feeling, 345–347
  Language Charts, 344–345
  resources for, 353
  Responding to Plot, 348–349
Little Cloud, 53
Lost in the Museum, 67

M

Magazines for children, 22
Making Sense, 235
Making Text Connections, 288–291
Making Words, 157
Mangione, Cheryl, 89
Mathematics, 20
Me on the Map, 17
Media/technology
  alphabet knowledge and, 129–130, 134
  background knowledge resources and, 22
  comprehension of text and, 297
  cross-checking and, 243
  fluency and, 233
  informational text structures and, 82
  monitoring reading and, 307
  phonemic awareness (PA) and, 152
  phonics instruction and, 165
  Radio Reading and, 228–229
  reading response web resources, 353
  resources for, 28, 365
  sight word learning and, 221
  television and, 21, 71, 82

vocabulary meaning and, 279
writing/spelling and, 375
Mediated strategies. *See* Phonics
Metacognition, 298
Methodologies. *See* Assessments; Learning methods
Monitoring Logs, 302–303
Monitoring reading
   Critter, 298–299
   discussion, 298
   English Language Learners and, 301
   further ideas/activities, 304–305
   home-schooled children and, 306
   Monitoring Logs, 302–303
   Monitoring Strategies Checklist, 338–339
   Monitoring Think~Along, 300
   Pause~Think~Retell, 301
   resources for, 307
Monitoring Strategies Checklist, 338–339
Monitoring Think~Along, 300
Morning Message, 3–4
Movies/videos. *See* Media/technology
Multimedia. *See* Media/technology
Music
   alphabet knowledge through, 128–129
   background knowledge and, 20
   fluency and, 231
   resources for, 28
   Writing from Songs, 356–357

N

Neurological Impress Method, 222–223
News about Me, 35–37
Nonfiction structure, 49
Norms. *See* Standards
Nouns, *see Common Nouns*

O

Object Exploration, 13–14
Oral language. *See also* Alphabet recognition/knowledge; Fluency; Storytelling
   choral reading and, 227
   enhancement of, 23–28
   fluency and, 207–208, 232
   independent reading and, 241, 291
   Oral Reading Miscue Analysis, 266–268
   as reading foundation, 1–2
   resources for, 28
   sense of story and, 70

Oral Reading Miscue Analysis, 266–268
Owl Moon, 82

P

Pain and the Great One, The, 350
Parent~Recommended Topics, 357–358
Pattern Books, 213
Pause~Think~Retell, 301
Phoneme Deletion and Substitution, 180–183
Phoneme Segmentation, 177–179
Phonemic awareness (PA)
   Break and Make, 144–146
   discussion, 126, 136
   First Sounds, 137–142
   further ideas/activities, 147–149, 147–150
   I Spy Rhymes, 137
   Phoneme Deletion and Substitution, 180–183
   Phoneme Segmentation, 177–179
   Put It Together, 143
   resources for, 152–153
   Sound Boxes, 142–143
Phonetic spelling, 377–378
Phonics
   books with specific vowel sounds, 162–163
   Explicit Phonics, 155
   further ideas/activities, 160–161
   instruction in, 125–127
   Making Words, 157
   Phonics: Consonants, 187–198
   Phonics in Context, 159
   resources for, 165
   teaching of, 154, 156
   Whole~Part~Whole Phonics, 158
Phonics: Consonants, 187–198
Phonics in Context, 159
Picture books, 344–345
Plot Relationships Chart, 62–64
Poetry
   fluency and, 227, 231
   I Spy Rhymes, 137
   phonemic awareness (PA) and, 136, 147
   phonics instruction and, 160
   Rhyme Detection, 174–176
   Text Tapping and, 355–356
   use of, 9
   writing/spelling and, 372
Precommunicative spelling, 377
Predicting with Pictures, 17
Predict~Sample~Confirm, 236
Preview in Context, 271–272

Print concepts
- assessment of, 86–87, 100–102, 117–118
- for English Language Learners, 54
- further ideas/activities, 57–58
- home-schooled children and, 59
- *Language Experience Approach (LEA)* and, 54–55
- *Learning about Print Through Writing* and, 55–56
- learning methods and, 50
- *Shared Reading* and, 52–54
- *What Can You Show Us?* and, 56

Programs. *See also* Teaching strategies
- book talks and, 9
- home-school reading and, 8

Progressive Storytelling, 25
Public libraries and home-schooled children, 11
Puppets, 26, 28
- sense of story and, 70
- writing/spelling and, 363

Put It Together, 143
Puzzles. *See* Games/puzzles

Q

Quickdraw/Quickwrite, 19

R

Reading independently. *See* Independent reading
Radio Reading, 228, 228–229
Rain Forest Babies, 77
Rainy Day Fun, 284
Rathmann, Peggy, 295
Reading aloud
- background knowledge and, 18
- book choices for, 26
- importance of, 50
- sense of story and, 70

Reading comprehension. *See* Comprehension of text
Resources
- alphabet knowledge and, 134–135
- background knowledge and, 22
- cross-checking and, 243
- fluency and, 233
- informational text structures and, 84
- literature responses and, 353
- monitoring reading and, 308
- motivation for reading and, 12
- oral language and, 28
- phonemic awareness (PA) and, 152–153
- phonics instruction and, 165
- print concepts and, 60
- sense of story and, 72
- sight word learning and, 221
- vocabulary meaning and, 279
- writing/spelling and, 362, 375

Responding to Plot, 348–349
Retelling, 336–337
Retelling of stories, 119–123, 336–337
Rhyme Detection, 174–176
Rhyming. *See* Poetry
Rosie's Walk, 350
Ruby the Copycat, 295
Rylant, C., 350

S

Sam's Sandwich, 291
Schema. *See also* Background knowledge of children
- importance of, 13

Science, 19
Scrambled Text, 78
Semiphonetic spelling, 377
Sendak, M., 56, 350
Sense of story
- further ideas/activities, 57–58
- home-schooled children and, 71
- *Plot Relationships Chart* and, 62–64
- *Simple Story Elements* and, 61–62
- *Story Faces* and, 67–69
- *Story Star* and, 65–66

Shared Reading, 4–5, 52–54
Shared Writing, 354–355
Shelving. *See also* Classroom environments
- classroom libraries and, 10

Show and Tell, 18
Show and Tell~Question~Connection, 23–24
Sight words
- *Associative Learning*, 214–215
- *Basic Sight Vocabulary* (assessment), 246–251
- *Common Nouns* (assessment), 252–257
- discussion, 209
- *Explicit Instruction*, 210–212
- further ideas/activities, 216–217
- home-schooled children and, 218–220
- *Pattern Books*, 213
- *Word Wall*, 215–216

Simple Story Elements, 61–62
So You Want to Be President, 78
Songs. *See* Music
Sound blending, 148
Sound Boxes, 142–143
Sound isolation, 149
Sound substitution, 150
Spelling and literacy. *See also* Writing
    developmental spelling, 366
    Developmental Spelling (assessment), 389–392
    developmental stages of, 377–378
    Directed Spelling Thinking Activity (DSTA), 369
    discussion, 341–343
    English Language Learners and, 368, 371
    further ideas/activities, 372–373
    Have~A~Go, 366–368
    home-schooled children and, 374
    resources for, 375
    Spelling Workshop, 370
    That Reminds Me..., 370–371
    Writing (assessment), 379–380
    Writing Observational Checklist (assessment), 387
    Writing Rubrics (assessment), 380–386
Spelling Workshop, 370
St. George, Judith, 78
Standards of *Elementary Reading Attitude Survey*, 39
Story Faces, 67–69
Story Frame, 284–286, 338
Story grammar, 49
Story maps, 65–66
Story Star, 65–66
Storytelling. *See also* Oral language
    audio books and, 10
    direction of reading and, 57
    home-schooled children and, 11, 27
    importance of reading aloud, 8, 343
    Progressive Storytelling and, 25
    retelling as assessment method, 119–123
    Shared Reading and, 4–5
    Shared Writing, 354–355
    use of Big Books for, 53
Structured Repeated Readings, 223–226
Substitutions of sound. *See* Sound substitution
Summer Wheels, 344
Surveys, *Elementary Reading Attitude Survey*, 38–46
Sweeney, Joan, 17

T

Teacher~Assisted Reading, 222–223
Teaching methods. *See* Learning methods; Teaching strategies
Teaching strategies
    Book Boxes, 14–15
    Brainstorming, 16–17
    Expand~a~Sentence, 24
    Favorite Book Show and Tell, 5–7
    Knowledge Chart, 15–16
    Morning Message, 3–4
    Object Exploration, 13–14
    Predicting with Pictures, 17
    Progressive Storytelling, 25
    reading enthusiasm and, 8
    Shared Reading, 4–5
    Show and Tell~Question~Connection, 23–24
Technology. *See* Media/technology
Television. *See also* Media/technology
    background knowledge and, 21
    informational text structures and, 82
    sense of story and, 71
Tenth Good Thing About Barney, The, 344
Text structure. *See* Informational text structures; Phonics
Text Tapping, 355–356
That Reminds Me..., 370–371
Think Aloud, 281–283
Three Little Pigs, The, 62
Transitional spelling, 378
Twinkle, Twinkle, Little Star, 128

U

Using Alphabet Books, 129–130

V

Very Hungry Caterpillar, The, 70
Viorst, J., 344
Vocabulary meaning
    Four~Square Vocabulary Grids, 274–276
    further ideas/activities, 277
    home-schooled children and, 278
    Preview in Context, 271–272
    Vocabulary Connections, 272–273
    Word Frames, 273

W

Wells, R., 129
What Can You Show Us?, 56
Where the Wild Things Are, 350
Whole~Part~Whole Phonics, 158
Word Detective, 237–238
Word Frames, 273
Word Wall, 215–216
Words per Minute, 258–261
Writing
    assessment of alphabet knowledge through, 169
    cross-checking and, 241
    daily classroom routine for, 3–4
    Developmental Spelling (assessment), 389–392
    direction of reading and, 55–56
    discussion, 344–345
    English Language Learners and, 354–355, 359–360
    Expository Writing and, 79–81
    further ideas/activities, 361–363
    home-schooled children and, 352, 364, 374
    home-schooled children and informational text structures and, 84
    home-schooled children and print concepts and, 59
    Let Me Tell You About..., 359–360
    and literacy, 341–343
    literacy and, 354
    literature responses and, 348, 351
    monitoring reading and, 302–303
    Parent~Recommended Topics, 357–358
    publishing ideas, 363
    Quickdraw/Quickwrite, 19
    resources for, 365
    Shared Writing, 354–355
    sharing of, 8
    sight word assessment and, 253
    Text Tapping, 355–356
    vocabulary meaning and, 277
    Writing (assessment), 379–380
    Writing from Songs, 356–357
    Writing Observational Checklist (assessment), 387
    Writing Rubrics (assessment), 381–386
Writing from Songs, 356–357
Writing Observational Checklist, 387
Writing Rubrics, 381–386

Y

Yolen, Jane, 82